PRESCHOOL EDUCATION

*A Handbook for the Training
of Early Childhood Educators*

Contributors

RHETA DE VRIES, Ph.D.
University of Illinois at Chicago Circle

LYNN DORMAN, Ph.D.
University of Massachusetts at Boston

ELLIS D. EVANS, Ed.D.
University of Washington

LOIS M. FEARS, Ed.M.
Hampton Institute, Virginia

WILLIAM L. GOODWIN, Ph.D.
University of Colorado

ALICE S. HONIG, Ph.D.
Syracuse University

LEON JONES, Ed.D.
Howard University

RONALD K. PARKER, Ph.D.
The City University of New York
Institute for the Development of Human
Resources, New York City

DONALD L. PETERS, Ph.D.
The Pennsylvania State University

RUPERT TRUJILLO, Ph.D.
University of New Mexico

PRESCHOOL EDUCATION

*A Handbook for the Training
of Early Childhood Educators*

RALPH W. COLVIN

and

ESTHER M. ZAFFIRO

Editors

Foreword by
William Smith

SPRINGER PUBLISHING COMPANY
New York

Copyright © 1974
Springer Publishing Company, Inc.
200 Park Avenue South
New York, N.Y. 10003

This work was developed under a grant from the U.S. Office of Education, Department of Health, Education and Welfare. However, the content does not necessarily reflect the position or policy of that Agency, and no official endorsement should be inferred.

This handbook was the primary objective of the National Leadership Project in Early Education and Child Development, which was funded by the Early Childhood Branch of the Bureau of Educational Personnel Development under the auspices of the State College of Arkansas. The project was directed by Ralph W. Colvin, Ph.D., and conducted in collaboration with Esther M. Zaffiro, M.S.E., and the ten Fellows who contributed the contents of this book.

74 75 76 77 78 / 10 9 8 7 6 5 4 3 2 1

Library of Congress Cataloging in Publication Data

Colvin, Ralph W
    Preschool education.

    1. Education, Preschool—Handbooks, manuals, etc.
I. Zaffiro, Esther M., joint author. II. Title.
LB1140.2.C663   372.21   74-79411
ISBN 0-8261-1620-5

Printed in the United States of America

Contents

Foreword

In the late 1960s, upon my arrival at the Office of Education, a number of efforts were being made in the Bureau of Educational Personnel Development, spearheaded by Dr. Joan Duval, chief of the Early Childhood Branch, to meet the critical shortage of early childhood training programs and trained early childhood personnel. The undertaking had been sparked by several important developments.

The movement in many parts of the United States for statewide kindergarten programs had created a serious need for a large number of qualified staff members. Evidence resulting from the Head-Start Program in low-income areas had triggered demands on the part of parents and citizens from various socioeconomic levels who had not been involved in the program. They had begun to realize that their children, too, could benefit from a preschool experience and were no longer content to accept the sterile notion that their children's formal schooling should begin in the first grade. The demand did not come from the higher-income families since they have traditionally sent their children to private nursery schools or have engaged private tutors to compensate for the lack of formal schooling in the kindergarten years.

The economy was another factor that encouraged greater adoption of statewide kindergarten programs. As the cost of living continued upward, no longer permitting middle-class women the luxury of not working, these eventually expanded to include preschool programs. Preschool education was also promoted in low-income areas, especially for the sake of mothers who desired to get off the welfare rolls by working.

Day care centers similar to those that had been developed under Head Start by social agencies, such as settlement houses and churches, began to abound and provide custodial care for young children. American educators finally came to see the value of people such as Jean Piaget, Jerome Bruner, Robert Hess, and Maria Montessori, who had shown that young children were capable of learning in a structured setting at a much earlier age than had been thought. I can recall listening to Dr. Mario Montessori in his home a few years ago as he described in detail the theoretical and very practical framework that his mother used so successfully in her work with young, disadvantaged children in the forgotten bowels of poverty in Europe.

When all these forces are considered, it becomes clear that the early childhood education movement had its base in sociopolitical, economic, and theoretical, as well as pedagogical, roots.

The developments described above show that, unlike a number of educational movements in the United States, the energizing of early childhood education was not based on rhetoric but rather on solid theoretical and practical foundations. The only problem was that institutions of higher learning, especially those with teacher-training functions, did not view early childhood education as a priority, as a discipline, or as being worthy of inclusion in a significant way in their institutional format. Furthermore, in states that had not adopted preschool programs, most institutions had neither the training design nor the faculty competence to develop such a program. In some states most of the competence and initiative were found at the local level where child-center advocates spanned the elementary-to-kindergarten-to-preschool period with trial-and-error methodology. Their saving grace was their intuition, their experience, and any contacts they might have had with learning theorists at nearby universities.

The focus of our national program in the early 1970s was on building a leadership cadre whose theoretical and field-based training would equip it to move into institutions of higher learning to sponsor, develop, or simply manage early childhood education teacher-training programs. It was our intent to equip this new leadership cadre with a shared experience bank derived from 52 Office of Education Early Childhood Personnel Training Programs. The articles in this book draw from this bank of experiences and should, therefore, be of great value in the training of preschool educators.

The evidence resulting from five years of early childhood teacher training programs shows the critical importance of three dimensions in any preschool education program: (1) collaboration between the home and community, the school or day care center, and the university; (2) the early identification, diagnosis, and prescription of and for young children with learning and behavioral problems; and (3) the documentation and analysis of the processes leading to success or failure in preschool programs for the purpose of transferring and adapting these processes to different settings.

As I look to the future, I am convinced that no career or vocational field has as great a promise as that involving young children and their families. For this reason we must define competence in this field and make efforts to recruit people who best meet the standards set. We must make better use of theory and develop evaluation methods that best suit our purpose. I hope this book will assist us in these tasks and push us a few more steps toward our goal.

William Smith
Director, Teacher Corps

Introduction

We address this handbook to those who will be responsible for planning, implementing, and evaluating programs for the training of early childhood personnel. Comprehensive and individualized services for young children —including community, nursery, preschool, kindergarten, and primary school programs as well as day care in its many forms—will require the services of persons from many fields: education, recreation, social welfare, and health care, as well as the academic disciplines. The task is so immense that within each of these vocational areas it will draw upon personnel of widely varying levels of education and experience. Also, both for manpower and effectiveness of service parental involvement will be essential in every aspect of programming. Child and family needs can only be met by the full spectrum of public and private, profit and nonprofit community agencies.

Thus, our target audience is broad and inclusive: multidisciplinary, multilevel, and interagency. It includes leaders in the helping professions, as front-line activists, and those in the many academic disciplines concerned with the content of early childhood instruction. Each profession and discipline must incorporate a teaching-learning ladder with participants at one level training those below as they themselves are trained from above, in a continuous learning-while-doing chain of interaction. This chain must also link up with those capable of recruiting, inspiring, and educating: parents, students, and community volunteers, as well as administrators who can facilitate interagency communication, cooperation, and constructive action.

The present work is designed to prepare people to serve in leadership roles; it may be used in college courses, for in-service upgrading of personnel, and in the short-term training of community leaders.

This book has its origins in the pioneer research and programs of the Children's Bureau, the aggressive outreach and program development of the Office of Economic Opportunity, the training impetus of the Educational Professions Development Act of 1967, the focusing of priorities by the White House Conference on Children of 1970, and the coordinating efforts of the Office of Child Development. These thrusts—both the cause and effect of increased knowledge, mounting social pressure, and political responsiveness—have created and sustained a revolutionary movement which radiates optimism, stimulates creative planning, and inspires devotion.

Accumulating research indicates that the optimal development of all children—whether handicapped or talented, disadvantaged or privileged—requires early, individual, and personalized services. Agencies and parents representing children with special problems; advocates of civil rights, social action, and welfare reform; Women's Liberation activists; and the ever-increasing population of working mothers are realizing a common cause and insisting upon greatly improved and enlarged early childhood and family services as the right of all children. Legislators are responding by passing educational and social welfare legislation that will bring about an unprecedented expansion of early childhood personnel training and employment opportunities as well as services for children and families.

This handbook is the product of the ten Fellows and two staff members of the National Leadership Project in Early Education and Child Development that emerged from the Early Childhood Leadership Training Institute, Bureau of Educational Personnel Development, United States Office of Education. This Leadership Training Institute, centered at the State College of Arkansas, was responsible for providing technical assistance, training, evaluation, and dissemination services to 52 Early Childhood Personnel Training Projects financed by Office of Education grants. Traditionally, Bureau Institutes perform such services through a panel of established consultants. Here, entirely new procedures were pioneered.

First, four basic issues were identified: (1) a critical shortage of leadership personnel of national stature to direct university, state, and federal early childhood personnel training programs; (2) a general deficiency in applying and communicating theory and research in professional training; (3) a failure to inspire in trainees a theoretical orientation and research attitude toward the development of services to families and children; and, (4) serious defects in evaluation theory, methodology, and techniques.

To provide for the Institute's service responsibilities to Office of Education programs, while at the same time coping with these four basic issues, a learning-through-service format was established and efforts were made to identify ten young professionals showing high potential for national leadership in the training of child development personnel. Nominations were invited from the 1700 members of the Society for Research in Child Development, consultants on various federal advisory panels, and other authorities in the areas of early education and child development, as well as prominent leaders and agency officials involved in the development of Black, Chicano, and Indian professionals. Approximately 200 nominations were painstakingly processed on the basis of extensive data. After screening candidates to thirty in number, the Institute staff submitted data on each to a consultant panel of five early childhood authorities who individually ranked them. Selections made on the basis of the most favorable totals of these ranks resulted in the appointment of ten Fellows who were unusually well-trained and experienced, as well as remarkably varied in terms of professional, educational, social, cultural, religious, geographical, and racial backgrounds. In accepting appointments, Fellows and their employers each agreed that at least 1/5 of the Fellows' time would be devoted to the Institute, that extensive travel would be involved, and that each Fellow would receive an Institute stipend of an additional 1/5 of his current salary.

Thus this handbook evolved in the context of a closely shared, two-year, interdisciplinary group experience of twelve early childhood specialists with: professional training and practice in the behavioral sciences, a vital interest in the development of children and parents as well as the training of personnel to service families, and the immediate objective of exchanging leadership training and experience for the provision of technical assistance, training, evaluation, and dissemination services to the 52 Office of Education Early Childhood Personnel Training Programs.

The establishment of a shared frame of reference, intimate communication, and active collaboration involved bimonthly full group, periodic subgroup, and frequent small group meetings at highly selected locations throughout the United States; much individual study, observation of programs, and reporting; and frequent telephone and mail contacts. Full group sessions first included attendance at two national, policy-establishing early childhood meetings which provided close contact and discussion with authorities who remained available and were constantly consulted throughout this project. Three subsequent meetings involved intensive study and close interchange with leadership personnel of three programs of high research output and definite theoretical orientation of representative points of view. The University of Minnesota Institute of Child Development with its developmental orientation, and the University of Kansas Department of Human Development with its behavioral focus, were selected because they had received the preponderence of nominations in a poll of the members of the Society for Research in Child Development regarding university programs with the highest level of excellence in the training of early childhood personnel. This intensive study of model programs included a session at the University of Colorado Early Childhood Special Education Demonstration Laboratory with its clinical orientation and exploration of four different educational curricula. With special concern for minority group and individualized instruction, a series of sites were visited in each of three locations: New York, Atlanta, and Albuquerque. In order to better serve and study the 52 Office of Education personnel training programs, the group focused its energies on the development of the *Site Visit Questionnaire for the Study of Personnel Training Programs in Early Childhood Education and Development.* Repeatedly revised in course of application, this Questionnaire became the basic format for gathering and organizing information for this book.

Collaboration is never a simple process; it is difficult even when experienced superficially. In this situation it was lived personally and in depth. Though the *Site Visit Questionnaire* had evolved readily with all Fellows contributing and compromises easily made, both chapter organization and content assignments took considerable time and effort before a generally satisfying format and individual writing responsibilities were determined.

With a cookbook orientation, we sought to describe in detail the sequence of experiences encountered in program development. However, we found ourselves mired in redundancies as we encountered the constantly recurring phenomenon of the problem identification-theorizing-planning-implementation-evaluation cycle. From such preliminaries evolved the present organization: first, the role of theory in program development; then, the immediate material and interpersonal community; next the derivation of objectives, content, and methods; then, the issues of evaluation and measurement; and finally, dissemination.

Content assignments went a similar course. Comprehensiveness was soon compromised; it would necessitate writers covering areas of low interest and minor competence. Each Fellow was asked to present a series of topics of prime interest and expertise. These were synthesized and teams, balanced regarding theoretical and practical orientations, were developed to assume responsibility for each major area. Activities fell into the five broad categories of theory, community, curriculum, evaluation, and dissemination.

DeVries and Parker lead off by exploring Piagetian, behavioral, and analytic psychologies to identify within each theory its concept of the child and its approach to fostering the child's development. Then, on the basis of many site visits to projects throughout the United States, these authors observe the application of theory in program development with the unhappy conclusion that there are few instances of rigorous application of theory, and there is even reason to question the potential of any one established theory to produce a theoretically derived, completely consistent, and appropriately broad curriculum offering.

Considerable personal experience underlies Trujillo's discussion of the community. First of all he speaks as a Chicano from New Mexico who is intent upon presenting "somebody's community" as preferable to that of "nobody's community" and in recognition of the nonexistence of "everybody's community." However, with fine judgment he does identify common dimensions and illustrates with broadly representative examples, many of which were achieved from consultation with David Hoffman, who recently completed a comprehensive study of early childhood programs.

Peters, Honig, Fears, and Dorman represent a balance of those who have devoted their lives to the teaching of children and the teaching of adults to work with children. They bring to their core chapters on planning, implementation, and management a wide knowledge of the literature, tempered by considerable first hand experience. They aim their exposition at the primary target of educating personnel to work with young children while keeping in mind the ultimate target of the preschool child and his family.

Goodwin, Jones, and Evans, share responsibility for evaluation and measurement. Goodwin directs his fine wit to the pros and cons of evaluation, and then addresses himself to evaluation models and difficulties encountered in their application. Jones discusses the methodology of the evaluator-consultant as he assists the decision maker in appropriately defining concepts and evolving objectives. Evans presents measurement with a balance of reservation and enthusiasm, discussing both the broad issues and specific measures in current use. His "Annotated Bibliography of Published Tests and Scales" will be of much assistance to the reader.

Peters concludes with a discussion of dissemination, balancing the responsibility to inform with the need to respect privacy. He well illustrates the conflict that often exists between individual rights and the interests of society.

Although the Fellowship group originated from widely diverse backgrounds and viewpoints, their two years of frequent and intensive contacts provided a bond of affection and respect, a fund of shared professional, social, and personal experiences, and a sound basis for communication and cooperation. Though topics have been developed by Fellows individually or in groups, there has been a communal responsibility for this project, in whole and in part. Initial outlines and three drafts of each paper were submitted to the entire group with each member being responsible to all others for both verbal and written commentaries. Immediately prior to final revisions, the group presented an American Psychological Association Post Doctoral Institute: Early Childhood Program Development. This experience allowed each to discuss his contribution and benefit by participants' comments and criticisms. Thus, we have shared unusual opportunities to evolve a common set of basic definitions, resolve inconsistencies, correct errors, avoid redundancies, and fill voids. Also, the heterogeneity of the group and its varied experiences together have broadened the point of view of each participant in such a fashion that cross-references and transitions became natural rather than studied.

As interaction brought cohesiveness to this interdisciplinary group, so also these last several years has the field of early childhood education and care recognized the necessity for the combined efforts of planners, community representatives, front-line activists, parents, and evaluators. However, despite this rapprochement and mutual respect among participants, discontent abounds. Recurrent confrontations indicate widespread feelings of disenchantment with legislative provisions, developmental theories, popular methodologies, exemplary evaluation models, research contributions, and widely used measurements; each is seen as deficient in meeting the demands placed upon it. This general dissatisfaction provides an appropriate start for exploration of new approaches to the education and care of young children and their families.

We hope that this book, which has largely been developed by young minds evolving in new settings, will assist those who are developing programs for the training of personnel for improved family and child services.

Ralph W. Colvin
Esther M. Zaffiro
State College of Arkansas

Biographical Sketches of Editors and Contributors

Ralph W. Colvin draws on an extensive professional background in areas concerned with young children, including the gifted, handicapped, disadvantaged, and retarded. A doctoral graduate in clinical psychology from Duke University, he has, over the past two decades, directed training programs, conducted major research projects, and published widely under the auspices of such organizations as the Astor Home for Children, the Kennedy Child Study Center, the New York Association for Brain Injured Children, and the Child Welfare League of America. Dr. Colvin's numerous other affiliations, as teacher or consultant, include the Department of Special Education at Columbia's Teachers College; the Department of Health, Education and Welfare; the Mayor's Committee on Mental Retardation (New York); and the Governor's Council in Early Child Development (Arkansas). He is past president of the American Academy on Mental Retardation.

Rheta DeVries is currently at the University of Illinois at Chicago Circle, where she is associate professor in the College of Education and acting head of the Department of Human Development and Learning. Following graduation from Baylor University, she taught in Illinois public schools for four years, and then studied at the University of Chicago, where she earned a Ph.D. in psychology. She was director of a research project entitled "Cognitive Development during the Years Five to Seven," in the Champaign, Illinois, public schools, and has published several journal articles on this subject. Her current research and writing, in collaboration with Constance Kamii, focuses on the definition of a Piaget-derived curriculum for young children.

Lynn Dorman divides her professional life between teaching and writing. She served as an instructor in psychology at State College at Framingham and assistant professor of psychology at Wheaton College, and currently has appointments as assistant professor at the University of Massachusetts and lecturer at Boston University's Metropolitan College and School of Education. In collaboration with Freda Rebelsky, she is co-editor of *Child Development and Behavior*, as well as co-author of *Everyone Should Know About Kids*, and is now co-editing an eighteen-book series on life-span developmental psychology. Dr. Dorman received her doctorate in developmental psychology from Boston University, and a postdoctoral fellowship from the University of California.

Notably, she also brings to the present volume the benefit of several years' experience, earlier in her career, as a kindergarten teacher in Farmingdale, New York.

Ellis D. Evans received his M.S.Ed. and Ed.D. from Indiana University. He has conducted extensive research in the field of childhood education and has contributed numerous articles to scholarly journals. Author of *Contemporary Influences in Early Childhood Education,* he is also co-author of *Children and Youth: Psychosocial Development* and *Development and Classroom Learning,* as well as editor of two volumes concerned with child and adolescent behavior and development. Dr. Evans is a professor of educational psychology at the University of Washington, where he has taught since 1964.

Lois M. Fears holds a B.S. degree in home economics from A & T State University in Greensboro, North Carolina; a graduate diploma in early childhood education from the Eliot-Pearson School in Medford, Massachusetts; and an Ed.M. from Tufts University. Currently acting departmental chairman, Department of Early Childhood Education, at Hampton Institute, she has also been providing technical assistance to Head Start programs on a local, state, and national level since 1965. For two summers she was education director of the Newport News, Virginia, Head Start program and has conducted numerous workshops on the various facets of curriculum development for young children.

William L. Goodwin, an associate professor in educational psychology and chairman of the Division of Foundations and Research Methodology at the University of Colorado, received his Ph.D. from the University of Wisconsin, and studied as a postdoctoral fellow at Harvard University. He has been a research associate at the Research and Development Center for Cognitive Learning at the University of Wisconsin and has served as director of four SESAME, Title III, ESEA projects at Bucknell University. A frequent contributor of articles and reports to professional journals, Dr. Goodwin has written and edited several books, including a textbook co-authored with Herbert Klausmeier, *Learning and Human Abilities: Educational Psychology.*

Alice S. Honig is currently completing her doctoral dissertation at Syracuse University, where she is also assistant professor in the Department of Child and Family Studies of the College for Human Development. For the past ten years, she has been Program Supervisor on the research staff of the Syracuse University Children's Center, which provides day care for low-income infants and preschoolers. Her publications include articles on early education, including the effect of an intervention program on Piagetian sensorimotor processes. She has recently published a book with J. Ronald Lally, *Infant Caregiving: A Design for Training.*

Leon Jones completed his graduate work at the University of Illinois and the University of Massachusetts, where he received his doctorate. His area of specialization is educational research and evaluation, with emphasis on methodology. Dr. Jones' most recent paper, "The Operationalization of Fuzzy Concepts: Methodological Research and Applications," was presented at the 1972 annual conference of the American Educational Research Association. He is now an associate professor in the School of Education at Howard University.

Ronald K. Parker, a past director of the Child Development/Day Care Resources Project for the Office of Child Development, Department of Health, Education and Welfare, spearheaded a national task force of eighty professional consultants charged with developing day care resources nationwide. While with this project, he co-edited three handbooks defining means of operating day care programs for infants, preschoolers, and school-age children, as well as a training handbook for teachers that was published by the Office of Child Development. Overall, the project produced sixty-five publications covering all aspects of child development and day care. Dr. Parker, who earned his doctorate at Vanderbilt University, is the author or editor of numerous other books and articles. He is now an associate professor of psychology and principal investigator of the Cognitive Development Project of the City University of New York, as well as director of the Institute for the Development of Human Resources, in New York City.

Donald L. Peters, an associate professor of human development at Pennsylvania State University, is coordinator, as well, of the early childhood education programs of its College of Human Development. He also directs the Pennsylvania Daycare Study, a state-wide evaluation of early child care programs. His interests are varied, ranging from early childhood program development and research on cognitive development to research and evaluation of personnel training. Dr. Peters has written many articles in these areas and is the author of two books: *Early Childhood: The Development of Self-regulation* and *Early Childhood*. He received his Ph.D. from Stanford University.

Rupert A. Trujillo has developed a number of programs related to the education of minorities. Currently assistant dean of the College of Education at the University of New Mexico, where he earned his doctorate, he has been a director for Head Start and field coordinator in charge of a community project for the hardcore unemployed. Other assignments have included director of Teacher Corps at New Mexico State University, where he was responsible for developing an innovative bilingual teacher preparation program with emphasis on community participation. Dr. Trujillo, who completed a postdoctoral fellowship in early childhood education at Arkansas State University, has served as consultant to the U.S. Office of Education and the popular children's TV series, Sesame Street, as well as numerous urban and rural projects.

Esther M. Zaffiro attended Lee College, University of Chattanooga, and received her B.A. and M.S.E. degrees from the State College of Arkansas, where she held a fellowship in early childhood education. She functioned as research associate in the preparation of this book and also contributed editorial services. She is active in state and community educational and social welfare organizations, and was appointed by Governor Rockefeller to his Task Force on Early Childhood and his Commission on the Status of Women. She is at present a member of the faculty at Ashland College, Ashland, Ohio, where she teaches courses in early childhood and supervises students who plan to enter the child care or early childhood education field. She is also coordinator for the Ashland Community Day Care Center, a recently opened facility combining Head Start, college nursery school, and educational day care programs with a laboratory for college students.

PART I

THEORETICAL FOUNDATIONS AND THEIR REFLECTIONS IN PRACTICE

Chapter 1

Theory in Educational Practice

RHETA DEVRIES

How would education be different if teachers and administrators were required to justify their activity on the basis of behavioral science research or theory? When this question was presented to a group of school psychologists, counselors, and teacher supervisors, a moment of stunned silence was followed by scattered laughter punctuated by a single response: "We would strike!" This flippant reaction seems to express a typical attitude among those concerned with practical aspects of education. Theory and research are apparently viewed as alien to their interests and needs, and perhaps somewhat threatening.

Many educators say, "We don't care about theory. We're interested in what works!" While such a view reflects a necessary pragmatic concern, it overlooks the fact that a judgment of some teaching effort as having "worked" depends on the educator's theory of what constitutes learning, what behavior indicates its occurrence, and what kind of learning is important. The aims of this chapter are to convince the reader that theory *does* matter, that it is an inescapable fact of every educational practice, and that the educator must know the theory behind every educational practice.

First, let us clarify what is meant by theory. Theory is often used in a restricted sense to refer to the formal conceptualizations of behavioral science, where it provides a deductive system to guide the researcher in studying human behavior. The researcher uses theory to assist in the selection of variables to observe, in the formulation and testing of hypotheses, and in the interpretation of findings. Theory enables the behavioral scientist to go beyond empirical facts to interpret, explain, or generalize

The author wishes particularly to thank Dr. Constance Kamii for her critical reading of this manuscript and for her many helpful suggestions. Appreciation is also expressed to Dr. Tom Lickena, Dr. Lorraine Wallach, and Dr. Lawrence Kohlberg for helpful comments. In addition, the following persons generously shared their views on the role of theory in training teachers: Dr. Millie Almy, Dr. Barbara Biber, Dr. Urie Bronfenbrenner, Dr. Cynthia Deutsch, Mrs. Elizabeth Freidus, Dr. Ogden Lindsley, Dr. John Maier, Dr. Marie Piers, Dr. David Weikart, and Dr. John Wright.

from facts gathered in a systematic way, and then to modify the theory accordingly.

In this chapter, however, theory is discussed in a broader sense (which includes the restricted meaning) as an assumption, attitude, belief, or philosophy about human behavior. In this sense, everyone has theories about such aspects of human behavior as intelligence, motivation, perception, learning, developmental change, personality, normal and abnormal behavior, and interpersonal and group behavior. Perhaps informal ideas should not be called theories. Nevertheless, in the broader sense of the term, there is no sharp line of demarcation between the theories of the behavioral scientist and those of the layman philosopher. Each has some kind of evidence, systematic or unsystematic, objective or subjective, upon which his ideas rest.

In the remainder of this chapter, the educational implications of different theoretical orientations will be discussed, with special reference to the education of young children. This begins with a consideration of how educational practice can be affected by theoretical notions about the nature of (a) the child, (b) developmental change, (c) intelligence, (d) motivation, and (e) sex, culture, and ethnicity. Illustrations are drawn from various formal theories, particularly those of Sigmund Freud, Erik Erikson, B. F. Skinner, and Jean Piaget.[1] Following this general discussion, these four theories are considered in further detail. A comparison of the psychoanalytic theories of Freud and Erikson illustrates how modification in theory is accompanied by modification in practice. Comparison of the theories of Skinner and Piaget clearly illustrates how vastly different theories result in vastly different educational goals, teaching methods, and evaluation criteria. Finally, the alienated relationship between educators and behavioral scientists is discussed, and a rapprochement is suggested as the process through which education (especially early education) can mature into a scientific discipline.

EDUCATIONAL IMPLICATIONS OF DIFFERENT THEORETICAL ORIENTATIONS

Theoretical notions about human nature and behavior can be categorized into three general points of view which describe the most basic theoretical differences in the field of early education.[2] Kohlberg (1968) conceptualized these as maturationist, cultural-training, and cognitive-developmental, and traced their historical stream in education, philosophy, and psychology.

The maturationist views the child's development as primarily predetermined by internal factors that unfold best in a benign environment without adult cultural pressures. Neill's (1960) Summerhill approach represents the extreme educational application of this theoretical orientation. The cultural-training point of view assumes that development is primarily determined by external factors, and that it is best fostered through direct teaching of cognitive, moral, and cultural knowledge. The program of Bereiter-Engelmann (1966) is an application of this view.

The cognitive-developmentalist assumes that development results from a natural interaction between the child and the environment, and that education must provide an environment with resources which the child uses in actively constructing his own knowledge. An example of this view is the Kamii-DeVries (Kamii, 1971, 1972; Kamii & DeVries, 1974; DeVries & Kamii, in press) Piaget-derived curriculum for young children.

With this introductory perspective, let us turn to more specific consideration of theoretical notions which have a vital effect on educational practice.

It is hoped that the reader will reflect upon the following questions concerning his or her own theoretical biases:

1. What theories do I hold concerning children and their development?
2. What do my behaviors with children or my teaching about children imply about my theoretical beliefs?
3. Are my behaviors concerning children consistent with my theories?

Assumptions Concerning the Innate Nature of the Child

Beliefs about the basic nature of the child affect many educational practices. Let us first consider the implications of differing theories regarding the child's innate equipment. Theories range from Locke's extreme view that the child's mind is a "blank slate" totally determined by his environment, to the opposite notion that he is totally determined by biological or theological factors over which the environment has no control. At the former extreme, the child at birth is considered to possess no equipment relevant or important to socialization or educational goals. He may be seen as a more or less intact physical system, but lacking psychological attributes or behaviors which contribute to development. This judgment leads to a cultural-training belief in the omnipotence of the environment in determining the child's development. The socializer must therefore take an active, directive role in shaping the individual and must accept responsibility for the outcome of training.

The other extreme position—total determination by biological or theological factors—probably does not exist in pure form. Such a view would obviously lead to a totally pessimistic approach to education. In general, one's degree of pessimism regarding the efficacy of educational efforts depends on the degree of determinism attributed to such factors. However, the more common orientation seems to be that the newborn possesses at least some innate equipment relevant to changes required by the social world. How this equipment is conceptualized makes a difference in how one deals with children. Important dimensions of this conceptualization include: (a) intrinsic valuation, (b) specific kinds of innate characteristics, (c) relative activity or passivity, (d) potential for change, and (e) universality.

Intrinsic Valuation. Value judgments regarding the attributes of the child are critical because the educator decides whether to foster or discourage the behavioral expressions of these attributes. If an innate or a learned characteristic is viewed as undesirable, educational goals will be cast in terms of discouraging, repressing, or somehow changing this aspect of the child. Consider the educational stance resulting from the following negative valuation expressed in an undergraduate text on religious education of children (Benson, 1942):

> Child nature is no different today from what it was a thousand years ago. . . . In spite of all we can do in an educational way, the child will go in the wrong direction. . . . Before education can perform its proper task among men it must recognize that this task is not to lift a rising race but a falling one. The natural inclination of the child is downward . . . in their earliest hours children have tendencies away from as well as toward God. (p. 7)

Compare the above negative view of the child's intrinsic nature with the following excerpt from Neill (1960), a description of the self-regulated child: "Self-regulation implies a belief in the goodness of human nature; a belief that there is not, and never was, original sin" (p. 104). This belief led Neill to establish his Summerhill school, where students were given relatively complete freedom. He directly attributed his educational approach to his view of the nature of the child which was inspired by Rousseau and Freud:

> Well, we set out to make a school in which we should allow children freedom to be themselves. In order to do this, we had to renounce all discipline, all direction, all suggestion, all moral training, all religious instruction. We have been called brave, but it did not require courage. All it required was what we had—a compete belief in the child as a good, not an evil being. My view is that a child is innately wise and realistic. If left to himself without adult suggestion of any kind, he will develop as far as he is capable of developing. (Neill, 1960, p. 4)

Whether or not one agrees with either extreme view of the child, it seems clear that the way in which one structures educational practice is affected by one's valuation of the child's basic nature. A negative valuation can lead to either of two opposite kinds of practice: an environmental structure that may be authoritarian, rigidly controlling, repressive, or even punitive; or a totally permissive structure characterized by apathy, indifference, and neglect. Positive valuation tends to lead to deliberately established structure, permitting the child to exercise, express, or satisfy inherent tendencies or needs. Positive valuation thus tends to result in attempts to maximize autonomy and de-emphasize control.

Specific Kinds of Innate Characteristics. In addition to the practical effects of one's positive or negative valuation of the child's innate psychological attributes, the kinds of attributes the child is believed to possess also affect educational practice. These attributes vary widely from specific traits, such as selfishness or curiosity, to more general characteristics, such as instincts, drives, or biologically based processes.

The various theoretical notions about attributes can be generally grouped in terms of whether the child is viewed as a miniature adult or as qualitatively different from the adult. The adultomorphic, egocentric belief that the child's psychological makeup, like his physical appearance, is parallel to the adult's leads to imposition of adult standards of behavior on the child. The child's basic psychological characteristics are viewed as quantitatively different from the adult's in much the same way that his size is different. While quantitative height and weight differences are obvious, it is also obvious that the child possesses the major species-identifying physical attributes at birth. Thus, the adult-miniature belief can lead to postulation of child *psychological* characteristics which are qualitatively like those of the adult, as well as to educational efforts which attempt to foster learning by the same methods used with adults.

In contrast to the adult-miniature theory, belief in qualitative differences between the child and the adult leads to quite different educational practices. This view that the child is psychologically different in kind, in comparison with the adult, requires an educational approach which provides for the child's uniqueness.

One example of the adult-miniature belief is S. Freud's theory that the instinctual infantile sexual energy of the infant remained qualitatively the same into adulthood. The behavior of adults was viewed as primarily determined by innate sexual instincts which differed from the infant's only in the locus of cathexis (oral, anal, genital) and in the degree of control and channeling of their energy. This postulation of sexuality as a basic characteristic of the child led S. Freud (1924) to say:

> Experience must have taught educators that the task of moulding the sexual will of the next generation can only be carried out by beginning to impose their influence very early, and intervening in the sexual life of children before puberty, instead of waiting till the storm bursts. Consequently almost all infantile sexual activities are forbidden or made disagreeable to the child. . . . (p. 321)

Another adult-miniature theory regarding the psychological characteristics inherent in the child is that of Skinner (1961, 1968). His operant
conditioning model postulates the child's basic psychological attributes in
terms of potential for external control. Primary principles of reinforcement
state that observable behavior tends to be repeated if followed by a pleasant
consequence and tends not to be repeated if followed by a neutral or unpleasant consequence. In addition, behavior may also be prompted by
antecedent stimulus cues associated with a behavior and its consequences.

One application of this theory to education has taken the form of
behavior modification through behavior analysis (Evans, 1971; Bushell,
1970a, 1970b; Becker, Thomas & Carnine, 1969; Krasner & Uhlman, 1965;
Lindsley, 1970). A teacher using this method decides what behavior is
changeworthy, counts the frequency (rate) at which the behavior is occurring, institutes reinforcement procedures, and then counts the rate of the
behavior to find out whether it has changed.[3] The reinforcement procedures
vary, depending on the behavior to be changed and on individual differences
in reinforcement preferences. Application of this behavior modification
technique requires thinking in terms of strengthening, weakening, maintaining, extinguishing, and putting operationally defined behavior under stimulus control.

Contrasted to adult-minature theories about the kind of innate psychological attributes possessed by children is the theory of Jean Piaget
(Piaget, 1952, 1970; Piaget & Inhelder, 1969). He postulates biologically
based (but not maturational, in the above sense of that term) invariant psychological functions of assimilation and accommodation which operate to
enable the child to know and adapt to his environment. Hunt (1969)
pointed to this process as the source of "intrinsic motivation" which, he
argued, is inherent in an organism's natural and spontaneous information-
processing and action. Piaget's work inspired R. White (1959, 1963) to
conceptualize effectance and competence motivation as universal. This
theory postulated that from birth infants are motivated by a feeling of
efficacy to interact continually with their environment. Satisfaction resulting
from experiencing the effects of one's actions is viewed as causal in motivating behaviors usually described as curious, exploratory, or playful.

These Piagetian views of the child lead to an educational stance which
recognizes the active role of the child in constructing knowledge. Kamii
(1971) pointed out the importance, from a Piagetian perspective, of fostering the child's excitement, curiosity, resourcefulness, and confidence in his
ability to figure things out. The Piagetian early childhood teacher does this
by encouraging the child to see and solve problems that are based on the
child's spontaneous interests. Based on Piaget's theory, Hunt (1969) concluded that the teacher should follow the child's spontaneous interests
rather than try to prescribe learning. These Piaget-derived views suggest
the importance of child directiveness in learning (not to imply a laissez-

faire approach), individualization of educational experience, and permitting the child to discover and correct his own errors.

Relative Activity or Passivity. Langer (1969) discussed the importance, with respect to human nature, of the activity-passivity dimension of theoretical orientations. He pointed out that beliefs differ radically depending upon whether one thinks of man as spontaneously initiating his own actions or as simply responding to environmental stimulation. For the educator, the implications pertain primarily to the locus of initiative. Differences in viewpoint are reflected by whether the teacher looks to the child for the direction of educational efforts or whether the teacher assumes the directive role.

Environmental arrangements and classroom management techniques can even reflect critical differences in this respect. Belief that the child is a passive respondent may be reflected in such practices as traditional neat rows of desks, the teacher as lecturer, homogeneity of specific learning objectives, other conformity demands, or individualization of instruction determined by the *adult's* logical analysis of difficulty.

Belief that the child is an active initiator may be reflected in such practices as are found in open education (Brown & Precious, 1968; Ridgeway & Lawton, 1965; Rogers, 1970; Spodek, 1970). Classrooms are generally arranged informally, with a wide variety of activities available for the child's choosing. The teacher functions more as a resource person, as a facilitator of the child's pursuit of his own objectives, and as a challenger and expander of those objectives. Group conformity is minimized, and expectations are expressed in terms of pursuit of some constructive activity. The teacher provides assistance and guidance when the child requests it and attempts to ask questions and provide information that leads the child to a higher level of learning. (Goodwin, in chapter 8 of this volume, provides a helpful chart on the relative contributions of teacher and child to content and processes of learning and discusses the Educational Development Center as an exemplar of high contribution on the part of both teacher and child in an informal classroom.)

An informally arranged classroom does not always imply an attitude of trust in the child's pursuit of learning. Even in such a situation it is possible for the teacher to structure learning activities directly, and to demand rote learning of adult logic. Similarly, the classroom which "looks" traditional may be operated in such a manner as to foster child initiative. Analysis of individual cases would be required to determine which theoretical view is being expressed, and whether or not contradictory practices are being utilized by an individual teacher.

Potential for Change. The degree to which the child's basic equipment is viewed as complete determines the degree of optimism the educator feels regarding his effect upon the child. As Ausubel (1958) noted, belief in the essential preformed nature of the individual leads the socializing agent to feel that he can foster only slight improvements in what the individual is destined to be. Such a view permits the educator to avoid much responsibility for the outcomes of his training efforts; the cause of both failure and success rests with the child. If important psychological attributes are believed to develop, rather than to exist at birth, educational implications depend on the way in which development is conceptualized. This is discussed in the following section.

Also related to the issue of the organism's initial relative completeness is the issue of the degree of malleability considered possible. It is clear from the foregoing that a preformationist bias leads to a belief in limited malleability. In contrast, belief in the infinite plasticity of human nature results in unlimited optimism concerning the individual's potential for change.

Universality of Human Nature. The belief in human psychological characteristics as universal can lead to homogeneity in educational approach. If one expects all children to be alike in some way, expectations and demands will be generally applied, and apparent deviations will be ignored, rejected, or actively squelched. The extent to which characteristics are universally attributed determines the degree of homogeneity in practice. The more aspects of human nature that are believed to be universal, the greater the tendency to treat individuals alike, to demand conformity, and to expect similar educational outcomes. Conversely, the fewer the characteristics that are believed to be identical among children, the greater the tendency to provide for educational needs viewed as unique to the individual, to permit diversity, and to expect educational outcomes to depend upon the individual's unique capacities.

The degree of specificity of the characteristic considered universal qualifies the above-mentioned extrapolations. If one believes that specific characteristics are learned rather than innate, one would tend to treat individuals differently. For example, Piaget's (1950) postulation of the functional invariants of assimilation and accommodation leads an educator to view all children as using these basic processes in their efforts to organize or construct their experiences. However, this postulation leads to a view of children as differing in the content of experience, in the aspect of experience focused upon, and in the degree to which progress occurs in construction of knowledge.

Nature of Development

One's belief about the nature of the child can also influence one's belief about the nature of developmental change. This issue is particularly critical for the educator because he is directly concerned with fostering change. Topics selected for this discussion of developmental change are:

source; course; cause; scope and limitations; and interrelatedness of different aspects of development.

Source of Change. Sources of developmental change can be generally characterized as internal and external to the child. If the source is believed to be completely external, the educator may assume all responsibility for determining what change is to occur, when it is to occur, and how it is to occur. This cultural-training view, exemplified by behavior modification and programmed learning, assigns a psychologically passive role to the child. Even where the child manages his own behavior modification and thus decides what behavior to modify, external reinforcement is still viewed as the source of change.

Where the source of developmental change is believed to rest within the child, the educator is concerned with defining directions of change identical to, or compatible with, the directions emanating from the child. Spontaneous interests and voluntary participation in educational activities are encouraged. The teacher leaves the what, when, and how of change to the child's initiative, and the child is encouraged to be psychologically active. Even where the teacher provides specific materials or offers specific activities (such as asking the child if he wants to paint or play a game), the child is never forced to participate and the child's own active, internal processes are still viewed as the source of change. The best example of this theoretical perspective is the Kamii-DeVries Piaget-derived curriculum. Other child-centered programs, particularly those influenced by psychoanalytic theory, also reflect belief in an internal source of change. However, belief in internality of change in these programs is generally restricted to socioemotional change. Paradoxically, in psychoanalytic programs, cognitive change tends to be treated as if externally caused (for example, number may be taught by an associationistic method which reflects Skinnerian principles).

Course of Change. The basic difference in theoretical orientations to the course of developmental change concerns whether the child changes quantitatively or qualitatively in his general patterns of response and mode of organizing experience (Kohlberg, 1968; Ausubel, 1958; Langer, 1969; Flavell, 1970). Qualitative developmental change refers to a change in the *kind* of response pattern and in the mode of organizing experience. Quantitative developmental change refers to *increase in amount* of responses and in amount of experiences organized.

The cultural-training theory of Skinner expresses belief in quantitative developmental change. Change is viewed as successive approximations to a terminal objective. It is thought to occur continuously through the addition of many elements, with organization of experience becoming more complex but not different in kind. Such a view leads to the expectation that the child can acquire adult-level patterns of response, even if only partially, and that such patterns are equivalent in kind to those of the adult. From this perspective, the educator's task is to choose the content to be added to the child's repertoire, and to directly teach responses to specific stimuli. Behavior modification and programmed learning certainly reflect the quantitative belief, and many examples may be cited from the Montessori method in early education. For example, Montessori teachers realize that five-year-olds can understand little, if any, of the representational meaning of maps of the world; but five-year-olds are encouraged to color maps of the countries in each continent, to put together map puzzles, and to put each country's flag on it. Such educational methods seem to express a faith that the addition of many little elements of geography will finally add up to the adult's knowledge.

In contrast to Skinner's view, the theories of Freud, Erikson, and Piaget reflect belief in qualitative developmental change. Change is viewed as occurring in an invariant sequence of discontinuous stages. Such a belief calls for early education geared to patterns of organizing experience which are psychologically different from those of the older child and the adult. The educator expressing this theoretical orientation is more likely to accept child behavior that reflects ideas, reactions, and beliefs which are inappropriate or incorrect from the point of view of adult logic, rather than to demand adult-level responses. The teacher refrains from imposing adult ways on the child since the child must first develop through intervening stages. Again, however, we find that the psychoanalytic theories of Freud and Erikson take the qualitative perspective only with regard to socioemotional development, while Piaget's theory views both socioemotional *and* cognitive development from this perspective.

Cause of Change. Beliefs about developmental causality are closely related to beliefs about the source and course of change. Again the central issue is whether one conceives the prepotent factors to be primarily internal or external to the child. The greater the belief in the efficacy of external factors, the more likely the educator will take an active role in directing the child's learning experiences. The educator who considers change as primarily externally determined will probably focus on such external factors as teaching methods and materials (for example, Montessori and Distar) rather than on the reactions and psychological processes of children.

This view is well illustrated by the Bereiter-Engelmann (1966) (now Becker-Engelmann) approach and is also reflected generally in the everhopeful investment of educational resources in commercial materials. The search for the better textbook or technique of material presentation seems to reflect a belief that somewhere there is the stimulus which will elicit the desired response, somewhere there is a method which will succeed even in the hands of a poor teacher. Teaching from this perspective tends to take a teacher-directed or even authoritarian form of "telling."

The educator who considers developmental change as internally determined focuses more on the child than on methods and materials. The teacher will take a less directive role (although some directiveness may also be present) and will attempt to capitalize upon the child's interests and motivations in the educational enterprise rather than imposing prescribed content and activities. Belief in developmental change as stemming from the child's interaction with environment leads the educator to take a pessimistic view of his efficacy in directly or quickly modifying qualitative aspects of the child's thinking. The teacher will more likely assess the child's qualitative level of internal organization and then attempt to act as a facilitative part of the interactive environment (see Kamii, 1971; Kamii and DeVries, 1974).

Scope and Limitations of Change. Beliefs about limitations of change potential rest heavily on beliefs about the nature of the child and other aspects of developmental change. Views regarding the scope of possible changes are generally focused upon the interactions of (a) the child's innate capacity, (b) his developmental level, and (c) the adequacy of his environment.

Regardless of how a teacher conceptualizes individual innate capacity for change, evaluation of this capacity as more or less limited will probably determine expectations and demands. The child may react to such expectations and demands by similarly expecting more or less of himself and by making more or less effort.

Developmental level considerations must be placed in the context of the previous discussion on the course of change. The teacher who views developmental change as a process of quantitative acquisition of bits of knowledge or skills will probably present the child with increasingly more complex tasks whose complexity hierarchy is defined by the adult view of complexity. Most school curricula are based on such a conception. Change potential from this perspective may be considered limited only by some variety of innate capacity, environmental inadequacy, or motivational restriction.

In contrast to the view of development as continuous quantitative change are the Piagetian and Freudian views of development as a discontinuous course with qualitative changes in the child's mode of experience. This leads to a concern for assessing the qualitative level and fostering progress to the next higher level rather than directly to the adult level or through successive levels defined by the adult's view of complexity. Change potential is considered limited at any point in time by the degree to which the individual's current level of development is well established, as well as by the degree to which the individual is aware of its limited adaptive use. For example, from the Piagetian perspective, the child at the concrete operational level cannot develop formal operations until he has well established his concrete operational thinking; and he also cannot develop formal operations until he recognizes that his concrete reasoning is inadequate to answer many questions he asks himself. Moreover, this change is also limited by inadequate maturation and experience; that is, the concrete operational child requires a certain degree of neurological development which derives both from hereditary factors and physical growth in order to become formal operational. The concrete operational child also requires experiences that provoke the intellectual exercise necessary for his active construction of formal reasoning ability.

Another contrast to the view of development as continuous quantitative change is the maturationist belief in change as resulting from an internally determined unfolding of preformed or prearranged patterns of behaviors or behavioral predispositions. This belief generally leads to an educational stance which is pessimistic about the extent to which development can be influenced. Environmental potential for bringing about change is considered limited, and one can only hope to bring about minor limiting or patterning effects, and to foster slight improvements on what the individual is destined to be. Specific attempts at improvement depend on the value judgment attached to the unfolding behaviors. The goal of education thus becomes that of exerting necessary control and restraint on those behaviors considered unacceptable, and of providing a benign, noncoercive environment in which the unfolding of acceptable behaviors can proceed unhindered.

Different conceptions of the nature of development will clearly result in different specific conceptions of readiness for certain educational experiences. The view taken influences whether one waits for readiness to appear "naturally" or whether one attempts to bring it about in some way. One's definition of readiness is influenced by whether one conceives it in terms of a set of prerequisite bits of information, a particular configuration of physiological and social characteristics, or a general structural mode of relating to experience.

These definitions of readiness influence the sequencing of educational experiences. Examples of readiness defined in terms of prerequisite factual elements are found in most school curricula, particularly in programmed instructional packages, in the Becker-Engelmann preschool curriculum, and in the use of standardized instruments for sequencing learning. Freudian and Eriksonian conceptions of development lead to definitions of readiness in terms of patterns of physiological and socioemotional characteristics. A cognitive-structure conceptualization of readiness, which is found in Piaget-based curricula, includes physiological and socioemotional characteristics.

Change potential may also be attributed to environmental factors. An assumption about environmental adequacy or inadequacy may lead to varied degrees of optimism concerning change potential. This is discussed in the section below on beliefs about cultural or ethnic characteristics. If one considers certain environmental characteristics as necessary for optimal developmental scope, the absence of these will result in pessimism and, perhaps, in abandonment of effort toward educational objectives. For example, many educators approach inner city children, children of minority groups, children from poor families, children with only one parent in the home, etc., as severely limited in potential for change. They may even conclude that educational efforts are severely constrained or virtually useless. Caldwell (1967) examined research evidence bearing on common beliefs concerning the optimal learning environment for the child under three years of age, and concluded that this evidence contradicted some common beliefs and raised questions about the general truth of others. For example, the belief that the child's own home is the optimal environment for learning seems to be true only when the home provides a warm and nurturant emotional relationship and varied sensory and cognitive input.

Another notion pertaining to the scope and limitations of developmental change, a notion with clear educational implications, is that of the *critical period*. If one believes in the existence of a critical period, a time when an individual is especially susceptible to environmental influence on a particular aspect of development, timing of appropriate experiences will be determined accordingly. If one believes that, once the critical time has passed, later experience will be ineffective, no effort will be made with an individual whose critical period is believed to have passed. The institution of Headstart preschool programs seems to have been implicitly based on the assumption that a critical period exists for the development of readiness for academic schooling.

The psychoanalytic view expresses a certain belief in a critical period. It holds that very early educational intervention is necessary in order to bring sexual instincts under control. S. Freud (1935) noted, "Educators have a limited time during latency to develop the mind before the sexual instinct bursts forth in puberty and overwhelms the child wth its force, marking the end of his educability" (p. 83). According to this view, if this impulse training is not completed early, older children are difficult, and the school must devote its efforts to completing this training rather than to intellectual development.

The Skinnerian theory also leads to a belief in the early timing of education. This environmentalist position holds that early education is important for preventing the establishment of competing response patterns that would impede later learning.

Maturational theories (such as those of Gesell and Lorenz) which postulate genetic determination of behavior patterns are discussed by Kohlberg (1968), he noted that this position leads to the belief that early cognitive training is a waste of time and later periods are more critical for intellectual development. The extreme point of view in this regard is based upon the belief that biologically based critical periods exist in which the individual can acquire certain learnings. Thus, attempts to train these abilities before or after these periods are either completely useless or much less effective.

Some notions pertaining to individual readiness for particular educational experiences seem to rest on a vague belief in critical periods. The educator who resignedly attributes failure of educational efforts to lack of readiness and who advocates passive waiting for readiness to appear reflects a belief in the critical periods hypothesis which absolves him of responsibility in developing readiness. However, Erikson's psychosocial theory does not take such a passive vew of the responsibilities of socializing agents in assisting individuals to successfully resolve the crises of the critical periods described by this theory.

Kohlberg discussed a cognitive-developmental point of view based largely on Piaget's theory and concluded that this view suggests that many forms of cognitive training (such as teaching the solutions to mathematical equations) are inappropriate at the preschool level because the child has not yet developed the prerequisite cognitive structures. Therefore, timing of specific educational efforts depends on the development of this structures. However, Piaget's theory does not reflect a belief in critical periods for this development.

Interrelatedness of Changes. A conception of various developmental changes as proceeding relatively independently may lead to separation in efforts to foster these various changes. A view of changes as interdependent tends to result in programs which attempt to integrate educational efforts. If one construes a primary objective of education to be broadly cognitive (as Piaget describes cognitive development), one would be more concerned with the thinking processes of an activity than with the content of the activity. For example, a Piagetian teacher would consider it equally useful for a child to work with different lengths of paper in making a collage or to participate in charting the heights of various children on a wall. The cognitive structuring of seriation and transitivity [4] are viewed as possibly arising from any number of different types of experiences. However, if one construes a primary objective of early education to be uninhibited artistic expression, the collage activity would be viewed as better for realizing this objective. If one defines objectives in terms of solutions to arithmetic problems, words read, and words written, the concern with general changes, such as in reasoning processes or in the acquisition of healthy self-concept, tends to be minimized.

Nature of Intelligence

The contrasting conceptions of intelligence of adherents of the psychometric approach and of Piaget lead to different educational practice. The psychometric assumption that intelligence is unchanging throughout life led psychologists to construct tests with statistical norms such that individuals tested on different sets of questions at various points in their lives would perform at the same I.Q. level. Intelligence is thus operationally defined in normative quantitative terms, that is, in terms of relative position on a curve of correct answers to questions largely dependent on knowledge of culture-bound factual information.

Piaget's (1950) research on cognitive development in children led him to challenge this definition and to propose a developmental conception of intelligence. In contrast to the psychometric notion, Piaget vews intelligence as changing qualitatively from infancy to adulthood. He defines intellectual growth in terms of changes in reasoning that underlie answers to the same tasks at different stages of development. Individuals are assessed in terms of their reasoning about such ordinary phenomena as space, time, wind, clouds, dreams, and quantity. Performance is assessed in terms of a universal sequence of development rather than in quantitative comparative terms.

These two conceptions of intelligence are not just theoretically different. Psychometric and Piagetian tasks actually tap different aspects of cognitive functioning. This was demonstrated by Kohlberg and DeVries (1969) in a study of children's performance on 22 psychometric and Piagetian tasks. Factor analysis separated psychometric and Piagetian tasks into different factors. The results of this study were confirmed in a later study by DeVries (1974). Thus, the two different definitions of intelligence actually lead to different information about intellectual functions. Kohlberg and DeVries suggest that these might be more useful than psychometric tests in assessing psychoeducational efforts because Piagetian measures provide an assessment of an individual's general organization of experience which is not limited to direct cultural learning.

Educators in general rely on the psychometric conception of intelligence. Let us consider the ramifications of this theoretical orientation in educational practice. First of all, intelligence is equated with I.Q. Since the standardization design results in a numerical score which remains relatively stable over time, intelligence thus tends to be viewed as innately predetermined and fixed.

If the teacher believes intelligence is unchangeable, he cannot conceive his role to be that of improving it. All that is left is to improve the individual's store of information. Belief in the I.Q. as such an absolute measurement can lead a teacher to label individuals as more or less able, and to extend this as an expectation in all areas of functioning. If it is true that such expectations affect the individual's self-concept and tend to influence behavior in the direction of the expectation, the I.Q. can take on a self-fulfilling prophecy function.

Belief in intelligence as having at least some innate base which cannot be changed by educational experience leads to belief in the limitation of the effect of teaching. The degree to which the educator believes teaching can change a student's intelligence depends on the degree to which intelligence is considered determined by innate factors. The more it is believed to be innate, the more the teacher is pessimistic concerning the efficacy of training, especially for students with low I.Q. scores. The teacher may make little effort to bring about change in individual performance level. Since failure to learn is attributed to a deficit in the child, this perspective would lead to a view that early education is useless for poor children, who can be predicted to fail in school. On the other hand, the teacher who believes in the efficacy of environmental determinants, and in a limited innate determination of intelligence, will take a more optimistic attitude toward the efficacy of educational efforts and will be more likely to set higher goals for pupils. This view in extreme form could lead to unrealistically high or inappropriate expectations and to pupil frustration.

Since intelligence tests have generally been reserved as the special bailiwick of psychologists, educators have tended to assume that assessment of intelligence is outside their province. The awe with which a teacher may approach psychometric tests stems from one or more of the following: (a) the teacher's respect for authority results in a faith in the experts; (b) the teacher may not know the test content or the theoretical and empirical rationale on which it is based; and/or (c) the test can be designed, administered, and interpreted only by those trained in this special competency. It is understandable, therefore, if a teacher concludes that since the tests are constructed by experts who use strict and arduous standardization procedures, assessment of intelligence is not to be left to the ordinary teacher.

Teachers do, however, administer group tests yielding an I.Q. score, and they do know the content of these group tests. Since these are also constructed by experts, the teacher's awe of standardized tests may be unaffected by the fact that he or she is permitted to administer them. After all, the procedure for arriving at an I.Q. score for an individual is purely mechanical and involves no interpretation. However, knowledge of the content of these tests may lead to contempt, especially when the test results conflict with the teacher's evaluation of an individual.

A teacher's belief that assessment of intelligence is outside his or her capability is reinforced by the fact that individually administered intelligence tests are considered more reliable assessments than group tests. When a child has learning problems, a specialist is called in to administer an individual test in order to discover the child's *real* ability level. Thus, for many teachers, the I.Q. acquires a certain mystique that becomes attached to intelligence itself. Since I.Q. and intelligence tend to be viewed as synonymous, the teacher who considers himself incapable of measuring I.Q. is led to conclude that he cannot trust himself to evaluate intelligence. Thus, educational practice tends to separate itself from assessment of the intellect whose growth its efforts are supposed to foster!

Another unfortunate result of the isolation of intelligence from educational practice is that educators tend to operate with a fragmented theory of the child and development. Intelligence tends to be viewed as apart from motivation, learning, and socioemotional development. With intelligence outside the province of their expertise, what is left for educators but to focus on teaching specific knowledge and/or promoting socioemotional development?

Piaget's theory of intelligence leads to a situation that is quite different from that resulting from the psychometric conception. Since intelligence is seen as changeable over time and only partly determined by hereditary factors, this perspective leads to an optimistic view of the efficacy of educational experience. Unlike the teacher influenced by psychometric theory, the Piagetian teacher tries to promote the child's improvement of his intelligence. Since the source of intellectual development is internal to the individual, however, teaching does not take the form of direct instruction. Rather, the teacher makes materials available and acts as part of the environment with which the child interacts. Since it is the child who constructs his knowledge, the teacher leaves the initiating role to the child in selecting and engaging in activities. From Piaget's perspective, the development of intelligence is very much the valid concern of the teacher.

Since the Piagetian teacher tries to facilitate the development of intelligence, he or she must also be able to evaluate it. The teacher continuously assesses the nature of children's thinking through observation of play, as well as through occasional administration of Piagetian tasks.

Piaget's theory of development leads to a holistic theory in which intelligence is inseparable from all other aspects of development. In fact, it leads to establishing socioemotional objectives as foremost, with cognitive objectives an integral part of these socioemotional objectives (see DeVries & Kamii, in press, and Kamii and DeVries, 1974 for further elaboration).

Piaget (1964) distinguishes between the learning and the development of the child. He points out that learning is opposite to development in the sense that the former is provoked from external sources, whereas the latter occurs as a spontaneous process governed by internal structures. Since learning occurs within the limits set by developmental level at any point in time, development always explains why any specific learning is possible. Learning is limited in scope of application, whereas a developmental change is more likely to generalize to a broad scope of application.

Nature of Motivation

As was noted above, one unfortunate result of isolating intelligence from the province of education is the tendency also to view motivation as apart from intelligence. The question of motivation is related to the preceding discussion on various beliefs concerning the source of developmental change, since beliefs about motivation hinge upon some of the dimensions already mentioned. For example, the view that motivation originates out-side the individual leads to the assumption of at least some responsibility by the educator, although other socializing agents may also be considered responsible. The opposite view—that the source of motivation is internal —leads to blaming the child for its absence and crediting him for its presence. (Whether motivation is considered to be present or absent often depends on whether the child exhibits an interest in the objectives which the *educator* thinks are important.)

The view of learning as a reactive process occurring through condi-tioning also has implications for motivation; it may result in the extreme view that motivation is unnecessary for attainment of educational goals. Many behavior modification methods reflect a belief that motivation is unnecessary in order to bring about meaningful behavioral change.

Hunt's (1963) radically different conception of motivation as in-hering in the individual's adaptive intellectual efforts to comprehend his experience places motivation in a central and inextricable position with regard to learning. This view tends to lead a teacher in the direction of (a) capitalizing on spontaneous or induced individual interests as the major context for learning, (b) permitting individuals to pursue different learning goals, (c) expecting individuals to differ in amount of time necessary for learning, and providing ample time for mastery of learning. Representative of this approach are the "open school" and the Piaget-derived program being developed by Kamii (1971) and DeVries (1974).

Sex, Culture, and Ethnicity

No discussion of the practical educational expressions of one's beliefs about children would be complete without considering the effects of beliefs pertaining to sex, culture, and ethnicity. Behavioral differences among per-sons grouped on the basis of these characteristics have historically been of interest to behavioral scientists. However, the popular controversies have not yet led to consensus as to whether observed differences are due to biological or social factors (Cole & Bruner, 1971; Maccoby, 1966a). De-spite the lack of empirical justification for assigning superior status to any sex, culture, or ethnic group, it is well known that such assignments are made throughout the world. In the United States, inferior status is ascribed to females, non-Western cultures, and minority ethnic groups. The inferior status of these groups is accompanied by social devaluation and discrimina-tion (see, for example, D'Andrade, 1966; Cole & Bruner, 1971), which operate to perpetuate the inferiority myth and often encourage conformity of such groups to behaviors ascribed as inferior.

Education and the behavioral sciences have reflected society's ascription of inferior statuses and have actively perpetuated their continuation. This has been due largely to the failure to recognize the primary role of learning in determining behavior, to a misplaced faith in biological determinants of social behavior, and to the failure to recognize the situation-dependent nature of behavior. For example, a large body of evidence indicates that the behavioral differences between sexes are due primarily, and perhaps totally with regard to psychological characteristics, to cognitive learning of social roles (Kohlberg, 1966; D'Andrade, 1966; Hamburg & Lunde, 1966; Maccoby, 1966a).

Learning is also obviously a primary determinant of cultural and ethnic differences. Recent thinking and research make it clear that many old assumptions and beliefs concerning the nature and accommodation of differences must now be discarded or revised. Two important points are:

1. Research-based conclusions about differences are frequently invalid due to the use of testing situations employing procedures, language, materials, testers, etc., with which one group, but not the other, has had little or no experience. Current controversy regarding standardized tests of intelligence reflects a growing concern among both professional and lay groups about the limitations to the validity of these psychometric measures. In particular, their use with persons having a background of experience different from that of middle-class whites has been called into question. Cole and Bruner (1971) cite examples of research which contradict previous findings of incompetence in other cultural groups when methodology is altered so that it is culturally appropriate. One research group (Cole, Gay, Glick & Sharp, 1971) concluded that "cultural differences reside more in differences in the situations to which different cultural groups apply their skills than to differences in the skills possessed by the groups in question." It is therefore imperative that behavioral scientists carefully scrutinize their data for situational or other bias.

2. Educational and other social institutions communicate that certain arbitrary sexual, cultural, or ethnic characteristics are inferior when other characteristics are perpetuated as the standard to be achieved. Such euphemisms as "weaker sex," "culturally deprived," and "culturally deficient" clearly label groups as inferior. Reference to groups as "culturally disadvantaged" may be used by some to refer to conditions of economic, social, or political discrimination which have resulted in a group's lack of opportunity to develop and compete on an equal basis with others. However, the term "culturally disadvantaged" has been used so widely as a synonym for the terms more explicitly attributing deficiency that it has become just as anathema as those terms. Simkins, Williams, and Gunnings (1971) noted that even "biculturation" (Valentine, 1971) is used to denote inferiority when the bicultural model weighs the characteristics of

one culture more favorably than the other. Simkins et al. concluded that the only acceptable model is that of cultural difference which leaves room for a change in the social system to accommodate and weigh with equal favor the characteristics of the minority group.

When belief in the inferiority of a group is coupled with belief in learning as the primary determinant of characteristics ascribed as inferior, the majority group may attempt to influence conformity to those characteristics that are ascribed as superior. A serious ethical question arises when the methods of behavioral science (and of medical science) are used to alter the behavior of individuals without their consent. A well-intentioned behavioral scientist or educator may violate the rights of an individual when he attempts to "help" him behave in conformance to majority standards. Such attempts have been defended by Krasner and Ullmann (1965): "If a person is being supported by society (as in a psychiatric hospital), then it is appropriate for an authorized agent of society to alter his behavior. On the other hand, behavior modification is inappropriate if the person is a self-supporting, contributing member of society. . . . The ultimate source of values is . . . the requirements of the society" (p. 363).

The great danger in this point of view, of course, is that society can develop a system of arbitrary values which define sex, cultural, or ethnic characteristics as not meeting "the requirements of the society." How does one define a "contributing member of society"? How does one assign individuals to psychiatric hospitals or to other positions in which societal support is provided? The fact that blacks are disproportionately represented in mental institutions and prisons suggests that societal values may be operating to define ethnic characteristics as deranged or criminal. One particularly promising approach is that of Szasz (1961), who questioned the labeling of mental and emotional disorders as "illness" and suggested that they be considered "problems in living" instead. Such a perspective opens the possibility of more broadly considering the individual in his environmental context. This issue is a complex one, and the discussion here merely points out the need for self-awareness regarding beliefs held toward individual members of different cultural, ethnic, or sex groups.

Perhaps it is appropriate here to point out that up to this point we have discussed the importance of the educator's theory about children in general. However, a teacher expresses that general theory specifically in classroom practices with regard to specific children, at specific times, and in specific ways. The extent to which a child may be psychologically damaged by communication of a teacher's beliefs that the child's sex, culture, or ethnicity (or other characteristic) is inferior or worthless cannot be calculated. Similarly, the extent to which a child may be psychologically enhanced and facilitated in development by communication of a teacher's belief that the child is intrinsically worthwhile also cannot be calculated.

EDUCATIONAL IMPLICATIONS OF THEORIES OF
FREUD, ERIKSON, SKINNER, AND PIAGET

References to the theories of Freud, Erikson, Skinner, and Piaget have been made in our previous discussion of the dimensions where theoretical differences result in differences in educational practice. However, let us consider the ramifications of some aspects of these theories in more detail. The attempt here is not necessarily to be complete in presenting each theory, or even to be current regarding changes in a theory. The goal is simply to demonstrate that particular theoretical beliefs lead to particular educational practices.

Theories of Freud and Erikson

The early Freudian psychoanalytic perspective (S. Freud, 1924; A. Freud, 1935) placed a negative valuation on the basic nature of the child. Children were considered by S. Freud as "polymorphously perverse" and full of "actively evil" impulses. This view of the nature of the child as basically bad dictated that the role of the socializing agents (parents and teachers) must be to provide consistent pressures on the child to conform to society's demands for control of impulses. Freud (1924) wrote: "For it is indeed one of the most important social tasks of education to restrain, confine, and subject to an individual control . . . of the sexual instinct . . ." (p. 321). The Freudian perspective of humans as basically affective and nonrational beings, whose behavior is primarily determined by innate sexual instincts, leads to a view of the socialization process as one of changing this basic nature. Domination by the pleasure principle must be replaced by the reality principle, thus enabling the child to behave in a socially acceptable manner. However, the child is viewed as vigorously resisting attempted restraints on his gratification of oral, anal, and genital impulses to engage in such "naughty" (A. Freud, 1935, p. 49) behaviors as thumb-sucking, lack of bladder and bowel control, playing with excreta, cruelty to animals, and masturbation and other sexual activities.

Developmental change, from the Freudian standpoint, is primarily a matter of neutralizing instinctual energy and transforming it into ego energy through the processes of repression, reaction-formation, substitution, and sublimation. Some restriction on instinctual gratification is necessary to force the functioning of these processes which, if successful, result in energy freed from instinctual objectives and made available for more socially acceptable aims. The child's ego and superego begin to develop in the context of situations where enough gratification exists but some impulse gratification fails to occur. The psychoanalytic teacher thus attempts to foster this development by demanding that the child postpone gratification, learn to endure a degree of pain, and altogether renounce sexual pleasure.

Freud postulated a sequence of universal stages in which instinctual energy shifts from oral to anal to genital areas of the body. The basic internal conflict between instinctual desires for sensate pleasures in these areas and the demands of society that the instincts not be gratified directly must be constructively resolved for normal development. The particular stage of development for an individual child dictates the kind of conflicts with which the teacher should be concerned. The socialization pressures are viewed as necessarily resulting in fears and anxieties on the part of the child. The psychoanalytic educator focuses upon thwarting direct instinctual gratifications and promoting the ability to delay and rechannel gratification. Diversionary tactics are utilized, and socially acceptable activities are offered as substitutions. For example, Anna Freud (1935) suggested that sand and water play may provide a substitute for play with urine and feces, and use of chalk and paint may be encouraged as impulse sublimation. Role playing and other forms of play are viewed as the vehicles through which the child works out conflicts and problems.

Mental life was viewed by S. Freud (1924) as arising largely from instinctual conflict: ". . . he has evolved for himself a mental activity in which all these relinquished sources of pleasure and abandoned paths of gratification are permitted to continue their existence, a form of existence in which they are free from the demands of reality. Every longing is soon transformed into the idea of its fulfillment . . ." (p. 382).

Anna Freud (1935) spoke of the "guerrilla war" between the child and the educator in which the child struggles against relinquishing his sensually satisfying behaviors. She noted that "step by step education aims at the exact opposite of the child's instinctive desires" (p. 58), that "education is not content to break the child of a habit which it regards as bad, but it strives to put every obstacle in the way of its re-emergence" (p. 67). This view of the child's nature led her to conclude: "The earliest educators and the little child are opposed to each other like two hostile factions. The parents want something that the child does not want. The child pursues his aims with a wholly undivided passion; nothing remains to the parents but threats and the employment of force" (p. 89). On the other hand, A. Freud (1924) cautioned against "the injurious effect of too great repression" as well as "the lack of all restraint" (p. 104). She recommended "the right proportion of instinct-gratification and instinct-restriction" (p. 105).

This educational stance called for some modification in the harsh and often punitive child-rearing practices of the day. However, severity was still considered necessary in the very early years to help the child become less dominated by his instincts. This summary of early Freudian theory suggests that the belief in a basically evil child led to educational and child-rearing practices which, if not as harsh or punitive as then-current practices, required external coercion by adults in order to promote neutralization and rechanneling of instinctual energies.

Anna Freud (1965) later wrote about normal development in a more positive vein, without, however, contradicting her earlier position. Noting that "the possibilities for beneficial intervention in the developmental realm are almost as unlimited as those for harmful interference with development" (p. 233), she emphasized the role of the mother figure in promoting the critical development of imitation, identification, and introjection. The latter were viewed as somehow linked to the development of pleasure in achievement and to "the inner urge toward maturation, i.e., toward progressive development" (p. 81). Pleasure in achievement was described in terms of task completion and independent problem-solving in play. A. Freud commented that if the child did not have sufficient satisfying experiences in play, pleasure in achievement would be retarded. The child would derive pleasure, instead, from praise and approval from others. She cautioned that overnight change in a child's behavior should be regarded with suspicion, noting that "regression is normal and that . . . the slow method of trial and error, progression and temporary reversal is more appropriate to healthy psychic growth" (p. 99).

With regard to the teacher's role, Anna Freud said, "It is the task of the teacher to match the child's needs for occupation and expression with the material offered and not to create a sense either of boredom or of failure by lagging too far behind or by anticipating needs before they arise" (p. 91). She further pointed to "the common mistake of giving the highly intelligent children more food for intelligence; talking to the particularly verbal; and giving the bodily active more opportunity for action" (p. 233).

Traditional nursery school curricula tend to reflect the more positive view of the child in this later psychoanalytic position, to reject behavioristic views. However, a closer look at many practices associated with psychoanalytic thought reveals that they are also influenced by other psychodynamic theories and do not represent Freudian theory alone.

Modifications in Freud's theory by ego psychologists (see, for example, Hartmann, 1958; Hartmann & Kris, 1945; Hartmann, Kris & Loewenstein, 1946) also lead to an orientation to practical dealings with children which is different from early Freud. The primary modification in theory by neo-Freudians is the postulation of innate rational ego energy which is separate and distinct from irrational instinctual energy. The significance of this difference is that it leads to a view of the child as possessing both an innate good and bad instinct. The socializer's task, then, becomes that of developing the already existing good capacity rather than repressing and transforming the instinctual energy from its self-gratification focus. The focus is upon adaptation with regard to reality relationships. Not all interchange with the environment is viewed as conflictual, and adaptive coordinations are considered possible without the frustration of instinctual drives by exigencies of reality.

Erikson's theory is selected for particular focus here because his extensions and elaborations of Freud's theory are acclaimed by other ego psychologists (see, for example, Rapaport, 1959) and because this theory is considered an important one in most graduate-level child-personnel training programs.

Erikson describes eight stages in the human life cycle, each of which is characterized by a phase-specific developmental task that must be solved. The discussion here is limited to the first three stages of early childhood with which this book is primarily concerned: trust versus mistrust; autonomy versus shame and doubt; and initiative versus guilt.

While Erikson's stages parallel the psychosexual stages of Freud, the tasks and their adaptive coordinations are not only intrapsychic but also psychosocial in nature. The focus is upon the relationships between the child and his milieu, and particularly emphasizes the specific external social demands upon the child as important to the outcome of his development. Appropriate social contact and communication are necessary for proper development that is gauged in terms of adaptive, rational coping with social demands.

Erikson's first three stages are critical periods in which the child's healthy, adaptive resolution of the crisis of each stage determines to what extent he later possesses a sense of basic trust, is autonomous, and has initiative. The degree to which the child fails to make a healthy crisis resolution determines to what extent he later feels a sense of basic distrust, is ashamed and doubtful in his relationships, and is handicapped by guilt.

The role of the socializing agent during the first year of life is to provide stimuli in the proper intensity and at the right time so that the infant can accept them. A mutuality in regulation between the child and his caretakers is important for the development of a reliance on the sameness and continuity of the external environment. It is also important for the infant's development of a feeling of trust in himself and the capacity of his organs to cope with urges. During the latter part of this first stage, healthy coping involves incorporation of experiences as the infant seeks to experience stimulation in a more active fashion. He bites, focuses his eyes on objects and follows trajectories to take them in visually more thoroughly, discerns and localizes particular sounds, reaches out, and grasps.

In the second stage, when the child is resolving the crisis of autonomy versus shame and doubt, the task of the educator is to permit the child's gradual development of the ability to withhold and let go voluntarily. This requires considerable patience on the part of the adult, since control of bowel and bladder functions constitutes an important aspect of this crisis. If demands are too rigid or too early, the child will be deprived of the experience of willingly and by free choice exerting this control, and he will feel ashamed and doubtful about his ability to control himself. This crisis also involves all experiences of withholding and letting go, and the facilitating adult permits the child to drop and throw, push and pull. The child is presented with firm expectations of self-control, inhibition, and regulation, and he is encouraged to accept and comply with these.

The third-stage crisis focuses upon the establishment of initiative versus guilt. Problems of this period pertain largely to the Oedipal wishes directed toward the parent of the opposite sex. The child's identification with the parent of the same sex leads to a desire to usurp that role with the opposite-sex parent. Jealousy and rivalry are experienced. The feeling of power resulting from increased imagination and locomotive ability results in secret fantasies and guilt. Castration anxiety arises as imagined punishment for fantasies.

The role of the parent and educator during this period is to foster identification and assist the child in resolving the Oedipal crisis. Successful resolution provides a basis for a high but realistic sense of ambition and independence, and for perseverance in pursuing social goals. Through identification, the conscience becomes firmly established and the child develops a sense of responsibility. Adults should promote feelings of equality and worth, encourage the child's feeling of being "grown-up" when sharing obligations, exhibiting discipline, and making things. Successful social adaptation in this third stage results in the development of moral responsibility and superego development.

Developmental potential is determined by the degree of success in resolving important crises. During early childhood, the Oedipal crisis is paramount as the child struggles with frustrations over the lack of gratification of his sexual interest in the opposite-sex parent. A. Freud said, "The task of education in the case of the little child would be to check alike the evil wishes which are directed against his brothers and sisters and his father, and the longings for his mother, and to prevent their materialization." Also, the educator attempts to promote healthy resolution of this conflict through fostering identification with that parent and internalization of moral values.

The role of experience in personality development is critical in determining behavior since an individual's past history reflects repressed impulses and conflicts. Patterns of earlier experiences of love and hate, rebellion and submission, etc., are repeated. While general behavior is determined by the part of the body invested with instinctual energy at a particular time, individual uniqueness results from the particular content of experiences pertaining to the interaction of instinctual energies with environmental forces.

In addition to Erikson, other neo-Freudians—such as Jones (1968) and Ekstein and Motto (1969)—advocate educational methods that differ considerably from the early, more repressive approach of the Freuds. It would seem that psychoanalysis and other psychodynamic perspectives have contributed to education a greater appreciation of individual differences, especially in terms of unconscious motivations. It also offers teachers an avenue of increased self-awareness and growth necessary for the most effective teaching.

Bank Street College of Education in New York City and The Erikson Institute in Chicago are probably the best current examples of early childhood educational programs which are strongly influenced by psychoanalytic theory. However, other psychodynamic theories and cognitive-developmental theories are also acknowledged as sources of their educational practices (Biber, 1959; Biber & Franklin, 1967; Biber, Gilkeson & Winsor, 1959; Shapiro, undated). The Erikson Institute stresses an integration of Erikson's theory with that of Piaget (personal communication). The result of this eclecticism is that the psychoanalytic influence is expressed in a manner quite different from the early writings of the Freuds. For example, the teacher rejects "threat, fear, and punishment as psychologically corrosive mechanisms of control" (Biber, Gilkeson & Winsor, 1959, p. 4), and focuses upon developing a relationship of trust and positive valuation between herself and the child. Moreover, the Erikson Institute particularly emphasizes the importance of the ego development of the teacher as basic to the ability to have a healthy influence on children.

Theories of Skinner and Piaget

Behavior modification through behavior analysis is perhaps the clearest example of the educational application of behavioral science theory and research. This application has succeeded in bringing together the psychological laboratory and the real-life environment of classrooms. The behavior modifier uses empirical techniques which are systematic and objective and which are derived from theory based solidly on research. The theory is readily transferable into clear practical application because its principles and language are relatively simple to understand and they possess a "commonsense" appeal. Results of behavior modification techniques are often dramatic, and the effectiveness of this approach in changing extreme problem behavior is impressive.

From the scientific perspective, behavior analysis is commendable in that it produces teachers who follow the scientific method of gathering objective data, analyzing it, planning educational procedures based on empirically derived theoretical principles, implementing these systematically, and evaluating the effectiveness of the procedures by comparative analysis of pre- and post data. The teacher is actively experimental, varying components of procedures to maximize effectiveness.

From the clinical and child-development perspective, behavior analysis is commendable in a number of ways. It can produce teachers who respect individual behavioral differences and take them into account in planning tailor-made educational experiences. Also, the systematic procedures of reinforcement possess a consistency which enforces consistency on the part of the teacher. It can serve to reduce arbitrariness and negativeness in the teacher's demands on, expectations of, and rewards and punishments of the child. The child may thus experience greater security and less anxiety and frustration if the environment is one in which communication is clear and he knows what to expect.

Behavior modification tends to result in demands on the child that are reasonable in terms of his ability to succeed. Change is expected to occur in small increments, from the child's starting point (entry behavior), and the teacher may be less frustrated and more tolerant of less than perfect behavior. These techniques can make the teacher more confident and self-respecting as a result of demonstrated efficacy and competence.

Behavior modification can also result in greater confidence and self-respect on the part of the child who experiences pleasure in behaving in ways which make him feel in more control of himself and bring the rewards of social approval. Where behavior obnoxious to others is modified, the positive effects of this change in attitudes, feelings, and behavior toward the child can obviously be far-reaching. Behavior modification provides an extremely optimistic outlook on the potential for behavior change, and is especially welcome to those attempting to change severely disturbed or asocial behavior.

However, on the negative side of the clinical and cognitive-developmental ledger, some serious concerns exist. The view of the child as qualitatively like the adult in psychological characteristics can (though not necessarily) result in arbitrary imposition of adult standards on the child. The deliberate shaping of a child's behavior to resemble that of the adult is not defensible if this assumption of similarity is untrue. A large body of child development theory and research, particularly the work of Piaget, challenges this assumption and argues that the child is psychologically qualitatively different from the adult. This point of view is elaborated below.

Thus, even though the behavior modifier attends to such individual differences as reinforcer preferences and tailors procedures for the individual, he may be exhibiting a lack of respect for the child by forcing conformity to behavior which is meaningless to the child. For example, a child may learn to count and to follow a procedure which yields the correct answer to a mathematical equation. However, if he does not know the meaning of the numerical terms, what he probably learns is that in school one uses a nonsense code to answer a teacher's nonsense questions. Moreover, imposition of inappropriate standards of behavior may actually interfere with or distort development. The child experiencing such modification may pay a high price for the rewards of conformity. Where the changed behavior seems arbitrary to the child, he may develop an unhealthy dependency on the external world for definitions of good behavior and fail to develop the internal direction which forms the basis for feelings of competence and self-respect.

One important issue regarding the use of behavior modification concerns the values which determine selection of behaviors to be modified. This issue is both ethical and logical. The problem of deliberate misuse of this technique for control of others for one's own ends will not be discussed here. Rather, the question of what to modify entails consideration of appropriateness, priorities, and breadth of effects.

The concern of a cognitive-developmental psychologist for the appropriateness of behavior selected for change pertains to its relationship to developmental change; an example of inappropriate change is given below. The concern for priorities is related to that of appropriateness, but also involves the more general question of economy of time and effort. Given that a particular behavior change can be brought about through operant conditioning procedures, does it require more time and effort (on the part of both teacher and child) than would be expended at a later stage of development? Does the behavior change occupy time and effort better devoted to other learning? Does it take more time and effort than is warranted by the import of the change? The latter question refers to the possibility that behavior modification techniques may be utilized to change a host of superficial behaviors which have no long-range effects and occupy time better spent on focusing on behavior with better payoff potential.

The focus of behavior modification upon overt, observable behavior and upon narrow goals for change results in a lack of breadth which calls into question its all-purpose educational utility. Two examples illustrate the present serious narrowness with which behavior modification is frequently applied. The first example is an experience of a teacher-educator currently using behavior modification as a central part of early education training. He instituted a behavior modification procedure to attempt to eliminate his five-year-old daughter's nocturnal bedwetting. She was allowed to select a toy (from a supply of toys she selected) each morning following a dry night. After an entire week of dry mornings, she could select a toy from a more expensive group. The procedure was highly successful in terms of controlling the bedwetting behavior. The child almost immediately showed two consecutive weeks of dryness. However, the sensitive father noticed that his daughter's sleep simultaneously became disturbed, with physical thrashing and bad dreams. He halted the modification procedures and concluded that he preferred to tolerate the bedwetting behavior than create what he considered a psychological disturbance.

The second example pertains to a report given at the Second Annual Symposium on Behavior Modification (held in 1971). Among many papers describing similar dramatic changes in children with severe behavior problems was one study which reported the successful modification of a hyperactive boy's classroom behavior. The teacher and the entire class cooperated in providing reinforcement for his sitting at his desk and attending to his work. In addition, his desk was fitted with a device which emitted small candies (which he shared with his classmates at the end of a day) at intervals while he was at his desk.

The general satisfaction of the symposium audience with the results indicating increased time at desk perplexed this writer, who was impelled to ask one of the symposium leaders the following questions: Why don't behavior modifiers attempt to assess effects of their procedures other than the specific effect selected for change? Taking the study described as an example, why isn't the investigator also concerned with at least mentioning, if not actually measuring, positive changes in self-concept which likely accrued to the boy who became able to control his hyperactive behavior and received the warm social approval of teacher and peers? What about the change in the teacher's feeling about her ability to deal effectively with a serious problem? What about the likely change in attitudes of parents, teacher, and other children toward the problem child? What about the likely change in patterns of social interaction of the problem child and his peers? Why don't behavior modifiers silence some of the criticism of their work by attempting to document such efficacious effects? The answer of the prominent behavior modifier was, "We don't know how."

It would be unfair to intimate that no behavior modifiers recognize or are concerned with other effects or the context of their procedures. However, such concerns are not generally articulated or studied in a systematic way. (The current work of T. Risley on language in the natural context may be an exception.)

It should be noted that behavior modification offers to educators only a technique. It does not provide assistance in making curriculum decisions. One danger is that the use of behavior modification may result in a deemphasis of curriculum as the teacher focuses on changing overt behaviors that are frequently superficial. Another possible negative result may be that a poor curriculum is more efficiently pursued. The image of an orderly group of children behaving just as the teacher wishes may lull the teacher into an uncritical attitude toward the curriculum content and method.

It may be that behavior modification should not be used with normal children, but should be reserved for use with children who are severely retarded or disturbed. Even in these cases, behavior modification should probably be used only until social behavior is brought under enough control that other methods can be effective. If behavior modification is to be used at all, it must be used wisely. It must take into account its effects within the broad developmental context and become concerned with broadening its efforts to include effects of reinforcement procedures beyond target behaviors.

The theories of B. F. Skinner and Jean Piaget, as vastly different theories of learning, clearly result in different educational goals, different teaching methods, and different evaluation criteria for ascertaining whether learning has occurred. The Skinnerian early education derivative is exemplified most clearly by the academic program developed by Bereiter and Engelmann (1966) and extended by Becker and Engelmann. The Piagetian derivative which best reflects that theory was begun by Kamii (1971) and is being developed by Kamii and De Vries (1974).[5] The practical effects of the theoretical differences between these two approaches can be illustrated by an example of divergent evaluations of children's acquisition of cognitive abilities studied by Piaget.

Engelmann (1971) attempted to teach seven kindergarten children conservation of substance, weight, and volume, speed, and specific gravity by teaching them such verbal rules as, "It will float because it's lighter than a piece of water the same size." Kamii and Derman (1971) then administered a posttest to the four children available on the day of their visit. They found that although the children had indeed learned the verbal rule, they often used it inappropriately and made statements characteristic of the preoperational child. For example, one child predicted that a cake of soap would sink "because it is heavier" and an identical cake of soap would float "because it is lighter!" When the examiner called the child's attention to the fact that she had placed identical cakes in both sinking and floating prediction piles, she did not show any sign of awareness that her statements were illogical. Preoperational answers were given many times as explanations of predictions and observations. For example, an object was said to sink or float because it is "light" or "heavy," "small" or "big," "skinny," "made of wood," or because "the air went out" (a bottle sank when the cap was removed and the air went out).

The significance of this study for our discussion on theory is that two different theories led to two different conclusions about learning and to two different conclusions about teaching. Engelman concluded that use of the verbal rule indicated that learning of logical principles had occurred. He accounted for inappropriate use of the rule and preoperational answers in terms of incomplete rules, the need for better programming, and the need for a longer period of instruction. Kamii and Derman concluded: *"Since the children did not have the prerequisite abilities for the construction of a single hypothesis, they could not possibly have attained the precise concept of specific gravity, no matter how long they had been taught many rules"* *(p. 135).*

Engelmann stated: "It is possible to teach children a wide variety of discriminations, including those that involve logical structure" (p. 126). He advocated teaching of verbal rules as the most efficient method to promote learning. Kamii and Derman, on the other hand, pointed out that *"both logical and physical knowledge must be structured slowly, beginning at the sensorimotor level and integrating all the intuitive concepts that are necessary for the attainment of later cognitive abilities"* (p. 141). They advocated teaching for long-term learning by asking the "right" questions at the "right" time to facilitate the child's construction of many incorrect rules, prior to gradual construction of the rule which is correct from the adult's point of view. A later development in thinking about Kamii's Piaget-based curriclum is that the "right" times should be judiciously selected for teacher intervention. The teacher should not bombard the child with a stream of questions, but should instead encourage the child to experiment with materials and find out how objects react to his various actions.

Piaget's theory emphasizes that developmental change is change in the individual's basic structure of cognitive organization. This point of view leads to the conclusion that not all behavioral change indicates structural change. Followers of Skinner do not recognize structural change, but view all behavior as reversible and modifiable.

The demonstration of extinction (behavior reverting to previous, undesirable action) is considered particularly important as proof of the fact that the behavior modifier actually has the behavior in question under the control of procedural manipulations. If extinction cannot be demonstrated when reinforcement procedures are suspended, the behavior modifier considers his procedures to have failed.

This view is quite in contrast to the position of developmentalists such as Piaget, who would consider the success of the extinction attempt to indicate a superficial behavioral change and its failure to indicate a possibly deeper and more lasting change in the individual's cognitive structure.

The methods of behavior modification are coercive, from the child's perspective. Piaget's (1932) theory clearly calls for conditions of non-coerciveness as necessary for the child's development into a fully autonomous person whose behavior is controlled from within rather than from without. While this does not imply complete permissiveness or passivity on the part of the teacher, it does indicate that to the degree the child is forced to behave in response to external controls, he will not be able to develop internal controls.

The controversy between behaviorists and developmentalists illustrates the primary issues in early childhood education: What kind of learning are we attempting to promote? How do we know when this learning has occurred? How do we teach in order to facilitate this learning? Different theoretical orientations appear to lead to different answers. If the educator is to provide the best education for young children, he must first be fully aware of the theory behind practice. Only then can he critically examine the theory and research of behavioral science and use its findings as a base for practice.

EDUCATION AND BEHAVIORAL SCIENCE

This chapter began by stating that educational practice is alienated from behavioral science theory and research. The reader may rightly protest that the exclusion of theory and research from education is not total. Prospective teachers do study what behavioral scientists say, and educators draw upon the resources of behavioral science to some extent. However, it seems fair to say that educators do not derive from behavioral science a coherent framework to guide their day-to-day operation. Should this be the case?

Why do educators fail to apply in the classroom the theories and findings of behavioral science? The first reason is probably historical. When behavioral science came into existence in the nineteenth century, education already had a long history and its own well-established traditions. As a newcomer to an old profession, behavioral science had difficulty in convincing educators that it had something new to contribute to education.

The second reason may be found in the contrast between the theoretical focus of behavioral science and the practical focus of education. In questioning whether or not behavioral science *can* provide practical guidance, educators offer the following reasons:

1. The aims of educators and behavioral scientists are basically different. Behavioral scientists seek to establish organized knowledge, while educators seek to formulate policies for action.

2. Little research is directly relevant to educational practice because researchers usually deal with laboratory situations which are typically far different from classrooms, and the focus of research is too distant from classroom concerns. Moreover, researchers do not translate their ideas and findings into the action language of educators.

3. Research findings and theories are frequently contradictory, and since behavioral science has not finished its task of confirming a coherent theory of behavior, practical application often cannot yet be drawn with certainty. It's no wonder that educators often conclude that formalized theories have nothing to offer them and that they must "just be practical."

In light of these well-founded skepticisms and many past frustrating attempts to apply behavioral science theory and research to educational practice, must we conclude that a rapprochement is hopeless or useless? The argument presented here is for rapprochement. Rapprochement is suggested as action that would strengthen both education and behavioral science, and give education a well-deserved role in behavioral science. Rapprochement is suggested because education and behavioral science share many of the same concerns, and because their expertise is complementary.

Parallel concerns of educators and behavioral scientists suggest that closer collaboration would be mutually beneficial. In a very broad (and admittedly oversimplified) sense, one can say that behavioral scientists spend more time in attempting to understand behavior, and educators in attempting to change it. It seems reasonable to expect that improved understanding of behavior would result in more effective attempts to change it, and that results of attempted change would lead to improved understanding. The fact is that the parallelism in concerns which should have led to a healthy interaction has in general continued as a distant parallelism in separate worlds.

Behavioral science offers its theory and research findings and methods from which education can select and build upon. The behavioral science approach and methodology can be adapted to the specific needs of education. Through behavioral science, education can render conscious its implicit theories and begin to direct its practice according to its own research-based theory.

In view of the present incompleteness of behavioral science, however, it would be a mistake for education simply to pursue an uncritical grafting operation of behavioral science theory upon practice. Rather, education should capitalize on the strengths offered by behavioral science, while at the same time recognizing its limitations.

Education offers to behavioral science a real-life milieu for theory testing, and can thus contribute to the development of more lifelike concepts and theories. In the educational setting, behavioral science can gain insights into human behavior which are not possible in more sterile laboratory settings. However, progress in behavioral science requires the collaboration of educators. Without their active participation and their unique questions and problems, behavioral scientists are unlikely to evolve a coherent educational focus.

The rapprochement suggested here between education and behavioral science is actually a call for the development of a behavioral science of education. Establishment of such a discipline requires changes in both education and in behavioral science. To a degree, educators need to become behavioral scientists, and behavioral scientists need to become educators.

It is clear that intelligent use of behavioral science requires the acquisition of its knowledge and skills. Educators who become their own behavioral science masters will reject the temptation to borrow inappropriate measures or methods. They will insist upon a behavioral science of education which focuses upon the problems of human learning and development in the educational setting.

Behavioral scientists who attempt to address themselves to clarifying theory and to answering educational questions by doing research in the natural behavioral context will be likely to resist the temptation to focus only on those aspects of behavior which are easily observed and quantified, but which are too often superficial and meaningless. They will feel the need to deal with the host of disorderly facts and variables of the educational milieu, and will thus feel the need for devising new methods for answering educational questions.

In order to best serve the interests of children, behavioral scientists must cooperate with teacher-training institutions in developing educational professionals whose specific practice is guided by behavioral science more clearly applicable to the educational setting than is now the case. The assimilation of education into behavioral science should result in significant accommodation on the part of behavioral science itself.

The questions common to the concerns of educators and behavioral scientists are difficult ones. Several lines of research are particularly needed to bring clarification on the theory-practice question: (a) the relationships between the beliefs and practices of educators need to be investigated; (b) more specific practical implications of specific theories need to be derived and field-tested; and (c) methods of evaluating educational practices need to be developed which consider both the negative and the positive effects on the child as well as the broad and long-range developmental effects.

The opening question of this chapter has been only partially answered. Since educators' beliefs about children and learning influence their practices in significant ways, it seems important to examine implicit beliefs and their educational implications. Without a clear conceptualization of intuitive, implicit beliefs, decisions affecting the lives of children cannot be made on the basis of the best knowledge available, and fads and commercial advertising may be too influential in connection with those decisions. The time is long overdue for educators to use the theories and methods of behavioral science in their approach to developing and evaluating curriculum objectives and teaching methods. The time is also long overdue for behavioral scientists to be more concerned with practical applications of their science. If research and theory building are pursued in the educational context as a collaboration of educators and behavioral scientists, a behavioral science of education can perhaps become a reality.

NOTES

1. Perhaps it is only fair to sensitize the reader to the writer's Piagetian bias. It is hoped that this bias is not reflected in unfair treatment of other theoretical positions.

2. This section owes a heavy debt to Ausubel (1958), Kohlberg (1968), Langer (1969), and Shapiro (1971). Their ideas were a source of both specific content and inspiration.

3. The reader unfamiliar with these principles of behavior modification is advised to consult Bijou & Baer (1961) for a particularly concise presentation.

4. Seriation involves the transitive comparison of many elements along a

certain dimension. It requires the ability to see, for example, that if A is greater than B, and B is greater than C, then A is greater than C.

Transitivity is the ability to coordinate simultaneously many pairs of relationships so that any element of a seriated group can be viewed as simultaneously greater than one element and less than another. For example, B is at the same time greater than A and less than C.

5. See chapter 2 by R. Parker in this volume for a discussion of differences in Piaget-based curricula.

REFERENCES

Ausubel, D. P. *Theory and problems of child development.* New York: Grune and Stratton, 1958.

Baldwin, A. L. *Theories of child development.* New York: John Wiley, 1967.

Becker, W. C., Thomas, D. R., & Carnine, D. Reducing behavior problems: An operant conditioning guide for teachers. Urbana, Ill.: ERIC, 1969.

Benson, C. H. *An introduction to child study.* Chicago: Moody Press, 1942.

Bereiter, C., & Engelmann, S. *Teaching disadvantaged children in the preschool.* Englewood Cliffs, N.J.: Prentice-Hall, 1966.

Biber, B. The implications for public education of research in learning. New York: Bank Street College of Education Publications, No. 56, 1959.

Biber, B., & Franklin, M. The relevance of developmental and psychodynamic concepts to the education of the preschool child. *Journal of the American Academy of Child Psychiatry,* 1967, 6(1).

Biber, B., Gilkeson, E., & Winsor, C. Basic approaches to mental health: Teacher education at Bank Street College. New York: Bank Street College of Education Publications, No. 62, 1959.

Bigge, M. L. *Learning theories for teachers.* New York: Harper & Row, 1964.

Bijou, S. W., & Baer, D. M. *Child development.* Vol. 1. *A systematic and empirical theory.* New York: Appleton-Century-Crofts, 1961.

Brown, M., & Precious, N. *The integrated day in the primary school.* New York: Agathon Press, 1968.

Bushell, D. *A token manual for behavior analysis classrooms.* Lawrence, Kans.: University of Kansas, Department of Human Development, 1970a.

―――. *Behavior analysis classroom.* Lawrence, Kans.: University of Kansas, Department of Human Development, 1970b.

Caldwell, B. M. What is the optimal learning environment for the young child? *American Journal of Orthopsychiatry,* 1967, 37(1), 8-20.

Cartwright, D. Lewinian theory as a contemporary systematic framework. In S. Koch (Ed.), *Psychology: A study of a science.* Vol. 2. *General systematic formulations, learning, and special processes.* New York: McGraw-Hill, 1959.

Cole, M., & Bruner, J. S. Cultural differences and inferences about psychological processes. *American Psychologist,* 1971, 26(10), 867-876.

Cole, M., Gay, J., Glick, J., & Sharp, D. *The cultural context of learning and thinking.* New York: Basic Books, 1971.

D'Andrade, R. G. Sex differences and cultural institutions. In E. E. Maccoby (Ed.), *The development of sex differences*. Stanford, Calif.: Stanford University Press, 1966.

De Vries, R. Relationships among Piagetian, psychometric, and achievement measures. *Child Development*, September, 1974.

DeVries, R., and Kamii, C. *Piaget for early education. Book 3. Group games*. Englewood Cliffs, N.J.: Prentice-Hall, in press.

Ekstein, R., & Motto, R. *From learning for love to love of learning*. New York: Brunner/Mazel, 1969.

Engelmann, S. E. Does the Piagetian approach imply instruction? In D. R. Green, M. P. Ford, & G. B. Flamer (Eds.), *Measurement and Piaget*. New York: McGraw-Hill, 1971.

Erikson, E. H. *Childhood and society*. New York: Norton, 1950.

————. Identity and the life cycle. *Psychological Issues*, 1959, *1*(1).

Evans, E. *Contemporary influences in early childhood education*. New York: Holt, Rinehart and Winston, 1971.

Flavell, J. H. *The developmental psychology of Jean Piaget*. Princeton, N.J.: D. Van Nostrand, 1963.

————. An analysis of cognitive-developmental sequences. *Genetic Psychology Monographs*, 1971.

Freud, A. *Psychoanalysis for teachers and parents*. Boston: Beacon Press, 1935.

Freud, S. *A general introduction to psychoanalysis*. New York: Washington Square Press, 1924.

Hall, R. V. *Managing behavior*. Merriam, Kans.: H. & H. Enterprises, 1970.

Hamburg, D. A., & Lunde, D. T. Sex hormones in the development of sex differences in human behavior. In E. E. Maccoby, *The development of sex differences*. Stanford, Calif.: Stanford University Press, 1966.

Hartmann, H. *Ego psychology and the problem of adaptation*. New York: International Universities Press, 1958.

Hartmann, H., & Kris, E. The genetic approach to psychoanalysis. *Psychoanalytic Study of the Child*, 1945, *1*, 11-30.

Hartmann, H., Kris, E., & Loewenstein, R. W. Comments on the formation of psychic structure. *Psychoanalytic Study of the Child*, 1946, *2*, 11-38.

Hunt, J. M. *Intelligence and experience*. New York: Ronald Press, 1961.

————. Motivation inherent in information processing and action. In O. J. Harvey (Ed.), *Motivation and social interaction: Cognitive determinants*. New York: Ronald Press, 1963.

————. *The challenge of incompetence and poverty*. Urbana, Ill.: University of Illinois Press, 1969.

Jones, R. *Fantasy and feeling in education*. New York: Harper & Row, 1968.

Kamii, C. K. Evaluation of learning in preschool education. In B. S. Bloom, T. Hastings, & C. Madaus (Eds.), *Handbook on formative and summative evaluation of student learning*. New York: McGraw-Hill, 1971a.

————. A sketch of the Piaget-derived preschool curriculum developed by the Ypsilanti early education program. In S. Braun & E. Edwards (Eds.), *History and theory of early childhood education*. Worthington, Ohio: Jones, 1972b.

Kamii, C. K., & De Vries, R. Piaget for early education. In R. K. Parker (Ed.), *Preschool in action,* Second Edition. Boston: Allyn and Bacon, 1974.

Kamii, C. K., & Derman, L. Comments on Engelmann's paper: The Engelmann approach in teaching logical thinking: Findings from the administration of some Piagetian tasks. In D. R. Green, M. P. Ford, & G. B. Flamer (Eds.), *Measurement and Piaget.* New York: McGraw-Hill, 1971

Kamii, C. K., & DeVries, R. *Piaget for early education.* Book 2. *Knowledge of the physical world.* Englewood Cliffs, N.J.: Prentice-Hall, in press.

Kessen, W. *The child.* New York: John Wiley, 1965.

Kohlberg L., A cognitive-developmental analysis of children's sex-role concepts and attitudes. In E. E. Maccoby (Ed.), *The development of sex differences.* Stanford, Calif.: Stanford University Press, 1966.

———. Early education: A cognitive-developmental view. *Child Development,* 1968, *39,* 1013-1062.

Kohlberg, L., & DeVries, R. L. Relations between Piaget and psychometric assessment of intelligence. Paper presented to conference on The Natural Curriculum of the Child, Urbana, Ill., 1969.

Krasner, L., & Ullmann, L. *Research in behavior modification: New developments and implications.* New York: Holt, Rinehart and Winston, 1965.

Langer, J. *Theories of development.* New York: Holt, Rinehart and Winston, 1969.

Lindsley, O. R. Children are not retarded. In G. Fargo, C. Behrns & P. Nolan (Eds.), *Behavior modification in the classroom.* Belmont, Calif.: Wadsworth, 1970.

Maccoby, E. E. Sex differences in intellectual functioning. In E. E. Maccoby (Ed.), *The development of sex differences.* Stanford, Calif.: Stanford University Press, 1966a.

———. *The development of sex differences.* Stanford, Calif.: Stanford University Press, 1966b.

Maier, H. W. *Three theories of child development.* New York: Harper & Row, 1965.

Marx, M. H. (Ed.). *Theories in contemporary psychology.* New York: Macmillan, 1963.

Maslow, A. H. *Motivation and personality.* New York: Harper, 1954.

McCurdy, H. G. *The personal world.* New York: Harcourt, Brace and World, 1961.

Neill, A. S. *Summerhill.* New York: Hart, 1960.

Patterson, B. G., & Gullion, M. E. *Living with children: New methods for parents and teachers.* Champaign, Ill.: Research Press 1968.

Piaget J. *The origins of intelligence in children.* New York: International Universities Press 1952.

———. Development and learning. In R. E. Ripple & V. N. Rockcastle (Eds.), *Piaget rediscovered.* Ithaca, N.Y.: Cornell University, 1964.

———. Piaget's theory. In P. H. Mussen (Ed.), *Carmichael's manual of child psychology.* Third Edition. New York: John Wiley, 1970.

Piaget, J., & Inhelder, B. *The psychology of the child.* New York: Basic Books, 1969.

Pinard, A. Piaget-based intelligence scales. In preparation.

Pinard, A., & Laurendeau, M. A scale of mental development based on the theory of Piaget: Description of a project. *Journal of Research in Science Teaching,* 1964, *2*, 253-260.

Rapaport, D. Introduction: A historical survey of psychoanalytic ego psychology. *Psychological Issues,* 1959, *1*, 5-17.

Ridgway, L., & Lawton, I. *Family grouping in the primary school.* New York: Agathon Press, 1965.

Rogers, V. R. *Teaching in the British primary school.* London: Macmillan, 1970.

Shapiro, E. The developmental-interaction approach to education. Mimeographed paper. New York: Bank Street College of Education, undated.

Simpkins, Williams, R., & Gunnings, T. What a culture a difference makes. *Harvard Educational Review,* 1971, *41*(4), 535-541.

Skinner, B. F. *Science and human behavior.* New York: Macmillan, 1961.

————. *The technology of teaching.* New York: Appleton-Century-Crofts, 1968.

Spodek, B. *Open education: The legacy of the progressive movement.* Washington, D.C.: National Association for the Education of Young Children, 1970.

Szasz, T. *The myth of mental illness.* New York: Paul B. Hoeber, 1961.

Tuddenham, R. Psychometrizing Piaget's theory. Paper presented at Conference on Ordinal Stages of Development, Carmel, Calif., 1969.

Valentine, C. Deficit, difference, and bicultural models of Afro-American behavior. *Harvard Educational Review,* 1971, *41*(3), 137-157.

Wallen, N. E., & Travers, R. M. W. Analysis and investigation of teaching methods. In N. L. Gage, *Handbook of research on teaching.* Chicago: Rand-McNally, 1963.

White, R. W. Motivation reconsidered: The concept of competence. *Psychological Review,* 1959, *66*, 297-323.

————. Ego and reality in psychoanalytic theory: A proposal regarding independent ego energies. *Psychological Issues,* 1963, *3*(3).

White, S. H. The learning theory tradition and child psychology. In P. H. Mussen (Ed.), *Carmichael's manual of child psychology.* Third edition. New York: John Wiley, 1970.

Chapter 2

Theory in Early Education Curricula

RONALD K. PARKER

The dual purpose of this chapter is to examine specific reflections of theory in Piagetian curricula and to review and critique the reflections of two theoretical approaches to language curricula. Specifically, the Piagetian curricula of Kamii, Lavatelli, Sprigle, and Weikart are comparatively analyzed in terms of their objectives, content, and methods. Selected preschool language development curricula emanating from theoretical positions of the neobehaviorists and psycholinguists are analyzed in terms of the adequacy of the theoretical conceptualization and the resulting curriculum.

Certain principles and beliefs about what children should learn and how this learning should take place are held by individuals concerned with the development and education of young children. In many cases these principles and beliefs are implicit in the ways individuals interact with children; in other cases, curriculum developers have made their principles and beliefs explicit as they presented a particular curriculum conceptualization.

Since theory building in child development has been the historical domain of psychologists (Baldwin, 1967; Langer, 1969; Maier, 1965), it is not surprising that conceptualizations of curriculum and educational practices have not, in general, felt the impact of formal theory. A recent publication (Parker, 1972) presented 13 conceptualizations of preschool curricula by some of the leading preschool curriculum developers. Parker and Day (1972), in a comparative analysis of these curricula, examined the degree to which formal theory in child development influenced each curriculum conceptualization. In general, little attention was paid to child development theory, and heavy emphasis was placed on the empirical research literature to determine the characteristics of the curriculum. Piaget (Kamii, 1972; Hooper, 1972) and Montessori (Banta, 1972) were the only two theorists who offered guidance in developing a *comprehensive* early

The author gratefully acknowledges the substantive contributions of Sueann R. Ambron and Gary I. Danielson to this chapter.

41

education program. Some developers used theoretical leads when developing certain program components; Karnes (1972), for example, used Guilford's Structure of the Intellect (1967) model for guidance in developing her cognitive activities. In general, however, theoretical references were made only in passing.

Our purpose in highlighting the specific curriculum reflections of a theorist derives from the thesis propounded in chapter 1 that *teachers* will profit by consciously using a theoretical orientation in their implementation of a preschool curriculum. With the aid of a theory-based curriculum, teachers will presumably be clearer in specifying their assumptions about child development, be consistent in curriculum implementation by establishing congruence between classroom behaviors and the theory, and be able to function more successfully by understanding theoretical principles and converting them into practice. Karnes (1972) reported that her teachers were able to *successfully* use the theoretical model of the Illinois Test of Psycholinguistic Abilities (Kirk & McCarthy, 1961) in better understanding language development and in developing language activities suggested by the theory. Finally, preschool curricula based firmly on theoretical positions will enable researchers to make more refined comparisons of the effectiveness of different approaches to early education, with the ultimate benefit that empirical support will emerge for certain approaches over others.

PIAGETIAN THEORY AND
EARLY EDUCATION CURRICULA

Since Piaget is generally recognized as the leading theoretician in child development and his influence is being felt in conceptualizations of early education programs, this section examines that influence and its expression in several preschool curricula. As an aid to the reader interested in examining the reflections of other theorists on early education curricula, the Appendix supplies the names and addresses of some major curriculum developers.

Before discussing the specific Piagetian curricula, four issues merit brief discussion: relevance of Piaget's work to educators; Piaget's view of critical periods in intellectual development; training for the acquisition of basic concepts and logical operations, and aspects of Piaget's theory with particular relevance to preschool curriculum.

Relevance of Piaget's Work to Educators

The work of Jean Piaget in genetic epistemology is of particular relevance to the educator because of his conceptualization of intelligence: intelligence is developmental in format, substantive in content, and operational in behavior (Sigel, 1969).

Let us elaborate briefly on these characteristics. In the development of intelligence Piaget describes four periods in terms of invariant sequential behaviors: the sensorimotor period (birth to about two years), the preoperational period (two to about seven or eight years), the period of concrete operations (seven or eight to about eleven or twelve years), and the period of formal operations (eleven or twelve through adolescence). Furthermore, Piaget provides information on substantive content. He describes the acquisition of concepts that reflect logical operations in such content areas as classification and seriation (Inhelder & Piaget, 1964), number (Piaget, 1952), space (Piaget & Inhelder, 1967), and geometry (Piaget, Inhelder & Szeminska, 1960). Finally, by specifying the process involved in acquiring substantive content, Piaget delineates a psychology of intelligence that is operational in behavior.

The congruence between Piaget's theory and the educator's use of the theory, of course, depends on a conception of the educational endeavor as guiding a developing organism through stages of intellectual growth, providing him with the appropriate organization of the environment, and introducing information at the appropriate time levels and in an appropriate manner (Sigel, 1964).

Piaget's View of Critical Periods in Intellectual Development

Identification of the early years as a critical period in intellectual development is frequently cited as a justification for preschool programs. Kohlberg (1968), in an article about early childhood education, noted:

> The major factual considerations leading to the notion of a preschool critical period in cognition derives from neither animal nor institutional studies. The real basis for stressing preschool cognitive programs comes from the belated recognition by educators that differences in the child's educational achievement are primarily due to the characteristics of the child and of his home environment rather than the child's elementary schooling, as such. (p. 1048)

Piaget's theory, according to Kohlberg (1968), does not imply critical periods in intellectual development:

> Insofar as the critical periods concept implies (a) sensitivity to stimulation at a definite chronological time span, (b) greater sensitivity to stimulation at earlier than at later periods of development, or (c) irreversibility of the effects of early stimulus deprivation. The position does hold that there are special sensitivities to stimulation at definite stages of develop-

ment, and it implies that the effectiveness of stimulation is contingent upon its match with a given level of development. The child's perception of the world is determined by his stage of cognitive organization, and a stimulus is only a stimulus if it can match or be assimilated to already developed schemata. (p. 1048)

Acquisition of Basic Concepts and Logical Operations

The acquisition of basic cognitive structures is reflected in mastery of such concepts as object permanence, causality, and the conservation of mass, weight, and volume, thereby indicating the attainment of various levels of logical operations. Since Piagetian preschool programs focus on basic concepts, the issue of training for the acquistion of these cognitive structures, basic concepts, and logical operations must be addressed.

The literature on training for the acquisition of basic concepts and operations has been reviewed by Sigel (1964), Flavell (1963), Kohlberg (1968), and Hooper (1968, 1972). The evidence from the training studies was described as inconclusive or at least that children could not be taught a logical operations function unless they had reached a particular level of cognitive maturity.

Consistent with the results of the reviews, recent experiments in teaching and learning, in Geneva, demonstrated that it is possible, within certain limits of the child's current level of operations, to speed up the acquisition of basic concepts and operations (Sinclair & Kamii, 1970).

Hooper (1968) made the point that the role of learning and educational experience is not denied by Piaget, but they are qualified chiefly through emphasis on the self-regulation (equilibration) process. Through self-regulation the individual's actions operate to alter cognitive structures. Piaget, therefore, acknowledged "the potential effect of the right kind of experience at the right time for the developing organism" (p. 424).

Piaget's Theory and Preschool Curriculum

At least seven facets of Piaget's theory are identified by various authors (Ginsburg & Opper, 1969; Kamii, 1970; Kohlberg, 1968; Sigel, 1969) as having particular relevance to preschool curriculum.

1. There are qualitative differences between adults and children in their beliefs about reality and their general cognitive processing (Ginsburg & Opper, 1969).

2. Intellectual development occurs in an invariant sequence of stages (Sigel, 1969).

3. Each stage in the development of intelligence is characterized by

the presence or absence of specific cognitive operations (Ginsburg & Opper, 1969).

4. At each stage the intellect operates as a coherent whole so that every concept that the child possesses at a given time is related to the network of all the other concepts he has built (Kamii, 1970).

5. Knowledge is not a copy of reality that is passively received; rather, it is the result of an active construction on the part of the child (Kamii, 1970).

6. The child's active construction of knowledge occurs in his confrontations with the physical and social environments (Sigel, 1969).

7. Intellectual development can be accelerated by emphasizing cognitive, conflict, match, and sequentia ordering of experiences and active self-selective forms of cognitive stimulation (Kohlberg, 1968).

Descriptions of Preschool Curricula Based on Piaget's Theory

Current efforts to apply Piaget's theory to preschool curricula will be described with respect to three points: objectives, content, and method. These preschool curricula were selected because the developers claim to base them *primarily* on Piaget's theory, written materials are available describing the program, and the curriculum contains at least three components, e.g., classification, seriation, and number components. The Piagetian preschool curricula are:

1. Constance Kamii's Ypsilanti Early Education Program
2. Celia Lavatelli's Early Childhood Curriculum
3. Herbert Sprigle's Learning to Learn Program
4. David Weikart's Cognitive Curriculum

While some of the programs reflect the viewpoint of the director alone, others represent the results of a group effort. For convenience and clarity, however, the programs will be referred to by a single sponsor's name.

Constance Kamii's Ypsilanti Early Education Program

The Ypsilanti Early Education Program developed by Kamii and others during a four-year period (1966-1970) has recently been revised by Constance Kamii and Rheta DeVries (1974).

Objectives. Kamii distinguishes between the tasks used in Piagetian research and the theory underlying the studies. Rather than teaching Piagetian tasks, she and DeVries take a broader view of the pedagogical implications of the epistemological theory. While emphasizing the long-range goals of education, such as formal operations and socioemotional maturity, they advocate (1) strengthening the preoperational process of thinking, and (2) stressing cognitive processes rather than behavioral objectives. This dual strategy is seen as the best way to achieve long-term goals. For example, the long-term goals of classification and seriation

> are not to enable children to make little matrices and arrange little graduated sticks, but to use the process of classification and seriation to isolate relevant variables and to generate and test hypotheses in dealing with real world (Kamii, 1970, p. 18).

In addition, a distinction is made between physical knowledge and logical-mathematical knowledge. Physical knowledge activities which encourage the child to build his repertoire of exploratory actions and strategies are stressed as of primary importance. In the context of feedback regarding the results of actions on objects, the child develops physical abstraction, out of which reflective abstraction arises.

Some of the most important objectives from Kamii's perspective of preschool are outlined under the heading of socioemotional and cognitive objectives.

Socioemotional objectives are: (a) to develop intrinsic motivation to learn, which is described in terms of children busily doing things, exhibiting curiosity, confidence, and creativity; (b) to control one's own behavior, that is, exhibiting the ability to make decisions and plans, to carry them out, and to evaluate actions, and the ability to respect rules and authority when appropriate; (c) to develop good relationships with peers, which means playing with other children, discussing things with other children, and respecting the rights and feelings of other children; and (d) to develop good relationships with adults.

Cognitive objectives are: (a) to build physical knowledge of objects; (b) to build a repertoire of social knowledge from people; and (c) to build logical-mathematical knowledge appropriate for children in the preoperational period.

Content. In selecting and organizing content, Kamii's (1970) philosophy is to

> (a) select the materials . . . to give a variety of appropriate choices to the child, (b) make a diagnostic evaluation of the child's level of functioning and train of thought once he has chosen an activity, and (c) follow up on his interests in light of this diagnostic evaluation. (p. 43)

In terms of content for a curriculum designed primarily to assist cognitive development, the critical areas, according to Kamii, are logical knowledge and physical knowledge. A third area—representation—helps the child to structure his knowledge progressively and symbolize it.

The content of Kamii's program includes: (a) logical knowledge (classification, seriation, number and spatial reasoning and temporal reasoning); (b) physical knowledge (knowledge about the nature of matter); and (c) representation. Piaget distinguishes three types of representation: indices, symbol, and sign. He refers to *indices* when part of the object (e.g., the bottom of the bottle) or marks causally related to the object (e.g., footprints in the snow) are sufficient cues for representation of the entire object. He refers to *symbols* when imitation, make-believe, onomatopoeia (e.g., uttering "quack, quack"), three-dimensional models, or pictures are used to symbolize the referent. The term *signs* is used when words and other signs (e.g., algebraic signs) can be be utilized in symbolizing (Kamii & Radin, 1970).

Method. The method of the Ypsilanti Early Education Program will be reviewed in the context of teacher roles, as well as of the selection and organization of learning activities and content.

Piaget identified three sources of knowledge: physical (feedback from objects), social (feedback from people), and logical-mathematical (feedback from the cognitive structure that the child has already built). In a Piagetian preschool, therefore, the role of the teacher cannot be one of simply transmitting knowledge directly to children.

> In physical knowledge, for example, if the child believes that a block will sink, she encourages him to prove the correctness of his statement. . . . She lets the object give the feedback from the child's own actions on objects. This is how she indirectly builds the child's initiative, curiosity, and confidence in his own ability to figure things out.
>
> In the teaching of social knowledge, teaching in a Piagetian preschool is not different from traditional teaching, i.e., the teacher simply tells the answer and reinforces the correct responses. (Kamii, 1970, p. 37)

Social knowledge can only come from feedback from people so the teacher feels quite free to tell a child that something is called a record player or magnet.

The role of the teacher in the logical-mathematical realm is not to reinforce the "correct" answer but to encourage the child's process of reasoning from his point of view. In classification, for example, the teacher uses an interactional method in which the child's thoughts and feelings are assessed and the child's immediate interests serve as the basis for the social-teaching exchange to proceed. If we prematurely impose adult logic on young children, according to Kamii, the lesson they will end up learning is that there is one correct answer and the answer always comes from the teacher.

In the selection and organization of learning activities, Kamii's approach is similar to that of traditional child-development philosophy. However, the way Kamii uses the traditional activities is different: activities and content are organized to maximize the cognitive benefit to the child. The daily schedule includes free activity time, group time, playground time, juice time, and bathroom time. The free activity time is the longest and most important block of time during which the children choose what they want to do from the range of possibilities that the teacher provides. The materials she selects to put in the classroom are, therefore, crucial (Kamii, 1970).

Periodically the program has included home visits made by the teacher once every two weeks on the half-days when the child is not in school. The purpose is to conduct individual tutorial sessions with each child, and to involve and instruct the mother in the educative process. The content of the home visits parallels the classroom activity. This aspect of the program is very clearly spelled out, even to the extent of a compilation of a catalog of home teaching activities determined to be effective because they benefit the child, make sense to the mother, and are structured so they can be continued by the mother in the absence of the teacher.

Celia Lavatelli's Early Childhood Curriculum

Lavatelli's Early Childhood Curriculum is a commercially available set of materials, teacher's guide, and volume describing how Piaget's theory can be applied to instructional programs for four-, five-, and six-year-olds.

Objectives. The major objective of the Early Childhood Curriculum is not to change drastically those preschool practices which have stood the test of time, but to provide the cognitive underpinning that will make the preschool more intellectually challenging (Lavatelli, 1970b). More directly, the program is designed to assist children in acquiring logical ways of thinking.

Specific objectives for each lesson are given in terms of mental operations and language models in the teacher's guide. Language is used to support mental operations, so that as a child is learning a particular mental operation the teacher is modeling the appropriate language structure. In the lesson on one-to-one correspondence, for example, the identifying properties of objects and matching objects by a one-to-one correspondence of properties are described as the mental operation. Language models for this same lesson include: "noun phrases with one or more adjectives (a small, round, red bead); coordinate sentences with directions for more than one action (find all the red beads and put them on the string); prepositions (*on* the string, *off* the string, *next* to the table)" (Lavatelli, 1970b, p. 9).

Content. The curriculum content (illustrated in Table 2.1 on pages 54-55) is organized around three main themes: classification; number, space, and measurement; and seriation. The program is planned with a developmental sequence in mind; the last set in each series requires the most advanced mental operations (Lavatelli, 1970b).

Method. The methods used in Lavatelli's program will be described as they relate to the structure of the training sessions and the teacher's approach. The core of this

> Piagetian program is a short, structured training session that the teacher conducts several times a week with five or six children. During these training sessions, children work with concrete materials, solving problems designed to foster development of intellectual skills in operations in classification, number, space and measurement, and seriation. (Lavatelli, 1970b, p. 1).

The length of these training sessions depends upon the attention span of the children. Initially they can be as short as ten minutes and gradually increased. Since the training sessions are meant to be enjoyed, they should be carried on in an informal, zestful way with each child actively engaged in working with materials at his own pace (Lavatelli, 1970b, p. 3).

In implementing the program, the teacher should have a good understanding of the development of the thought processes in each content area; this understanding will provide guidelines for choosing materials and knowing what to say to the children. The approach used by the teacher is to present the material to the child, then transform the material in some way, ask the child questions about the transformation and, finally, ask the child to justify his answer.

Herbert Sprigle's Learning to Learn Program

The Learning to Learn Program developed by Sprigle (1968) stimulates the cognitive development of four- to seven-year-old children through a sequential preschool curriculum of planned learning experiences. The program's theoretical foundation is that mental development proceeds along an orderly sequence of motor-perceptual-symbolic phases with periods of transition. "According to Piaget's formulation, spoken language comes only after the development of mental images which, in turn, develop out of repeated encounters with objects the child can move and manipulate. This second stage of mental imagery is replaced by the third stage of symbol formation which enables the child to talk about things in their absence" (Sprigle, 1970, p. 3).

The major concepts on which the program is grounded are that early childhood education is the beginning of the educational process, that the first few years of school should provide the child with opportunities to learn how to learn, and that every child has a drive toward increased competence and looks to adults for guidance relevant to this growth. Many Piagetians would not agree with Sprigle's interpretation of Piaget's thinking about the relationship between language and thought. Nor would they accept the goal of "learning to learn" as a major objective.

"This is not an instructional, direct-teaching, content-oriented, skill-development program. Rather, the primary emphasis is on learning to learn" (Sprigle, 1970). The objectives of the program are to establish early childhood education as the beginning of a continuous educational process and to help the child learn how to learn. Furthermore, each session (game-like activity) has specific objectives. Under "classification," for example, the following specific objectives are listed:

> To learn that items can be arranged into categories by some type of system.
> Given the information, to learn names by categories and items.
> Given the criteria of how items are categorized and descriptions of how items meet criteria, to separate items into categories.
> To recall information to separate array of items into two, three, four, or five categories.
> To combine subcategories into general categories, using criteria of attributes and/or function.

For a game labeled "absolute course," where children stepped over or crawled under yardsticks of varying heights, the specific objective was to develop the child's awareness of his own body in relation to an object (Van De Riet & Van De Riet, 1969).

Content. The Learning to Learn Program has a three-year sequential curriculum of planned learning experiences (beginning when children are four years old and continuing through first grade). It is based upon game-like activities which begin with concrete, three-dimensional manipulative materials and proceed to *higher-level* two-dimensional materials relying on language and communication. The flexible, loosely structured games stress conversation, problem-solving, and decision-making. Content, competition, and right/wrong answers are de-emphasized while thinking, reasoning, and expression of ideas are reinforced.

The curriculum attempts to develop attitudes and behaviors that promote learning. These include attention, concentrating, effort, perseverance, flexible mental set, sensitivity to the structure of a stimulus, strategies of problem-solving, decision-making, information-gathering, effective communication, learner responsibility, confidence and self-worth, and many others (Sprigle, 1970).

Children acquire these skills and concepts (Van De Reit & Van De Reit, 1969):

1. Information-gathering and processing through the use of all the senses.

2. Observation, identification, and labeling of objects.
3. Attention to and concentration on attributes that discriminate one object from another.
4. Classification.
5. Identification of classes and subclasses.
6. Identification and classification on the basis of reduced clues.
7. Use of guesses and hunches to advantage.
8. Decision-making.
9. Use of past learning to make decisions.
10. Problem-solving.
11. Reasoning by association and classification.
12. Anticipation of events and circumstances.
13. Expression of ideas.
14. Use of imagination and creativity.
15. Conventional communication.
16. Operations on relationships.
17. Exploration of number and space.

The substance of the program's curriculum is divided into two broad sections: language communication and number space. The specifics of content are elaborated in Table 2.1 on pages 54-55.

Method. The method in Sprigle's Learning to Learn program will be outlined in terms of the teacher's role and the daily schedule.

Teachers in the program are child-oriented rather than subject matter-oriented. Their approach is to pose problems for the children, ask questions, and stimulate interest and curiosity. Since one aim of the program is that the children learn from their own activities and thoughts, the teacher must be perceptive and sensitive to how the child works with and uses the materials.

The first cognitive activities of the day take place in a morning circle group with the teacher. Conversation, singing, or clapping ensues, with the teacher initially supplying most of the stimulation and the children later participating more spontaneously. Cognitive experiences (such as counting and reading a calendar) are included in this session.

A free activity period follows for approximately two hours. The child has freedom of movement and choice of a variety of materials available in the classroom. During the two-hour activity two or three children at a time are taken from the classroom by the teacher to an isolated place free from visual and auditory distractions. Here the children are exposed to the structured curriculum lasting from 10 to 30 minutes, depending upon the lesson. Later, the teacher introduces a follow-up activity on the content learned in the small groups.

Parental involvement is considered a crucial part of the Learning to Learn Program. Because most parents work, meetings are scheduled on

Sunday. The meetings are divided into three parts: general announcements, videotapes and discussion, and describing the curriculum and how it is related to suggested home activities. The showing of videotapes of the classroom has been especially effective. Parents enjoy seeing their children in action, and can better understand the activities they can do at home as follow-through on school programs. The teacher's behavior provides a model for parents and the parents can understand how children can learn more effectively with parental help (Sprigle, 1970).

David Weikart's Cognitive Curriculum

The cognitively oriented curriculum developed by Weikart (1969) during the five years of the Ypsilanti Preschool Project is a carefully structured program, and is based primarily on principles derived from Piaget's work on cognitive development. In addition, the principles of sociodramatic play and impulse control suggested by Sara Smilansky, and of specially developed language techniques called "verbal bombardment," and the adaptation of Bereiter and Engelmann's language patterning, are incorporated into the program. This program provides a preschool intervention experience for low-income three- and four-year-old children (Weikart, 1969, pp. 2–3).

Objectives. The two broad objectives of Weikart's program are: (a) to help the child develop logical modes of thought in order to gain knowledge about himself and objects, to see relationships between himself and things in his environment, and to group and order objects and events; and (b) to help the child develop the capacity to manipulate symbols and thus to act on and represent the environment.

Specific objectives for content areas are indicated in the daily plan. In one illustration during planning time, the temporal relations goal of understanding sequence of events was pursued through the activities of recalling the events of yesterday and talking about the sequence of the day (McClelland, 1970).

Content. To implement the objectives, four cognitive skill areas have been defined: classification, seriation, spatial relations, and temporal relations.

Classification, for example, is defined as learning to recognize likenesses and differences among objects and to group them on this basis. "It is an outgrowth of the child's ability to identify the objects in this world. A child in the pre-operational stage may group objects in various ways—there is no right or wrong way. The teacher reinforces the child's growing awareness that things go together because they share certain attributes" (McClelland, 1970).

The activities pertaining to each of these content areas are implemented along three levels of representation—index, symbol, and sign—into which the levels of operation (direct physical-motoric level and verbal level) are integrated. Thus, there is a three-dimensional framework into which program activities have been planned.

Method. The methods used by teachers to implement the cognitive curriculum will be discussed in the context of the structure of the classroom and the daily schedule. "In the cognitive program, the classroom is set up in specific ways to facilitate and reinforce certain goals. While this structure undoubtedly contributes a frame of reference for the children, it is only one of a variety of elements used by the teachers to provide experience with the concepts and content areas of curriculum" (McClelland, 1970).

The daily schedule includes planning time, working time, group meeting for evaluation, cleanup, juice and group time, activity time, and circle time. One hallmark of the cognitive program is the planning time at the beginning of the day, during which the child makes plans for working time. The child gains experience in carrying a task through to completion, in sequencing events, and in thinking before acting.

Supplementing the preschool sessions are afternoon visits to the children's homes by the teacher. The purpose is twofold: to engage the mother in the process of her child's education, and to extend school activities to the individual child in the home. The teacher suggests activities that the mother can engage in with her child during the week and points out household activities which can be structured to include the curriculum (Weikart, Adcock, & Silverman, 1969).

Comparative Analysis of Piagetian Preschool Curricula

The four programs described will now be compared with respect to the major aspects of their program which relate to curriculum objectives, content, and methods.

Preschool program objectives can range from broad educational goals to specific aims for a single lesson. The Piagetian programs reviewed identified both types of objectives. Kamii and Sprigle placed their primary emphasis on long-range goals. The long-range goals of formal operations and socioemotional maturity were identified by Kamii. Sprigle stressed the goal of the learning-to-learn process, a goal that might not be accepted by all Piagetians as appropriate. The development of logical modes of thinking was the long-range goal of Weikart's and Lavatelli's curricula. Weikart also mentioned the importance of the development of the capacity to manipulate symbols.

Since the preschool curricula discussed were based on Piaget's theory,

TABLE 2.1

Content Areas of Preschool Curricula
Based on Piaget's Theory

Kamii, C. Ypsilanti Early Education Program

CLASSIFICATION	SERIATION	NUMBER	SPATIAL REASONING	TEMPORAL REASONING	OTHER
Uniting, disuniting, re-uniting Grouping things that are identical/similar Inventing one's own criteria and using them consistently Shifting the criteria to group and regroup objects in different ways Thinking independently rather than depending on others to judge the correctness of the conclusion	Comparing and ordering Arranging a series of graduated cups, dolls, etc., from biggest to smallest, or vice versa, by comparing relative differences	Arranging, dis-arranging, and rearranging Establishing numerical equivalence by one-to-one correspondence Fostering the logical process which underlies conservation	Development of child's structuring of space from topological space to geometric space Development of static space into more dynamic transformations Reconstruction of sensorimotor space on representational level	Structuring time into sequence, but not intervals Development of a sense of speed--slow or fast	Physical knowledge Representation (a) Index--part of object, marks causally related to object (b) Symbol--imitation, make-believe, onomatopoeia, three-dimensional mode, pictures (c) Sign--words and other signs

Lavatelli, C. S. Early Childhood Curriculum: A Piaget Program

CLASSIFICATION	SERIATION	NUMBER, MEASUREMENT, AND SPACE OPERATIONS	OTHER
One-to-one correspondence Multiple classification Complementary classes Class inclusion Hindsight and foresight Intersection of classes Combinations and permutations	Seriation of length with intersection of new unit Seriation of two sets of objects Seriation of length and color Multiple seriation Transitivity	Conservation of number Conservation of number: one-to-one correspondence without physical correspondence Conservation of liquid Conservation of quantity with and without visual correspondence Horizontal and vertical reference points Conservation of surface area Conservation of length: introduction to measurement Spatial transformation A model and representation of the model	Specific language models used by the teacher with each lesson

Sprigle, H., Learning to Learn

CLASSIFICATION	SERIATION	NUMBER, SPATIAL REASONING	OTHER
Learning that items can be arranged into categories by some type of system; Given the information, learning the names of categories and items belonging to each category; Given criteria of how items are categorized and description of how items meet criteria, separating items into categories; Recalling information to separate array of items into two, three, four, or five categories; Combining subcategories into general categories, using criteria of attributes and/or function	Anticipating and describing events of a story from a book; With a story sequence of two pictures, choosing an appropriate ending; From a choice of two pictures; With a story sequence of three pictures, choosing an appropriate ending; From a choice of two pictures; From an array of seven-eight pictures, choosing any number of pictures to make a story	Development of the child's concept of spatial relationships through kinesthetic and spatial cues; Development of the child's ability to classify by color, size, and sequence; Development of the concepts of equivalence, spatial relationships, and estimation; Development of the child's ability to recognize, seriate, and write the numerals 1 through 9; Development of the child's ability to deal with more abstract mathematical concepts	To help the child learn ways to gather, relate, organize, and apply information in a meaningful and useful manner in the following areas: visual, auditory, organization, part-whole relationships, and problem-solving; To help the child experience satisfaction in possessing knowledge and being able to use it for independent accomplishment; To help the child learn to communicate knowledge and ideas verbally

Weikart, D., Cognitive Curriculum

CLASSIFICATION	SERIATION	SPATIAL REASONING	TEMPORAL REASONING	OTHER
Grouping on the basis of: functional and relational, perceptual attributes, gross discriminations	Ordering objects on the basis of size, quantity, or quality	Expressing orientation of the child's body and of other objects in space (motoric and verbal expressions)	Dealing with time in terms of periods having a beginning and an end; Learning that events can be chronologically ordered and time periods can have variable lengths	Levels of operation: verbal, motoric; Levels of representation: object, index, symbol, sign

55

it is not surprising that curricula content overlaps. Each curriculum included such areas as classification, seriation, and spatial relations; additionally, most included number and temporal relations. Kamii's and Weikart's curricula content appeared to be particularly similar. Both programs developed from the Perry Preschool Project and, until 1966, Kamii and Weikart were working together. Based on the current literature, however, Kamii's curriculum presently seems more sophisticated in Piagetian content than does Weikart's. Furthermore, Weikart's cognitive curriculum contains almost nothing that deals with the content area of numbers. In terms of development, the content of Sprigle's program has been evolving over the past six years and includes the widest age range (from four to seven). Sprigle also included more number content than the other programs. Lavatelli put considerable stress on language content. In addition, Sprigle's and Weikart's programs both emphasize language more than Kamii's program.

There are a number of variations in the methods used by Piagetian programs. Both Kamii and Sprigle stated that they are process-oriented rather than content-oriented. In Sprigle's program the children are taken from the classroom in small groups to a place with less distraction for a brief period of structured cognitive games. Similarly, the structured lessons in Lavatelli's program are given in small groups. Sprigle also uses a group "morning circle" to introduce some cognitive activities in large groups. Weikart and Kamii describe the importance of "planning time" when children plan what they will do for the day, but free activity time is identified by Kamii as the most important time of day. In Kamii's program children are given a choice of materials, cognitive functioning is diagnosed, and the teacher follows up on the child's interest during individual time.

Method differences can also be viewed in terms of the role of the teacher. Kamii sees the teacher's role as that of providing an environment in which the child can construct his own knowledge rather than receive directly transmitted knowledge. Lavatelli emphasized the teacher's role in asking the right question. Sprigle saw teachers as child-oriented rather than subject-oriented. Weikart stressed the importance of the teacher's commitment to a particular curriculum frame of reference and the teacher's taking the children and goals rather than methods and activities as the starting point for teaching in the cognitive curriculum.

All these Piagetian programs draw heavily on traditional early education curricula. In addition to unique activities, Kamii uses many of the same activities as a traditional program, but with more focus on cognitive development. Lavatelli's and Sprigle's programs are largely structured cognitive activity periods to be used along with a traditional curriculum. Weikart's cognitive activities subtly permeate the basically traditional program.

Future Directions of Piaget's Theory
Applied to Early Education

Having discussed the rationale for using Piaget's theory as a framework for preschool education and having described Piagetian preschool curricula, it is appropriate to mention both some problems and two applications of the Piagetian approach. The difficulty of identifying or training highly skilled teachers required to implement a Piagetian curriculum and the lack of fully developed, evaluated, and exportable curricula are among the problems of adopting a Piagetian orientation. It seems desirable that teachers in a Piagetian preschool program have a thorough knowledge of Piaget's developmental theory, and that they be able to probe and assess where children are developmentally, with respect to various concepts, and to provide an appropriate cognitive task for the child. To elaborate on the second problem, the preschool curricula vary in their development, but the authors have generally approached the problem globally rather than by way of a careful component analysis and thorough evaluation.

Two areas of potential application of Piagetian orientation identified by Sullivan relate to evaluating teaching sequences and psychoeducational assessment. Piaget's genius at elucidating the concepts which children have of the world is a promising tool for teachers. Teachers could use some of Piaget's probing techniques to explore concepts they are trying to teach, to see how well the child has grasped a concept, and at what level of operation the child is functioning (Sullivan, 1967, p. 34).

THEORY AND LANGUAGE CURRICULA

Curriculum Components

Preschool curricula may be arbitrarily divided into their educational components—such as art, language, mathematics, music, and social studies—or into such areas as physical-motor, sensory-perceptual, and social-affective. The components of a preschool curriculum often are assembled by examining a variety of theoretical positions within a curriculum component. For example, in designing activities to promote esthetic development in art, music, and dance, the curriculum developer may lean more heavily on the theorists in fine arts rather than exclusively on the writings of developmental psychologists or general theorists.

To illustrate the reflections of diverse theories in shaping curricula, we have selected the curriculum component of language development.

Language Component Focus

An examination of language components may have special value because the majority of curricula emphasize a language component; language skills interact with a variety of other components; and many curriculum developers and program operators who emphasize language do not understand the conceptual issues in language development. (While this section focuses on the development and acquisition of one language, the field of early childhood bilingual education is equally important and has recently been reviewed by John and Horner, 1971.)

During the last decade special attention has been focused on language development in preschool education. This has resulted directly from the discovery that large numbers of preschool children exhibit severe language deficits and from the increasing attention of psychologists to the interaction between language and cognition (Cazden, 1972; Palmer & Fein, 1974).

At the same time, pioneers in the relatively new field of psycholinguistics have sought to understand the manner in which language exerts control over verbal and nonverbal behavior, and how the language-user acquires the skills and abilities that linguistic theorists indicate he must acquire (Jacobovits & Miron, 1967; McNeill, 1968).

While great strides have been made in the area of psycholinguistic theory during this period, the practical application of theoretical implications has lagged far behind. This section of the chapter will attempt to evaluate, very briefly, the manner in which several preschool programs have made an effort to use specific theoretical approaches in the development of language curricula; it will also explore the manner in which psycholinguistics can aid in the development of preschool language programs. However, there will be no attempt here to make an in-depth evaluation of the merit of the individual theories of language development.

Theoretical Positions

The wave of controversy created by two general theoretical positions has added to the difficulties of the preschool educator who must decide what position he will take in the language component of his program. Broadly speaking, these two positions may be termed *neobehaviorist* and *nativist*.

The neobehaviorists include a range of theorists from Skinner (1957) to Osgood (1957), who have maintained that the principles of conditioning and learning which have been extensively explored in the psychology laboratory can be logically extended—albeit with modifications—to language behavior. In this conceptualization the social environment is considered a vital and necessary shaping force, without which language would or could not develop.

The nativists, characterized by such men as Chomsky (1965), Lenneberg (1967), and McNeill (1968, deny the primary importance of the social environment in the development of language. They maintain that the fundamental basis of language cannot be explained by learning theories, even when those theories are represented by multilevel, mediational models. Instead, they propose various forms of innate language mechanisms which variously affect and control language development.

Not only is the job of the preschool educator made difficult by these grossly different theoretical approaches, but it is further complicated by the fact that subtle differences among the proponents of either group imply different approaches to the task of language training. For example, McNeill favors an approach to language development which emphasizes that the child is born with a preprogrammed set of linguistic categories, while Slobin favors a linguistic developmental theory in which the child is assumed to be born with a predisposition to learn a set of linguistic categories of an unspecified nature (Smith & Miller, 1966). Both of these positions offer slightly different implications for the development of language training programs.

Many issues involved in the controversy have often been obscured because the contributing theorists frequently concern themselves with different aspects of language development (John & Moskovitz, 1970) without clearly indicating this fact. Staats (1968) observed that, since Chomsky's successful attack upon Skinner's operant theory of verbal behavior in 1957, there has been some tendency to discredit all behavioristic approaches—the premise being that if you have discredited one behavior theory, you have discredited them all. This was, indeed, implied by Chomsky himself in an introduction to his reprinted article in 1967.

On the other hand, Staats (1968), while agreeing that individual learning theories cannot deal comprehensively with language, proposed that experimental evidence would indicate that an integrated learning theory *can* offer the most helpful approach in studying language development. In support of a learning-theory approach, he argued:

> The psycholinguists have almost no contact with the determining events for language development and thus can make no positive statements in this area. . . . A learning theory approach (on the other hand) does have the capability of making explanatory statements . . . and generating . . . procedures for doing something about the development of language behavior and of treating problems in this area. . . . The work of linguists and psycholinguists is extremely important [in providing] a precise description of language [and] what it is a child has to learn. Based on this information we may better devise materials for training the child . . . . When a child does not develop language as expected, or in any case of language pathology, we must look to the learning conditions involved (and in some cases to the biological conditions). If we wish to *produce*

language development we must manipulate the learning conditions. (pp. 157-158)

Building on a behavioristic base, Osgood (1957) conceptualized psycholinguistic abilities as composed of three dimensions: levels of organization; psycholinguistic processes; and channels of communication. Two levels of organization—the representational or mediational level, and the autonomic or involuntary level—were postulated. Psycholinguistic processes were classified in terms of reception, organization, and expression. Channels of communication referred to the sensorimotor paths by which linguistic symbols were received or produced.

Using the Osgood conceptual model as a base, three groups of investigators attempted to construct compensatory language training programs: Dunn and Smith (1965), with the Peabody Language Development Kit; Hodges, McCandless, and Spiker (1967); and Karnes (1972, with her Ameliorative Program. Our discussion is limited to the Peabody and Ameliorative curricula.

There are many pitfalls in the Peabody Language Development Kit (PLDK). These were outlined in detail by Rosenberg (1971), but can be summarized in three statements: the kit is not based on a model of language that has empirically proven itself capable of characterizing human language; the authors have not demonstrated how the language exercises were generated from the theory; and the kit was not validated by adequate experimental evidence before publication.

The single research effort that has most extensively explored the differential effects of several language programs over an extended period of time (several years at this point) is the work of Merle Karnes (1972). The basic assumption behind her Ameliorative Program is that the environment of low-income children is inappropriate for the development of skills necessary to succeed in school. The program involves three daily 20-minute structured learning periods covering math concepts, language, and science-social studies.

The instruction models were derived from Osgood's conceptualization of psycholinguistic functioning (1957) and the Guilford Structure of Intellect (1967). The instructional strategy involved a low teacher-pupil radio, immediate correction of incorrect responses, and reinforcement using praise of appropriate responses.

While the Ameliorative Program is one of the best examples of a well-defined attempt to utilize a theory based on psycholinguistic principles, it is subject to many of the criticisms listed previously concerning the PLDK. Because of its conceptualization, the program is included here even though the curriculum is presented in such a brief fashion in the publicized materials that evaluation of specific aspects is made nearly impossible. Basically, the program involves the use of the Illinois Test of Psycholinguistic Abilities (ITPA) (Kirk & McCarthy, 1961) as a diagnostic instrument, with appropriate language training based on those portions of the test in which the child has demonstrated deficiencies.

Another example of an attempt to use a neobehaviorist approach as a theoretical base for a preschool language program is Adkins' University of Hawaii Language Curriculum (1968), which was designed to attack the linguistic and cognitive deficiencies of children from low-income families in Hawaii. Its goal was to foster the development of cognitive skills by using language as the vehicle. Basically, the program consisted of a modified Bereiter and Engelmann (1966) procedure that was revised to teach basic syntactic patterns as well as words and phrases which occur with high frequency in standard dialects of English but not in the Hawaiian subcultural dialect. The curriculum was mimeographed and assembled as a manual. Carefully sequenced grammatical structures were presented to the children in small increments. Reinforcement for mastery of the material was given through operant procedures on a variable schedule. Pattern practice was used as the child's repertoire of syntactic structures grew (Adkins, 1968).

The language program began with the assumption that the child knew nothing about the mastery of standard English. Each child was permitted to progress at the rate necessary to complete each part of the sequence, which started with the use of simple identity statements and expanded to more difficult constructions.

In an example of a purely Skinnerian approach, Sapon (1968) directly implemented the principles of operant behavior theory to study the language behavior of children. His Verbal Behavior Laboratory was designed to develop procedures, programs, and materials to shape and establish specific behaviors appropriate for effective participation in formal primary school activities.

The basic theoretical orientation involved the experimental analysis of behavior utilizing a three-term contingency model (consisting of control stimulus, response, and consequence of the response) to promote generalization and maintenance of verbal behavior outside the school setting. The program was designed so that no behavior was introduced until its requisite antecedent behavior "bits" had been established and a given criterial level of performance exhibited. The environment was specifically designed to promote optimally the acquisition of each new behavior. One of the main components of the program was an extension of matching of sample behavior to the field of language development.

Evaluation

When all the evidence is considered, it must be generally conceded that the traditional behavior theories are inadequate to fully explain the intricacies of language development. It must also be acknowledged that, at this time, neither the linguists nor the psycholinguists have provided an adequate theory of linguistic *performance* for the student of language behavior (Rosenberg, 1971) or for the preschool educator. It is not difficult to understand, therefore, why a review of cognitive and language preschool sentence patterns to systems of communication strategies" (Bartlett, 1970). dicated that many language programs were diffuse, unclear and, at best, pragmatic attempts to increase language performance. An additional confounding factor is that each program defines language, per se, in a different manner. These definitions range from "limited subjects of vocabulary and sentence patterns to systems of communication strategies"(Bartlett, 1970).

The preschool educator lacks not only an adequate performance model, but also an adequate method of measuring language development (see chapter 10). Rosenberg (1971) emphasized the extent to which the field of linguistic measurement is out of contact with the mainstream of research and theory in the language sciences. Using the Illinois Test of Psycholinguistic Abilities as an exemplar of a widely used, much-publicized test based on Osgood's theory as a case in point, he stated: "It is not based on a viable model of linguistic competence and performance [and] does not reflect in any obvious way recent work in the area of developmental psycholinguistics." He also maintained that Osgood's revision of his theory toward a transformational approach was completely ignored when the ITPA was revised in 1968 (Kirk, McCarthy & Kirk, 1968).

One becomes more aware of the inadequacies of the instrument by an examination of the standardization materials that do *not* accompany the test kit itself. The 12 subtests were standardized on a sample defined as "those children demonstrating average school achievement, average characteristics of personal-social adjustment, sensorimotor integrity, and coming from predominantly English speaking families" (Paraskevopoulos & Kirk, 1969). However, when used with predominantly low-income children, factor analysis demonstrates that the 12 supposedly independent subtests can be partitioned into anything from one to three factors. Parker (1969), for example, found that there were only three primary factor loadings for the ITPA: visual, auditory, and closure. All these findings cast doubt on the appropriateness of this instrument as a diagnostic base or evaluative index for language training programs.

Proposed Approach

The literature contains a number of suggested avenues which might profitably be explored to aid in the construction of a theoretically adequate training procedure and assessment index. Cazden, Baratz, Labov, and Palmer (1971) examined a number of folk beliefs which seem to have permeated the world of preschool language programs and which are typical of the level of conceptualization of many of the programs reviewed. Although these myths have been found to be in error when subjected to rigorous experimentation, they persist in many preschool programs because they correspond to commonsense notions of how language develops.

The first myth is that children learn language by imitation. In a general way, this must have some effect on language learning, since children speak the language of their parents, but research evidence indicates that it is not the entire answer. A second myth is that children learn language by being corrected. Children do learn some things by being corrected, but not grammar per se. Corrections usually occur during misstatements of fact, clarification of word meanings, etc. A third, and important, myth is that learning a nonstandard dialect is not learning a true language. Commonly ignored is the fact that all dialects of a language are systematic and highly structured language codes. This leads to a belief that nonstandard English is merely a form of "bad" or incorrect English rather than a highly systematized dialect of the language. The implications of this finding for preschools lends support for those who advocate treating English as a second language when it is begun after the first language or dialectic form has been established.

Rosenberg (1971) suggested six hypotheses that obviously need experimental validation, but might serve as a focus for the development of a language training program. They are:

1. Language training should be preceded by an adequate assessment of the nature of the language disabilities present in the child.
2. The program should recognize the minimal contribution to first language acquisition of environmental variables.
3. A language training program should reflect the likelihood that experience is related more to transformational and semantic development than to syntactic and phonological development.
4. A language training program should be based upon specific knowledge of the nature of the interaction between the speech of the child and the speech of the adult.
5. The program should consider carefully the implications of the possibility of a critical period for the operation of the innate biological component of first-language acquisition.
6. Since active participation appears to be characteristic of the behavior of a normal child acquiring a first language, it seems reasonable to suggest that a language training program for a child with retarded language development should include an attempt to insure active participation. (pp. 18-20)

Another area worthy of empirical investigation is the usefulness or necessity of a sequentially arranged learning hierarchy in language development. Cazden (1972) pointed to evidence which suggests that a careful understanding of learning hierarchies might well be more important for planning evaluations than for actually sequencing learning materials.

The area of language assessment is the second of the two areas that must be carefully explored if it is to be a viable part of preschool education and not just a means of providing quantifiable data for journal presentation.

Again, Rosenberg (1971) listed several factors which he felt were the minimal requirements of any language assessment device:

1. It must be based upon an adequate characterization of the structure of the adult language.

2. It must reflect our knowledge of normal language development.

3. It must be able to differentiate between underlying linguistic competence and observable linguistic performance as it is constrained by such factors as memory, attention, time limitations, and motivation.

4. Scoring will have to reflect dialect idiosyncrasies.

5. Items should be grouped for scoring according to whether they reflect primarily motivational development or learning.

6. The items should reflect the full range of linguistic competence: phonological, syntactic, and semantic. With respect to syntactic competence this would include (a) morphological rules; (b) grammatical categories; (c) basic sentence types; (d) grammatical relations; (e) structural equivalence; (f) transformations; and (g) discourse structures.

Semantic competence should include (a) the lexicon; (b) paraphrasing; (c) the ability to detect ambiguities; (d) sentence understanding; and (e) production of sentences using novel semantic input. (pp. 11-13)

If psycholinguistics is to aid in the development of preschool language programs, it will have to act in both of these areas, namely, the development of adequate language assessment devices and the creation of a workable theory of language performance that can be the base of a language training program. Unfortunately, it is difficult to find theorists who are interested in the practical applications of linguistic theory to the preschool arena. But the time to act is now. The many preschool programs and the increasing number of day-care centers provide a fertile, ongoing testing ground for applied theory. The naive manner in which linguistic theory has been used in many preschool programs reflects how badly help is needed. It is a waste of both time and money for the preschool educator, without considerable expertise in linguistic theory, research, and methodology, to try to develop his own language materials. His lack of knowledge creates a void that seriously reduces the effectiveness of his overall program. The psycholinguist can fill that void and thereby contribute to the construction of a theoretically sound language program.

SUMMARY

Reflections of theory in curricula were approached by examining theoretical influences in comprehensive preschool curricula and in the language component of a curriculum. Piaget's influence on early education was used to illustrate the impact of a particular theory of child development on the preschool curricula of Kamii, Lavatelli, Sprigle, and Weikart. While these programs have a number of features in common, variations on the theme were presented in terms of objectives, content, and method to underscore the fact that a variety of curricula can be inspired by one theory.

The curriculum component of language development was selected to illustrate the reflections of diverse theories in shaping language development curricula. A profile emerged of the field of early education totally committed to language development without having adequate curriculum materials (i.e., theoretically sound and clearly operationalized) and valid measuring instruments. This status analysis should signal us to proceed with caution in designing and implementing early language curricula.

REFERENCES

Adkins, D. *Development of a preschool language-oriented curriculum with a structured parent education program.* Final Report. Education Research and Development Center, College of Education, University of Hawaii, 1968.

Athey, I. J., & Rubadeau, D. O. (Eds.). *Educational implications of Piaget's theory.* Waltham, Mass.: Ginn-Blaisdell, 1970.

Baldwin, A. L. *Theories of child development.* New York: John Wiley, 1967.

Banta, T. J. Montessori: Myth or reality? In R. K. Parker (Ed.), *The preschool in action.* Boston: Allyn & Bacon, 1972.

Bartlett, E. . An analysis of published preschool programs. Paper presented at the meeting of the National Association for the Education of Young Children, Boston, November 1970.

Bereiter, C., & Engelmann, S. *Teaching disadvantaged children in the preschool.* Englewood Cliffs, N.J.: Prentice-Hall, 1966.

Cazden, C. B. Evaluation of learning in early language development. In B. S. Bloom, T. Hastings, & C. Madaus (Eds.), *Handbook on formative and summative evaluation of student learning.* New York: McGraw-Hill, 1972.

Cazden, C. B., Baratz, J. C., Labou, W., & Palmer, F. H. Language development in day-care programs. In E. Grotberg (Ed.), *Day care: Resources for decisions.* U.S. Department of Health, Education, and Welfare, Washington, D.C.: U.S. Government Printing Office, 1971.

Chomsky, N. *Aspects of the theory of language.* Cambridge, Mass.: M.I.T. Press, 1965.

————. Review of Skinner's verbal behavior. In L. A. Jacobovits & M. S. Miron (Eds.), *Readings in the psychology of language.* Englewood Cliffs, N.J.: Prentice-Hall, 1967.

Dunn, L. G., & Smith, J. A. *Peabody language development kit.* Circle Pines, Minn.: American Guidance Service, 1965.

Flavell, J. H. *The developmental psychology of Jean Piaget.* Princeton, N.J.: Van Nostrand, 1963.

Furth, H. G. *Piaget for teachers.* Englewood Cliffs, N.J.: Prentice-Hall, 1970.

Ginsburg, H., & Opper, S. *Piaget's theory of intellectual development: An introduction.* Englewood Cliffs, N.J.: Prentice-Hall, 1969.

Guilford, J. P. *The nature of human intelligence.* New York: McGraw-Hill, 1967.

Hodges, W. L., McCandless, B. R., & Spiker, H. H. *The development and evaluation of a diagnostically based curriculum for preschool psychosocially deprived children.* Final Report. University of Indiana Project No. 5-0350, U.S. Department of Health, Education, and Welfare, 1967.

Hooper, F. H. Piagetian research and education. In I. E. Sigel & F. H. Hooper (Eds.), *Logical thinking in children.* New York: Holt, Rinehart and Winston, 1968.

————. An evaluation of logical operations instruction in the preschool. In R. K. Parker (Ed.), *The preschool in action.* Boston: Allyn & Bacon, 1972.

Inhelder, B., & Piaget, J. *The early growth of logic in the child.* New York: Norton & Company, 1964.

Jacobovits, L. A., & Miron, M. S. (Eds.). *Readings in the psychology of language.* Englewood Cliffs, N.J.: Prentice-Hall, 1967.

John, V. P., & Horner, V. M. *Early childhood bilingual education.* New York: Modern Language Association, 1971.

John, V. P., & Moskovitz, S. Language acquisition and development in early childhood. *National Society for the Study of Education Yearbook.* Chicago: University of Chicago Press, 1970.

Kamii, C. K. Piaget's theory and specific instruction: A response to Bereiter and Kohlberg. *Interchange,* 1970, *1*, 33-39.

————. Evaluation of learning in preschool education: Socio-emotional, perceptual-motor, and cognitive development. In B. S. Bloom, J. T. Hastings, & G. Madaus (Eds.), *Handbook on formative and summative evaluation of student learning.* New York: McGraw-Hill, 1971.

————. An application of Piaget's theory to the conceptualization of preschool curriculum. In R. K. Parker (Ed.), *The preschool in action.* Boston: Allyn & Bacon, 1972.

Kamii, C. K., & DeVries, R. *Piaget for early education.* New York: Prentice-Hall, 1974.

Kamii, C. K., & Radin, N. A. framework for preschool curriculum based on some Piagetian concepts. In I. J. Athey & D. O. Rubadeau (Eds.), *Educational implications of Piaget's theory.* Waltham, Mass.: Ginn-Blaisdell, 1970.

Karnes, M. B., Zehrbach, R. R., & Teska, J. A. The conceptualization of the ameliorative curriculum. In R. K. Parker (Ed.), *The preschool in action.* Boston: Allyn & Bacon, 1972.

Kirk, S. A., & McCarthy, J. J. The Illinois Test of Psycholinguistic Abilities: An approach to differential diagnosis. *American Journal of Mental Deficiency,* 1961, *66,* 339-412.

Kirk, S. A., McCarthy, J. J., & Kirk, W. D. *Illinois Test of Psycholinguistic Abilities.* Revised Edition. Urbana, Ill.: University of Illinois Press, 1968.

Kohlberg, L. Early education: A cognitive-developmental view. *Child Development,* 1968, *39,* 1013-1062.

Langer, J. *Theories of development.* New York: Holt, Rinehart & Winston, 1969.

Lavatelli, C. S. A Piaget-derived model for compensatory preschool education. In J. L. Frost (Ed.), *Early childhood education rediscovered.* New York: Holt, Rinehart & Winston, 1968.

————. *Piaget's theory applied to an early education curriculum.* New York: Learning Research Associates, 1970a.

————. *Teacher's guide to accompany early childhood curriculum: A Piaget program.* New York: Learning Research Associates, 1970b.

Lenneberg, E. H. *Biological foundations of language.* New York: John Wiley, 1967.

McClelland, D. *Ypsilanti preschool curriculum demonstration project: The cognitive curriculum.* Ypsilanti, Mich.: High/Scope Educational Research Foundation, 1970.

McNeill, D. On theories of language acquisition. In T. R. Dixon & D. L. Horton (Eds.), *Verbal behavior and general behavior theory.* Englewood Cliffs, N.J.: Prentice-Hall, 1968.

Maier, H. W. *Three theories of child development.* New York: Harper & Row, 1965.

Osgood, C. E. A behavioristic analysis of perception and language as cognitive phenomena. In *Contemporary approaches to cognition.* Cambridge, Mass.: Harvard University Press, 1957.

Palmer, F. & Fein, G. *Language and cognitive development.* New Jersey: General Learning Press, 1974.

Paraskevopoulos, J. N. & Kirk, S. A. *The development and psychometric characteristics of the revised Illinois Test of Psycholinguistic Abilities.* Urbana, Ill.: University of Illinois Press, 1969.

Parker, R. K. *The effectiveness of special programs for rural isolated four-year-old children.* Final report. Project No. 9-D-018, U.S. Department of Health, Education, and Welfare, 1969.

————. (Ed.) *The preschool in action.* Boston: Allyn & Bacon, 1972.

Parker, R. K., Ambron, S., Danielson, G. I., Halbrook, M. C., & Levine, J. A. *Overview of cognitive and language programs for three-, four, and five-year-old children.* Atlanta: Southeastern Educational Laboratory, 1970.

Parker, R. K., & Day, M. C. Comparisons of preschool curricula. In R. K. Parker (Ed.), *The preschool in action.* Boston: Allyn & Bacon, 1972.

Piaget, J. *The child's conception of number.* New York: Humanities Press, 1952.

Piaget, J., & Inhelder, B. *The child's conception of space.* New York: W. W. Norton, 1967.

Piaget, J., Inhelder, B., & Szeminska, A. *The child's conception of geometry.* New York: Basic Books, 1960.

Rosenberg, S. Problems of language development in the retarded: A discussion of Olsen's review. In H. C. Haywood (Ed.), *Social-cultural aspects of mental retardation.* New York: Appleton-Century-Crofts, 1971.

Sapon, S. M. *Operant studies in the expansion and refinement of verbal behavior in disadvantaged children.* Final Report. Contract No. OEO-2401, Office of Economic Opportunity, 1968.

Sigel, I. E. The attainment of concepts. In M. L. Hoffman & Lois V. Hoffman (Eds.), *Review of child development research.* Vol. 1. New York: Russell Sage Foundation, 1964.

————. The Piagetian system and the world of education. In D. Elkind & J. H. Flavell (Eds.), *Studies in cognitive development.* New York: Oxford University Press, 1969.

Sinclair, H., & Kamii, C. Some implications of Piaget's theory for teaching young children. *School Review,* 1970, *68,* 169-183.

Skinner, B. F. *Verbal behavior.* New York: Appleton-Century-Crofts, 1957.

Smith, F., & Miller, G. A. (Eds.). *The genesis of language: A psycholinguistic approach.* Cambridge, Mass.: M.I.T. Press, 1966.

Sprigle, H. *Inquisitive games: Discovering how to learn.* Teacher's Guide. Chicago, Ill.: Science Research Associates, Inc., 1968a.

————. *Inquisitive games: Exploring number and space.* Teacher's Guide. Chicago, Ill.: Science Research Associates, Inc., 1968b.

————. *The learning to learn program.* Jacksonville, Florida: Learning to Learn School, Inc., 1970 (mimeographed).

Staats, A. W. *Learning, language, and cognition.* New York: Holt, Rinehart & Winston, 1968.

Sullivan, E. V. *Piaget and the school curriculum: A critical appraisal.* Bulletin No. 2. Toronto, Ontario: The Ontario Institute for Studies in Education, 1967.

Van De Riet, V., & Van De Riet, H. *A sequential approach to early childhood and elementary education.* Phase I. Grant Report. Grant No. OEO CG-822 A/O, Office of Economic Opportunity, 1969.

Weikart, D. P. *Ypsilanti preschool curriculum demonstration project.* Ypsilanti, Mich.: High/Scope Educational Research Foundation, 1969.

Weikart, D. P., Adcock, C., & Silverman, C. *Ypsilanti preschool curriculum: A demonstration project.* Ypsilanti, Mich.: Ypsilanti Public Schools, 1969.

APPENDIX

INFANT AND PRESCHOOL PROGRAM RESOURCES

Addresses of Infant Program Resources

Caldwell, Bettye
Center for Early Development and
   Education
College of Education
University of Arkansas
814 Sherman Street
Little Rock, Arkansas 72202

Fowler, William
Demonstration Program in Infant Care
   and Education
Ontario Institute for Studies in
   Education
Toronto, Canada

Gordon, Ira
Parent Education Program
Institute for Development of
   Human Resources
College of Education
University of Florida
Gainesville, Florida 32601

Huntington, D., Provence, S., and
   Parker, R.
Day Care: Serving Infants
Office of Child Development
400 6th Street, N.W.
Washington, D.C. 20013

Karnes, Merle B.
Educational Intervention at Home by
   Mothers of Infants
Institute for Research on Exceptional
   Children
Department of Special Education
403 East Healey Street
Champaign, Illinois 61820

Keister, Mary Elizabeth
Group Infant Care Project
University of North Carolina
Greensboro, North Carolina 27412

Lally, J. Ronald, and Honig, Alice
The Children's Center
100 Walnut Place
Syracuse University
Syracuse, New York 13210

Levenstein, Phyllis
Mother-Child Home Program
30 Albany Avenue
Freeport, New York 11520

Painter, Genevieve
Infant Education. San Rafael,
   California: Dimensions Publishing
   Co., 1968
(P.O. Box 4221, San Rafael,
   California 94903)
Teach Your Baby. New York: Simon
   and Schuster, 1971.

Parent and Child Centers
Office of Child Development
400 6th Street, N.W.
Washington, D.C. 20013

Schaefer, Earl
Infant Home Stimulation Program
Graham Child Development Center
University of North Carolina
Chapel Hill, North Carolina 27514

Sparling, J., and Land, M.
Infant Day Care Program
Graham Child Development Center
University of North Carolina
Chapel Hill, North Carolina 27514

Weikart, David
Ypsilanti–Carnegie Infant Education
  Project
High/Scope Educational Research
  Foundation
125 N. Huron
Ypsilanti, Michigan 48197

Whitney, David, & Parker, R.
Infant Explorer Program
Universal Education Corporation
1501 Broadway
New York, New York 10036

	ART	COGNITIVE	LANGUAGE	MATHEMATICS	MOTIVATION	MUSIC	PHYSICAL-MOTOR	READING	SCIENCE	SENSORY-PERCEPTUAL	SOCIAL-AFFECTIVE	SOCIAL-STUDIES
ADKINS		X	X	X	X	X						
ALFORD	X	X	X	X		X	X		X	X	X	
BECKER	X	X	X	X		X		X	X		X	
BOGER	X								X	X		
BOGIN		X										
CALDWELL		X	X	X		X			X	X		
CATLETTE	X	X	X	X	X	X	X		X	X	X	X
DEUTSCH		X	X									
GRAY		X	X		X	X			X	X		
HARMS	X									X		
HARRIS	X	X	X	X	X	X	X		X	X	X	
HENDERSON		X	X	X	X					X	X	
HODGES		X	X	X	X		X		X	X	X	
KARNES	X	X	X	X	X	X	X		X	X	X	X
LANE	X	X	X		X	X	X		X		X	X
LESSER		X	X	X						X	X	
McKILLIP		X		X								
MEYER	X	X	X						X	X	X	
NEDLER		X	X	X		X	X		X	X		
NIMNICHT		X	X		X					X		
O'HARE	X	X	X			X		X	X			
PALMER		X	X						X	X		
REEBACK			X									
RESNICK		X	X	X			X	X		X		
ROBISON	X	X	X	X		X			X		X	X
SPAULDING					X						X	
SPRIGLE	X	X	X	X	X					X		
STERN		X	X	X					X			
WHITNEY	X	X	X	X	X	X	X		X	X	X	X
WOOLMAN	X	X	X		X			X	X	X		

Preschool Curriculum Resources Index

An "X" indicates that the program has written curriculum materials and resources in that area.

Addresses of Preschool Programs

Adkins, Dorothy
University of Hawaii Preschool
   Language Curriculum
Center for Research in Early
   Childhood Education
1776 University Avenue
University of Hawaii
Honolulu, Hawaii 96822

Alford, Roy
Appalachian Preschool Education
   Program
Appalachia Educational Laboratory,
   Inc.
P. O. Box 1348
Charleston, West Virginia 25325

Becker, Wesley
Engelmann-Becker Program
University of Oregon
Follow Through Project
Eugene, Oregon

Boger, Robert
Classification and Attention Training
   Program for Preschool Children
Institute for Family and Child
   Research
Home Management House, Unit 3
Michigan State University
East Lansing, Michigan 48823

Bogin, Nancy
Experimental Prekindergarten and
   Demonstration Center at New
   Rochelle
City School District
Washington School
60 Union Avenue
New Rochelle, New York 10801

Caldwell, Bettye
Center for Early Development and
   Education
College of Education
University of Arkansas
814 Sherman Street
Little Rock, Arkansas 72202

Catlette, Naomi
San Felipe Kindergarten
San Felipe School
Southern Pueblo Agency
San Felipe
Algondones, New Mexico 87001

Deutsch, Martin
Institute for Developmental Studies
New York University, School of
   Education
239 Green Street, Third Floor
Washington Square
New York, New York 10003

Gray, Susan
The Demonstration and Research
   Center for Early Education
   (Darcee)
John F. Kennedy Center for Research
   on Education and Human
   Development
Box 151
George Peabody College for Teachers
Nashville, Tennessee 37203

Harms, Thelma
Harold Jones Child Study Center
Child Study Center Institute of
   Human Development
Institute of Human Development
2425 Atherton Street
Berkeley, California 94704

Harris, Florence
Developmental Psychology Laboratory
   Preschool
Developmental Psychology
   Laboratory
University of Washington
Seattle, Washington 98105

Henderson, Ronald
Tucson Early Education Model
Early Childhood Education Center
1515 East 1st Street
Tucson, Arizona

Hodges, Walter
The Behavior Oriented Prescriptive
    Teaching Approach
Early Childhood Education
Georgia State University
Atlanta, Georgia

Karnes, Merle
Karnes' Preschool Program
Institute for Research on Exceptional
    Children
Department of Special Education
403 East Healey Street
Champaign, Illinois 61820

Lane, Mary
Cross-Cultural Family Center
1969-1970
Nurseries in Cross-Cultural Education
San Francisco State College
1600 Holloway Avenue
San Francisco, California 94132

Lesser, Gerald
Childrens Television Workshop
    "Sesame Street"
Children's Television Workshop
1 Lincoln Plaza
New York, New York 10023

McKillip, William
Early Mathematical Learning Project
Department of Math Education
College of Education
University of Georgia
Athens, Georgia 30601

Meyer, William
Center for Research and Development
    in Early Childhood Education
Psychology Department
331 Huntington Hall
Syracuse University
Syracuse, New York 13210

Nedler, Shari
Early Childhood Education Learning
    System
Southwest Educational Development
    Lab (SEDL)
800 Brazos Street
Austin, Texas 78701

Nimnicht, Glen
The Responsive Program
Far West Laboratory for Educational
    Research and Development
Claremont Hotel
1 Garden Circle
Berkeley, California 94705

O'Hare, Robert
Instructional Concepts Program
Southwest Regional Laboratory for
    Educational Research and
    Development
11300 La Cienega Boulevard
Inglewood, California 90304

Palmer, Frank
Concept Training for Two to Five
    Year Olds
Educational Research and
    Development
State University of New York at
    Stony Brook
Stony Brook, New York 11790

Reeback, Robert
Oral Language Program
Southwestern Cooperative Educational
    Laboratory
117 Richmond Drive, N. E.
Albuquerque, New Mexico 87106

Resnick, Lauren
The Primary Education Project
208 M. I. Building
Learning Research and Development
    Center
University of Pittsburgh
Pittsburgh, Pennsylvania 15213

Robison, Helen
Project Child
Bernard M. Baruch College
City University of New York
17 Lexington Avenue
New York, New York 10010

Spaulding, Robert
The Durham Education Improvement
    Project (EIP)
Institute for Child Development and
    Family Studies

School of Education
San Jose State College
San Jose, California 95114

Stern, Carolyn
Preschool Language Project
Early Childhood Research Center
1063 Gayley Avenue
Los Angeles, California 90024

Whitney, David
The Discovery Program
Universal Education Corporation
1501 Broadway
New York, New York 10036

Woolman, Myron
The Micro-social Classroom
6 East 82nd Street
New York, New York 10028

Chapter 3

The Program and Community Participation

RUPERT TRUJILLO

The diversity of interpretations of *community participation* has generated heated arguments, discussions, fears, and frustrations. Persons in positions of authority—program directors, civic club officials, businessmen, school officials—often perceive the concept in terms of unreasonable demands, a confrontation with militants, busybodies, rabble-rousers, and the like, who will not listen to reason. Many individuals consider community participation a nonproductive activity, reflecting the assumption that "we" (program personnel) know best what "they" need and what is good for "them." Some go even further, justifying their action or inaction on the basis that those who "demand" are, at best, stupid or, at worst, outsiders who are using the community for their own aims. Such attitudes provide the focus for this chapter, which will examine the arguments, pro and con, underlying the assumptions and propositions relative to community participation. This broad goal requires the presentation of information which will broaden and clarify community participation and which the reader may use as a guide. Additionally, practical techniques and exemplars are presented to help the reader in achieving true community participation—if that is his objective.

Community participation in early America was as expected as a home-cooked meal. No one really asked how, when, why, or where—participation was expected of all members of a given community. However, with advanced industrialization and technology, the specialization syndrome set in: professionals moved in the direction of specialization, nonspecialists were relegated to "left field," and schools assumed more of the "home functions" for children.

RATIONALE FOR COMMUNITY PARTICIPATION

The entire spectrum of group dynamics (i.e., the relationship between the individual and the group) and communities has been widely discussed.

75

Allport (1962) wrote: "the norm (that is, the average of the judgments), instead of being a 'one-way agency' of the group acting upon the individual, is circularly involved in the process of the formation of the group itself. The 'group' depends on this norm no less than the norm upon the 'group' " (p. 12). Parsons and Shils (1951) elaborated:

> The social system is, to be sure, made up of the relationships of individuals, but it is a system which is organized around the problems inherent in or arising from social interaction of a plurality of individual actors rather than around the problems which arise in connection with the integration of the actions of an individual actor, who is also a psychological organism. (p. 6)

The Community as a System

A multitude of propositions and counterpropositions could be cited in this regard, but for the purpose of this chapter the writer takes the position that in the most fundamental sense a community is a social system which in turn is a structuring of events, happenings, or patterned relationships. Thus, a social system has no structure apart from its functioning.

Basically, social structures are contrived systems. Men contrive systems to satisfy specific needs. Systems are held together by psychological rather than biological or physical conditions. Social systems are hinged in the attitudes, perceptions, beliefs, motivations, habits, expectations, and experiences of human beings. For a social system to function efficiently, its members must agree on what constitutes appropriate and required behaviors for group members (Katz & Kahn, 1966).

The systems begins to break apart as segments generate dysfunctional activities. This occurs because all parts are interrelated: any activity of one part has implications for other parts and for the total operation. And since systems (communities) are dynamic, all systems experience some degree of dysfunction. At best, a system is a moving equilibrium.

Program personnel must be aware of group support that exists in relation to a specific program. Failure to recognize community mores and to obtain support can have highly dysfunctional consequences.[1] Additionally, if a segment of the community fails to accept the objectives or methods of achieving the objectives (as in the case of a few parents who feel they should manage the program budget), the management of the program will be seriously affected. A system can be optimally effective only if the majority of its members are in accord with given beliefs.

Communication

Programs need effective communication networks so that decision-makers can utilize in positive ways the energy generated by dysfunctional activities.

An example: a group from the community confronts the director. Viewed in one way, this can be dysfunctional. However, since community projects should be helping persons to make decisions relative to their perceived needs in relation to the conduct of their own lives, the activity of the dissenting group can be viewed as legitimate and functional because it helps the director modify the program on an ongoing basis.

How do these factors relate to community participation and to the development of an early childhood education program? For one thing, program officials should be cognizant of the interactions of the subsystems and of their possible consequences to a program. Few situations are as disruptive to the program director as working with a staff that is in constant friction with a subsystem of trainees. Some program directors may be oblivious to the friction and hostility because they listen to *what* is said rather than to *how* it is said. Many times the hostility is not even verbalized! Nonverbal communication has as much relevance as, if not more than, verbal communication.

When communication is poor, people often attempt to "work out" a situation by attacking the direct, immediate problem rather than realizing that the difficulty usually lies in a hidden cause or causes that precipitated the problem.

If a program is to be truly effective, the director must gain the support of most members representing the program's community—faculty, staff, or various social, political, educational, and economic agencies or groups. This is possible only if close attention is given to establishing and maintaining an open communication network.

Money as a Factor

Several factors serve to strengthen the rationale for community participation. First, if federal monies are involved in the conduct of a project, community participation is essential. Rightly so—the government has not moved in this direction in idle speculation. Rather, this approach is founded on data which indicate a positive relationship between effective programs and high levels of community participation. For example, the Federation of Independent Community Schools (Wray, 1971)

> since May of 1969, has accomplished far more than was originally anticipated by the initiating group of parents. In less than two years, a firm beginning has been made in establishing and developing a new and alternative urban school system that can both enhance and transcend the cultural diversity represented in Milwaukee's inner city, North and South. (p. 1)

Parents and Children

A second factor which strengthens the rationale for community participation emphasizes the importance of the relationship between the child and his home environment (Gordon, 1970, pp. 1-2). The child's personality is shaped by parental behaviors and attitudes, but his physical setting also plays a vital role before and during school years. How, then, can low-income parents, preoccupied with bare existence, provide much in the way of academic guidance, direct instruction, language interaction, or cultural activities for their children? How can parents who are grappling with or for life provide consistency in child management and discipline? A parent's own emotional security, self-esteem, attitudes toward school and education, and beliefs in internal versus external control of the environment greatly influence the child.

Studies summarized by Bloom, Davis, and Hess (1965) demonstrated that the home is the most important influence on a child's intellectual and emotional development. Strickland (1971) concluded, on the basis of a longitudinal study conducted in Milwaukee, that "maternal intelligence was the most reliable single indicator of the level and character of intellectual development of the children" (p. 4). A longitudinal study conducted at the Fels Institute by Kagan and Moss (1962) indicated that important behavioral changes which occur in a child during the first years of school are closely related to his identification with his parents.

Thus, if parental factors do influence child behaviors, attitudes, and performance, programs should involve parents to increase the possibility of obtaining optimal results. Regardless of ethnicity, socioeconomic level, and other factors, most people usually want to be good parents, and are concerned with and interested in their children's well-being. Their weaknesses or deficiencies, however, must be shared by educators and the educational system. If parents have negative attitudes toward educators or education, educators have to some extent contributed to the development of those attitudes. If parents cannot verbalize their needs, we must ask ourselves how well we would do with only a third-grade education— or is it possible that parents who attended our schools were not provided with opportunities to verbalize, particularly in relation to their lives and needs? Perhaps we were too busy attempting to teach these parents only the natural regions of the United States and how to diagram sentences.

Social Action and the Poor

Typically, some community agencies have worked from the *assumption* that poor people are not interested in the education of their children and that they lack the necessary skills and abilities demanded in planning and administration. There is also the underlying fear on the part of program personnel that too much parental skill and ability might result in a "take-over."

Many examples across this land demonstrate that when "poor people become involved in successful social action on important issues in their own behalf, their interests extend over a greater period of time, their feeling of helplessness does lessen, and their skills, and activities do change gradually" (Haggstrom, 1968). Two cogent examples can be drawn from the black people's struggle for freedom and from the Chicano movement, with its deliberate aim of undoing the traditional stereotypes of the Mexican-American.

A few years ago, not many sociologists would have predicted that poor blacks from poverty areas would, with some help, organize their communities in such a way that timid, ultraconventional members of the black middle class would follow them into a militant struggle for freedom. Unquestionably they have accomplished some of their goals, but their struggle will continue.

The Chicano today is unwilling to accept discrimination, ridicule, or other forms of downgrading. Institutions and agencies at all levels are under pressure to respond more effectively to the needs, language, and culture of the Mexican-American. While the Chicano movement has not been as effective as the black movement in terms of middle-class Spanish-speaking participants, it is gaining momentum.

Organized poor people have increasingly responded from the vantage point of power: they have engaged in rent strikes and taken successful actions against owners of slum buildings; they have picketed stores that sell merchandise at inflated prices; and they have formed countless consumer cooperatives. In the course of such varied involvement, the poor have—with help, to be sure—acquired organizational and planning skills as well as other managerial qualities which once did not characterize persons from poverty areas.

Interdependency

Another rationale for community participation is the interdependence among people, organizations, and agencies in any community. This interdependence requires that action be initiated on both sides of the track. If community leaders proceed from the assumption that low-income people are indifferent, lazy, and content, then the community can expect difficulties.

Social systems evolve and change (and even merge) to meet their needs. Communities will come together in efforts to satisfy such basic needs as survival, food, and safety. Social needs relative to cultural pride, values, feelings of belonging, or inner control will also bring about group cohesiveness.

The energy that exists in all segments of each community can be dissipated in positive or negative directions. An analogy can be drawn here. It is well known that children "live up" to our expectations: if they are considered "troublemakers," they will be. To a large extent the same applies to communities: categorize a community in negative terms and the expectations will be met.

Researching and Utilizing Community Resources

The role of program personnel, then, is to help affluent community members demonstrate, through action, a willingness to work with—not for— the less affluent. Failure to recognize and exercise this vital role can scar a community and have dysfunctional consequences. Many fine examples of affluent communities working with the less privileged will be documented here and presented as exemplars.

Program directors must understand that most projects are funded at levels that do not permit all the activities required by program people. It is important therefore, that the director or some staff member know specifically the kinds of services and personnel that are available in conducting a program. Is there a home for the aged in the larger community? (Residents in these homes need help and also want to help.) Are there middle-class persons who have time and are willing to help by tutoring, sewing, cooking, collecting clothing, or building classroom furniture? What human resources are available in the community at large—dental, medical, or other skills (e.g., crafts, photography, agriculture)? Can any agencies, groups, or car dealers be drawn upon for transportation needs? Have businessmen been asked to donate new, used, damaged, or discarded items that can serve the program in some capacity? What kinds of programs similar to yours are operating in the area? If their activities overlap with yours, is it possible to complement their services?

The final justification for community participation is that parents are exercising a legitimate right to social involvement when they demand a voice in programs. The educational system has always been responsive, to some degree, to the wishes of certain elements in the communities. Paradoxically, certain successes of the system have sharpened the differences between the underprivileged and the privileged. The schools have generally better meet the needs of the affluent, and most curricula typically fail to consider cultural differences. In addition, better equipped libraries and physical plants are usually found in the affluent neighborhoods. The most vocal critics of schools today are minority group members who feel that their educational needs are not being met. They are insisting on the right to select staff, develop programs, and be involved in decision-making (Hoffman, 1971). In short, each community has groups of persons —some affluent, some poor—who can make or break a project. No longer can a project expect to function as a "domesticated" organization immune to public scrutiny.

Definition of Community

The preceding material equates a community with a social system, and therefore with a structuring of events or happenings as opposed to physical parts. One can argue that there are such things as total communities (i.e., a community comprising all businesses and every social, educational, economic, and civic organization within given boundaries). An alternative approach, one that is based on the concept of pluralism, would be to define a community as nothing more than several self-sufficient groups living within certain boundaries and forming distinct social systems with their own needs, communication networks, goals, etc. Still another approach is to view a community in terms of a series of small communities or as a complex of competing communities.

Consensus on a definition of community is probably not possible or really necessary; however, by borrowing from the terminology of social psychology and mathematics, the following workable definition can be offered: *A community is a group of persons living within certain physical boundaries, sharing common attitudes, perceptions, beliefs, motivations, habits, and expectations; the group may be mutually exclusive, intersecting, or nonintersecting with other groups, depending on a specific activity.*

It appears that if a group is to share beliefs, etc., there must be some important dimension that brings about group cohesiveness. Dimensons such as the following serve to give project personnel some indications of the nature of a given community: linguistics; ethnic composition; political situation; religious factors; economic conditions; or any combination of these.

Of all the points mentioned thus far, one of the most important for program directors is the fact that a community is not static. As Hughes (1936) stated, "A social system is a moving equilibrium . . ." (p. 186). By keeping this concept in mind, the director avoids the mistake of feeling that since everything in a program is going well today, it will continue to do so.

Justification of Community Participation

The words "community participation" often conjure unpleasant thoughts in the minds of many persons, but this need not be the case. One must recognize that there is a direct correlation between the number of persons in an organization and the additional organizational activities required by staff members. Therefore, when a program director decides in favor of community participation, in a sense he is asking for more work. How does one justify this additional work? How does one justify community participation in general?

First, programs are presumably set in motion to help people—children, adults, trainees, or others. The more resources available to a program, the more effective the service can be. Second, there is a direct correlation between programs identified as significant and the degree of community participation within them. The Federation of Independent Community Schools presents a good example. A group of parents decided that the urban school, as they knew it, had failed to reflect the cultural diversity in Milwaukee's inner city. The Federation was therefore designed, with technical assistance from Marquette University and the University of Wisconsin (Milwaukee), to insure two conditions that were very important to the founding parents:

> 1. That each community school remain completely independent in all areas of the decision-making process so that each school would respond in its own ways to the cultural and educational needs of the community in which it functions.
> 2. That all independent schools in Milwaukee (meeting the designated screening criteria) would work together to discuss mutual problems and coordinate common services and resources. (Wray, 1971, p. 1)

Seven independent community schools, serving nearly 2,000 children, are Federation members. Each school is very different from the public school in the neighborhood. Each school retains its independence and autonomy but works cooperatively in areas of mutual concern. One of the strongest factors in these schools is the high level of voluntary parental involvement (Wray, 1971, pp. 1-13).

Another good example is the Hough Parent and Child Center in the black ghetto of Cleveland, Ohio. The director of the Council for Economic Opportunity decided to involve community leaders and agency representatives in discussing funding possibilities. A planning committee of ghetto area residents, community leaders, and agency representatives was selected. Within a month the groundwork was laid, and the Family Service Association of Cleveland was designated as administering agency. However, because committee meetings were not well attended, parent membership was increased from one-third to one-half; meeting times were changed to more convenient daytime hours; transportation and babysitting services were provided; and parents were contacted before each meeting. The result was greater participation.

A year later, 1968, the Hough Parent and Child Center was funded by the Office of Economic Opportunity. The committee and administering agency selected the director and associate director, while a policy advisory committee replaced the larger planning committee. Sixty percent of the advisory committee members were parents elected to one-year terms by all parents involved with the center. Other advisory members represented various organizations: volunteer agencies, the health unit, the board of education, family service agencies, etc. The advisory committee not only participated in policy formation; it also served in leadership development training. The committee offered ideas and suggestions from the community and was instrumental in mobilizing community resources. The next step involved changing the policy advisory committee into a board of directors, which then assumed major responsibilities for the entire program.

Too often, community participation is taken to mean participation only by those in a particular "target area" served by a program. This stems from a limited conception of community. To restrict participation to a target population is to ignore, to the detriment of the program, valuable services and resources. It is important that program directors and staff understand two points of view: on the one hand, we speak of total community participation; on the other, we speak of community participation by low-income persons only. The latter condition appears to be nearly impossible and often not as fruitful as when representatives of a broad spectrum of the community participate in project initiation and decisions. A good example is the Community Coordinated Child Care project in Westchester County, New York. Representatives to the meetings, which resulted in the creation of dozens of day-care centers and staff training, included all community elements: poor parents; concerned, affluent housewives; educational personnel; local businessmen; etc. An additional reason for including broader community participation is that program personnel typically are not exclusively poor persons. Both viewpoints can have strengths and weaknesses. A director may find himself in a conflicting situation because of the position taken by his advisory board with regard to broader participation.

Realizing these condtions, the writer presents the following definition of community participation (with a personal bias that the approach selected has positive implications for children, parents, neighborhoods, and communities): *Community participation means mutual initiative and involve-*

ment of persons from target area neighborhoods and the community at large, or special communities of professional people with the resources and skills to help with specific program problems. Initiative may come from staff, parents, or other community members.

Administrators of the Pennsylvania Day-Care Program (McInerrey, Durr, Kershner & Nash, 1967) feel so strongly about involving diverse viewpoints that they insist that one of the their strongest points is their use of both parents and nonparents as staff members. Each has a contribution to make because each lives differently, and each has a legitimate role in the process. Professional staff members have been trained in specialized fields to provide specific expertise known to be useful to children or parents of young children. Services come about through parental initiative and/or parental requests.

A program must reflect the nature and character of the people living within its community. The ethos of the community, that which is socially accepted, should be woven into the program operations. In a sense, the goal of most programs is predetermined—the product of a union between cultural ethos and academic scholarship.

The target population should participate from the beginning and for as long as the program continues, the degree varying according to parental interest, family situations, personal health, and other individual considerations. The program director must exercise leadership in this area, co-ordinating efforts, capabilities, resources, interests, services, and ideas—an activity that is both crucial and most difficult. Generally speaking, poor people are heavily dependent on outside forces, as in the following examples:

1. A poor person is much more likely to have contact with the police than is a middle-class family member.
2. Urban renewal programs disrupt poverty neighborhoods, scattering families in various directions.
3. Schools which tend to be impervious to the concerns of the poor tend to impose school standards and definitions on their neighborhoods. The same applies to other institutions—settlement houses, recreation programs, youth councils, and boys' clubs.

An additional factor that must be kept in mind in insuring a successful program is that the director as a professional will not be accepted automatically, regardless of his orientation and commitment. He and his staff will have to demonstrate through *action,* not *verbiage,* their real convictions. As Bey (1971) stated: "You might be identified as a specific oppressor because of the position you hold; position alone is enough for many disadvantaged to identify you with the power structure, regardless of your political and social convictions" (p. 3).

FACTORS THAT CAN FACILITATE OR
IMPEDE COMMUNITY PARTICIPATION

Parental Concerns and Input

This section attempts to show how community leaders, grassroots persons, educators, and institutions can impede or facilitate community participation. Many activities, such as the Child Development/Day-Care Workshop, conducted in Warrenton, Virginia, in July 1970, have generated a number of explicit concerns about child-care development programs in rural and urban settings. These concerns have been voiced by grassroots persons from black, Indian, Chicano, Appalachian, Ozarkian, and migrant communities (Hoffman, 1971).

Parents at the workshop asked to be involved in decision-making activities affecting their children. They wanted a voice in staff selection, hiring, and firing. They expressed a need for more males and other family members, such as teen-agers and grandparents, to work in programs. Additionally, grassroots persons expressed the advisability for professional administrators and staff to be from a background similar to that of the program's population.

Parents feel that their experience and knowledge relative to a given community should be utilized in the training of professional staff and other program personnel; thus, training programs should incorporate indigenous personnel into their activities. (Specific ways to accomplish this are presented later in this chapter.)

Relevant curriculum is also considered extremely important. Parents want their children to learn about drug abuse since such instruction is as vital for the survival of their children as is reading, if not more so. They also want the curriculum to recognize and reflect their heritage and culture.

Parents see a disparity between the rich, stimulating environments in the classroom or community center and the unavoidable bleak home environment of the child. They feel that this factor places a psychological strain on the child as he attempts to determine why all those "beautiful things" exist in centers, but not in his home (Hoffman, 1971). Program personnel can minimize this disparity by conducting workshops for parents. Inexpensive items and materials found in most homes may be converted into useful learning aids in school and at home. Such activity serves to give parents specific skills as well as tasks to perform at home. In addition, the utilization of parents' skills (such as quilting, sewing, and cooking) helps to create a more positive attitude toward the program (Lally, 1971). Teachers can demonstrate that they believe parents really care about their children's education. In the Syracuse center the teachers send a note home every day—appropriately titled "Memo to Mommy"—describing what the child did, enjoyed, and experienced.

Many parents developed negative feelings toward programs because sociologists, researchers, community developers, and educators have conducted study after study without any visible benefits for the "target" residents. The poor do not want to be "studied" again; they have little appreciation for research, and are impatient with the scholar's concern for substantiation. The scholar tends to forget what the disadvantaged cannot—that life can never wait until all the data are analyzed. Important decisions (i.e., survival) must be made on the spot, regardless of lack of evidence (Silberman, 1965). Because they feel that most programs have failed to respond to the needs of the disadvantaged, many parents favor community-developed and community-controlled schools and projects.

Generally speaking, programs with extensive community input do not differ substantially from traditional programs. Both stress cognitive development; however, grassroots parents see the need for a different context if their children are to gain ethnic and cultural pride, self-esteem, and bilingual competency. Fully aware of the consequences of not being able to cope with political, social, and economic forces, these parents want their children to receive education relevant to these topics.

Such concerns can be viewed as positive or negative, depending on one's point of reference. Take, for example, the desire of parents to be involved in training professional staff. Program personnel can ask, "What can they as parents possibly say to us?" Every community has its cultural ethos and identity. Who is in a better position to know conditions in the ghetto or barrio than those who live there? To involve parents in a linking role is to increase continuity between the program and the home, thereby increasing the potential of a better life for all. Failure to utilze such a resource is asking for a half-relevant program—or no program at all.

The Dr. Martin Luther King Family Center in Chicago provides a good example of the kind of input a program director can obtain from parents. The center originated in a research institute but is now community-controlled. Because black parents entered the scene, the entire operation took on a black orientation; among other things, parents initiated activities designed to help the black child build a positive self-concept. Their Freedom School for Black Children redefines development, competence, linguistic skills, and cognitive systems within a black frame of reference (Hoffman, 1971). The following description of the King Family Center in *Freedom School for Young Children* (1970) serves to emphasize this point:

> Because of the daily experiences which "simply omit blacks" it is necessary to emphasize for the children cultural experiences which take into account "the black experience." Culturally-based songs, rhythms, stories

and pictures are part of the child's everyday school life. Vacation days to celebrate black heroes are a part of the world. Considerable verbalization, the use of mirrors, etc., all relate to his growing self-image. The symbols of Black Revolution are communicated as part of everyday experience—not in an angry and defiant mode, but rather in an ego-enhancing and supportive manner. That the child is beautiful, delightful to be with, worthwhile in his own right, and black, is evident to the teacher, parents and child.

Educators and Community Leaders

True, the involvement of grassroots parents enhances a program, but another factor should be considered. Poor people have been powerless since the day one. They have not had the opportunities to learn certain skills, to gain positive attitudes, and to have worthwhile experiences leading to productive lives.

By virtue of their lower social status, the poor are more dependent on a larger number of powerful persons (educators included) and organizations. They see such persons and organizations in power as lacking adequate rationale for often unpredictable decisions and actions. They are even further downgraded by hostile, condescending attitudes that implicitly or explicitly communicate the inferiority of the poor. Not all educators or power figures exhibit such behavior, but powerful persons can typically be divided into two types: the callous or punitive, and the benevolent. Both types have tended to treat the poor as inferior, working *for* them instead of *with* them, reaching down to relate to them.

The dependency of poor people also limits their scope of operation, as a result of which two prerequisites for attaining an "equal" power base have been lacking: (a) early childhood environmental conditions which provide motivation, hope, self-confidence, skills, and positive attitudes for action, thus insuring relatively permanent aspects of the personality; and (b) provision of social status for "proper" role behaviors, enablng individuals to make important decisions for their futures.[2] Educators and community leaders need to find ways of remedying the situation and helping poor parents become less dependent.

The Director's Roles

One of the main jobs for a program director, then, becomes that of bringing people from divergent groups together to plan activities cooperatively. The term *divergent* is critical here—people necessarily have divergent points of view. Yet, if we are to ameliorate the negative social and racial conditions in our country, we must be willing to work together and provide opportunities for the less affluent to make decisions about their lives. In the process, the poor help administrators to make meaningful decisions; but more important, they gain experience in administration and decision-making.

Program directors must invite persons from the target population to serve on committees and policy boards at local, state, and national levels. As Hoffman (1971) explained:

> The experience and training received in policy-making roles could have a major impact on the skills and the attitudes of a significant segment of the low-income population. To the extent that serving on policy committees helps parents develop both the self-confidence and skills necessary for self-determination and leadership, programs can help powerless people achieve political influences far beyond specific concerns for their children. (p. 43)

Marshall (1969) conducted a study utilizing data from the Greater Los Angeles Community Action Agency. He found that target persons, after serving on the Board of Directors, developed a positive sense of personal power. They learned their real power in relation to politics. Self-esteem and aspirations were also changed in a positive direction, and the people became much more active as community leaders. The writer, in his work with several federal projects, has also witnessed this phenomenon time and again.

A real possibility of producing negative consequences exists, however. When disadvantaged persons are placed on boards with already powerful figures—educators, businessmen, politicians—loss of faith in the "system" by the poverty representatives often ensues. When those in power refuse to share any power, manipulating the poor for their selfish ends, the latter go back to their neighborhoods and often do their best to insure the downfall of the program. When power is shared, however, the discipline of a divergent group should operate to make each person's thrust serve the purposes of the group and not those of an individual or special-interest sector.

A discussion of family-related factors that tend to impede the school achievement of disadvantaged children was presented by Riessman (1962). (A word of caution is in order: not all families exhibit the following characteristics; and those that do, exhibit them in varying degrees.) According to Riessman, program directors and other personnel working with the culturally different student should consider five points: (a) the lack of an "educational tradition" in the home; (b) the student's inadequate motivation to pursue a long-range educational preparation for a career; (c) his poor estimate of self; (d) his antagonism toward the school and the teacher; and (e) his poor health and diet, along with a noisy, disordered home environment where learning is difficult if not impossible (p. 4).

Aside from these points regarding home environment, it should be noted that parents communicate their expectations and attitudes toward themselves and their children. If the expectations are low, performance will quite likely be low. The director must try to involve parents in teaching and helping roles that afford pride, love, and a feeling of self-satisfaction. Since parents and siblings serve as models, this new feeling is passed on to the children and can help to counter the five above-mentioned points. Parents begin to express good feelings and attitudes about the program and to provide continuity between activities in the program and the home (Hoffman, 1971).

Programs such as those under I. Gordon (1969) in Florida, J. R. Lally at the Children's Center in Syracuse (1971), and R. Trujillo at New Mexico State University have utilized parents in teaching roles. In the Syracuse Children's Center program, paraprofessional "child development trainers" make weekly home visits and help parents with teaching sensorimotor tasks, encouraging infant language development, and providing other care-giving skills. A weekly workshop in the day-care center is held for parents, who are encouraged to build toys from broken toys, to create mobiles or games for their children, and to learn tie-dyeing or how to "make" books for preschoolers by using old magazine pictures. Sewing clothes for themselves and their children is popular, but in all cases the parents choose their own activities.

Institutions

Many times persons administering educational programs fail to recognize that all institutions—social, educational, economic, and political—have an impact on the population in general but on the disadvantaged in particular. The disadvantaged, as is well known, pay higher interest rates than do middle-class families; they are more likely to be used by unscrupulous politicians, and are forced to interact with social welfare workers who often render subjective and unpredictable decisions. Though education tends to be the equalizing factor in our society, education is not impervious to other influences, and the problems a child brings to school cannot be solved solely by educational remedies. If a child cannot read, a number of situations may be operating against him: inadequate food, clothing, or shelter, or electricity or water at home that is "on today, off tomorrow." Problems more important than learning to read occupy the child's mind. In other words, social, political, and economic factors impinge upon him, his parents, and his home.

A few examples illustrate the point. Many settlement houses run recreation programs that meet their own criteria. While these criteria are based on some rationale, code, or guidelines, they often do not reflect understanding of and consideration for the patterns and life-styles of the participants. Neighborhood youths cannot engage in accustomed modes of behavior and still participate in settlement house activities; as a condition for participation, they must, involuntarily and without understanding why, dissolve friendships.

Economic deprivation and the inability to obtain or maintain long-term, adequate employment are frequently conjoined with substandard housing and with exorbitant rents to slum landlords who care only about one thing: collecting the payments (Bey, 1971). In addition, restrictive building codes imposed by housing boards force many a large family to remain in an overcrowded house, even if and when the family has funds to add a room. The regulations may stipulate that an architect must be engaged to draw the plans and that an engineer must render decisions concerning stress capabilities of beams—this in addition to the usual contractor's costs. Needless to say, the additional fees for professional services make the project financially prohibitive.

The poor are rated "bad risks" by banks, and invariably find themselves squeezed by finance companies demanding higher interest rates on loans. Families that buy more than they can afford run the risk of having their belongings repossessed or their wages garnished.

Until a few years ago, facilities for medical and psychiatric care or legal aid were practically nonexistent for the poor. If care was available, it was usually inadequate.

The attempt to seek categorical assistance or general relief is a dehumanizing experience. Agencies are often deliberately rude in their efforts to discourage applicants. Rules, regulations, and red tape become so overwhelming that poor families are left at the mercy of totally uncomprehensible forces.[3]

In 1972, in some parts of the United States, quasi-feudal systems were still in operation. Thousands of people work the land, and plant and harvest the crops in exchange for a "house" rented from the landowner, credit at the company store, and the "privilege" of financing all purchases through the owner. In rural areas, storekeepers exploit customers by selling goods at prices considerably higher than those in surrounding areas. Higher profits for company stores, Indian trading post owners, and chains operating in ghettos are the norm—and their policies amount to increased poverty for the captive buyer.

This has become such a defensive proposition for both urban and rural peoples that some countermeasures have been taken. Successful cooperatives have been organized in both urban and rural settings. In several urban areas, poor people are bussed from the ghettos to the suburbs to take advantage of lower prices. In El Paso, Texas, a large discount store has recently been opened in the barrio.

City Hall regulations often work directly against programs and poor people. In connection with one program, the writer found a city regulation which limited the amount of floor space that could be added to an existing structure. If a large family lived in a house with a floor area of 700 square feet and wanted to add another room, only 10 percent of the existing floor space could be added. The reader can calculate the size of the mansion after the addition!

Not all institutional personnel sit around and scheme against the poor. For each of the examples cited, there are others of a different nature. In the city which imposed the 10 percent restriction on house additions, the writer was instructed by a sensitive, high-level city official to draw and submit the plans according to regulations and then to meet with him and explain the real needs of the family. Ignoring portions of the regulations, the official approved the plan and many others like it. In addition, he always sent the "right" inspector to approve the building. He did not, nor did we want him to, compromise on safety standards, but his common-sense approach enabled families to obtain floor space consistent with their needs.

In a planned early education program, concerned representatives of the power structure—school personnel, bank representatives, and individuals from other agencies—met every week for months with the director to explore ways of financing and providing bussing to the program's classrooms. With a population of semirural disadvantaged children to be served, the budget did not allow for transportation costs!

Program personnel must be aware of the local situation and must have the desire, interest, and "intestinal fortitude" to do what is consistent with the needs of "their people." In short, the director has the responsibility of determining how to utilize the resources in his community to insure the most effective program.

ORIENTATION FOR PROJECT/ COMMUNITY UNDERSTANDING

The preceding material points to critical issues in administering a program. At the very core of each program lies the dilemma of bringing people with differing values, beliefs, concerns, orientations, and needs together into a working relationship. This is no easy task, for the staff, trainees, and target population may represent different linguistic and cultural backgrounds. Orientation of the staff and trainees to the basic issues and needs of the community, and of the community to the potentials of the program, is one of the most crucial factors in administering a program. There is no one optimal way of accomplishing this because it is impossible to predict all the unique variables of each program. With this in mind, a number of techniques and ideas that have been successfully implemented across the country are presented. It is hoped that the reader can, with modifications, utilize the information to fit his particular situation.

In a real sense a program calls for a marriage between academic scholarship and cultural ethos. On the surface it may appear that this union would be impossible and to some extent even undesirable; however, upon closer scrutiny, one must realize that the two worlds do exist and that it is invaluable to create a meaningful relationship between the two. Scholarship is dedicated to the search for truth which will, in the end, benefit the disadvantaged; but the disadvantaged live under tremendous pressures and want relevance now. Thus, the scholar is reminded to keep in touch with reality.

Identification of Community Representatives

Where and when does one start? Every project should be based on the needs of the target population as expressed by "true" representatives of that population. Many a program has failed because program personnel identified and listened to "false" representatives.

Program directors should involve different segments of the community even during the conceptualization stage, so that parents and other community forces can have a voice in the direction of the program. It is much easier for community representatives to understand the nature of the program if they have been involved from the beginning. One can expect difficulties if the first community contact is made when the trainees arrive or sometime thereafter. After initial broad participation, an advisory group may be selected. This group, though smaller in membership, should also be representative of the area.

Staff selected for a program need orientation to the program and to the community. (See also chapter 6 where staff selection is treated.) The utilization of community representatives from the beginning—including a voice in staff and trainee selection—facilitates orientation by the community. Some of the techniques presented in the following pages serve to bring the orientation into focus by working within community or program components. Depending on the size of the program and on time and budget constraints, staff and trainee orientation may be conducted simultaneously or separately. The techniques can be modified in any manner consistent with the needs and objectives of the program.

Orientation? Of Course!

Prior to the delineation of specific techniques, a rationale for the activities is presented. A primary training objective should be the integration of components. If we proceed from the assumption that the program is designed for a specific community and that, in most cases, the target population is from a cultural background different from that of the trainees and staff, we must provide orientation to bridge this difference.

We are all products of our cultures, and our behavior is shaped by cultural factors. Many persons conduct training by providing opportunities for program personnel to "learn about the community." In many cases, this calls for learning another language to communicate effectively. Language must be considered necessary for communication in another culture, not as an end in itself. Speaking the target population's language and understanding their customs and value systems are essential if staff and trainees are to gain support and respect from the people. Without this support and respect, they cannot render meaningful and worthwhile service. Program personnel will encounter difficulties if they lack the sensitivity to live and work effectively with persons in the target area.

Learning about the other culture and the people of that culture is both important and desirable, but an equally important factor must be considered: program personnel should examine their own motivations, interests, expectations, objectives, and ability to cope with the demands of the program. It is critical that the program trainee or staff member understand himself. Jones (1968) summed it up when she stated, "Trainees have to become aware of themselves and how they affect others; of how they have been shaped by American culture; of how they react in unfamiliar situations" (p. 7). Attitudinal change does not occur overnight. Attitudes formed over twenty or more years are not likely to be transformed in a few months. There must be a concern with increasing awareness of self so that the person may decide whether change is needed.

The following exercises are presented with no notion that the order or format must be followed. It is up to the director and the staff to make decisions relative to the exercises and format to be used.

Community Description

Several approaches can be utilized to give staff and trainees a flavor of the culture and the people in the target area. If at all possible, community members should be enlisted to provide firsthand information. This can be done by utilizing such methods as the "fishbowl technique" (described later on this section), where community representatives, sitting in a small circle, with staff and trainees sitting in the outer circle, help program personnel to gain perspective in relation to persons and culture. This also serves to help program trainees begin the self-analysis which is so important but which generally will not occur unless the trainer or program director presents this as one of the objectives.

Another technique for community description calls for the assignment of tasks to be performed by program trainees in the community. All trainees should not have identical tasks, and alternate ways of achieving the objectives should be provided. The data may be written, recorded on video- or audiotape, presented in the form of a play, or role-played. Assignments might be made individually, by teams of interns alone, or by teams composed of parents, trainees, and staff.

Objectives for each activity must be behaviorally stated. For example:

Today we shall attempt to learn about Ward #3. We want to gain some perspective relative to the residents and the physical, social, political, educational, and economic conditions in the ward. Trainees will be grouped into teams of three.

Team A will gather data on physical conditions of Ward #3. The team will draw a map showing the boundaries; describe conditions of streets, sidewalks, lighting, traffic, etc.; describe housing conditions; and specify and meet two other objectives.

Team B will gather data on educational conditions. The team will describe the outside appearance of educational facilities, and examine a school zoning map and record the nature of the zoning.

(Continue in this manner with other teams and objectives.)

Teams are brought back at a specified time to present their findings. Parents should be at the sessions to set the record straight or to provide additional input. This type of activity provides valuable information and is much more effective than any series of lectures.

Communication Facilitators

Communication is essential if programs are to succeed. The process can be facilitated by using games; the following usually serve as good beginners. (Community people should participate in this process.)

Game 1. Two by Four. Explain the nature of communication: verbal, nonverbal, and body language. *The Silent Language* (Hall, 1959) and *Body Language* (Fast, 1970) are excellent resources. Explain the value and necessity of communication in our society. Instructions for the group follow:

Step 1. Choose a stranger or someone you do not know too well. (Take a chair with you.)

Step 2. Sit behind your partner (he faces away from you so that you are speaking to the back of his head). The listener may not talk, ask questions, or take notes.

a. The first minute, talk about yourself (time allotted may vary);
b. The second minute, talk about your ambitions, your role, or your expectations, etc.;
c. The third minute, talk about the program.

Step 3. Reverse positions (now your partner sits in your chair facing the back of your head), and repeat Step 2 a, b, and c.

Step 4. How well did you listen?

a. Invite another team of two to join you.
b. Your job is to role-play your partner. You attempt to recall and relate to the other three as many things as you remember about your partner, his expectations, etc., and his reactions to the program.
c. Bring the total group back together—people remain in the same seating arrangement; however, all face the center of room—talk about names, places, roles, communication, etc.

A variant on this game is part of the Syracuse program's process of selecting paraprofessionals as child development trainers (Lally, 1971). Paraprofessionals are asked to role-play what a director can do in this project. They also role-play what a parent expects of the program.

Game 2. Block Buster. Use many blocks of various shapes and colors. Divide the blocks into as many bags as you have groups, and give each group one bag. Participants sit on the floor or at tables, or both.

Step 1. During this activity, you may (or may not) talk. (The leader decides whether he is after communication as such or is interested in group process. For this example let us assume that the group is not to talk.)

Step 2.

a. Open the bag and empty the blocks on the table or floor.
b. Build a structure using all the blocks. Judging for the best structure will take place when all groups are finished. (This activity can be used to obtain certain objectives, such as encouraging a timid individual or group to react, etc.)
c. After the judging is over, decide as a group (no talking) which shapes and colors of blocks you want for the next structure.
d. Once you decide, move about the room (no talking)—beg, borrow, barter, or steal the desired colors and shapes of blocks your team needs.

Step 3. Bring the total group together and discuss the process, the product, the objectives, etc.

Game 3. Tonteria (Foolish Thing). The large group is divided into small groups which sit on the floor or around tables. Each group is provided with a large piece of clean paper and a box of crayons. The leader gives instructions but allows no group talking through Step 2.

Step 1. Have each group draw a picture with all members participating. Tell the group that no restrictions, no boundaries, and no judgment will be made.

Step 2. Have some parents, staff members, or someone else move about during the activity, nodding in approval or disapproval.

Step 3. Have one observer (predetermined based on desired outcome, i.e., confrontation between trainer and director, trainee and director, trainee and trainee, trainee and parents, etc.) confront a group by verbally ripping a group's project apart (e.g., you used too much red; your product lacks balance; your product is too large, too small).

Step 4. Bring the group together in a large circle and analyze the activity.[4]

Problems invariably surface during training. If they are viewed as challenges and used as learning opportunities, they contribute in large measure to a program trainee's involvement and assumption of responsibility. Coping with problems results in learning that serves to prepare a person for his immediate or future role. Ability to cope is probably one of the best indicators of the trainee's potential. Wight and Bing (1969) quoted Hopkins in this connection:

> Many of the problems which the trainee should deal with in a program . . . are generated out of the processes of the program itself, out of the very ambiguity. The processes are to an extent unpredictable, they can throw the trainees on their own resources, create anxiety, and in some cases even hostility among trainees. The trainer's risk is to keep the trainees zeroed in on the problems, encourage them to diagnose what is going on, define the problem, devise a solution, and take action on it. In cases like these the trainer is acting as an internal consultant to the trainees, keeping them attuned to the task and assisting in the sensitive work of analyzing. . . . (p. 66)

Modified T-Groups. T-groups are typically associated with sensitivity training which has group process and interpersonal dynamics as the major focus. Thus, the content of a group's discussion is the process of the group (the happenings within the group). Quite often in T-groups anything happening outside the group is not considered important to the discussion. The trainer in the T-group has the specific role of facilitating, observing, and reporting group members' feelings and reactions as regards other persons in the group. This type of group is considered trainer-led because the trainer plays such a vital role in the process.

In contrast, the modified T-group has the group leader playing a very different role: he guides group members in conceptualizing and generalizing their experiences and in becoming aware of the social forces which impinge upon them and others. In this manner, the major focus in the modified T-group is to help participants deal with forces outside the group.

A hypothetical example of a stuation where a modified T-group might be utilized is as follows: A trainee is left in charge of a group of children. The supervisor comes into the room and sees fit to "correct" the children verbally and physically. The trainee takes exception to the approach and lets the supervisor know it. Several days later, the supervisor returns. This time a parent, a regular teacher, and the trainee are in the room. The supervisor causes a child to cry. (Note that a hypothetical situation is being presented; consequently no child need be present.) The parent gets several other parents to join her in calling a meeting with the administration. During the meeting, accusations and counteraccusations are cast about —parents against supervisor and supervisor against trainee. The trainee, according to the supervisor, is to blame for the mess because "the trainee went about the community spreading rumors."

With a modified T-group session, the incident can be used to help all trainees—not just the one involved—to conceptualize and generalize the experience. More importantly, it can be an extremely effective instrument for examining social forces and implications.

Critical Incidents. "Critical incidents" can be utilized alone or in conjunction with such activities as community description, modified T-groups, and fishbowl. This activity involves the use of actual incidents involving persons in previous programs—for example, between a trainee and a parent or between two trainees. The real purpose of this activity is to introduce personnel to typical kinds of situations that arise in programs. The incidents can be recounted verbally, but role-playing can serve an important function by allowing participants to determine how well acquainted they are with the culture, the program, the language, etc. There are no right or wrong answers for the open-ended incidents. They merely point out how the participants reacted during the actual occurrence. In addition, staff members can use the activity to gain better understanding of the trainees' values, goals, or judgments. It is possible to utilize this technique in understanding social, personal, and job-centered issues.

Biographical Descriptions. Use of biographical descriptions can follow or be linked with any of the preceding techniques. The objective is to present detailed information about a person who is perceived as being particularly antagonistic, puzzling, difficult to deal with, or irrational. The biographical description attempts to provide insight into his values, expectations and aspirations. Attempts must be made to demonstrate how the individual has been influenced by his culture—religion, family customs, traditions, and social status. The person being discussed is not present or identified by name. Later, in a one-to-one session, a supportive person who is particularly skilled in interpersonal relations should discuss with him the perceptions which others have of him, with the objective of helping him become more aware of his effect on others. This will allow him to make decisions about modifying his behavior if he so desires.

Role-Playing. This is probably one of the most widely used techniques in group work. Basically, the process calls for some person to play his own or another's role. A good way to extend this technique is to have one group role-play a given situation, with no attempt to talk about ways in which the situation should have been handled and with no effort at solving the problem. Another group observes the role-playing, develops a number of group alternate solutions, and reports back to the original group for interaction and group discussion. This also helps program personnel gain insight into trainees' modes of behavior, leadership potential, etc.

Fishbowl. One of the most effective orientation activities can be the fishbowl. Depending on the program, time limitations, and number of participants, this technique can be conducted for the benefit of community members, trainees, or staff. The objective can be to provide information about the community for staff and/or trainees or to provide information relative to the program for community members and/or trainees. This technique can be far more effective than a lecture-type orientation. The process calls for the staff to sit in a small circle and for the trainees to sit in a larger outer circle. The staff interacts with no intention of addressing the trainees. The discussion deals with staff opinions, concerns, and expectations about the program in general. Program aspects such as objectives, limitations, budget, and problem areas are brought to light. At the end of the discussion, those sitting in the larger circle are given the opportunity to comment, ask questions, and present opinions and ideas.[5]

COMMUNITY PARTICIPATION EXEMPLARS

As stated earlier in this chapter, there is a positive correlation between effective programs and a high level of community participation within the program. The following paragraphs illustrate how program parents and other community members have participated in programs.[6]

The Story-Reading Program (Harding & Macklin, 1969)

This program at Cornell University was aimed at examining the influence of story-reading on the language development of young disadvantaged children. Twenty children were chosen for the experimental group and 20 for the control group, and both groups were matched for age, sex, socio-economic status, and race. Teen-age story readers from working-class homes were trained during the first year. Initially, the girls made weekly home visits to help mothers set a story-reading time, learn new ways of obtaining and holding children's interests, and select books for children. The second year these readers were replaced by mothers, caretakers, or siblings.

Appalachia Preschool Education Program (Alford, 1969)

At Charleston, West Virginia, three-, four-, and five-year-olds from low-income rural families were chosen, and the program was home-oriented to fit the needs of small rural school districts. It was so structured that the number of qualified preschool teachers needed was reduced; transportation difficulties for children and parents were eliminated; program costs were about one-half the amount needed to run a conventional kindergarten; and parents could participate fully. Television, home visits, and a mobile class-room served as vehicles to conduct the program. Taped television programs were aired five days per week. Parents were helped by home visitors who explained the theme for the following week, gave suggestions to complement the taped programs, and helped parent-child communication. A mobile unit was moved from site to site to provide instruction for groups of 10-15 children for one and a half hours per week.

A Demonstration Program:
Group Care of Infants and Toddlers

Sponsored by the University of North Carolina at Greensboro, this program was unique in at least two ways: (1) children came from both middle-class and low-income backgrounds, and (2) the program was explained during initial meetings with the parents, where information about the child and the parents' views of the child's needs were gathered. Based on information provided by parents, cue cards were then developed for each child. The attempt was made to provide care at the center which was almost identical to that received at home. The cue cards were updated through the interaction between the parents and center personnel. The aim was to provide "truly" individualized care.

Family Educare System

Comprehensive programs in Hempstead, New York, offered help with child care, child development instruction, and family and community involvement to varied populations. Obtaining family involvement and strengthening family ties were key objectives. Services through Educare included full-time, half-day, after-school, weekend, evening, intermittent, and open-ended programs tailored to fit family needs.

Parent Education Programs

Both Ira Gordon (1969) at the University of Florida and J. R. Lally at Syracuse University (1970) trained indigenous women from poor families to be parent educators and child development trainers. Mothers were provided with nutritional and child development information. They were encouraged to help their children learn and to enjoy this teaching interaction with the child. Since a great deal of hostility toward middle-class workers had been evidenced in the past, the parent educators received extensive pre- and in-service training in establishing rapport and reducing defensiveness and hostility.

Project CHILD

The Curriculum to Heighten Intelligence and Language Development, at Bernard Baruch College, City University of New York, served black and Puerto Rican families with prekindergarten and kindergarten children (Robinson, 1969). The goals of one of the program components, Parent Project, were (a) to help parents obtain, evaluate, compare, and assess their children's school learning, and (b) to have parents develop a curriculum for home teaching to reinforce school teaching. Two-hour meetings were held weekly; parents were paid $2.00 for each session attended. Babysitters were furnished during the meetings. Activities such as role-playing, demonstrations, committee work, trips, group evaluation, and planning were carried on during the sessions. A number of positive outcomes resulted, one of the most significant of which was that parents offered to help teachers select culturally relevant curriculum content. Parents also assisted teachers in classroom implementation.

Project Know-How

Conducted at Florida State University, this program was designed to work with children aged 12-24 months and their parents. One objective was to strengthen and stabilize the family processes related to socialization of the children. Mothers helped to plan daily schedules for the children. In the morning, mothers served as instructional aides; after lunch the children took a nap while the mothers learned about nutrition, budgeting, child development, cooking, and home management. Family role relationships, such as division of labor, role support between mother and father, and decision-making, were topics for course work. Results revealed that positive, supportive behaviors in relation to children were exhibited by program parents upon completion of the program. Use of physical punishment was common prior to and at the beginning of the program, but this was replaced by negative speaking.

National Capital Area Day Care Association

This program was conducted in poverty areas of the nation's capital. One objective was to provide jobs and teacher training for people in the community. Parents could progress on a career ladder from aide to day-care assistant, to assistant teacher, and then to teacher. Monthly parents' meetings were held at each of 16 centers. Parents had a voice in policy formation and in selection of center personnel. The Parent's Advisory Council (PAC) was elected from these groups. The PAC was involved in establishing policies, hiring personnel, identifying needs, and presenting ideas to the larger body of parents for possible implementation.

Dr. Martin Luther King Family Center

A unique idea was tried here; four black ghetto fathers and their nursery school children who attended the Family Center Preschool served as subjects for the model. The underlying assumption was that black ghetto fathers have not been approached directly enough to obtain their involvement in positive emotional experiences with their children. The process for this model took form in several objectives:

1. Try to establish a mutually trusting working relationship to insure that the father's masculine role is not undermined.
2. Have program fathers persuade other fathers to join to obtain a better understanding of community problems and to contemplate solutions.
3. Relate father-child activties to the father's work or to an outdoor activity.
4. Develop an all-male group.
5. Plan programs which require participation of wives, children, and fathers.

This approach was quite successful: more fathers entered the program, and activities involving teen-agers, mothers, and other children in the community became commonplace.

Parents' Community Cooperative Nursery School
(Smith & Davies, 1970)

One of the most significant programs involving a community was located in Menlo Park, California. Begun under the leadership of Francis Oliver, a community resident, this program demonstrated that:

(a) funds could be raised by communities (parents raised $10,000 toward a new building);

(b) black people could run a successful school; and

(c) parents could, with some help, write proposals, by-laws, and regulations, and hire teachers.

The parents held meetings in different homes on Thursday evenings and Friday mornings. They typed, cleaned, taught, attended community meetings, made movies, helped on field trips, and attended courses for self-improvement. Both parents and teachers developed the instructional program.

Grandview-Crestview Parent Child Center

A program for migrants conducted in Grandview, Washington, by Martin G. Yanez was designed to provide such educational services as child development instruction, communication skills, and language development for migrant children and parents.

Parents were involved in educational activities which aided them with child training during the first three years. Topics such as discipline, nutrition and health, motivation, self-concept, and how children learn were covered. Training sessions for parents took the form of discussions, as well as participation in educational activities provided by the program for the migrant children. Home visits and counseling services were offered to all families. Adult classes in auto mechanics, nutrition, home economics, planned parenthood, etc., were offered. Fifty percent of the policy advisory board was composed of migrant parents. Also serving on the board were a doctor, a nurse, and other community representatives.

DARCEE

The Demonstration and Research Center for Early Education, at George Peabody College for Teachers (Nashville, Tenn.), was funded by the National Laboratory on Early Childhood Education and the Office of Economic Opportunity (OEO) through Project Head Start and has been in existence for a number of years at the time of this writing. DARCEE's three functions—research, training, and demonstration—were directed at improvng the ability of disadvantaged children to learn. Both rural and urban children and their parents served as the population. Middle-class subjects were identified for comparison groups. The process had been conceived for longitudinal studies of parents, children, and other closely related family members. There was interest in helping the mother become a more effective educational change agent for her child. Each mother was given instruction in planning and organizing her life to demonstrate its importance in becoming a better teacher. Mothers who had undergone DARCEE training were utilized in a Mother Home Visitor Program, training new mothers as paraprofessionals.

Another DARCEE component involved home visitation to obtain cooperation from mothers. Materials were brought to the home and demonstrated, and exercises were assigned weekly. The home visitor spent one hour or more weekly at each home, and the visits extended over six months. Planning was individualized. The visitor followed the mothers even though some moved, some went to school, and others obtained new jobs.[7]

Ypsilanti-Carnegie Infant Education Project

This was one of the better known and respected early education programs at the time of the writing of this chapter. The program attempted to assess the effectiveness of systematic intervention by public school teachers in preventing intellectual deficits in disadvantaged children. The rationale for this home visiting program was:

1. Preventive programming must begin before the disadvantaged child reaches age three because the framework of the intellectual growth of the child is complete by then.

2. Preventive intervention is potentially successful when it is presented as a home-teaching program for both mother and infant (Weikart & Lambie, 1969, 1970), where the home worker sees herself as a guest in the home as she helps the mother in sensitive ways to become aware of and a contributor to her infant's development and learning.

Christian Action Ministry

The procedure by which the following exemplar came to be written is itself an example of community participation in early childhood personnel training. The university participant in the collaboration informed the community organization about the possibility of submitting a joint description of their work for consideration as an illustration in this chapter. The book outline and first draft of this chapter were read by three persons from the community organization, and a brainstorming session was held to consider the important points to include. After the university participant wrote a first draft of the description and presented it to the group, it was revised according to their suggestions and finally approved.

In another instance, a community organization and a state university implemented a unique model of collaboration in which both would realize goals pertaining to early childhood education. Christian Action Ministry (CAM), a nonprofit community organization of 13 black churches in the West Garfield Park area of Chicago, was interested in finding the most effective curriculum for use in its day-care centers and in training community residents. The College of Education at the University of Illinois at Chicago Circle was interested in developing a specialized training program in early childhood education, in extending its responsiveness to community needs, and in doing curriculum research. CAM initiated the exploratory contact with the College of Education, and the entry into a working relationship came only after CAM examined the orientation and biases of the faculty member with whom they would be working and decided that these coincided with their own educational philosophy. The aims of the collaboration were:

1. To train indigenous residents in child care and development, and in curriculum development and research.

2. To implement, field-test, and evaluate the Piaget-derived early education curriculum which was begun by Dr. Constance Kamii in Ypsilanti, Michigan, and which was made available through a legal agreement between the university, Dr. Kamii, and the Ypsilanti public schools.

3. To produce a written curriculum particularly suited to realizing the learning potential of the community's children, based on the field-testing experiences.

4. To accomplish the foregoing goals in the context of genuine community control.

Mutual agreement on all decision-making aspects of the program was required. Much time was devoted to assuring clear communication and to hearing all points of view on any issue. Depending on the nature of the decision, the level of necessary agreement varied. For many decisions, agreement was necessary only between the director of the CAM-St. Barnabas Day-Care Center and the participating university faculty member. Other decisions required consensus between CAM's Council or Day-Care Board and other university representatives, such as the dean or associate dean of the College of Education, the chancellor, or legal counsel. Consensus decisions were made on the goals of the research, a proposal for funds (granted by the Spencer Foundation), personnel to be hired, and accountability and use of funds.

The community organization in this situation was better able than many community groups to exert full control because of its financial investment in the program. CAM provided the day-care center's basic operating expenses through its own state and private sources. Funds for the curriculum research came jointly to CAM and the university, and these were supplemented by funds from the university's Urban Education Research Program (DeVries, 1971).

Rough Rock School

The following exemplars, as well as others, were documented by John and Horner (1971).

Rough Rock is an isolated community of 1,200 in the heart of the Navajo Reservation in northeastern Arizona. The main occupation is sheepherding; average income is $700. The population of the school district is widely scattered throughout an area of 115 square miles; 95 percent are non-English-speaking and 90 percent have no formal education. In September 1966 the Rough Rock Demonstration School was opened with classes from pre-school through grade 6, and a grade level has been added each year. In the 1968–69 school year there were 408 students. Classes at Rough Rock were divided into four phases: Phase I—Head Start; Phase II —Follow Through (kindergarten-grade 2); Phase III—elementary; and Phase IV—upper elementary. Originally the main emphasis in the school was on a locally developed English as a second language program, with instruction in Navajo reading for the older children. However, over the years, a steadily increasing program of spoken Navajo and Navajo culture and history developed, and in the 1968–69 school year Navajo was the medium of instruction in Phases I and II. In the proposed program for 1969–70, the language used during the school day was divided as follows: Phase I—4 hours spoken Navajo, 2 hours spoken English; Phase II—4 hours spoken and written Navajo, 2 hours spoken English; Phases III and IV—2 hours spoken and written Navajo, 4 hours spoken and written English.

Historically, Indian education in the United States has been characterized by outside control of the school on the one hand and parental distrust and antagonism on the other. Rough Rock's innovative philosophy of parental and community involvement was initially met by parents and community with suspicion and a reluctance to participate. This attitude changed first to one of deference, later to one of critical and concerned involvement. Rough Rock attempted to bridge the traditional separation between school and community. Among the innovations were a seven-member, all-Navajo school board that exercises real authority in developing school program and policy, a system of parent teams, and school visits and talks by leading Navajo elders and artisans.

Parents who were not members of the teams were encouraged to visit the school, stay several days, live in the dorms, eat in the cafeteria, and observe in the classrooms. One benefit of parent teams and visiting parents was that every child in the school had a parent or close relative living in the dormitory at some time during the school year. Parents were also encouraged to take children home for the weekend, a policy discouraged in the traditional Indian boarding schools where parents met numerous obstacles in arranging such visits. Unlike the traditional schools, Rough Rock was not plagued with a "runaway" problem. At this writing more than 12,000 visitors from 42 states, 8 foreign countries, and 86 Indian tribes had visited this school.

Santa Fe Community School

The 65 children in this urban school were selected in proportion to their different backgrounds as represented in Santa Fe: low- and middle-income English-speaking (white and black), Spanish-speaking, and Indian. The program, begun in September 1968, offered tuition on a sliding scale. The school was divided into a lower school (3-6 years old) and an upper school (5-9 years old). The school hoped eventually to include children up to 12 years of age. The entire school program was bilingual, with English and Spanish used in all classes. All children in the lower school began by learning basic concepts in both Spanish and English. For 15 minutes daily all lower-school children were brought together for "Circle Time," which included games and songs in Spanish, as well as the learning of Indian songs and dances. Upper-school pupils supplemented the oral Spanish program with texts.

The basic stated goal of the school, which was started by the joint efforts of parents and educators, was to combine a multilingual, multicultural experiment with individualized instruction. Parents elected members to the board of trustees of the school and also served on various committees. For a small fee the school provided a day-care service for working parents. One Saturday each month the parents attended school with their children and engaged in a variety of activities ranging from repair jobs to picnics. Parents were also free to participate on school trips, such as visits to Indian pueblos for celebrations and dances.

Applied Language Research Center

In the elementary schools selected for this program, the student enrollment was almost 100 percent Spanish-speaking. The bilingual program started formally in September 1966 in four pilot grade 1 classes in two public elementary schools in the El Paso Independent School District. Control classes were set up with instruction in oral Spanish for 20 minutes daily. A grade level was added each year, and by September 1968 the experimental program had reached the grade 3 level, with a total of 17 experimental classes in several schools. The program was planned to continue through grade 6. The overall goal was to produce literate, bilingual students. Parental interest was encouraged; newsletters in both Spanish and English were sent to parents, keeping them up-to-date and explaining changes in the program. Parents and children were bussed together to the Lab for program demonstrations three or four times a year. The Lab reported at the time of this writing that both fathers and mothers were beginning to attend the demonstrations.

Good Samaritan Center

Located in a predominantly (92 percent) Spanish-speaking, low-income neighborhood (population about 20,000) in San Antonio, Texas, this pre-school program served children who lived in the neighborhood and spoke only Spanish. Some of the parents were third- and fourth-generation Mexican-Americans who spoke no English. The staff held regular meetings with them and asked them to observe their children in class and to meet with the teacher for a discussion of problems. Parents were also encouraged to take home simple conceptual materials to use in teaching their children.

In 1968-69, the Urban Educational Development Center of San Antonio, in an attempt "to create change in the community by doing things with people," formed three parent groups: (1) parents of three-year-olds enrolled at Good Samaritan, (2) parents of three-year-olds not enrolled at Good Samaritan, and (3) a group of civic leaders. The third group was included so that they might develop insight into community problems. The activities included supervising children going to and from school, attending meetings with school and community officials, visiting the school to observe children and discuss methods and techniques with staff, and volunteering as teacher's helpers and as hosts at private home gatherings to demonstrate school and community services. Before each activity, parents were personally contacted and then sent a letter of invitation.

SUMMARY

Some broad objectives, together with a rationale for community participation, was presented. The argument was made that a community is a viable and powerful force that can make learning meaningful and therefore effective. A case was built for the establishment of a learning community beyond the traditional concept of formal school, which was considered far too restrictive, unreal, and isolated. Furthermore, the author feels that America will remain a great country only to the extent that more meaningful relationships are established between the affluent and the less affluent. The people of this country must move quickly to redress the wounds that are inflicted upon the poor, the outcasts, and the "different." Our society can ill afford not to recognize this issue, and it must take positive action to ameliorate negative conditions.

The relationship between parents and children in terms of educational considerations was presented along the following lines. The child's personality is shaped by parental behaviors, aspirations, and attitudes. The child's physical setting also plays a vital role in molding his behavior before and during school years. Those of us who work in "disadvantaged schools" have come to realize that not "being in," and that not having a fair chance as an adult—a parent—certainly reflect themselves in loss of motivation and hope in the child as early as first and second grade, particularly if a child finds himself in a nonsupporting school or in one permeated with racism.

Finally, the author advocates that our society reorder its priorities and pool its resources in order to enhance the learning careers of our children.

NOTES

1. *Functions* are those observed consequences which facilitate adaptation or adjustment of a given system; *dysfunctions* are those observed consequences which lessen the adaptation or adjustment of the system (Merton, 1957).

2. The spirit of these paragraphs was influenced by speakers such as Drs. Frank Riessman (Washington, D.C., 1969), Simon Gonzales (Los Angeles, 1970), and Warren Haggstrom (Washington, D.C., 1968). Time and space do not permit full and detailed information relative to studying and understanding a community and its power structure. The reader is referred to Hunter (1953), Warren (1965), Hoffman (1971), and Saranson and Ganzer (1969) as excellent sources for the topic.

3. The nature of the three preceding paragraphs was influenced by a panel discussion held in Washington, D.C., 1969. Drs. Joe Paige, Warren Haggstrom, Bill Smith, and others were in attendance.

4. The games presented are examples of activities which have served the writer well in various programs. Some ideas are original; others have been borrowed and modified from various workshops conducted across the country.

5. Techniques, ideas, and activities presented here were obtained from various sources, including workshops and institutes conducted in different parts of the country. Special recognition is given to Albert Wight and John Bing

(1969) whose *Handbook for Cross-Cultural and Community Involvement Training* is recommended for details on many of the techniques cited.

6. The reader is referred to Hoffman (1971) for a comprehensive listing of, and abstracts on, projects in the United States which have had extensive parental involvement.

7. For a more complete treatment of DARCEE the reader is referred to Demonstration and Research Center for Early Education (1969) and to Gray and Klaus (1970).

REFERENCES

Alford, R. W. A home-oriented preschool program in rural Appalachia. Paper presented at the meeting of the National Association for Education of Young Children, Salt Lake City, November 1969.

Allport, F. H. A structoronomic conception of behavior: Individual and collective—I. Structural theory and the master problems of social psychology. *Journal of Abnormal and Social Psychology,* 1962, *64,* 3-30.

Bey, A. D. Improving your relationships with paraprofessionals. *Career Development,* 1971, *1*(2), 1-2.

Bloom, B. S., Davis, A., & Hess, R. Compensatory education for cultural deprivation. Based on working papers contributed by participants in the Research Conference on Education and Cultural Deprivation. New York: Holt, Rinehart and Winston, 1965.

Demonstration and Research Center for Early Education. *Intervention with mothers and infants: Annual progress report.* Nashville, Tenn.: George Peabody College for Teachers, 1969.

DeVries, R. Collaboration between UICC and CAM. Paper presented at meeting of Leadership Development Project, Atlanta, Ga., October 1971.

Fast, J. *Body language.* New York: M. Evans, 1970.

Gordon, I. J. The Florida parent education program. Unpublished manuscript, University of Florida, College of Education, 1970.

———— (Ed.) *Reaching the child through parent education: The Florida approach.* Gainesville: Institute for the Development of Human Resources, University of Florida, 1969.

Gray, S. W., & Klaus, R. A. *The early training project: A seventh year report.* Nashville, Tenn.: Demonstration and Research Center for Early Education, George Peabody College for Teachers, 1970.

Hall, E. T. *The silent language.* Garden City, N.Y.: Doubleday, 1959.

Harding, J., & Macklin, E. The Cornell story-reading program. Paper presented at meeting of Society for Research in Child Development. Urbana: ERIC Clearinghouse, University of Illinois, 1969.

Hoffman, D. B. *Parent participation in preschool daycare.* Atlanta, Ga.: Southeastern Education Laboratory, 1971.

Hughes, E. C. Ecological aspects of institutions. *American Sociology Review,* April, 1936, *1,* 186.

Hunter, F. *Community power structure: A study of decision-makers.* Chapel Hill: University of North Carolina Press, 1953.

John, V. P., & Horner, V. M. *Early childhood bilingual education.* New York: Modern Language Association of America, 1971.

Jones, D. *The making of a volunteer.* Washington, D.C.: Office of Education, Peace Corps, 1968.

Kagan, J., & Moss, H. A. *Birth to maturity: A study in psychological development.* New York: John Wiley, 1962.

Katz, D., & Kahn, R. L. *The social psychology of organizations.* New York: John Wiley, 1966.

Lally, J. R. Syracuse University Children's Center: A day-care center for young children. Syracuse, N.Y.: Department of Family and Child Development, Syracuse University, unpublished manuscript, February 1970.

————. *Development of a day-care center for young children: Progress report.* Syracuse, N.Y.: Syracuse University Children's Center, PR-156 (C6), 1971.

Marshall, D. R. The politics of participation in poverty: A case study of the Board of the Economic and Youth Opportunities. Unpublished doctoral dissertation, University of California at Los Angeles, 1969.

Martin Luther King Family Center. *Freedom school for young children.* Chicago: The Center, 1970.

McInnerey, B. L., Durr, B., Kershner, K. M., & Nash, L. A. *Preschool and primary education: Annual program report to Ford Foundation.* Harrisburgh, Pa.: State Department of Public Instruction and Welfare, 1967.

Merton, R. *Social theory and social structure.* New York: Free Press, 1957.

Parsons, T., & Shils, E. A. (Eds.). *Toward a general theory of action.* New York: Harper & Row, 1951.

Riessman, F. *The culturally deprived child.* New York: Harper & Row, 1962.

Robinson, H. F. *CUE project child: The parent program.* New York: City University of New York, 1969.

Saranson, I. C., & Ganzer, V. J. Social influence techniques in clinical and community psychology. In C. D. Spielberger (Ed.), *Current topics in clinical and community psychology.* New York: Academic Press, 1969.

Silberman, C. E. *Crisis in black and white.* Vintage Book, 1965.

Smith, L., & Davies, M. *Research on a community-initiated preschool program.* Menlo Park, Calif.: Parents' Cooperative Nursery School, 1970.

Strickland, S. P. Can slum children learn? *American Education,* July 1971, 3-7.

Trujillo, R. Rural New Mexicans: Their educational and occupational apsirations. Unpublished doctoral dissertation, University of New Mexico, 1968.

Warren, R. L. *Studying your community.* New York: Free Press, 1965.

Weikart, D. P., & Lambie, D. Early enrichment in infants. Paper presented at annual meeting of American Association for the Advancement of Science, Boston, 1969.

————. *Ypsilanti-Carnegie infant education project: Proposal for filming grant.* Ypsilanti, Mich.: High/Scope Educational Research Foundation, Inc., 1970.

Wight, A., & Bing, J. *Handbook for cross-cultural and community involvement training: A draft handbook*. Estes Park, Colo.: The Center for Research and Education, 1969.

Wray, J. The federation of independent schools. Unpublished pamphlet, The Federation of Independent Community Schools, 2637 N. 11th St., Milwaukee, Wisconsin, 1971, 11.

PART II

PROGRAM PLANNING
AND IMPLEMENTATION

In Part II the focus is upon both the theoretical and practical decisions relative to program planning, implementation, and management that must be faced by persons responsible for early childhood education personnel training programs. Serious attention is directed toward the basic considerations affecting program purposes, personnel selection and organization, instructional content and delivery, and information dissemination.

The need for such an undertaking was expressed by Howard (1968) in the following way:

> The faculties of many college and university institutions, which are currently creating or expanding programs for teachers of young children in order to meet the demand for qualified people in this field, find little guidance for their decisions regarding what specialized provisions should be made for teachers of young children. Professional literature offers little help. A review of the literature and rather extensive correspondence with the United States Office of Education, the Department of Elementary, Kindergarten, and Nursery Education of the National Education Association, the National Laboratory on Early Childhood Education International, The National Association for the Education of Young Children, and more than two dozen noted experts in the field of early childhood education failed to uncover a single study regarding characteristics of exemplary undergraduate preservice teacher education programs in the field of early childhood education. (p. 1)

When one considers the resources available to the training program administrator concerned with the education and training of early childhood teacher trainers, or of the trainers of teacher trainers, an even greater void is discovered.

The task, then, of defining the decision points (and the alternatives at each) in developing programs for early childhood educators, from paraprofessionals through doctorate graduates, is not without hazards. Still, from the ex-

113

perience accumulated through program visitation and consultation and through reading and discussion, some beginning efforts may be made. In doing so, it will be necessary to emphasize the generic decisions of program administrators. Realistically it would be impossible to include discussion of all possible decisions, and we shall therefore focus upon key decision points and the major options available at each.

Administrators and planners responsible for early childhood personnel training programs will not all face the same sets of decisions. Each program will develop a "personality" of its own and, like the people involved, each will have an individuality and a uniqueness that is valuable and worthy of note. Each program will be characterized by its own goals, theoretical orientation, operating context, personnel, content, and means of delivery. Each has the potential to provide new insights into the ways and means of developing quality early childhood personnel to meet the growing needs of society. These program characteristics are the concern of the chapters that follow.

In dealing with these topics, an attempt has been made to present chronologically the decisions involved. Some of the decision points clearly precede others. However, a linear temporal sequence may not always be realistic, and it certainly is not crucial. Many decisions may be made simultaneously, or be revised or modified at various points in program development. By the same token, many decisions are (or should be) interrelated, with later decisions contingent upon prior decisions or upon constellations of decisions. Indeed, some of the decision points discussed will not occur in every program—that is, there may be operating constraints posed by choice of settings, institutional requirements, certification, or other governmental regulations that effectively remove decisions from the hands of the program administrator or program planner. In any event, the attempt here is to provide one possible framework for the integration of the decisions faced in the program planning, implementation, and management areas.

Chapter 4

Program Planning and Program Goals

DONALD L. PETERS AND LYNN DORMAN

Program planning is a part of all phases of program development. However, from the outset, a clear conceptualization and definition of the ultimate program are vital. No program can be all things at all times, and a clear sense of definition will guide efforts in development, maximizing the utilization of existing resources. Program goals, if broadly derived and explicitly stated, can provide the parameters of the program definition.

Deriving program goals is not a simple task; nor is it merely an intellectual exercise. Multiple considerations may be taken into account when defining program goals. Because of situational variation, different training levels, geographical and sociocultural constraints, and so forth, it is impossible to prescribe specific goals or program content that would have generalized applicability for every early childhood personnel training program. Nevertheless, some guidelines may be offered to help program personnel derive a unique and appropriate set of goals for their program. At the same time, it should be remembered that even within a particular program a continuous process of retailoring may be required as new needs and insights develop.

The sources of information which may assist in specifying program goals are suggested in Figure 4.1. It should be noted that a distinction is being made here between program goals and learner objectives. Program goals are global, concerned with ultimate outcomes and multiple content areas, and provide the overall directionality for the program. Learner objectives are specific, measurable, narrow in content, and functional for instruction. Program goals provide the referent for administrative decision-making. They do not, in themselves, constitute adequate criteria for the development of instruction. Refinement is necessary, through the efforts of the program personnel, to provide detailed learner objectives. These objectives may then provide the guidelines for the development of specific program components.

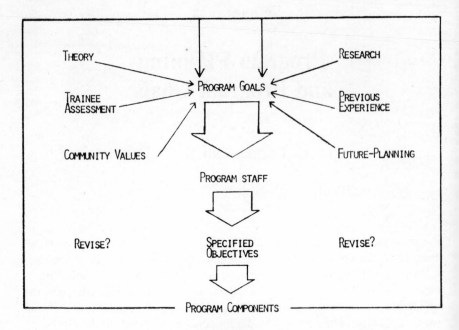

FIGURE 4.1

Sources of program goals. The loop recycles until congruence
is achieved between the program developed and the sources of
program goals.

THEORY

A clear and explicit theoretical orientation for the program will assist in
the program development process, including the selection and setting of
program goals. In particular, it will influence the relative stress provided
for different content areas and the priorities assigned to particular goals.
As such it provides a value structure against which inputs from other sources
are weighed.

The theoretical orientation—the nature of the child and of development—discussed in chapter 2 can provide important inputs for decisions at
all points of program development and implementation. A vital point of
departure is to make explicit the foundations on which an early childhood
education program is based. Additionally, however, consideration may be
given to the theoretical orientation (if any) of the programs for the early
childhood personnel being trained. The program for trainees could have a

theoretical orientation different from that of the program(s) for children. For example, the training program for Montessori teachers may be based on different premises about learning than the Montessori program for young children. Analysis of the Montessori method may indicate a "discovery-based," hierarchical arrangement of learning tasks for children to be learned through manipulation of didactic materials. This implies an "appropriate" set of teacher (directress) behaviors which could conceivably be taught through the use of behavior modification techniques.

Frequently, more attention is paid to the theoretical basis of programs for children than to the theoretical basis of programs for their teachers. This probably should not be the case. The selection or formulation of a theoretical (or philosophical) position vis-à-vis the training program involves choices. Program development personnel may choose to adopt or adapt existing personnel training models or early childhood program models, or they may choose to formulate their own innovative model.[1] At the heart of such choice is the conceptualization or model of man and the theory of learning with which one feels comfortable. Alternatives include at least those that fall into three major categories: psychodynamic or phenomenological (psychoanalytic, Eriksonian, Rogerian, etc.); behavioristic (Skinnerian); and information processing or other cognitive models (Piagetian, etc.).

Detailed discussion of each is clearly beyond the scope of this text. Hitt (1969) has suggested some of the contrasts that may be derived. These include:

1. Man can be described meaningfully in terms of his behavior or in terms of his consciousness.
2. Man is predictable or unpredictable.
3. Man is an information-transmitter or information-generator.
4. One man is like another or is unique.
5. Man lives in an objective world or in a subjective world.
6. Man is knowable in scientific terms or is more than we can ever know about him.

Such a list only touches the surface of the differences involved. Moreover, it emphasizes the extreme positions without acknowledging the many intermediate positions between such contrasting viewpoints. Hitt draws a conclusion worth noting. He emphasizes that the acceptance of a particular view has important implications for the everyday world. The choice "could greatly influence human activities in such areas as education. Thus, this ongoing debate is not just an academic exercise" (Hitt, p. 657). The point can be made in stronger terms. Just as one's theoretical orientation influences how one goes about educating children (see chapter 2), so the underlying theoretical or philosophical orientation affects the decisions of the program planner and curriculum designer of programs for early childhood personnel. For that reason it seems highly desirable that it be made explicit.

One could argue that in a situation of conflicting alternatives, a pragmatic or a theoretical approach may be desirable. Theoretical eclecticism or agnosticism may be advocated. Many programs do seem to proceed by selecting what appears to be best from the many theories, methods, and materials available. Such programs may fare well through an inductive bootstrapping approach.[2] However, some danger is involved. The eclectic position provides little theoretical framework from which deductions can be made; that is, since the framework is piecemeal and incomplete, it provides limited possibilities for deducing next steps or responses in new situations. This could lead to short-term "coping," the impossibility of evaluating and generalizing, a lack of internal consistency, or reliance on an implicit "naive" psychological model. When the underlying theoretical orientation of the program is made explicit and is shared among all possible decision-makers within a program, it is more likely that decisions will be consistent and congruent.

The theoretical position held for teacher training (paraprofessional through graduate) does not necessarily imply adherence to the same point of view at the level of programming for children. The two may be considered independently of one another. However, the advantages of consistency or congruency between these two dimensions should be assessed by program personnel, and the decision to opt for consistent or diverse program orientations should be made consciously.

Brief examination of a curriculum decision that is highly related to the choice of theoretical orientation may clarify the concerns previously mentioned. In planning a program for undergraduate student teachers, one could be faced with the choice of providing an in-depth, consistent training experience within a single orientation, or providing breadth through exemplars of and experience with a variety of program models. In one program, student teachers and graduate students are taught to plan and implement preschool programs according to the principles of operant conditioning. Additionally, much of the training curriculum is itself developed around operant theory. Students both undergo and learn to employ behavior modification techniques. As such, the program provides experience with the theoretical orientation, reinforced at several levels.

Another program illustrating the first option, although involving an alternative theoretical orientation, is that of the Center for Early Education in Los Angeles. This small institution has adopted a psychoanalytic orientation in its early education programs. The description of its training programs states, "Students . . . learn and apply psychoanalytic concepts, including the normal instinct and ego development of the growing child; common emotional problems in the early years . . ." (Center for Early Education, undated, p. 3.) An integral part of the training program conducted for para-professionals included a series of five unstructured seminars focusing upon "the development of an awareness of the unconscious motivation of be-havior." Each seminar session was conducted by a consulting psychoanalyst. In this case again, the theoretical orientation of the training program over-laps and is consistent with the orientation of the program for children. Each supports the other.

Alternatively, several personnel training programs maintain early edu-cation programs based upon a variety of theories. Where planned variation exists and several early education models are operating simultaneously (or through extra-institutional liaisons), it is possible to provide students with observation of or experience in a variety of programs. For example, the program at The Pennsylvania State University provides student teachers with experiences in up to four theoretical models of early education (oper-ant, Piagetian, responsive environment, and traditional). In such a case it becomes necessary for the theoretical orientation of the overall training program to differ from the theoretical orientation of some of the early education programs.

One potentially useful framework for early education programs derives from the combination of several ideas.[3] When program personnel are com-mitted to specification of competencies based upon performance and also have clear theoretical orientations, a system is required which permits the statement of performance criteria that tap multiple levels of thought. Steele (1970), recognizing this need, presented a method for assessing the intent and practice of instruction that utilized Bloom's taxonomy of educational objectives for the cognitive domain. Application of this system to the defini-tion of performance criteria for different content areas of a curriculum for early childhood educators provides a theoretically based framework for stating program goals and for other aspects of program development. A suggestive set of competencies dealing with early childhood education cur-riculum models that has been derived in this way follows.

Memory

1. Identify key figures in curriculum development, including Baer, Bereiter-Engelmann, Caldwell, Deutsch, Gordon, Gray, Heffernan, Honig, Kamii, Karnes, Lally, Lavatelli, Montessori, Neill, Nimnicht, Painter, Read, Weikart.
2. Identify major early childhood model curricula characteristics, includ-ing the specifying of objectives, special materials, teacher role, target populations, special methods, degree of parental involvement, motiva-tional strategies, and other unique features.
3. Name major reference sources appropriate to each identifiable pro-gram type.

Interpretation

1. Compare and contrast major early education curricula models along the major dimensions listed under 2 above.
2. Suggest likely areas of impact on children's development for each major curriculum for different target populations.
3. Suggest likely future changes and/or modifications of curriculum emphasis for each of three major early childhood program models.
4. Given specific research findings, indicate the implications of a specific program modification.
5. Explain major characteristics of different program models to others less well informed.
6. Given the basic characteristics of major early childhood education curricula, deliver orally or in writing a presentation outlining the important trends in early education curriculum development.
7. Given special conditions under which a program has never previously been tried, state the likely outcomes.

Application

1. Given a major theory/curriculum, prepare a single concept/skill plan, weekly or unit plan, overall or yearly plan.
2. Given a plan (see 1 above) based on one of the major early education curriculum models, apply with children.
3. Given a special population, select and apply appropriate curriculum components.
4. Apply process evaluation to both 2 and 3 above.

Synthesis

1. Utilizing components of several programs, develop a new total program for a specific population.
2. Given a specific child's problem and utilizing existing components, develop a program to alleviate the problem.
3. Given a specific curriculum and specific restraints on a problem, make appropriate adaptations.
4. Generate hypotheses concerning possible extensions of known curricula along any of several dimensions.
5. Integrate research and evaluation findings into major curricula and their components.

Evaluation

1. Specify appropriate standards for early childhood education curriculum evaluation for each of major programs.

2. Develop a scheme for process evaluation of curriculum component derived from a major program.
3. Critique evaluational research done on major programs for practice in relation to objectives, logical consistency, validity and reliability of data.

Formal Analysis

1. Probe and make explicit the underlying assumptions of each of three major early childhood education models.
2. Distinguish between components of major programs which have been deduced from theory or induced from empirical evidence.
3. Determine consistency of theory application.
4. Pinpoint inconsistencies of program design (if any).
5. Determine reasonableness of inferences/generalizations drawn.

RESEARCH

Existing literature and research findings may provide useful information for decisions concerning developing program goals. The consensus of professionals in the field may be solicited for potential content areas or emphases. For example, Howard (1968) attempted to determine the characteristics of exemplary early childhood teacher education programs by polling 20 experts in the field. These persons, holding positions of responsibility in professional organizations, teacher-training universities, and governmental agencies, were asked to recommend 10 institutions which they felt had exemplary programs. The institutions most recommended were then visited and studied. Some of the recommendations from this report that applied to program content included:

1. A broad liberal arts background rather than an intense specialization in one or two disciplines (p. 8).
2. An interdisciplinary approach (p. 8).
3. A division of approximately one-third of professional education hours in highly specialized courses for teachers of young children, one-third of the hours in student teaching experiences, and one-third of the hours in child development, educational psychology, and foundation courses (p. 10).
4. An emphasis on the interrelatedness of knowledge in the teaching of and learning by young children (p. 11).

Other sources of authority include a two-year study of the education of American teachers by Conant (1963) and a report by Koerner (1964). One study brought together a group of educators actively involved in teacher education projects (Smith, 1962). This group agreed upon five interrelated parts as essential to the process of teacher preparation:

1. A liberal education.
2. Specialized knowledge in their field.
3. Professional knowledge, including understanding of the role of the school and the contributions of the behavioral sciences.
4. Practice teaching under adequate supervision.
5. A unifying theory.

Allen and Hawkes (1970) cited another such list by Louis Fischer, who suggested that professional training for teachers should include:

1. A first-rate liberal education.
2. Broad knowledge of the sequence of human development from birth to maturity.
3. A working understanding of how people learn, of competing psychological theories and their evidence.
4. An understanding of principles and methods of educational research.
5. Some understanding of the total range of curriculum.
6. Knowledge of teaching means, methods, and materials.
7. Experience working with children in a variety of learning situations.
8. Experimentation in learning to handle oneself in a number of contexts—with teaching colleagues, administrators, and various members of the lay public, as well as with parents and children.
9. An acquaintance with a range of journals, newsletters, official publications, and organizations.
10. Knowledge of ways and means of gathering new knowledge.

The program administrator may accept or reject these potential goal areas or add new ones of his own.

Another form of authority that might be considered relates to research on successful teaching. It is difficult, at best, to draw firm conclusions from this broad area. Biddle (1964), Eisner (1963), Flanders (1964), and Johnson (1969) maintained that the problem is so complex that no one knows or agrees upon what factors most accurately characterize the competent teacher. When specific concern is directed toward the characteristics of the early childhood teacher, empirical data (but not the contradictions) vanish. As a result, Broudy (1969) contended that we "can define good teaching any way we like" (p. 583), and Goheen (1966) suggested that teacher behavior cannot be defined or analyzed and, therefore, "there will always be teachers who will break all the rules and yet be profoundly successful" (p. 221).

Ornstein (1971) provided a means for systematizing the nature of the research in this area, if not the findings. He suggested that teacher behavior research generally falls into one of three categories: (a) model systems, (b) instructional processes, and (c) teacher behavior characteristics.

Model Systems

The model system provides a scheme of complex but organized and inter-related elements of the teaching process. The model provides a prototype that directs attention to the systematic nature of teaching and learning. Some examples include:

1. The Flanders model (1960) involving teacher authority goals, interaction, and flexibility.

2. The Jensen model (1955) comprising seven categories of class productivity and class cohesiveness.

3. The Getzels and Thelen model (1960), which views the classroom as a social system governed by institutional roles and individual needs and three teaching styles: nomothetic, ideographical, and transactional. (Katz [1969] also clearly differentiated between teacher roles and teacher style with specific reference to preschool teachers.)

4. The Ryans communication of information model (1963a,b) including classification, evaluation, decision-making ordering, and transmitting.

Instruction Processes

Within this category are found procedures in which teacher behavior is usually described by a defined but abstract unit of measurement (Ornstein, 1971, p. 552). Such variables as "moves" (Bellack, 1966) or "acts" (Flanders, 1965) fall in this category. A series of responses or behaviors usually adheres in an "episode" (Smith, 1964), a "cycle" (Bellack, 1966), or a "pattern" (Flanders, 1965).

Teacher Behavior Characteristics

Here the focus is upon specific teacher behaviors. The difficulty lies in choosing which of the multitudes of possibilities are truly important. There appear to be few consistent relationships between teacher behavior and child learning, or between one teaching behavior and the criterion of child achievement (Ornstein, 1971). This, however, may reflect a limitation of our measurement systems more than an actual lack of relationship. Some recent progress in this area has been made by Thomson, Holmberg, and Baer (1971). Again, these alternatives may or may not be useful for particular programs or settings.

TRAINEE ASSESSMENT

By assessment is meant that some measurement technique may be employed to evaluate student entry behavior in such areas as literacy, previous experience, or prior learning. The concern here is not with selection criteria (discussed in chapter 6), but rather with procedures for seeking information relevant to curriculum planning for already enrolled students, with the intent of increasing the probability of their achievement success.

In the area of curriculum planning the administrator or program personnel may decide between the two major functions of assessment, namely: (a) utilizing student entry behavior to place students within specific programs or tracks, all of which lead to the same terminal objectives; or (b) utilizing student entry behavior to tailor a program with unique terminal objectives for each student.

The basic concern of both is individualized instruction and maximum potential for success, both within the program and in future employment.

Assessment for Student Placement

In an article Harold Mitzel (1970) clarified five different meanings of individualized instruction. Summarized, they were: (a) allowing the learner to proceed through content materials at a self-determined pace that is comfortable for him (rate tailoring); (b) allowing the learner to work at times convenient to him; (c) providing the learner with instruction beginning at a point appropriate to his past achievement; (d) providing remedial or special instruction to compensate for diagnosed difficulties; and (e) furnishing the learner with a wealth of instructional media and instructional methods from which he may choose or to which he may be assigned based upon his aptitudes.

Each of these imply attainment of the same terminal objectives for each student. The last three definitions also imply some assessment procedure prior to the initiation of instruction. The assumption is that placement, diagnostic or aptitude testing, by providing information that leads to tailoring the program to the needs of individual learners, enhances the probability of learner success in attaining the objectives. Such tailoring has been called "adaptive education" (Mitzel, 1970).

Assessment for the purpose of developing individualized instruction and for predicting success in training carries with it the general "dangers" of testing. Where assessment procedures and the interpretation of the results obtained fail to take into account ethnic, social class, and language differences, they may do more harm than good. Where one of the options open to decision-makers is to place people into remedial or special educational programs, too frequently such programs are filled with minority group members. Often this disproprotionate representation is the result of interpreting the tests rather than judging the students.

Assessment for Tailoring Outcomes

The possibility of individuality tailoring programs and terminal objectives to meet individual needs is based upon several assumptions. First, all students seeking training with a specific early education training program may not (and perhaps should not) be planning on employment in the same setting. For example, some students in paraprofessional training programs will find subsequent employment as classroom aides in public school systems, others in day-care facilities or child-care institutions, and some with Head Start or other programs. Some will go on to undergraduate education programs. Within an undergraduate teacher-training program, some students will find employment in preschools, and some perhaps in community-coordinated child-care facilities. Others may find employment in hospitals, social welfare agencies, or local, state, or federal administrative organizations. With rapid changes in the field of early education, the full range of possibilities is not yet known. The variety of settings thus indicated as possibilities, and the desires of students for particular settings, may be considered in tailoring a program to the student's needs.

Second, the variety of employment activities engaged in by trainees subsequent to their training may be quite broad. Depending upon the training level involved, the jobs are likely to vary from direct services to children (including but not limited to teaching) to administrative or supervisory roles in large field programs; from the training of parents and paraprofessionals to working with doctoral students; from keeping daily records to directing program evaluations; and from recording data to engaging in sophisticated research.

Third, the characteristics of the clientele with which the trainee will subsequently work may differ widely. Some examples of the variables here are age, socioeconomic background, ethnicity, sex, physical and mental health, mother tongue, second language, urban/rural background, the goal orientation of parents, number of siblings, or degree of social contact.

Katz (1970b) suggested several other dimensions upon which employment may vary: varieties of staffing patterns, varieties of organizational structures, variations in degree of community or parent control or influence over activities, varieties of physical plants and climates, and varieties of sponsorship, among others.

With such potential variety it is obvious that not all training needs can be met in one prescribed program. If the variation cannot (or if it should not) be limited through rigorous selection procedures, then flexibility in terminal objectives and in their related curriculum components seems desirable. To make this possible both the skills and knowledge base required for each category of employment outlet will have to be determined (empirically where possible) and employment aspirations and needs of individual trainees will have to be assessed.

Assessment of other student needs may also be considered. Students entering early childhood education programs come with a variety of background experiences, with cultural and ethnic biases, with aspirations, and with a variety of social and teaching skills. They are frequently articulate spokesmen of their own training needs. At the same time they may be insensitive to some of their own prejudices or shortcomings. Recognition of these individual differences is important.

In particular, it should be recognized that not all students share common values, backgrounds, and experiences. Nor are all students motivated by the same system of rewards. Assessment of these differences is essential if educational programs are to be developed which will capitalize on the language and culturally pluralistic resources of this nation.

Where trainees have had some previous experience in (or related to) early education, recurrent statements of needs emerge. Two such themes are: (a) concern for information and skills relevant to classroom management and discipline; and (b) concern for advice and experience in the working of educational "teams." Both of these concerns are repeatedly voiced by both teachers and paraprofessionals in early education.

Fuller (1969) presented a useful developmental conceptualization of teacher concerns. He suggested that students are not concerned about the problems of teaching before they have any teaching experience. However, during the initial stages of teaching or practice teaching, concerns focused upon the self are expressed. These early concerns center around the questions of (a) the relationships toward others, e.g., other teachers, the supervisor, and the principal; and (b) the adequacy of his or her own abilities, particularly in the area of class control or discipline. It is only later, after experience, that the teacher turns outward and expresses concern for the pupils. These later "mature" concerns of experienced teachers focus upon the ability to understand pupils' abilities, to specify objectives for them, to assess pupil progress, and so forth.

As training progresses, students at any level acquire more insight into their needs and alter their own objectives. With paraprofessionals in particular, as training proceeds and initial anxieties are overcome, tremendous enthusiasm develops and there is a rise in expectations and a desire for more training.

As indicated in Figure 4.1, it is desirable at frequent intervals to review the program and to compare it to the sources of program goals. In such a manner it will be possible to determine if congruency still exists.

PREVIOUS EXPERIENCE

Under the heading of previous experience are included three basic sources of information: the experience of the program staff, feedback from previous trainees, and job analysis of the prospective employment outlets.

Staff Experience

All early education personnel training programs are staffed with persons experienced in working with children and/or experienced in training early childhood education personnel. This previous experience, of course, provides a vital resource in establishing program goals and in all aspects of program development. Sole reliance on this resource, however, has its limitations. Since all experience is "past" experience, there is the danger of creating a "static" program, one which represents the status quo. The chief safeguard against such a danger is to insure that other inputs are assigned an important role in program development.

Previous Trainees

Programs with a history of training early childhood education personnel have a resource that is seldom utilized to full potential: their alumni. The program at Bank Street College of Education provides a notable exception. The previous trainees from this program provide some of the most important information for its revision and improvement. Trainees, after they have moved into the world of employment, are in an excellent position to illuminate "gaps" in a training program. The first time they run into a situation for which they have not been adequately prepared, they may provide new objectives, new competency statements, and even new areas of curriculum that might well be included in a program.

One vivid example will make the point. A recent graduate from a reputable baccalaureate-level early education program (not Bank Street) took a position as head teacher and administrator of a day-care center. She had almost all the skills required of the position—almost. But she had no training in or experience with bookkeeping, accounting, or budget management. No one knew this until the creditors came banging on the day-care center's door. Not knowing what to do, and apparently ashamed or afraid to ask, she had maintained a neat drawer full of invoices—none of which had been paid! This incident, probably atypical, suggests an addition to the training program from which she graduated.

Many suggestions can be offered by the alumni from any early education program. Means should be found for asking.

Job Analysis

Job analysis of prospective employment outlets provides another major source of information concerning the content of training programs. Prospective employers may be requested to specify in some detail the kinds of skills and experience that they would hope a new employee would have.

Indeed, with careful planning it may be possible to contract in advance with prospective employers for the placement of training program graduates —that is, through mutual agreement on potential candidates and the provision of training to meet their job specifications, arrangements may be made for guaranteed placement.

Where detailed information is not available, recruitment letters or employment opportunity files can provide some crude indications. Follow-up letters to employers after placing students may provide helpful feedback concerning the program's strengths and weaknesses.

Various task analyses may prove helpful. Task or job analysis in this sense requires identification and description of the minimal competencies required of a position. Although task analysis or the identification of prerequisite skills has been used extensively in industry, they are not well established in the field of education. Several empirical and logical strategies have been tried (McNeil, 1969; Gagne & Paradis, 1961; Miller, 1962), but, as in the analysis of teacher behavior, the results have not been particularly helpful at this point. The ten comprehensive curriculum models for elementary education personnel may yet prove a notable exception (Burden & Lanzillotti, 1971).

COMMUNITY VALUES

Most aspects of any educational program are heavily culture- and community-bound. Some training programs developed in the isolated university or college campus remain totally unresponsive to any real community needs. Middle-class students are taught how to teach "average" children and are given practice teaching experience with small groups of university offspring in idyllic laboratory schools. Little concern is directed toward the needs of culturally different children or toward working in settings that demand interaction with parents of diverse linguistic and cultural backgrounds.

Such programs produce teachers who are ineffectual or who may be harmful when employed in communities where the early education needs are the greatest.

Chapter 3 has addressed the issue of community involvement and participation in program planning and development as well as in its implementation. Where a personnel training program is tied to a particular community or where it is designed to meet rather specific needs, this type of involvement is essential. Where this is not the case, the issues of community needs and ethnic sensitivities should not be ignored. Every program goal, every program component, and every decision made may be subjected to questions concerning the value system from which it derives. For example: "Does this apply to children who speak little or no English?" "Does this method assume competition and motivation toward achievement?" "Would this be consistent with the behaviors fostered by the home environment of the children?" "What are the societal consequences of this decision?" "How applicable would this be when there are many children and little money?" "Whom have I excluded?" There are many, many more relevant questions. If the staff of an early education personnel training program are not sensitive to these issues, the new personnel they produce certainly will not be.

FUTURE PLANNING

Many people would agree that education is preparation for the future. The huge investments we make in terms of time, money, and human resources in the preparation of educational professionals and paraprofessionals are not for a short-term venture. While striving for immediate impact, it is the hope of everyone concerned with the education of early childhood educators that each one will have a long and productive career.

The 1975 trainee of 20 years of age will be but 45 in the year 2000. Assuming a productive career until age 65, the trainee we have facing us in our class today may still be teaching children in the year 2020. The five-year-old in an early education program in 1975 may be reasonably expected to be alive in the year 2050. What in our curricula is preparing children for the world in which they will live? What in our curricula is preparing them to create that world?

Questions such as this imply that educational thinking must take into account more of the future than is typical now. Alternative plans, policies, and programs must be weighed against the most systematic conjectures that can be developed about the future. Also implied is the notion that factors which seem decisive in the decision-making process in the current state of affairs may not be significant when viewed from a perspective o: the future (Weaver, 1971).

Shane (1971) defined the term "future-planning" as the study of the many possible alternative educational futures which could lie ahead, and the subsequent selection of those that seem most promising, followed by a deliberate attempt to create those particular educational tomorrows which are deemed most likely to serve learners of all ages (p. 186). He stressed that future-planning is planning *of* the future, not the traditional planning *for* the future. The future, because it has yet to come about, can bring with it any one of an infinite number of possible tomorrows.

Increased awareness of the necessity to build future-planning into curriculum is witnessed by the increasing number of books and articles on the subject: Hunnicut 1956; Shane, 1967; Shane and Shane, 1969 Toffler, 1970; Weaver, 1971; Shane and Nelson, 1971. Shane (1971, p 200) sorted the serious writings about the future into three categories: (a) statements regarding broad, current problems (e.g., pollution) and presumably promising practices intimately related to possible world futures (b) forecasts and conjectures as to likely happenings, assuming a surprise-free future, in the realms of science, international relations, etc.; (c) actual techniques and procedures of future-scanning and future-planning. The latter category includes several techniques worth discussing in slightly more detail.

Delphi

The Delphi technique has been described as an intuitive methodology for organizing and sharing "expert" forecasts about the future (Weaver, 1971). Typically the procedure includes a questionnaire that is mailed to respondents who remain anonymous to one another. Respondents first generate several concise statements of possible future events and give estimates as to the probability of each event occurring in the future. Responses from this first round are collated and returned to each respondent, who is then invited to revise his estimates.

Again the responses are assembled and reported back to the respondents. If a respondent's estimate does not fall within the interquartile range of all conjectures, he is asked to justify his position. The emphasis throughout is on what is *likely* to happen rather than on what the respondents would like to see happen, although the technique has been modified to obtain that type of information as well (Anderson, 1970; Cyphert & Grant, 1970).

Weaver (1971) saw the Delphi technique as having promising educational applications as a method for studying the process of thinking about the future, as a means of forcing people to think about the future in a more complex way than they ordinarily would, and as a planning tool.

ORPHIC

A system of future-planning with specific intent of influencing educational curriculum is ORPHIC (Organized Project Hypotheses for Innovations in Curriculum). ORPHIC builds on Delphi, but goes well beyond it. According to Shane (1971), the purpose of ORPHIC is to help educators to avoid blunders by enabling them to look ahead intelligently and systematically and to allow advanced study of plausible alternatives.

The basic steps of ORPHIC are:

1. An interdisciplinary trend census (similiar to Delphi).
2. A social consequences projection of trends.
3. A probability-difficulty analysis, i.e., estimating and forecasting the difficulty of either bringing about or impeding the change.
4. Exploring hypothetical sequences or events through scenario writing in order to examine and evaluate possible curriculum changes.
5. Arriving at a milestone appraisal or report (Shane, 1971, p. 204).

For a more detailed description of ORPHIC, see Shane (1971); for a detailed description of the original use of Delphi, see Helmer (1966b).

A recent study by Shane and Nelson (1971) gave an idea of the output that future-planning techniques may provide.[4] Respondents to this study made these predictions.

1. Early childhood education programs for two- and three-year-olds will be a universal reality by 1985.
2. There will be a rapid consolidation of federal education programs.
3. A substantial degree of differentiated staffing will be attained within the decade.
4. There is an even chance that performance contracting will be widely adopted. (Four out of five of the respondents felt it could occur quickly.)
5. There will be major changes in the preparation of teachers. These changes will include: (a) preparation of preservice students to work in teams or partnerships; (b) individualized instruction; (c) greater pupil participation in education; (d) multimedia instruction; and (e) routine use of sensitivity training.
6. Changes in teacher licensing and certification will be instituted and widely accepted by 1980 or 1985.
7. Flexible teaching partnerships will replace the self-contained classroom.

ON THE ISSUE OF RELEVANCE

On the campuses of most institutions of higher learning one hears the repeated cry that education is not relevant and that concerted efforts mus be taken to make it so. Students in colleges or schools of education are frequently more specific. They voice the concern that *their* courses are no relevant. Peter Wagschal (1969) made this comment:

> Without wishing to appear the picky grammarian, I am forced to admit that the clamor to "make education relevant" now strikes me as disastrously incompete and unintelligible. I can't remember ever using the word "relevant" without adding "to x". . . . So, when I read all the current articles on the relevance of American education, I always find myself filling something in to serve as the missing x.

Wagschal went on to question whether the missing x should be America as it is or America as it ought to be. He argued for the latter. However, such a statement in itself is too vague and misleading. He was right to question "to what?" But his answer was too simple.

The sources of input for curriculum planning discussed in this chapter provide more specific referents. For example, it would be appropriate to say that the curriculum designed and the objectives formulated should be relevant to the formation of the kinds of teaching behavior that is desired by the program planners and needed within its community context. Such a statement, while meeting Wagschal's objection, would not meet the concerns of those who insist upon a change in education. Nor is it likely that the program planner's and the student's views of relevance would be the same. Their differences in concern have been well documented (Fuller, 1969).

An alternative that is likely to be more pleasing to both sets of critics would be that the program designed and the objectives formulated should be relevant to the individual trainee, to his entry behavior, and to his aptitudes and aspirations—that is, relevance may be attained through individualizing and personalizing the education he receives. Adapting education to learner rates, or matching the methods to his aptitudes, is a means to individualized instruction. Adapting content to his aspirations and specific needs is one form of personalization, a step in the recognition of the learner as a person. This form of individualized education may be accomplished while still meeting the program goals derived from other sources.

Again, curricula may be developed to be clearly relevant to the employment skills that a job analysis indicates are important. However, today's jobs might not exist tomorrow, and a whole host of new professions or subprofessions may develop before the trainee has passed the prime of his working years. Therefore, it might be more important that the program foster the transfer of training to cover contingencies not accounted for or that it focus upon skills relevant to "learning to learn" or to the discovery of knowledge.

Ultimately, today's education should be relevant to the development of the skills and talents necessary for establishing learning conditions that are relevant for the future of young children.

SUMMARY

This chapter discussed the resources which may provide useful input for administrative decisions concerning the parameters of curriculum and the definition of goals and objectives. Each was treated at a rather abstract level. The intent was to provide suggestions of where to look for program input—not what to find; and the purpose is to suggest that all the sources named be used.

The theoretical orientation of the program was cited as part of the value structure against which all other inputs were weighed. This orientation could differ from the theoretical orientation espoused for the programs for young children. Whatever the orientation chosen, it was advocated that it be explicitly stated so that all possible decision-makers within a program would have it available as a referent for their decisions.

The literature and research findings were suggested as a second source of program goals. Such "authority" might provide a historical perspective for judging potential content areas or program emphases, and might suggest a useful framework around which to organize a program.

The assessment of trainee entry behavior and aspirations was suggested as a means of tailoring programs to the needs of trainees. Such individualization could be in terms of placing students into alternative tracks leading to the same terminal objectives, or altering terminal objectives for each student. Frequent reassessment was suggested to insure congruency between student needs and program goals.

The experience of the program staff was seen as an important contributor to program goals. However, a need also exists for supplementing staff experience with feedback from previous trainees and from employers. After they have moved into the world of employment, trainees are in an excellent position to reassess their training and to pinpoint program strengths and weaknesses. Means should be established to obtain this useful information and to incorporate it into the goals of the program. Similarly, employers could provide valuable information concerning the competencies they would hope a new employee would have. They, too, could provide helpful feedback concerning program strengths and weaknesses.

Since most aspects of an educational program are culture- and community-bound, it was suggested that programs be designed so as to be sensitive to cultural and ethnic variations. Where personnel programs were designed to meet community needs, community involvement was considered essential. In all cases the community can be an important force and a vital resource for the program.

Future-orientation is a part of all education. While striving for immediate impact, early education personnel training programs seek to meet future needs. The trainee of the present will be the teacher of the twenty-first century. The goals of a training program should include development of the skills and talents necessary for establishing the learning conditions of the future.

No one of the sources of program goals stands alone. In their entirety they provide a dynamic source of new ideas and of validating feedback which cannot be neglected if a program is to grow and develop in healthy ways.

NOTES

1. One reference source for models of teacher training is Joel Burden and Kaliopee Lanzillotti, *A Reader's Guide to the Comprehensive Model for Preparing Elementary Teachers.* Washington, D.C. American Association of Colleges of Teacher Education, 1971.

2. This kind of eclectic smorgasbord approach has on occasion been deliberately undertaken in planning early childhood programs. Sometimes it is called the "omnibus model" (Caldwell, 1971). Indeed, no one theory has an undeniable grasp on the truth, and no existent theory of learning or development provides guidelines for all situations.

3. The author is grateful to Tom Beasley, Barbara Bieler, Dorothy Gish, and Carol Quarton for their suggestions concerning the material in this section.

4. If one wants a set of more dramatic, though less systematically obtained, predictions of the way education may go (plausible alternative futures), Toffler's *Future Shock* is recommended.

REFERENCES

Allen, D., & Hawkes, G. Reconstruction of teacher education and professional growth programs. *Phi Delta Kappan,* 1970, *51,* 4-12.

American Psychological Association. Task force on employment testing of minority groups. Job testing and the disadvantaged. *American Psychologist,* 1969, *24,* 637-651.

Anderson, D. Clarifying and setting objectives using the Delphi technique. Paper presented at the annual meeting of American Educational Research Association, Minneapolis, Minn., 1970.

Bellack, A. *The language of the classroom.* New York: Teachers College Press, 1966.

Biddle, B. The integration of teacher effectiveness research. In B. Biddle & W. Ellena (Eds.), *Contemporary research on teacher effectiveness.* New York: Holt, Rinehart and Winston, 1964.

Broudy, H. Can we define good teaching? *Kappa Delta Pi Record,* 1969, *70,* 583-592.

Burden, J., & Lanzillotti, K. *A reader's guide to the comprehensive models for preparing elementary teachers.* Washington, D.C.: American Association of Colleges of Teacher Education, 1971.

Caldwell, B. Impact of interest in early cognitive stimulation. In H. Rie (Ed.), *Perspectives of child psychopathology,* Chicago: Aldine-Atherton, 1971.

Center for Early Education. *Practices and Beliefs.* Los Angeles: Center for Early Education, undated.

Conant, J. *The education of American teachers.* New York: McGraw-Hill, 1963.

Cyphert, F., & Grant, W. The Delphi technique: A tool for collecting opinions in teacher education. Paper presented at annual meeting of American Educational Research Association, Minneapolis, Minn., 1970.

————. The Delphi technique: A case study. *Phi Delta Kappan,* 1971, *52,* 272-273.

Eisner, E. W. Qualitative intelligence and the act of teaching. *Elementary School Journal,* 1963, *63,* 299-307.

Flanders, N. Diagnosing and utilizing social structures in classroom learning. In N. Henry (Ed.), *The dynamics of instructional groups,* Chicago: University of Chicago Press, 1960.

————. Some relationships among teacher influence, pupil attitudes, and achievement. In B. Biddle and W. Ellena (Eds.), *Contemporary research on teacher effectiveness.* New York: Holt, Rinehart and Winston, 1964.

————. *Teacher influence, pupil attitude and achievement.* Monograph No. 12. Washington, D.C.: U.S. Department of Health, Education, and Welfare, 1965.

Fuller, F. F. Concerns of teachers: A developmental conceptualization. *American Educational Research Journal,* 1969, *6,* 207-226.

Gagne, R. Some new views of learning and instruction. *Phi Delta Kappan,* 1970, 51, 468-472.

Gagne, R., & Paradis, N. *Abilities and learning sets in knowledge acquisition.* Psychological Monographs, 1961, *75* (Whole No. 518).

Getzels, J., & Thelen, H. The classroom group as a unique social system. In N. Henry (Ed.), *The dynamics of instructional groups.* Chicago: University of Chicago Press, 1960.

Goheen, R. The teacher and the university. *American Scientist,* 1966, *65,* 221-225.

Helmer, O. *Social Technology.* New York: Basic Books, 1966a.

————. The use of the Delphi technique in problems of educational innovation. Rand Corporation, p. 349, December, 1966b.

Hitt, W. Two models of man. *American Psychologist,* 1969, *24,* 651-658.

Howard, A. *Characteristics of early childhood teacher education.* Washington, D.C.: Association for Childhood Education International, 1968.

Hunnicut, C. *Education 2000 A. D.* Syracuse, N.Y.: Syracuse University Press, 1956.

Jensen, G. The social structure of the classroom group: An observational framework. *Journal of Educational Psychology,* 1955, *46,* 362-374.

Johnson, D. Influence on teachers' acceptance of change. *Elementary School Journal,* 1969, *70,* 142-153.

Katz, L. Teaching in preschools: Roles and goals. *Children,* 1970, *17,* 42-48 (a).

————. Early Childhood Education as a Discipline. *Young Children,* December, 1970, 82-89 (b).

Koerner, J. Findings and prejudices in teacher education. *School and Society,* 1964, *92,* 127-134.

McNeil, J. Forces influencing curriculum. *Review of Educational Research,* 1969, *39,* 293-318.

Miller, R. Task description and analysis. In *Psychological principles in system development.* New York: Holt, Rinehart and Winston, 1962.

Mitzel, H. E. The impending instruction revolution. *Phi Delta Kappan,* 1970, *51,* 434-439.

Ornstein, A. C. Systematizing teacher behavior research. *Phi Delta Kappan,* 1971, *42,* 551-555.

Ryans, D. Assessment of teacher behavior and instruction. *Review of Educational Research,* 1963, *33,* 415-441 (a).

————. Teacher behavior theory and research: Implications for teacher education. *Journal of Teacher Education,* 1963, *14,* 274-293 (b).

Shane, H. Future-shock and the curriculum. *Phi Delta Kappan,* 1967, *49,* 67-70.

————. Future-planning as a means of shaping educational change. In R. M. McClures (Ed.), *The curriculum: Retrospect and prospect.* 70th Yearbook of the National Society for the Study of Education. Chicago: University of Chicago Press, 1971.

Shane, H. G., & Nelson, O. N. What will the schools become? *Phi Delta Kappan,* 1971, *52,* 596-598.

Shane, H., & Shane, J. Forecast for the 1970's. *Today's Education,* 1969, *55,* 29-32.

Smith, B. O. *A tentative report on the strategies of teaching.* U.S. Department of Health, Education, and Welfare, Research Project No. 1640, 1964.

Smith, E. *Teacher education: A reappraisal.* New York: Harper & Row, 1962.

Steele, J. Assessing intent and practice in instruction. Paper presented at annual meeting of American Educational Research Association, Minneapolis, Minn., March 1970.

Thomson, C., Holmsberg, M., & Baer, D. The experimental analysis of training procedures for preschool teachers. Paper presented at meeting of Society for Research in Child Development, Minneapolis, Minn., 1971.

Toffler, A. *Future shock.* New York: Doubleday, 1970.

Wagschal, P. On the irrelevance of relevance. *Phi Delta Kappan,* 1969, *51,* 61-62.

Weaver, W. T. The Delphi forecasting method. *Phi Delta Kappan,* 1971, *52,* 267-271.

Chapter 5

Program Personnel

DONALD L. PETERS and LOIS M. FEARS

We have been considering the foundations and background relevant to the formulation of program goals for the training of early childhood education personnel. Based on this information, one could construct the "ideal" program for the particular personnel to be trained. Such an effort provides definition for the program and a sense of direction for all concerned. However, without the people in the program, both staff and students, there is no program at all. This chapter focuses upon "people-oriented" considerations in program planning, implementation, and management.

PROGRAM STAFF

A quality training program in early education requires the services of many people: personnel from the fields of education, medicine, social work, psychology, nutrition, etc. They all share a common interest in the development of the young child, and each person brings insights, theory, and facts which bear on the understanding of that development. The availability of such personnel will play a role in the formulation of the program goals (and their priorities), and will determine which goals will be carried out and how this will be done. Figure 1 in chapter 4 depicts the central importance of this translation and implementation role.

Unfortunately, many colleges and universities are experiencing difficulty in staffing both well-established and new programs with qualified personnel. Flexibility in staff criteria and staff organization is likely to provide the only short-term solution to this problem.

Classification of Staff Personnel

One way to meet staffing needs is to extend the range of personnel who may be associated with the program. The degree of association also

137

provides a means for classifying the potential staff. Four basic categories may be used: program personnel, program-related personnel, adjunct personnel, and consultants.

Program Personnel. This category consists of those persons most intimately related to the particular training program. Where the training program constitutes a unique funding unit, the program personnel are those whose salaries (or a portion thereof) are tied directly to their responsibilities within the program. Where funding is not a criterion, the program personnel are those who are readily identified with the program and to whom major program responsibilities have been assigned.

Program-Related Personnel. This category comprises persons with a significant interest in the program and from whom services are necessary if the program is to succeed. They are not, however, salaried in the program and do not have major administrative or educational responsibilities to it. For example, in an academic program for early childhood educators conducted at a college or university, not all the course work required of the trainees will be available within a single department or academic unit. Nor will all the personnel interested in the development of young children be based within one department. Personnel from other departments may provide services (in the form of new or modified courses, consultation, thesis supervision, and so forth) that are an important part of the program. Such persons, through their expressed interest in and commitment to service, constitute the program-related personnel; they are frequently listed on grant proposals as additional institution personnel resources.

Adjunct Personnel. The term *adjunct personnel* is frequently used for persons who are not directly related to the institution (college or university), but have particular expertise or services to offer on a recurring basis through external organizations, facilities, or arrangements. For example, if hospitals, child welfare agencies, school districts, and so forth, are used as practicum sites for trainees, with some portion of the instruction and/or supervision of the trainees provided by personnel of the practicum site, these personnel are frequently accorded adjunct status and title. Such status usually implies neither financial remuneration nor administrative or academic responsibilities. It is, however, more than a courtesy since it shows an active relationship, even if of a voluntary rather than a contractual nature.

Consultants. This category refers to persons with no direct affiliation with the training institution and for whom there need be no long-range commitment to the training program. Selected upon the basis of their particular expertise or contribution, their services may be employed temporarily on a financial or voluntary basis.

On occasion, longer-term consultant relationships may be arranged. Where particular expertise is lacking in a given area (for example, in evaluation), it may be advantageous to engage a consultant on a continuing basis to undertake specific responsibilities. Such arrangements may be further formalized through the subcontracting of entire components of the program. For example, one program conducted and administered by a local school district subcontracted with a nearby university for the production of in-service training materials and for the evaluation (both formative and summative) of the training program.

All four categories of personnel may provide considerable input into the program during all phases of development and implementation. All may be used to establish the qualified staff resources necessary for program functioning. The proportion of each, and the organizational framework in which they function, will vary from program to program depending upon the available resources and financial or other constraints.

Potential Consortium Arrangements

In situations where universities, institutions, agencies, and public schools are in geographic proximity, consortium arrangements may be established. Such consortia may provide a synthesis of information, enriched staff resources, and a diversity of services not otherwise available. The resulting enrichment and cross-fertilization may provide greater strength and program potential than the combined efforts of the individual programs would provide separately. At the same time, consortia arrangements may reduce the need for capital investments and staff expansions that would otherwise be required.

Several examples of consortium arrangements are noteworthy. The Atlanta University Center Corporation, a liaison arrangement among five colleges, provides for the shared facilities and cooperative efforts, thereby enriching all programs and increasing their efficiency in meeting national needs and priorities. The participating institutions are Clark College, Morehouse College, Morris Brown College, Spelman College, and the Interdenominational Theological Center.

Another example involves a coordinated set of programs for the training of master's-level personnel in early childhood education and child care. This program combines the resources of New York University and the University of Pittsburgh. Student entry occurs in either program, but the students spend approximately one-third of their studies at the other institution. One program emphasizes child development and child care from within a school of medicine, while the other emphasizes early education from the framework of a college of education; and the combination enriches both. The practical work experience at both institutions is quite different, thereby enriching the students' development and the diversity of their understanding.

There are, of course, some difficulties or limitations in connection with participation in consortia. Timing and scheduling considerations increase in difficulty. The scheduling and coordination of the trainee's time with that of the faculties must be dealt with. A faculty member may not be readily available for conferences with trainees because of part-time employment, transportation schedules, or other job obligations to his or her primary institution.

The self-interest of member institutions, a natural and unavoidable factor, should be recognized as an ever-present limitation of cooperative efforts. Colleges, like individuals, have trouble with "mine" and "ours" (Baskin, 1965). Nevertheless, as in the case of individuals, if a common purpose is strongly held, such difficulties can be resolved.

Communication is probably the greatest problem in the limitation of consortium arrangements. Communication within a college or university is frequently difficult enough, but when several institutions are involved the problems are compounded. Organization, geography, motivation, outstanding commitments, and traditions all make communication inherently difficult. New and separate communication networks may need to be established just for the consortium; and in an organization that is sensitive to its members, unusual care must be taken to keep everyone "in the know."

Money is not the measure of all things, but it is sometimes a useful measure of priorities. Limited funds may result in limitations on the cooperative endeavors that may be undertaken. All cooperative measures may not call for money, but where efforts do require a financial investment, desire alone cannot compensate for absent resources. While coordination may not be expensive, program operation is definitely costly

All these limitations, however real, should be kept in perspective Like many organizational limitations, they may restrict at one point but liberate at another, thereby opening opportunities for innovation and for expansion in new ways. They certainly do not make arrangements easy, but they may increase the potential for success.

Staff Recruitment and Selection

Given the four categories of potential staff resources and the presence or absence of consortia opportunities, a number of important but difficult decisions remain: issues of criteria, staff characteristics and balance, internal or external recruitment procedures, credential requirements, and staff patterns.

General Selection Criteria. A number of staff selection criteria, bordering on the obvious, may be suggested as generalities applying to all programs. Chichester (1956) suggested the following factors according to their relative importance: sociability (ability to get along with others); intelligence (ability to learn and think); training (education, technical knowledge); judgment (common sense); conscientiousness (sense of duty); physical traits (speech, manner, appearance); and drive (willingness to work hard).

Other studies list such qualities as general interest in children, ability to instruct, professional attributes, ability to maintain good human relations, and so on. Whether or not we are conscious of the fact, we are often more likely to be affected by the sociality of the applicant than by any other single factor. But to say that one factor is more important than another is like saying that the ignition system of an engine is more indispensable than the carburetor or the pistons. Ideally the selection criteria for personnel should be flexibly conceived, with focus upon the development of a staff that would be able to implement effectively the program desired.

One additional general criterion might be suggested: "compatibility of theoretical orientation." It is highly desirable that all members of the professional staff be involved in the selection or development of a theoretical orientation for the program. Unfortunately, this is not always possible. Where personnel are added during the later stages of program development, it may be appropriate to select them on the basis of their compatibility with the existing orientation. This may serve to reduce the possibility of fragmentation of effort and to increase staff cooperation. However, if variety of viewpoint is one of the desired goals for the staff of the program, selection on the basis of common theoretical bias would be inappropriate.

Specific Selection Decisions. There are several areas in which specific decisions relevant to staff selection may be defined. These include decisions concerning the source, sex, ethnic background, age, and specific qualifications of the potential staff person.

1. Source: Staff for a new program may be recruited from within the training institution itself, or sought elesewhere. There are pros and cons associated with either. Recruiting staff from within the institution may be more economical in terms of time and travel, and because such staff frequently may be utilized on a part-time basis (other academic or administrative responsibilities, funded from other sources, would constitute the remainder of their full work load). It may also permit the more rapid filling of positions. Since staff recruited from within the institution also have the advantage of being familiar with the organization and facilities, the time spent on orientation and familiarization is reduced.

On the other hand, new staff may bring innovative ideas and approaches to issues, as well as skills that were not previously available.

They are less likely to be complacent. Indeed, existing staff may be lacking in certain areas required for the success of the program, or they may be already too committed to take on new responsibilities.

2. Sex: It is generally known that females dominate the early childhood professions, both at the community level and in higher education. There may be virtue in attempting to redress this imbalance (Burtt, 1965) without sacrificing quality. It may be desirable to recruit and employ more male faculty members at all levels. Research conducted by Krapp and Lastinger (1954) on teacher recruitment provides the "classic" prescriptions of how this may be done (the two major areas are increased salaries and improved facilities). Equally, if not more appropriate, might be a basic change of attitude, removing the notion that early childhood is the exclusive domain of women.

3. Ethnic background: Projects employing faculties with varied cultural and/or ethnic backgrounds are more likely to provide a tolerant atmosphere where a greater interchange of ideas can occur. They are more likely to be sensitive to the ethnic and cultural differences in their trainees, and more capable of transmitting (through appropriate modeling) the sensitivity which the trainees will need in their future employment.

4. Age: Projects may give special consideration to recruiting young faculty with minimum or no previous experience, but who display potential for developing into outstanding teachers and/or administrators. In contrast, it may be desirable to recruit more mature and experienced personnel to implement the project's goals. The decision will rest upon consideration of existing resources and the desired staffing arrangements.

5. Specific qualifications: Obviously people are hired to do specific things. Occasionally there are specified "credential" requirements or detailed qualifications for filling particular vacancies. These have to be considered when seeking staff, and they are usually dependent upon how the position is defined. They may change if the position is defined as a "temporary," project-related position rather than as an institutional continuing commitment. Career potential, tenure, promotions, fringe benefits, and pay may be used to attract and *retain* staff personnel with the desired qualifications. They may also place unnecessary qualifications or credential requirements on the position. These initial commitments should be viewed in relation to the ultimate cost and resource factors involved in continual staff recruitment and retraining. Decisions of this sort may be obviated by short program length and by the nature of the funding. However, if the program is envisioned as becoming either a permanent or recurrent aspect of the overall institutional plan, early decisions may preclude later problems of staff recruitment and retention.

Additional Comments. To alleviate staff shortages and to increase the diversity of staff patterns, it may be possible and desirable to introduce relatively flexible criteria for selection—that is, practical and realistic considerations in implementing programs may imply the utilization of personnel with potential and skills, but without the usual academic credentials. ccording to Haberman and Persky (undated), this could be accomplished in at least two ways:

1. Give equivalence and recognition for achievement other than doctoral degrees to persons with successful experience in childhood education who have the abilities needed for preparing teachers and other personnel.

2. Require college staff to spend time in some form of direct involvement with preschool children in community-based settings.

Additionally, it may be desirable to select the best available staff, whether or not credentialed, and to develop a differentiated staffing pattern which minimizes the importance of weaknesses and maximizes the utilization of strengths. According to Oliver (1970), differentiated staffing seeks to make the best use of personnel. Teachers and other educators assume different (frequently nontraditional) sets of responsibilities according to carefully prepared definitions or task analyses of the functions to be performed. This goes far beyond traditional staff allocations based upon subject matter or other distinctions. It seeks new ways of analyzing essential teaching and administrative tasks and creative means of implementing new educational roles. Program-related personnel, adjunct personnel and consultants, as well as consortia arrangements, can all be used to supplement and make possible innovative organizational arrangements to meet program needs.

Staff Development

The success of a project depends on the quality of the staff working at all levels of the program. The act of employing staff is only a preliminary stage in the commitment of human development. Continued training should be provided on a frequent, regularly scheduled basis to obtain optimal results. Participative training, which directly involves staff in active give-and-take role playing, discussions, demonstrations, and other group interchange, is generally more interesting and effective than training which places participants in a passive role. Consideration at this point will be focused on three elements considered desirable in staff development for programs.

Preservice. Preservice for the training program is usually initiated by the program director. The staff and/or representatives of cooperating agencies or institutions may be involved. The preservice process, including number of meetings, hierarchical level of involvement on the part of cooperating institutions or agencies, areas of concern explored, and degree of agreement reached may vary according to program needs. The purpose of preservice training will in all probability vary from program to program Some of its goals may be to work out strategies of recruitment and selec tion of trainees, to explore the roles of the various staff members, and t secure commitment.

Preservice may also be planned to discuss strategies for meetin trainee needs. Staff have responsibility for knowing what their trainee bring to the learning experience and what they must take from it to b adequately prepared for employment. A staff team might be sent into community from which trainees are to come. There the team would asses the needs of the trainees, their socioeconomic status, the community i which the trainees would employ their skills, and the physical facilitie and educational materials available. Upon returning to the institutior preservice sessions could be beneficial in establishing competencies on th part of the staff to match the anticipated needs of the trainees and th community.

In-service Training. In-service training occurs after the trainees hav arrived at the institution, and it may continue through all phases of in plementation. To retain vitality, most programs require systematic in service training. As in preservice, relative emphasis will depend upo need and available resources. It is highly desirable that administrators an staff participate together in training which will benefit both as well a foster and strengthen the team concept. If the need is great, a program c staff in-service training may be developed that parallels the training pro gram. For example, if the staff has not previously had individual feedbac and counseling available for student trainees, and if this is a part of th program conceptualization, then in-service staff training may include rol playing and discussion to directly clarify problems or meet trainee need both curricular and personal.

Program needs should dictate the scheduling of staff meetings. It ma be desirable for staff to meet weekly to reflect on the past week's trainin experiences and capitalize on feedback from trainees for the followin week's events.

In order to make both preservice and in-service training interestin and more effective, administrators should take advantage of the increasin variety of training methods, techniques, and aids available. They shoul be no less creative here than they were in developing the program fc students. Some suggestions for teaching methods are included in chapter

Use of Consultants. A consultant is one who gives professional advic or service. For present purposes, we shall deal with four aspects of cor sultation.

The first area of concern is generic principles of consultation. Kiest (1969) listed some generic qualities of consultation appropriate for ar setting:

1. Consultation is a relationship solicited by the person needing help. Unsolicited consultative "help," however wise it may be, seldom achieves the mutuality of purpose that is vital to consultation.

2. The consultant relationship is temporary, and either party is free to terminate the relationship at any time. The client may be too polite to ask the consultant to leave and not come back, but if the client does not perceive the consultation as helpful, her "receiving set" is simply turned off and the consultant might as well go away.

3. The consultant's first obligation is to clarify problems and causes, thereby setting the focus for the consultation. The client may be asking how to achieve a predetermined result or what results should be sought. In either case, the first step is diagnostic.

4. Having helped the client to clarify the nature and cause of the problem for which consultation is sought, the consultant then helps in finding and evaluating alternative solutions.

5. It is the client's prerogative to accept and act upon, or to reject, any of these courses of action. Only to the degree that she finds the consultant's advice congenial will she make use of it. The consultant relationship does not provide for the enforcement of recommendations.

These points also have implications for consultant utilization in early childhood training programs.

Second, we shall consider the role of the consultant. Even though the program director invited the consultant, her perception of the consultant's role may not be very clear. The director may have been influenced by others to the extent that the invitation is not a true reflection of her desire to help.

The consultant can never be sure that a director has a clear interpretation of the consultant's role until he has conveyed it to the program director. The consultant should clarify the five principles listed above. He shares his expertise, but does not do the changing involved and does not require the program director to do so. He only helps to determine a course of action for the program to follow so that it can resolve its difficulties. The consultant helps define goals; he does not impose them.

Third, program directors may wish to consider certain functions within the role of a consultant. The latter may serve by meeting direct training needs or in-service staff training needs. Consultant service may best be utilized after trainees have returned to their respective jobs and have begun implementing and assessing areas where additional help is needed.

Consultants may also be used to provide levels of enrichment not otherwise possible with program staff. For example, invitations may be extended to nationally or internationally prominent educators to speak with trainees and staff. The charismatic nature of such persons may enhance the motivation and commitment of staff and students. This may also be a time to invite other college faculty so they may become informed about current thinking in early childhood education.

Other functions of consultants are: (a) to perform part-time jobs where full-time people are not needed or where the budget does not provide for them, especially with reference to valuation, research, educational auditing, and proposal writing; (b) to provide expertise and neutrality—for example, in mediating disputes among staff or in providing personal counsel to staff members or students; (c) to lend prestige and status to a proposal that can result in beneficial administrative decisions on the part of college executives, board members, or legislators in connection with program needs.

Fourth, whether the consultant addresses himself to matters of staff relationship, program stabilization, or academic milieu, his effectiveness may depend largely on the quality of the relationship he develops with the staff and trainees. The goal of developing a positive relationship goes beyond dealing with the issues that are present, although it is certainly part of the goal. Genuine two-way communication is the foundation on which any constructive relationship must rest. If consultation is to be more than the delivery of sterile bits of information, there must be an interpersonal exchange of both feelings and ideas.

The consultant may find the following information helpful: the number of people who will attend and their names; their roles in the model; how long they have worked in the program; and some estimate of their formal training, such as how many in-service sessions they have attended previously.

Payment of consultants should be arranged on an individual basis. Limits are frequently imposed by funding agencies, and program administrators should be familiar with the appropriate guidelines. Consideration should also be given to the advisability of engaging consultants on the basis of activities accomplished or products delivered rather than on a daily or hourly basis (Paul, 1971).

Staff/Institution Relations

No program exists apart from its contexts; nor do personnel perform their responsibilities except within a context of social relations. Consideration of ways of bringing about constructive and productive relations between the early childhood education personnel training program and the social structure within which it exists is important to the success of a program. Chapter 4 considered the relationship between program and the broader community. In this section some issues relevant to program and to the institution which houses it will be discussed.

Within a college or university structure there exists a political dynamic. Institutions vary in the nature of this dynamic, but all have their stresses and strains, and all have their rivalries. At any one time one area or discipline will seem to be supported more than others, and public and private jealousies will ensue.

For the past five or six years, early childhood education has been faring better than many other areas; and it seems likely to do so for several years to come. To take advantage of this situation, however, at the expense of other areas of the university is to invite trouble.

The selection of staff may make the case in point. Exceptionally plush salaries or unusually light teaching commitments may be viewed askance by other members of the institution. Similarly, staff selection which neglects established procedures will create concern for standards, and for their defense, when they might otherwise have fallen by the wayside with time.

Separatism is another danger. Where services might be gained from within the existing community, attempts to establish new sources of these services within a new program will be viewed as an infringement upon the realms of others. Such points of potential conflict should be avoided whenever possible.

While institutional change may seem to be desirable or expeditious, the framework for seeking such change should be chosen with care. Circumventing rules and regulations by seeking approved exceptions may be more prudent, in the long haul, than crashing ahead for a basic change. The proven exception may in the end establish the new rule without mustering the forces in defense of the status quo.

This is not to say that change should be avoided. Indeed, it may be one of the major goals of the program. However, it does suggest a tactful and judicious choice of methods. Persuasion through existing channels will frequently be more successful than insensitive disregard for tradition or direct challenge to authority.

PROGRAM TRAINEES

Just as the staff of a program for early childhood personnel training are considered important to its definition and implementation, so it may be said that the trainees themselves are the measure of its success. The makeup of the student body is crucial in defining the program's personality, and it is extremely important in determining the nature of the education that the student receives (Campbell, 1971). Therefore, the criteria for selection are central in the remainder of this chapter. In addition, the supplementary services a trainee may need are discussed.

The Trainee Selection Process

The area of student selection frequently turns out to be far more complex than it initially seems. Staff in all programs agree that they want the "best" students. This does not define what "best" means, or how the decision will be made, or how to get the student to apply and enroll, or what constraints impinge upon the selection process. Clearly, both program goals and legislated requirements must be served.

Program Goals. Early in program development, often at inception, a number of program goals will be set which bear directly upon trainee selection. These take various forms, some seemingly obvious, and others more subtle.

At the obvious end of the spectrum are decisions dealing with level of training (see chapter 6). The initial decision to develop a program of training for entry-level paraprofessionals in early childhood education focuses selection on prebaccalaureate persons without previous training in the area. That is, the level of training selected narrows the range of potential candidates.

As additional program goals place qualifiers on selection, the influence becomes increasingly subtle. For example, if the program intends to upgrade and provide employment for indigenous members of a particular community or area, the range of selection narrows still further. If the program objectives call for placing people on a career development track, or for eventually upgrading community residents to assume fully certified teaching positions in the area, the selection process needs to be more complex and the choice of participants is more limited. At an even more subtle level, if one of the program objectives is to increase ethnic understanding and tolerance, quotas may be imposed to assure diversity of ethnic background.

The selection process as of this point may be pictured as in Figure 5.1.

As can be seen, the process of selection rapidly becomes complex. Yet few administrators would be satisfied with the five-step procedure shown in Figure 5.1. For one thing, the decisions up to this point do not consider the potential student's aspirations, his or her desire to participate, or his or her capability of meeting the financial obligations of participation. Any selection procedure should take such additional factors into account if an appropriate "match" is to be made between student and program.

Other programmatic decisions involve such considerations as the number of program variations possible, the quotas for each, and the alternative means for tailoring programs for individuals.

Legislated Requirements. Legislated requirements take at least two

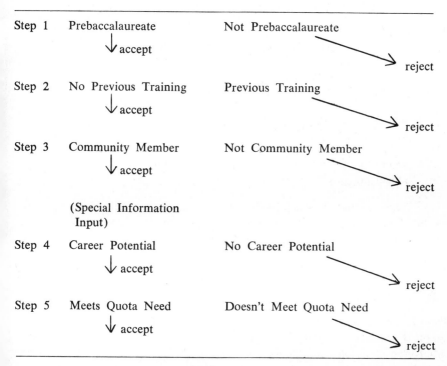

FIGURE 5.1

Hypothetical Trainee Selection Process

forms: those associated with the institution providing the training and those associated with funding or regulatory agencies. Included in the former category are quotas set upon the permissible number of foreign or out-of-state students, entrance requirements (i.e., test scores or previous educational background), class size, and scheduling requirements. Requirements associated with funding or regulatory agencies may pertain to socioeconomic status, ethnic or geographical representativeness, and sex ratios.

Major Issues in the Selection Process. Three additional issues important to student selection are worth considering at this point. Each deals with the process of decision-making. First, the question arises as to whether "clinical" or actuarial methods for selecting students are more useful—that is, are the student selection decisions of a committee of staff members better predictors of student program success than an actuarial equation for combining input on criterion variables? Dawes (1971), after reviewing the extensive literature on this question, concluded that they are not:

> It should not be surprising that actuarial methods are superior to clinical prediction. In principle, such methods have to be superior—for, in principle, it should always be possible to devise an actuarial method that simulates the clinician's behavior; thus, in principle, there is at least one method that does as well as the clinician, and there may always be one that is better. What is striking is that the only actuarial method considered in most of the research is that of linear combination of criterion variables— and this very simple actuarial method consistently does better than clinical judgment. (p. 181)

Even when the principles being followed by the decision-maker are valid, the computer following an actuarial approximation will perform better—i.e., it will apply the rules more consistently.

The second issue involves the whole question of testing. Test bias involves the question of validity. If a test accurately predicts a criterion, it is worth using—it has utility if the cost of administration does not exceed the cost of an incorrect decision (Cronbach & Gleser, 1965). In other words, as long as the criterion remains unchanged (e.g., success in a typical graduate program in early childhood education) and the test predicts the criterion accurately, the major consideration is the cost of test administration.

The difficulty arises when the predictor fails to predict. Marston (1971), among others, documented the increasing failure of the Graduate Record Examination to predict the criterion: success in a graduate program. This failure, more so than personal or social biases, may warrant discarding some of our most frequently used predictors. Further, as instruction is adapted more to individual needs and individual characteristics, the potential utility of individual selection instruments becomes greatly diminished. The criterion is no longer clear. This does not mean that individual assessment is useless. It means, rather, that the purpose changes from selection to matching students with personalized programs. (See previous chapter for an explanation of this role for assessment.)

The third issue involves the potentially adverse, though inadvertent, effects of selection criterion that may occur. Campbell (1971), for example, demonstrated how students with more highly focused interests are favored by the admissions policies of better schools. Those with broad interests are at a disadvantage when applying. He comments that this slant in the selection process may yield a more impressive-looking freshman class, but it may not be the best way to serve the needs of our culture. His evidence leads him to conclude that admission policies have unforeseen side effects.

The bias now in vogue, that of selecting those who have done well in high school and who score high on scholastic ability tests, favors applicants with scientific bents, those who are first borns, and those with narrow— or more accurately—highly focused interests.

Second, the usual admissions policies almost certainly have a homogenizing effect on the student body, cutting down on diversity.

Third, to the extent that the faculty controls admissions policy, they will sway the policy in the direction of admitting students that most closely resemble them. (p. 645)

The data and the conclusions presented by Campbell should certainly direct attention to the admissions policies of any program. At the least, careful investigation should be initiated to determine whether such biases exist in early education personnel training programs so that they may be assessed against program goals.

Selection Error. No matter how reliable and valid the selection procedures may be, if the number of applicants being considered is too small or inappropriate, program goals cannot be met. Before selection, the students must be found and convinced that the program is the one they want and need. This suggests a publicity effort focused upon areas that are likely to bring in the kinds of people desired. It also implies that such publicity should clearly state the programmatic objectives and admission requirements.

Even with the best of selection procedures, it should also be recognized that there will be occasional errors. Students will be admitted who later drop out or are requested to leave. Each such unfortunate occasion may be viewed as an opportunity for learning. Information should be sought to determine where things went amiss in the selection procedure or in the program, because this may assist in changing the system for the good of the students.

Services for Trainees

In addition to formal education, it is advantageous to provide trainees with a variety of other services to help insure program success: advising, counseling, tutoring or special help, and placement services. Each may serve general needs or be directed to the special needs of individual trainees. They may be the shared responsibility of the entire program staff, or they may be assigned to specific staff members or auxiliary personnel. For programs housed within colleges or universities, some or all of the services may be provided by other parts of the institution.

Advising. The advisory function frequently has two major components: program planning and career planning.

1. Individual Program Planning: In programs where many options are available and where trainees are given the opportunity to select and choose, they may need assistance to insure that they formulate the best educational program for their needs. They may need advice concerning routes to certification and/or graduation requirements. The advisor in such cases may make suggestions or act as a sounding board for student ideas. He may also serve a monitoring function to insure steady progress toward stated goals.

2. Career Planning: In generalized training programs, trainees frequently need information and advice for selecting their own career goals. They do not know the full range of employment opportunities, the educational requirements of each, or how to determine which is best suited for them. Even in specialized programs, trainees will have questions concerning their career plans, available career ladders, or the like. These needs may be readily met through informal contact with experienced staff personnel or through incorporating "career orientation" into the training program itself.

Counseling. Trainees are human beings, and human beings have problems. These may range from study-skill difficulties through problems of marital relationships, individual personality, or mental health. Usually such problems require individual attention and expertise that go beyond the capabilities of the academic program staff. For such cases a system of referral may be useful and desirable.

Tutoring. In the case of trainee academic difficulties, the best solution may be special individualized help. If time is available, this may be provided by program staff. In many cases more advanced students make excellent tutors for those who are less advanced. In some instances it may be desirable to establish a system of tutorial services, available to all who need it; in others it may be initiated as the need arises. In all cases, tutoring to serve special needs may serve as a useful adjunct to group instruction.

Placement Services. Training programs for early childhood education personnel have a moral obligation to assist trainees in finding employment. If adequate services are available through other components of the institution, this may relieve program staff of some responsibility. However, where programs are new, it is essential to publicize the program to potential employers and to make known to them that the program may offer a new source of prospective employees. If the potential employer is unaware of the program, he will not provide information concerning employment opportunities. If he is unfamiliar with the training provided, he will have difficulty in assessing the nature of the trainee's skills. Communication with potential employers should be an early effort of program staff.

SUMMARY

Issues relating to the people of the program—staff and students—were discussed. Several suggestions were provided for acquiring adequate program personnel, including adjunct and consulting relationships, the development of consortia, differentiated staffing, and generally flexible treatment of qualifications. Student selection and services were considered. The former was seen as a major issue which determines the "personality" of the program, and the latter as an additional means of insuring program success.

REFERENCES

Baskin, S. *Higher education: Some newer developments.* New York: McGraw-Hill, 1965.

Burtt, M. The effects of a man teacher. *Young Children,* 1965, *21,* 93-97.

Campbell, D. Admission policies: Side effects and their implications. *American Psychologist,* 1971, *26,* 636-647.

Chichester, J. Factors in teacher selection, *Phi Delta Kappan,* 1956, *37,* 245-247.

Cronbach, L., & Gleser, G. *Psychological tests and personnel decisions.* Urbana: University of Illinois Press, 1965.

Dawes, R. A case study of graduate admissions: Applications of three principles of human decision-making. *American Psychologist,* 1971, *26,* 180-188.

Haberman, M., & Persky, B. *Preliminary report of the AD HOC Joint Committee on the Preparation of Nursery and Kindergarten Teachers.* Washington, D.C.: NEA Association, undated.

Kiester, D. *Consultation in day-care institute of government.* Chapel Hill, N.C.: University of North Carolina at Chapel Hill Press, 1969.

Krapp, R., & Lastinger, S. Focal points for teacher recruitment, *Phi Delta Kappan,* 1954, *35,* 275-277.

Marston, A. Is it time to reconsider the Graduate Record Examination? *American Psychologist,* 1971, 26, 653-655.

Oliver, J. The meaning and application of differentiated staffing in teaching. *Educational Leadership,* 1970, *32,* 36-40.

Paul, A. Planning for inservice. *Team Exchange,* a quarterly publication of the Arizona Center for Early Childhood Education, University of Arizona, *1*(3), Winter 1971.

Chapter 6

Program Design
and Implementation

DONALD L. PETERS and ALICE S. HONIG

In the preceding chapters the resources for defining the parameters of an early childhood personnel training program, including its human element, were discussed. This chapter offers suggestions for program design and implementation. Although still at the abstract level of ideals and generalities, the attempt is to provide guidelines for moving from program goals to curriculum and specifiable program components.

In a sense, a systems analysis approach has been taken. Each aspect of the system must relate to the achievement of the particular goals of the system. Because goals will vary from program to program, some of the program decisions discussed will not be applicable to particular circumstances. However, the general process of (a) matching decision outcomes to program goals, (b) tracking sequences of decisions to insure their goal orientation, and (c) designing and selecting alternative approaches based on the particular characteristics of the operating environment, is felt to have general applicability.

PROGRAM REQUIREMENTS

Progress from the program goals toward a specific and functional program requires consideration of the resources available (both human and non-human) and of the program's organizational or operational requirements. These include specifications imposed by the institution or community housing the program, by relevant certifying or accreditation agencies, and by granting agencies when external funds are used. They also include obligations for innovation and change.

Throughout much of this chapter it will be assumed that the training program is conducted by an institution of higher education. This re-

155

flects the actuality of present-day practice rather than what needs to be or ought to be. There is a growing recognition that the preparation of educational personnel is a dynamic process, one that relates formal academic training with actual employment practice. As such, effective channels of communication and interaction between educational institutions and work settings are essential. Increasingly, there is greater emphasis on programs external to the college or university; programs based upon in-service, apprenticeship, or competency-based, career-ladder advancement.

Training Level

The training level to be pursued will be determined early in the conception of the program and will be based upon the perceived needs of the students as well as upon the program goals. Level specification may include, but not be restricted to, noncertificate and certificate paraprofessional training, associate of arts or junior college level, baccalaureate, master's, doctoral, or postdoctoral degree training. Alternatively, training level may be specified in terms of employment placements or roles. These include, but are not restricted to, school aide, classroom teacher, in-service trainer, teacher trainer, trainer of teacher trainers, program evaluator, administrator and personnel supervisor, as well as members of boards of education or of committees to plan for curriculum or institutional change in educational affairs.

The training level decided upon will be instrumental in determining many other factors of programming, such as staff requirements, institutional settings, trainee selection, ratio of supervisors to students, ratio of formal course work to field experiences in the curriculum, length of program, sequencing of required courses or training modules, provision of remedial aid in such areas as mathematics or language usage, and provision for recycling through areas where trainees may need further work.

Some programs specify the terminal degree of their course offerings in such a way as to preclude any trainees except those who are already very specially qualified. For example, Ph.D. programs may accept only entering trainees who already possess a master's degree. Other programs are geared to train entering paraprofessionals regardless of previously attained educational level. Still other programs make specific provision for training several different levels of students. Such programs may even conceptualize the different levels of students as interacting in such a manner as to facilitate and complement each other's training.

If several levels of training are undertaken, a decision about training personnel at different levels separately or together must also be made. Funding or staffing problems, as well as theoretical considerations, may figure in the decision. In any case, the responsibilities of staff members to different levels of trainees must be explicitly spelled out to prevent friction or lack of clarity of staff roles.

Another issue to be considered is whether higher-level trainees will have responsibilities in the education of lower-level trainees. One advantage of such a plan derives from the high level of motivation involved. Trainees given such responsibilities seek the personal and professional respect of the lower-level trainees for whom they are responsible. Motivated to model effective teaching, they are innovative and devote much time to their efforts. By working hard to develop their own expertise, they benefit themselves and those whom they teach.

If such responsibilities are to be an integral part of the program, behavioral objectives for the higher-level trainees should be identified and staff and program resources should be allocated for their achievement. Objectives in such areas as interpersonal skills, teaching skills, and supportive team management behaviors should probably be incorporated early in the higher-level trainees' program.

Several ethical questions may be connected with decisions about training level. The training program developer should have as clear a conception as possible of the available or potential employment opportunities for trainees upon completion of the program. This requires decisions and plans regarding an appropriate number of trainees to be accepted at each level, contact with potential employers (such as school superintendents), and provision of placement services.

One project recently completed an excellent training program for white paraprofessional teacher aides in a low-income white suburb, only to find that preschool aide jobs existent in the community were predominantly for black personnel to work in the inner city preschool facilities. The trainees who completed the program were forced to return to welfare rolls or to whatever unskilled jobs they could obtain. Had there been facilities for preschool care in their own economically depressed community, they would have been extremely well equipped by their training for employment there.

Program directors who find that there are uncertain job opportunities in the communities in which trainees live may decide to hold workshops to help solve the employment problems and simultaneously increase the trainees' commitment to working for solutions to their own community and job problems. For example, meetings may be called whereby community power structure representatives are invited to meet with educational trainees and program staff. Such a group could work together to find the feasible economic and political means to promote the creation of child-care centers, preschool programs, classroom aide positions, or afterschool and tutorial programs for older children. Establishment of such facilities would not only respond to community needs but would also provide jobs for qualified trainees completing the program.

The present "glut" of Ph.D.'s in terms of job market potentialities in certain fields should also be considered in decisions to accept certain numbers of students at the highest training levels. Prior planning and attention to the ethical implications of the training program for the students involved are thus important at every training level.

Other considerations—for example, the possible decision to furnish pay or other benefits to trainees who are doing student teaching—may depend on the training level or economic situation of the student teacher; this will be discussed in the practicum section.

Program Length

Decisions about program length will depend upon funding, training level(s), and program goals. Decisions, however, also need to be made about timing, distribution of training, sequencing, and other curriculum considerations.

Timing

Here the decisions to be made relate to questions of availability of trainers and constraints upon time. The trainees may well be involved in such decisions. Such involvement can tie together the trainee selection and level with the program's timing decisions, and thereby yield productive programming and maximal participation by trainers. The variety of options is wide. For example, in one ongoing program involved in training paraprofessionals with master's and doctoral candidates for reading and language skills, an initial summer workship was held for all trainees. Subsequently, one-third of the paraprofessionals were trained by and with master's degree candidates for consecutive three-month periods. In another ongoing program only summer training was offered because of job commitments by degree candidates. In still another program for day-care aides, both evening and daytime training programs were run simultaneously to accommodate the aides' working schedules.

The academic calendar and the availability of practicum sites will usually place constraints on the decisions. Where academic degree programs are involved, there may be institutional residence requirements to be considered.

Distribution of Training

Here the decisions relate to theories of learning and to maximum effectiveness of the actual training delivered. In allocating preservice and in-service training time to accomplish some goals, it may be more beneficial to distribute training over a longer period of time rather than to provide an intensive short training session. However, intensive short sessions may be more conducive to the achievement of other goals. For example, if the program objectives include the development of teamwork or compatible interpersonal relations of supervisory personnel and aides, intensive sensitivity-oriented sessions may provide the most effective means of attaining the objectives.

Sequencing of Training

Choice points about the insertion of training in a sequence of behavior will be dependent upon the program objectives and the underlying theory of learning. This involves considerations of prerequisites, course sequences and branches, the relationship of theoretical and practical experiences, the previous experience of trainees, and a number of other factors particular to the institution or program.

Certification

Present undergraduate early childhood education programs usually have two goals: to graduate the student and to certify him as a person competent to work in educational programs for young children. Similarly, many "career ladder" paraprofessional training programs have goals of general education and professional certification. The two goals, while frequently coterminous, may be considered as distinct (as is done, for example, in the Comfield Model for Elementary Education).

The administrator of a program that trains early childhood education personnel must be thoroughly familiar with the state certification requirements that should be built into his program. There are, of course, difficulties with certification requirements. Although designed to maintain standards, the process has frequently failed to relate to teacher performance, providing instead a set of credit-hour hurdles. As has been suggested, some form of competency-based or performance criteria certification may occur in the relatively near future. This change will also reflect the change in the role of the teacher from generalist to learning environment manager (Burden & Lanzillotti, 1969).

Certification requirements should be understood by the students themselves. This information will be valuable for their program planning and for understanding their curriculum content.

Institutional Requirements

Institutional requirements come in several forms, and include such things as basic or general education requirements, credits required for graduation, residence requirements, and time limitations. Some of these have been previously discussed; others will be discussed later in this chapter. Of concern at this time is the concept of the basic curriculum unit, the course. The course is: "A two- to four-hour a week, semester (or quarter) long segment—organized around some ascending order of difficulty within a complete program, but the organization of the material during the course is determined by the professor or the textbook" (National Center for Educational Research and Development, 1970).

Whether a particular course relates directly to program goals is sometimes open to question. Only occasionally are courses adapted to individual needs or differences.

Where flexibility in institutional requirements exists, the instructional module can be substituted as the basic curriculum component. The module is organized around a single or small number of objectives and is not associated with any fixed time interval. A pretest may be used to determinate the student's readiness to undertake the learning experience, and alternative methods of delivery may be designed. The student may then proceed as rapidly as his abilities permit.

The use of modules increases flexibility in developing programs for trainees, both in terms of the accomplishment of specific and general objectives and of developing unique sets of objectives for individuals.

BEHAVIORAL OBJECTIVES

Purposes of Establishing Objectives

Specification and implementation of the objectives of a program are integral parts of both planning and evaluation. They provide a means of translating theory into usable components and define the relevant information inputs at decision points. Several writers (cf. Dressel & Mayhew, 1954) discussed the purposes that the statement of educational objectives served in curriculum design and implementation. Some often-cited purposes included: directing ongoing classroom instruction, guiding the selection of content, defining the means for individualizing instruction and evaluating student progress, and focusing program evaluation activities.

Interest in stating objectives in behavioral terms is not new. Eisner (1967a) and Kliebard (1968a) traced the interest of curriculum-makers in behavioral objectives to the work of Bobbitt in the 1920s. Eisner examined Bobbitt's viewpoint on their importance in instructional planning and showed that the influence of his views extends to the present in the work of certain curriculum theorists such as Ralph Tyler, Benjamin Bloom, and David Krathwohl.

Similarly, Tyler (1971) quoted Rugg (1927) as specifying that the first task in curriculum-making is "the determination of fundamental objectives," and "consciously or implicitly, the curriculum-maker is always guided by his objectives in the selection of activities or other materials of instruction, and in their organization."

The long history of behavioral objectives has not led to their universal acceptance. Eisner (1967a) and Kliebard (1968a) both argued that the use of behavioral objectives has serious limitations. Eisner contended that there was insufficient stress on the extent to which the prediction of educational outcomes cannot be made with accuracy. He suggested that it is not even possible to state some objectives in behavioral terms (1967b). Others (Ebel, 1970) raised similar limitations. Kliebard (1968b) noted that emphasis on behavioral objectives "still borders on brainwashing or at least indoctrination rather than education" (p. 246). Still, the majority of curriculum planners advocate objectives for their utility value. They frequently provide clarity of role and task conceptualization even where 100 percent specification is not possible.

Specification of Objectives

A number of useful references are available pertaining to methods of specifying and implementing objectives (Mager, 1962; Bloom, 1956; Krathwohl, Bloom & Masia, 1964). Each of these sources offer slightly different rules for specificity and content of the behavioral statement. Krathwohl (1965) appeared to endorse this variability, suggesting that objectives might be conceptualized at three operational levels. At the most abstract level, the objectives are stated as broad, general statements that are useful for developing programs of instruction or for denoting types of courses that a student should take. We have discussed this level under the heading of program goals in previous chapters. At the second level, the broad objectives are refined into units of instruction. These are behavioral statements of the end points of instruction. At the third and most concrete level, the objectives are stated in the highly specific terms necessary for creating instructional materials.

In general, however, each formulation for constructing statements of objectives requires three basic ingredients: the performance criterion must be observable (i.e., it must occur in the form of external behavior); the behavior must be measurable; and there must be a standard stated or implied. The standard allows a decision as to whether the observed, measured behavior is satisfactory evidence of the achievement of the objective.

Objectives at the level of programs for children or for trainees may cover the cognitive, interpersonal, and intrapersonal domains.[1] They may require one or more performance criteria. Some examples approximating Krathwohl's level two with different performance criteria include:

I. *Cognitive*
  A. Objective specified: The trainees will learn the developmental gains and the sequencing of sensorimotor advances in the infant from 0 to 18 months.
  B. Objective operationalized:
     1. The trainee shall provide in writing an outline of four major accomplishments in the sensorimotor stage, including their hierarchical sequencing.[2]
     2. The trainees shall discuss orally four major developmental advances during the sensorimotor stage and specify the sequence thereof.
     3. Given a scrambled videotaped sequence of infant behavior, the trainee will specify the correct sequence of behaviors from less advanced to more advanced and list the behavioral prerequisites for each.

II. *Interpersonal*
  A. Objective specified: The trainee will learn successful techniques for the conduct of parent-teacher conferences.
  B. Objective operationalized:
     1. Given the records of a child with which he is familiar, the trainee will provide a written outline of topics to be covered in a parent-teacher conference. The outline is to be evaluated in terms of specificity, importance, degree of concern or encouragement, and possible suggestions to be communicated.
     2. Given the records of a child with whom he is familiar, the trainee will discuss with his supervisor the major points to be covered in a parent-teacher conference. He will indicate the importance, degree of concern or encouragement, and possible suggestions of each developmental advance or problem area.
     3. Given the records of a child with which he is familiar, the trainee will conduct a parent-teacher conference. The conference is to be observed and evaluated by the instructor according to the trainee's ability to specify advances or problems in development, possible suggestions discussed, tact and ease of relationship, rapport developed, and general friendliness.

III. *Intrapersonal*

A. Objective specified: As a result of undergoing training, the paraprofessional's self-image as an effective and useful person in society will be enhanced.

B. Objective operationalized:

1. The paraprofessional will list ten activities he expects to be able to do in his future employment situation that will benefit children directly.

2. The paraprofessional will role-play an oral presentation to a group of prospective trainees, expressing the value and satisfaction of the paraprofessional in working with children. The presentation is to be evaluated for statements of effectiveness, utility, and degree of personal conviction.

Additional Considerations

Objectives may be specified also in terms of the elimination of behaviors. For example, while coping skills for dealing with some classroom problems are not fully understood, certain teacher behaviors (cynicism, ridicule, severe punishment) are generally accepted as counterproductive. Objectives may be incorporated which specify the reduction or total elimination of such reactions in trying situations.

While behavioral objectives are best constructed for single performance criteria (e.g., one teaching skill), a series of such objectives may be grouped or clustered into performance modules representing more complex patterns of behavior. An example might be the grouping of objectives relating to question-asking, material organization and sequencing, and developmental assessment to form a cluster defining "teaching concepts to four-year-olds."

Finally, it should be remembered that no matter how carefully specified the behavioral objectives of a unit of instruction, or of a total program, they still constitute only a subsample of the learning accomplished or the behaviors changed. In a sense, the objectives constitute a minimal set of achievements sought, a set of basic standards to be reached. A program may indeed accomplish much more—in both the positive and negative directions. Without such minimal standards, however, it is difficult, if not impossible, to determine what *has* been achieved.

CURRICULUM COMPONENTS

All early childhood education personnel training programs will have curricula unique to their settings, resources, and purposes. However, several basic components seem to have generality, though their relative emphasis will vary. These include: a liberal education, knowledge of human development, knowledge of history and background of early education, knowledge of a basic content area, competence in interpersonal relations, competence in the practice of educational skills, and competence in the ways and means of acquiring new knowledge.

The first four constitute what is sometimes called the academic components of the program, or the knowledge base. The remainder may be referred to as the professional skill components. Alternatively, the liberal education component is sometimes considered separately as general education, with the rest deemed to be professional education. Neither division seems entirely appropriate. Indeed, the listing itself does not represent seven mutually exclusive areas of curriculum. They overlap and are interrelated, but are broken down here primarily for purposes of exposition. They certainly need not be separated in curriculum organization.

A Liberal Education

The arts and the humanities, the physical and social sciences—all contribute to an individual's comprehension of his world and his place in it. With growing affluence and leisure, each person needs a sense of identity and purpose and the flexibility that comes from active engagement in and understanding of the world in which he lives.

The relative emphasis on providing a liberal education is likely to follow a curvilinear path when considered against training level. At the paraprofessional level the concern is primarily upon basic communication skills (reading, writing, and speech) and less upon the broad liberal education background. At the baccalaureate level this component frequently takes on a major priority. At the graduate level the emphasis again diminishes, giving way to more specialized professional training. One paraprofessional training program conducted within a local school district included the following program goals for trainees:

> Each trainee shall be able to:
> (a) read and comprehend material written in English at a beginning college level pertaining to a variety of topics;
> (b) write English prose following the traditional and acceptable organization and rules;
> (c) write essays in English which relate judgments, assemble evidence, and draw conclusions in a manner adequate to facilitate written communications;
> (d) speak in a manner reflecting fundamental principles and methods of selecting, analyzing, evaluating, organizing, developing, and communicating information, evidence, and points of view for constructive influence in speech situations. (Stoudt, Hobbs & Peters, 1971)

These goals reflect value judgments which may be inappropriate in other settings and with different groups of trainees. They clearly ignore ethnic differences found among black, Puerto Rican, Mexican-American, and American Indian groups in our society. They do reflect one kind of emphasis placed upon "liberal education" for early education paraprofessionals.

At the baccalaureate level, programs frequently include course work or demonstrated competencies in the humanities (art, literature, languages, etc.), in the physical sciences (chemistry, mathematics, physics), in the biological sciences (biology, zoology, entomology, etc.), and in the social and behavioral sciences (psychology, history, political science, anthropology, sociology, economics), as well as in basic communication skills. At the post-baccalaureate level some breadth in these areas may still be required.

Human Development

Human development is usually studied on an interdisciplinary basis—that is, several major disciplines provide methods and findings that are important in understanding man from conception to death, as an individual within social, cultural, and physical contexts.

It is usually recognized that the study of child development provides an important component of teacher training. However, a broader conception of human development, with particular stress on the continuity and interrelatedness of different aspects of development, seems highly desirable.

At beginning levels, fundamental principles and landmarks in development usually suffice. At more advanced levels, consideration of alternative theories and their support, specification of developmental trends in the areas of physical or psychological development, intellectual development, emotional development, and social development seem warranted.

The study of human development includes at least:

1. An integrated bio-behavioral focus upon the processes of individual development from infancy through old age, and upon the family unit as the primary educative, economic, social, and psychological unit influencing the processes of individual development.

2. Study of the community as a collection of human beings and as a social organization interacting in a variety of ways. This includes the study of social organizations and their processes.

3. The interactional relationships of man with his physical environment, including the way in which the design and arrangement of man's physical environment both constrain and facilitate his behavior.

Early Education

As professionals and paraprofessionals in the field of early education, trainees may be expected to represent their field in a variety of social and employment contexts. As such they will need to understand its goals, background, and future directions. It seems reasonable to include, in their training curriculum, information concerning the history of early education, the principal programs and methodologies that have been developed, some of the key figures in the field, and the discernible evolutionary trends. In the case of paraprofessional training, this broad background may be at a conversational or recognition level. In more advanced training, a more comprehensive understanding of the philosophical, theoretical, and social foundations of program diversity may be expected. At more advanced levels the trainee may be expected to fully understand and employ the processes of program development.

This training may be issue-oriented—that is, the background, purposes, and directions of early education may be focused upon the critical isues faced in the field, with the arguments representing the many sides of each issue carefully drawn. A disservice is done to trainees at any level if they are led to assume that all persons—parents, community representatives, or educators—are in full agreement with the directions the field of early education has taken. They should be aware of counterarguments and alternative positions so that they may formulate their own position and communicate it to those with whom they interact. For example, in one program for day-care teachers, the trainees were confronted with reasons why day care might not be good for children, their families, or for society. These arguments were explored and the development of counterarguments was encouraged.

Finally, the field of early education is rapidly growing and changing. It may be desirable to emphasize this change and to make trainees aware of their roles in the process and their responsibilities for assessing the criteria for innovation. Trainees may be encouraged to see themselves as innovators and agents of institutional change, and they may be provided with the tools and strategies for assessing the innovations that they or others initiate.

Basic Content Knowledge

Where early education personnel are being trained for positions as aides or teachers in the early primary grades of public schools, there is a need for competency in the basic content areas of math, reading, the arts, the humanities, and the sciences. Specialty areas may be desirable. In such cases, students may develop programs which accomplish specialty area goals. In training programs concerned with the development of personnel for younger children, this area of curriculum will have a different emphasis: the focus will be directed toward the sciences and arts and geared to the child's understanding of his physical environment, social environment, and self-expression.

Interpersonal Relations

Early childhood educators must work with people. Movements toward educational teams and differentiated staffing place the "teacher" in contact with parents, subordinates, colleagues, supervisors, and community leaders as well as with children. They frequently are required to take on the role of "change agent," facilitating some aspect of the development of other individuals and groups. Recent literature suggests that the skills required for these roles can, and perhaps should, be taught (Buchanan, 1971; Dinkmeyer, 1971).

Some suggestions for inclusion in the curriculum for early education personnel are the examination of interpersonal conditions which facilitate personal growth, intensive interpersonal competency training, the study of group dynamics, and the study of the impact of socially defined roles upon relationship development and maintenance.

Professional Skills

Since teachers need the skills of their profession, instruction in teaching methods and technology should be part of their preparation. Such things as the development and utilization of plans and objectives, interactional skills for use with children, classroom management, and so forth, may be taught through classroom and practicum experiences. Within a training program they may be geared to the expected employment level of the trainee. Trainees who expect to teach young children should be provided with the opportunity to develop the skills they will need in that role. Trainees who later will be training teachers may be taught skills for working with children, but they should also receive instruction and experience designed to provide them with the skills they will need in teaching teachers. The same holds true for personnel who will be working with parents, graduate students, and so forth. Those being trained for leadership and management roles will need a variety of skills, including budgeting, planning, and administration.

Skills for Acquiring New Knowledge

For the professional the termination of a training program does not mean an end to study. To provide a means for continued growth and improvement in the field of early education, all workers in the field need to be skilled in acquiring new ideas and information. The skills necessary include those pertaining to the use of library resources, the reading of professional journals, participation in professional meetings, and conducting or participating in research and evaluation. The level of sophistication will vary with training level, but such skills represent an essential part of all programs.

NOTES

1. Programs may also include objectives for the sensor-motor domain.
2. Some examples of behaviors in different areas of development are: reaching for objects in the field of vision when the hand is not also visible; use of a support or stick to draw an object to oneself; varying the ways in which a new action may be carried out (such as throwing toys from a highchair) to see what happens if the action is varied; turning away from the line of sight of a ball which has rolled under a couch in order to locomote around the couch and retrieve the ball.

REFERENCES

Bloom, B. *Taxonomy of educational objectives: Cognitive domain.* New York: McKay Company, 1956.

Buchanan, M. Preparing teachers to be persons. *Phi Delta Kappan,* 1971, *52,* 614-616.

Burden, J., & Lanzillotti, K. *A reader's guide to the comprehensive models for preparing elementary teachers.* Washington, D.C.: American Association of Colleges of Teacher Education, 1971.

Dinkmeyer, D. The C-group: Focus on self as instrument. *Phi Delta Kappan,* 1971, *52, 617-619.*

Dressel, P., & Mayhew, L. *General education: Explorations in evaluation.* Washington, D.C.: American Council on Education, 1954.

Ebel, R. Behavioral objectives: A close look. *Phi Delta Kappan,* 1970, *51,* 171-173.

Eisner, E. Franklin Bobbitt and the "science" of curriculum-making. *School Review,* 1967, *75,* 29-47 (a).

————. Educational objectives: Help or hindrance? *School Review,* 1967, *75,* 250-282 (b).

Kliebard, H. The curriculum field in retrospect. In P. Witt (Ed.), *Technology and the curriculum.* New York: Teachers College Press, 1968a.

————. Curriculum objectives and evaluation: A reassessment. *High School Journal,* 1968, *51,* 241-247 (b).

Krathwohl, D. Stating objectives appropriately for program, for curriculum, and for instructional material development. *Journal of Teacher Education,* 1965, *16,* 88-92.

Krathwohl, D., Bloom, B., & Masia, B. *Taxonomy of educational objective: Affective domain.* New York: McKay Company, 1964.

Mager, R. *Preparing instructional objectives.* Belmont, California: Fearon Publishers, 1962.

National Center for Educational Research and Development. *Analytic summaries of specifications for model teacher education programs.* Washington, D.C.: U.S. Government Printing Office, 1970.

Rugg, H. Foreword. In *The foundations and techniques of curriculum-making.* Bloomington, Ill.: Public School Publishing Company, 1927.

Stoudt, H., Hobbs, J., & Peters, D. Huntingdon Area School District Paraprofessional training. Huntingdon, Pa., 1971 (mimeographed).

Tyler, R. Curriculum development in the twenties and thirties. In R. McClure (Ed.), *The curriculum: Retrospect and prospect.* Chicago: University of Chicago Press, 1971.

Chapter 7

Practicum

ALICE S. HONIG and LOIS M. FEARS

One of the most ancient and honorable methods of learning a skilled craft or profession has been actual experience with or apprenticeship to a master teacher. This method of teaching and learning through guided practice underlies a major portion of the education of early childhood personnel. In this chapter the history, purposes, and major elements of the practicum experience will be discussed, and the primary focus will be upon considerations that enter into decisions concerning the use and assignment of practica.

DEFINITIONS AND CONCEPTS

In the field of education, practicum has been designated by such terms as *on-the-job-training, field service, directed teaching, student teaching,* and *apprenticeship.* Often specified within these narrower designations are elements that are important to the conceptualization of practicum. Yee (1967), for example, in his glossary of student teaching terms, defined *student teaching* as "a prolonged period of laboratory experience in an actual classroom situation during which the student takes increasing responsibility for his preparation as a teacher under the direction of a college supervisor representing his teacher-education center and a cooperating teacher who is responsible for the classroom situation" (p. iii). Conant (1963), in his classic survey of 77 teacher-training institutions in the United States, used the designation *practice teaching* to define quite similarly a future teacher's participation in classroom activities under the guidance of a regular teacher and with the supervision of a professor of education.

In attempting to differentiate operationally some of these synonyms for practicum, Corman and Olmsted (1964, p. 3) pointed out that *apprenticeship* could mean that a trainee entered a practice situation without

171

any prior formal study of teaching whatsoever. They further contrasted *student teaching,* which may be of short duration and unpaid, with what they, in an experimental teacher-preparation program in Michigan, called *internships.* They designated *internship* as "an adequately supervised full-time teaching experience which follows an organized program of formal instruction in pedagogy and which precedes certification." Central to their definition was the requirement for supervision of the intern. The importance of internship experience derived, according to Corman and Olmsted, from the fact that application had not automatically or obviously followed the study of formal teaching methods and theory. They pointed out that seldom was there any necessary implication of theory for a preferred or exclusively correct course of action in a specific situation.[1]

These various terminologies refer to practice experiences provided at different time points to persons of differing skill levels. Practica may vary widely, for their function is to provide students an opportunity to acquire skills which may be more difficult to teach in the usual classroom situations, and to apply their classroom learning. Practica may range from observational experiences, with few direct contacts with children, to placement in actual job situations.

Work experiences in which a supervised trainee applies known skills in an integrated fashion at an advanced stage of personnel training are more frequently referred to as *internships.* The internship may occur concurrent with or subsequent to more formal classes in a training program; but in either case it entails a great amount of responsibility. The intern is often regarded as an almost fully trained person who is ready, upon completion of this supervised experience, to go out and work independently in his chosen field.

In a later section which surveys the history and usages of practicum, it will be noted that these semantic distinctions, based on both trainee competence level and timing of work-experience placement within a curricular sequence, have by no means been consistently adhered to in the literature. However, in our analysis of the major factors to be considered in providing practicum for trainees, we shall be using the term *practicum* to refer to any supervised experience which provides for the learning of skills in practical job or life situations. Practicum is likely to occur early in a training program rather than near its termination. The term *internship* will be reserved for advanced supervised work experiences which involve advanced skill levels and the assumption of great responsibility. These are programmed late in a personnel training program or upon termination of formal requirements. Student teaching may occur anywhere along this practicum-internship continuum. However, when a trainee carries out a long-term, paid, intensive teaching experience which assumes a great deal of advanced training, then internship seems a more appropriate designation for this experience.

PURPOSES AND IMPORTANCE

No matter which term is used, the purposes of practicum seem straight-forward. In teacher training, the first essential purpose of practicum has been to provide that peculiarly broad spectrum of practical teaching experiences which a classroom full of live and unique youngsters can provide for an inexperienced teacher—that is, practicum provides the realistic opportunity to learn and employ, under continuous supervision and evaluation, the skills of the teacher (Troyer, 1947).

Second, practicum can serve to make more meaningful and comprehensible the theoretical or methodological components of other courses which may appear to the trainee to refer often and unrealistically to the teaching of model children under optimal conditions. Practicum may be viewed as a connecting link in the curriculum continuum which can provide continuity to the other experiences planned with and for the trainee throughout his contact with the program.

Third, practicum provides a time for the trainee to test ideas in a variety of real but somewhat sheltered situations, and to study the results before entering service as a teacher.

Fourth, practicum has been utilized to motivate students. While trainees may be strongly oriented toward the application of skills and the provision of services, they may be less enthusiastic, for example, about the numerous methods or theory courses that may be required in a training program.

Fifth, insufficiencies in program planning or in trainee qualifications may be detected. Practicum can provide evaluative feedback as well as assistance in solving problems and correcting weaknesses. In addition, an opportunity is presented to screen out trainees who are not able to carry out adequate behaviors.[2]

HISTORY AND USAGES

The practicum, a component of so many teacher-training programs, has a long history as a training or curriculum method par excellence (Woellner & Wood, 1971). In his book on the historical development of student-teaching practices, Johnson (1968a) noted that in Europe some form of practice teaching was used in conjunction with the earliest efforts to train teachers professionally. Observation and emulation were considered the foundation of learning for the apprentice teacher. Apparently as early as 1438, in medieval England, teaching demonstration lessons before fellow students were established by William Byngham at Godhouse College as a method of training grammar school teachers. In the eighteenth century Pestalozzi conducted what we may consider the first modern teacher-training school. His trainees received little formal instruction; almost all their training involved practice teaching in some form.

The helping professions in general have been prominent in emphasizing the value of practical work experience in personnel training programs. Medical schools have internship and residency requirements in approved hospitals. Social work training institutions have been strongly committed to the concept of practicum and internship, which they sometimes refer to as *field placement*. Supervised case work trainees are given a great deal of responsibility in handling client problems.

In the field of mental retardation and special education, the importance of practical training experience for teachers and the specification of desirable practicum conditions have often been stressed (Fouracre, 1966; Mitchell, 1969; Smokoski, 1969). Anderson and Little (1968) urged that a variety of experiences with mental retardates be offered to teacher trainees from the freshman year onward. Delp (1968), arguing the merits of what he called an internship method for training special class teachers, emphasized the importance of including, from the very beginning of the program, practical work experience along with the course work and observation. The introduction of such experiences at program entry was designed to overcome some of the insufficiencies encountered in the traditional teacher-training program.

For the training of elementary and secondary school teachers, the importance of practicum as an essential ingredient has been broadly acknowledged (Cooper, 1969; Schorling, 1940). Sarason, Davidson, and Blatt (1962) felt that the practice teaching period was as important as lectures and assigned readings. Recent interest in designing innovative approaches to practical experiences testifies further to their importance (Gardner & Henry, 1968; Henry, 1970; Johnson, 1968b; Spodek, 1969; Whitelaw, 1965).

After his comprehensive study of teacher training, Conant (1963) advocated the elimination of all course requirements by the state, but he firmly stated, "I would have the competence of a future teacher tested by practice teaching under conditions set by the state and subject to state supervision" (p. 112) He emphasized that practice teaching is the one area of early education generally agreed to be a necessary training requirement. Conant's high regard for the value of practice teaching led him to recommend using only the most competent teachers for this purpose, paying them more and reducing their usual work load as a consequence of their training role with new teachers.

Shaplin and Powell (1964), in outlining significant new characteristics of practice teaching in recent years, concluded that internship (which they equated with practice teaching) should not be viewed as a sequel to professional preparation but as the very essence of the preparation. They proposed that we consider this internship not as a supplement to or culmination of a curricular sequence, but as an alternative to traditional teacher education.

In addition to the professional accord given to the importance of practical experience as a training tool, there is evidence that teachers who have completed teacher-education programs view student teaching as the best single factor and most valuable experience for preparation to teach (Gardner & Henry, 1968; Stiles, Barr, Douglass & Mills, 1960).

In the last few years there has been a growing acknowledgment of the important job roles which trained paraprofessional aides, who are often from linguistic and ethnic minority groups, can fill in health and educational settings (Bowman & Klopf, 1968). Practicum may be the most effective and economical component of a program to train such aides and paraprofessional staff. In such cases, on-the-job training may constitute the nucleus of supervised learning. Recently much attention has been given to selecting and training paraprofessionals as teachers of infants and toddlers. Emphasis has been placed on the importance of introducing the trainee very early to actual experiences with infants in every aspect of their development and functioning (Honig & Lally, 1972; Lally, Honig & Caldwell, 1973).

Although there has been an enormous recent growth in preschool educational attendance, Katz and Weir (1969) reported that most people who are now teaching preschool children have had no training for the job. They recommended practicum as the preferred training technique to remedy this widespread lack and urged that we show how to carry out teaching skills in actual classrooms.

THE RELATIONSHIP OF PRACTICUM OBJECTIVES AND PRACTICUM DECISIONS

Decisions concerning when and how to utilize practica should be based on the educational needs of trainees and on the objectives of the training program. Difficulties and drawbacks encountered in the administration of practicum experiences are directly related to insufficient attention to planning, particularly in the careful delineation of practicum goals and of provision for supervision (Kaltsounis & Nelson, 1968).

Objectives

Current educational emphasis is clearly on the specification of behavioral objectives for every aspect of teacher training [3] (Burden & Lanzillotti,

1969). Careful attention must be given to the considered and defined objectives to be achieved by practicum placement. The objectives may be derived from theoretical assumptions about the facilitation of learning or through an analysis of roles, skills, and work settings. (The reader will find it quite helpful, in formulating practicum objectives, to refer to the section in chapter 5 which deals with the sources of program goals and the specification of curricular objectives.)

During the formulation of practicum objectives, care must be taken to insure congruence of these objectives with those established for the educational consumer—in particular, the child in the classroom. For example, "experience in a rich sensory environment where the stimulation is planned and appropriate" is a valid objective for preschool children. In her practicum, a teacher trainee may have received intensive interpersonal skill training with youngsters. However, if she has not learned how to provide for a plethora of appropriate sensory experiences for young children, then congruence is lacking between the objectives as planned for practicum trainees and for the children.

The Practicum: Where?

Traditional practicum experiences have often occurred in a bright, airy classroom, among bright, well-scrubbed children; yet most educational settings are far from this ideal! Practicum experiences should be designed to help trainees gain insight into the cultures of the various ethnic and socioeconomic groups with whom they will be employed and skills that are effective for furthering the learning careers of such groups in particular.

Such skills may not be acquired by practicum alone. Supplementary techniques, such as microteaching and simulations, may be utilized as excellent adjuncts for sharpening the practicum tool to maximal efficiency. For example, mini-courses and workshops on how to cook Mexican foods or create bark paintings have been organized in order to increase teacher-trainees' sensitivity to the culture of the Mexican-American children whom they would ultimately be teaching. A number of such activities may be coordinated to provide a broad-based, multifaceted effort toward accomplishing program goals.

Practicum Time: When, How Long, and for Whom?

Determination of objectives should allow rational apportionment of trainee time to practicum in comparison to other curricular methods, such as lecture courses. If practicum objectives include the specification of a hierarchy of teaching competencies developed on the basis of performance criteria, decisions relative to the timing of practicum for trainees also become easier to make; the same is true for other curricular methods used.

The University of Massachusetts Model Elementary Teacher Education Program (METEP) stresses content knowledge, behavioral abilities, and human relation skills. Because METEP is a competency-based model, practicum begins at different times for individual students, depending on performance. Thus, instruction is fitted to the competency of the student, while at the same time the student is assisted in developing competencies required as objectives of the program. Also, because program objectives specify behaviorally what is required of the teacher trainee, attainment of these skills may be assessed prior to practicum. Other methods, such as role-playing or simulation, may be prescribed to prepare trainees for practicum if the prerequisites for entry have been set but not met. Thus, careful formulation of objectives aids in choosing potential methods for fulfilling these objectives as well as in decisions regarding the sequencing of methods and time allotted to any one method, including practicum.

The formulation of objectives should clarify what kind of practicum experience is to be undertaken, and whether or not orientation will be required of a trainee before entry into practicum. Behavioral definition of practicum objectives permits a comparison of present trainee competencies with ultimate competencies. Thus, decisions about trainee readiness for practicum can be based on some standard minimum set of required entry behaviors. Plans for pre-practicum training can then be made if a trainee is not yet functioning at this level.

A careful formulation of objectives should also facilitate decisions relative to distribution of practicum experiences compared to other course work for trainees of differing educational levels. One practical decision that could be made, for example, is to provide more practicum for paraprofessionals than is required or necessary for professionals in a higher degree program. Lazar and Brown (1971), concerned with the training of infant care workers (often paraprofessionals), proposed the following: "ideally, field activity should accompany every step of training; some programs design their training procedure in such a way that the shift from training to practice comes about through a gradual increase in the amount of actual work and a corresponding decrease in lecture and observation so that there is no marked transition between training and work" (p. 140).

In any case, the proper pacing of practicum experiences to match the developing skill and tempo of the trainee is of utmost importance. This may have far-reaching implications, especially for paraprofessionals. For example, in one program a paraprofessional, after a few months in practicum, was urged by her supervising teacher to assume major responsibility in planning and carrying out science and number concept lessons with five-year-olds. The teacher saw herself as helpful and generous in relinquishing classroom authority to the aide. Yet the paraprofessional became so frightened by the perceived "pressure" to assume such a level of responsibility too early that her absenteeism increased sharply and she ultimately left the program. Of course, such problems can arise at a higher level as well.

The practicum objectives will also simplify decisions on coordination of the timing and sequence of training for all levels of personnel. In many projects, paraprofessionals have served in the practicum simultaneously with graduate degree students. One goal of such programs is to teach the graduate students how to teach, supervise, and be responsive to and responsible for the paraprofessional trainee. Simultaneous training can also promote cross-cultural sensitization and language training if ethnic or racial differences exist among the trainees. Other programs have objectives which dictate the allotment of sequential training time to paraprofessionals and to teachers working toward professional degrees. Sometimes sequential training is planned because of staffing problems. Sometimes, however, an overly narrow conceptualization of differences in function for trainees at different levels is entailed in the decision to train such students separately.

Practicum: Credit or Not

Objectives can also have a bearing on the assignment of credit hours or certification of training for practicum work. For example, if paraprofessionals involved in the practicum desire to seek upward career mobility in their work and education, credit hours may be assigned to further such desires and to motivate good attendance and work habits in practicum. Credits may be given in such cases even though students in the regular college program may not have received credit for practicum in the past. The feasibility of this alternative will depend upon program/institutional arrangements and requirements.

Sometimes the transfer of practicum credits is also an issue. Detailed specification of the number of hours worked, the extent and nature of the supervision, and the work competencies demonstrated may facilitate a trainee's efforts to achieve recognition for such credits at another institution which does not routinely grant credit for practicum.

Another problem with regard to credit arises when trainees return to or begin college during their later adult years. In competency-based programs, a decision must be made with respect to granting credit for prior experiences, which may include child rearing, volunteer work in educational or social service settings, travel, or participation in a "Great Books" program. These experiences may have led to competency in skills which constitute part of the terminal program goals. Despite the lack of college supervision for such learning, some colleges have allotted practicum credits in such cases to facilitate the return of mature adults to educational degree programs.

Practicum: What It Is Not

Practicum experiences should never be set up just to fill staffing vacancies in an educational setting for young children. To require trainees to accept total responsibility for a group of children is unfair to both trainees and children. The children are deprived, at least initially, of teachers with expertise. For trainees, practicum should provide not only work experiences and specific skill learning, but also sufficient time to devote to observing experienced teaching models, to receiving feedback and suggestions from supervisory personnel, and to relevant skill-building activities. Nor should trainees be expected to provide schools with cheap labor (Whitelaw, 1965). This objection becomes more legitimate if we remember the distinctions made earlier between practicum and internship. Highly trained interns should be compensated for their work. Such an arrangement worked out between a school and a personnel training project may be mutually beneficial: good trainees can inject new ideas and enthusiasm into a school system in which they function as paid interns.

Practicum should not be conceived of simply as a way for degree candidates to increase the number of credits earned. Such a conception could engender resentment and might result in a decision to append applied experiences or practica as a minor component to a more formal curriculum.

Future Employment Roles

Consideration of the roles that the trainees will fill upon completing their training experience is important to the success of practicum assignment. How a teacher interacts with children makes a difference in their behavior (Butler, 1970). Does she let children initiate many activities? Does she give a high level of prompt positive feedback to children? Does she teach content matter thoroughly and yet release the children's creative powers to respond to the materials and concepts? What kind of roles does she model for children?

This notion of role-modeling is illustrated by Katz's basic distinction between two aspects of teaching: "role" and "style" (1970). By teaching "role" is meant that aspect of a teacher's behavior which concerns the duties, responsibilities, and functions expected of her by herself and by her clients. Clients may be children, parents, or employers. "Style" refers to the personalized flavor of a given role, so that one trainee may be outgoing, smiling, and loquacious compared to another, although both are expected to behave in certain ways and to perform certain tasks.

The objectives for practicum will depend on an accurate assessment of roles (job specifications) which the trainees expect, or may be required, to fill upon completion of the program. This assessment should optimally result in a high degree of individualization of placement in practica for educational trainees with differing future roles.

Trainee involvement in these decisions about future role expectations is extremely important for the success and relevance of practicum. The trainee should be encouraged, with the help of supervisory personnel or counselors, to explore her own strengths and weaknesses with respect to the roles and to the skills she will need for a given job situation. Practicum placement can then be tailored with greater accuracy and relevance to trainee needs and to program competence goals.

Katz (1970), in her analysis of teacher role models in early childhood education, clarified one subtle and potential source of difficulty. She discriminated three potential role models of childhood educators in preschool settings: "the maternal model," "the therapeutic model," and "the instructional model." If a preschool teacher trainee in a practicum experiences only the therapeutic model, for example, she will probably find it difficult to adjust and function in a job situation where planned and deliberate transmission of knowledge and skills to the children (the "instructional mode") is expected. Decisions for practicum placement, accordingly, should take into account potential role models with which a trainee may be expected to be familiar and competent.

In one program for training paraprofessional day-care aides, the improvement of interpersonal skills was considered the critical training objective. Sensitivity to and improved communication among workers at different educational or socioeconomic levels in a given day-care setting was the focus. Interpersonal roles were considered more important for the successful functioning of the day-care personnel being trained than the input of specific skills to help the children's cognitive development.

The importance of formulating objectives in planning and carrying out training programs with differing emphases cannot be overstressed. To illustrate further, Combs and Snygg (1959) defined the "good" person as one who contributes maximally to the adequacy of children and other persons, where adequacy is a function of positive self-reference, acceptance, and identification. Such a role model for a teacher trainee would indicate that practicum placement in preschool settings which represent predominantly laissez-faire play groups or rigidly structured academic preschools may be insufficient for such role learning.

Skills

Delivery of curricular experiences which meet the trainees' ultimate role needs will depend on at least two factors. The first task is an assessment of the specific skills each trainee needs to "fill in" her competency profile. Second, choices must be made of the most effective program delivery methods for the various jobs that trainees anticipate performing. The job skills so designated must be related to appropriate work areas where they can be learned.

These job competencies may be quite varied: they can include nutrition and dietetic skills for teacher aides who will prepare snacks and meals, cost-accounting methods for an educational supervisor who will be responsible for budget planning, techniques for reading stories to preschoolers, and ways to utilize a care-giving routine (such as diapering) to facilitate infant language and concept development in a day-care center.

Some skills have a more direct reference to materials or to the environment—for example, how to set up a terrarium, arrange an attractive reading corner, or use an electric saw to cut panels for a toy house (Bussis & Chittenden, 1970). These skills may be feasibly taught via special workshops or appropriate filmstrips as well as in a school setting. Some skills are more directly concerned with interpersonal relations. How does a trainee show a child that she honestly values his effort even though the quality of his work may be quite poor? How does she encourage creativity and self-expression and yet limit disorganizing behaviors by a child who is using messy materials such as paint or clay?

Some skills that a trainee may need to develop will actively involve her with both children and materials. For example, an imaginative trainee can increase a child's resourceful use of ordinary materials. She can encourage a child to notice and to take advantage of the potential for artistic, sensory, language, and concept learning inherent in cooking pancakes or in play with empty cans and a pail of water, wet sand, or sponge blocks in assorted shapes.

Skill-building in practicum will depend a good deal upon the kind of supervisory feedback a trainee receives to sharpen her observations of her own behaviors and to increase her diagnostic skills with children. Competency will also relate to how the trainee gets along with other adults in the situation.

Personal Development

Role definitions for the trainee may also involve an active change in self-concept during training. The trainee whose needs are met by careful attention to the planning of practicum placement, course study, and counseling may be helped to achieve increased self-comprehension and self-actualization. In this way, according to Shane (1970), a trainee begins to find answers to questions concerning role definition, questions such as (a) "Who am I?" (self-identity); (b) "What am I doing?" (self-orientation); and (c) "Where am I going?" (self-direction). Self-awareness and, hopefully, a wholesome self-concept develop as a trainee finds the answer to the first question. Through seeking and gradually through experience in acquiring an answer to the second question, the trainee progressively "finds herself" in the process of searching for inner integrity or self-satisfaction. She also develops the skills of social interaction and the coping behavior in which self-confidence resides. If all goes well, a successful answer to all three queries leads to desirable personal-social contributions, to acceptance by others, and to consequent personal happiness.

Creation of such a supportive emotional climate, particularly for paraprofessional trainees, often requires such innovative techniques as crisis clinics, group sharing of emotional reactions, and personal counseling to increase the positive self-attitudes and functioning of the trainees in their practicum behaviors and in their own families. It is presumed that, through a personalized curriculum continuum which includes practicum, one can contruct a responsive, effective educational milieu or matrix in which the trainee can safely discover the world and her own potential. She can become a productive, self-directed individual who is fully utilizing her skills and creative abilities.

SUPERVISION AND STAFF UTILIZATION

The basic purpose of supervisory personnel is to enhance the quality of trainee performance in practicum and, ultimately, on the job. Supervisors must be accurate appraisers of trainee skill level, trainee teaching style, and improvement rate. They should also be adept at demonstrating alternative roles, styles, and skills for a trainee. Finally, they must be knowledgeable enough about the trainees they supervise to be able to identify and vary the kinds and amounts of reinforcement which will be maximally effective in shaping more competent trainee behaviors. Sometimes effective praise for a job well done can be indirect, with no names mentioned. In a group session, where trainees talk about their practicum problems, a supervisor can describe an effective way a problem was handled by one of the trainees present.

Supervisory Personnel

Sarason, Davidson, and Blatt (1962) observed that a supervisor may be a master teacher but have no special skill or training in supervision. They felt that a supervisor should focus on far more than the technical or engineering aspects of teaching: lesson plans, curriculum materials, and special projects. Additional factors that must be considered include: the need to value highly a trainee's ability to arouse curiosity, her sensitivity to the contributions of children's ideas, and her recognition of individual differences among children; the need to be a good listener, observer, and facilitator (Cross & Nagle, 1970); the ability to motivate and extend the trainee's performance and lead her to self-evaluation; the necessity of possessing effective observation and conceptualization skills (ability to focus on salient points of behavior, to conceptualize such behaviors on a continuum from less to more appropriate, and to help raise trainee performance level); and the need for flexibility, adaptability, and maturity.

The supervisor must be clear about her own role in order to function in this flexible and sensitive relationship to a trainee. Corman and Olmsted's (1965) program for elementary school teachers in practice teaching (which they call *internship*) illustrated this clearly. Supervision was carried out by "consultants" who later described the qualifications which they felt were required to succeed in the position (in addition to special technical knowledge). This description included the following:

> 1. The intern consultant must be a person able to win the intern's respect by demonstrating, in actual practice, that she is a superior teacher. . . . The more successful consultants appeared to be those who were willing to "get their hands dirty," to illustrate their suggestions by demonstrations.
> 2. The intern consultant must be a person able to win the intern's trust. This meant that she must be able not only to guard confidences but also the privacy of events that she observed in the intern's classroom and which might have reflected unfavorably on the intern had they become known.
> 3. The intern consultant must be a person flexible enough to adapt to a variety of grades, school settings, and individual personalities and be able to resist substituting her own concerns for those of her intern. The real test came in being able to shift from one intern to another in both pacing and the substance of the guidance offered. . . . The consultant, if she wished to succeed, had to be perceptive enough, first of all, to determine the kind of teacher that the intern wished to become and wise enough to help the intern achieve that goal even though it might conflict with what the consultant herself valued.
> 4. The consultant must have that level of psychological security that would make it possible for her to accept strength in the intern as well as weakness. . . . Consultants were not immune to professional jealousy and while weakness in an intern was easy to tolerate, strength was sometimes more difficult to accept. (pp. 73-74)

The supervisory role may include a wide variety of duties, such as selection, orientation, and assignment of trainees to particular practicum settings, as well as observation and evaluation of trainee performance.

Demonstrations given by a supervisor can effectively improve trainee skills. Some demonstrations, such as a classification and seriation lesson, may require rather lengthy prior preparation. Sometimes, however, classroom events offer excellent opportunities for a supervisor to carry out brief, spontaneous demonstrations. For example, one supervisor was in the preschool classroom while a three-year-old (with poor articulation and very few words in his vocabulary) was climbing the jungle gym with a trainee's help. The little boy's shoe dropped to the floor. The supervisor immediately called out "Oh, Tommy, you dropped your toy car!" The child, usually so silent, looked up at the supervisor and explained, "No car. Shoe." The supervisor had made an on-the-spot demonstration of one way to encourage language by taking advantage of chance events in a child's life.

Whether the supervisory relationship is to be structured on an individual or a small-group basis is a decision that must be considered in any training program. Some programs are flexible enough to provide both the one-to-one relationship, which some judge to be most productive to change, and the team approach in assessing trainee behaviors and in planning strategies for future trainee development. Many projects involve not only trainees and supervisors but also cooperating personnel.

Of course, practicum supervisors may not necessarily be separate personnel. Provision of separate supervisory personnel for practicum will depend on funds available, institutional constraints, practicum site locations, and the availability of on-site personnel capable of assuming supervisory functions. Where several levels of practicum are undertaken—for example, where M.A.- and Ph.D-level educational personnel are being trained simultaneously with paraprofessionals within the same setting, it may be desirable to have on-the-premises supervisory personnel at least part of the time. The complex nature of the tasks and relationships being carried on may require on-the-spot assessment, judgment, or decision-making by the responsible supervisor.

With regard to a desirable ratio of supervisors to trainees, it is instructive to examine Johnson's data (1968c) from a national survey of student teaching programs. Both the frequency of visits to the trainee in practicum and the average number of trainees assigned per supervisor varied widely across the United States. Only four percent of responding institutions indicated a full-time supervisory load as low as 1 to 5 students, whereas almost one-third reported a load of 16 to 20 students. Since the quality of the educational personnel which a program produces may depend strongly on skills acquired through practicum, it is necessary to assess critically the loads of supervisory personnel. Serious decisions—such as reduction in the number of trainees—may have to be made if financial provisions for sufficient supervisory personnel have not been included in program planning.

Recent experiments have attempted to change the structure of delivery of supervisory services to trainees. Readling and Bloom (1970), in an article on team supervision, outlined such a new conceptualization. Instead of having the college supervisor work individually with students, they proposed that she work directly with a supervising teacher who benefited from her leadership and instruction. Thus the "team" consisted of teachers, trainees, and college personnel in a newly structured relationship which the authors called "a humanistic approach to accountability."

Critique of Supervision in Practicum

What kinds of criticism have professionals and practicum students raised with regard to their supervision experiences? In their book on the preparation of teachers, Sarason et al. (1962) noted that, as a result of inadequate supervision, trainees felt a lack of opportunity to raise questions, voice disagreement, and carry out their own ideas on how to act with pupils. Sarason and his colleagues also criticized many supervisory pre-practicum observation experiences, such as lab courses or field trips, as being artificially structured. The trainee in such cases knows what she is expected to observe and think. The authors believe that such an imposed conceptual structure does not permit a trainee to profit as much as possible from the learning potentialities of such experiences. Mayer (1961) also commented sarcastically:

> teaching practice is undoubtedly valuable for all concerned: the student gets a necessary taste of blood, the supervising teacher gets a free assistant and sometimes a little money from the school of education for instructing and reporting on her ward, the children have the fun of helping or bedeviling an inexperienced young adult. . . . The student must work along whatever lines the supervising teacher has established and cannot try out her own ideas. (p. 413)

Wilhelms, in a hard-hitting critique (1970), also castigated the frequent attitude of cooperating teachers which emphasizes only the perfecting of skills but does not foster student exploration. Practicum may then turn out to be the "start of an unremitting indoctrination into the very system we are all trying to break out of" (p. 23). The trainee needs to be able to grow into the kind of professional she wants to become.

Johnson and Knaupp (1970) analyzed trainee role expectations of supervisors. They found that student teachers wanted technical assistance in planning, conducting, and evaluating their instruction, but they wanted a free hand in finding their own ways to teach. The student teachers perceived very effective university supervisory behaviors as producing a positive, supportive atmosphere and personal manner and as helping with problems of self-evaluation, interpersonal relations, and job requirements. Edmund and Hemink (1958) analyzed the responses of student teachers to questions concerning ways in which practicum supervisors had been helpful or could have been more helpful. Most highly valued were personal encouragement by supervisors and constructive suggestions and criticisms. Trainees requested more observations by and conferences with supervisors.

SETTINGS

Practicum settings, when judiciously chosen, can facilitate both trainee learning and the supervisor's task. Too often, however, the settings are not wisely chosen. Sometimes they do not correspond closely enough to the real-life job settings to which trainees will be graduating. Such an objection was raised by Schooler (1965), who surveyed the organization and administration of practicum in teacher-training institutions across the United States. He labeled as inadequate the practice, established during the first half of this century, of placing trainees for only one or two periods a day in a local school or in a laboratory school. Schooler pointed out that this pattern did not provide a natural setting for teaching; nor did it provide the opportunity for a student to understand the functioning of the total school.

A recently completed, innovative teacher-training program set detailed behavioral objectives and provided intensive supervision. Yet many graduates complained, after their first working year, that the rich, stimulating experience had not prepared them for "the real world." Small university laboratory classes with as few as six children had constituted the practicum settings. In this optimal teaching environment the students flourished; but in their current job situations they found that overcrowded classes and discipline problems prevented them from teaching as successfully as they had in practicum.

Some innovative programs in teacher training use a graduated series of settings, consecutively experienced. Trainee skills necessary for successful functioning in community institutions with educational problems are learned and improved gradually. The procedure is a little like learning to swim well in a pool before trying to cross the English Channel! Another beneficial effect of using increasingly complex settings might be to mitigate what Alex (1970) called the "student teaching blues," which can be brought on by initially traumatizing experiences in difficult settings.

A readily available, convenient local setting may not be the most effective practicum setting. Some training programs have tried to broaden the choice of environments in which practica occur. Anderson and Little (1968) described a wide variety of practica for placement of trainees who were studying to be teachers of mental retardates: local clinics, state schools, university lab schools, summer camps, private and public schools, institutions, and agencies.

Setting Variety and Cultural Differences

Some programs have broadened even further the concept of practicum setting. The future job of a trainee or an educational administrator may involve working closely with an ethnically or linguistically varied parent population. Community control (in varying degrees) of educational settings is becoming more prevalent. A trainee may need firsthand experience with the living conditions and life-styles of different cultural groups. "Field experience" may then be taken quite literally! In some programs, trainees have worked in onion fields side by side with migrant workers. They have gone into bars and laundromats to talk to people. Learning to be responsive to the needs and aspirations of culturally different, economically disadvantaged parents may be the most relevant practical training for a future educational administrator.

Practica which provide for skill acquistion or improvement cannot neglect the social, economic, and personnel realities of the settings in which trainees will ultimately function. For example, the trainee may ultimately find employment with disadvantaged preschoolers who are hyperactive. Methods adequate for conducting story-time or concept-learning sessions in middle-class, university-run nursery settings may have to be altered radically in these new settings. For instance, the use of body motions, of materials tailored to specific child interests, and of different spacing of lessons may all be necessary to adapt the concept-teaching which the trainee has learned to the particular ecological conditions.

Planning for practicum should consider a variety of settings, populations to be served, and community characteristics. This last problem is explored more thoroughly in the chapter on community involvement in training education personnel. The *Comfield* teacher education model is a competency-focused, individually adaptive, and performance-based approach. This project reaches rural and semirural disadvantaged children from three culturally distinct groups in northwest Washington: the families of American Indians, Mexican-American agricultural workers, and descendants of Caucasian settlers from Appalachia. The use of such disaparate settings promotes a potential "multiplier effect" (program effects can spread among families not only in one cultural milieu but in several) as well as the "demonstration effect" of the project's ability to improve children's learning. Bank Street College's Institute for the Preparation of Educational Leadership at one period utilized strategically chosen sites across the United States in order to provide trainees with varied regional and subcultural practica settings.

Some urban childhood programs are able to provide practica in diversified settings within a large city school system. Trainees are placed in varied city schools, particularly those with a large population of disadvantaged children, for individualized practica. In recent years there have been increases in year-round Head Start centers, day-care facilities, prekindergarten experimental classes, and Follow-Through classrooms. These facilities, as well as traditional public and private schools, provide a wider selection of education settings than was previously available.

Creative City Settings

Urban areas with high population densities can also stimulate the creative use of uncharacteristic practicum settings, such as storefront academies. Another such innovative setting is the "contact laboratory" associated with the Teachers College model for preparing "teacher-innovators." This "contact laboratory" was set up so that trainees, after an initial apprenticeship in a normal public school setting, could offer educational and remedial programs to the children of the neighborhood. Thus, teaching candidates both served the neighborhood and satisfied their own needs for a setting where experimental teaching could be the norm. Additionally, research designs could be carried out to test the efficacy of these experimental teaching strategies (Joyce, 1969).

Despite the invigorating effects which practicum experiences across cultural or socioeconomic milieus can provide for trainees, the university-based laboratory school should not be underestimated as a potentially rewarding and important practicum setting. For example, "Project Change" at the State University of New York College at Cortland recently proposed to use the university laboratory school (which can be flexibly altered in structure) to carry out a planned variation in the number of grade levels present per classroom. Grade levels and grade mixes are to be experimentally varied to assess optimal setting conditions for practice teaching.

Setting Changes: Pros and Cons

If multiple opportunities for practica are offered to or required of trainees, the question of "switch or stay" arises with respect to a particular institution or locale. Even though no change in the level of difficulty (to be encountered in the next practicum) has been planned, project staff may still want to switch a trainee to another setting rather than have her continue at the same site.

The dilemma often inherent in this decision arises because of a potential conflict between the objectives for the trainees and those for the community adults and children whom the trainee serves. If the broadest possible trainee experience in practicum is an objective, redundancy of setting should be avoided. Trainees should be exposed to the greatest possible variety of settings. Planned sequential variation of practicum setting can result in maximizing content areas learned, exposure to different cultural and linguistic communities, and role repertoires. The trainee with the most diverse practicum experiences should be in a stronger position to function in a superior fashion in whatever educational setting she is employed.

On the other hand, decisions have been made to continue Teacher Corps teams on the same practicum site for two years, the rationale being that the trainees are more likely to become vital community participants. In addition, parents in poor communities may object to allowing their educational center or school to undergo frequent staff changes because of a training program's "arbitrary" decisions. Parents and professionals have pointed out that the education of children in public school systems suffers because of frequent professional staff turnover. In their home lives, low-income children may already experience inconsistent discipline and frequent changes of care-giver and dwelling place. Thus they may have a particularly strong need for sustained and consistent relationships with adults in educational settings. Continuous use of a given site for additional practicum may furnish the environmental and interpersonal stability and growth of trust necessary for a child's educational and personal growth.

Staying at the same site affords a trainee the chance to "follow up" the learning career of a particular child. She may need a long period of working in a community in order to understand more profoundly such problems as poverty and bilingualism in terms of a child's educational struggles and an institution's possible insensitivity to the dimensions of these struggles. Sometimes, therefore, the desire to increase the opportunities for a trainee to experience other settings may yield to such considerations or to staff cognizance of community needs.

ASSESSMENT OF PRACTICUM

Assessment of the effectiveness of the practicum experience may be formal or informal, but it is vital to the intelligent use and refinement of practicum as a teaching tool. The guiding principle of this process is to help the learner and to increase her ability to identify her own strengths and needs in order to plan for her further development (Troyer, 1947).

The focus of practicum assessment may not be on trainee competence alone. Worthy of investigation are other variables that may be closely related to practicum processes or outcomes. Such variables include the methods and quality of practicum supervision; trainee motivation, attitudes, and self-concept; and educational or developmental gains made by the children in the practicum setting.

Rating scales, case reports, final grades, personality inventories, and a host of other instruments have been used to assess practicum effects. A supervisor may simply prefer to observe and tally the frequency and conditions of incidence of selected trainee behaviors during the course of the practicum. The trainee's competency profile should then provide quick feedback on the success of the practicum procedures at different time points.

Tintera (1961) attempted to discover the effectiveness of various methods of practicum supervision, including conventional supervisor observation and case conference; supervisor observation supplemented by three voice tape recordings which were used in conference; and supervisor observation with three kinescopes of trainee performance. Measures were taken immediately after practicum and six months later. It was found that during the practicum period no particular advantages accrued to the student teacher who used either of the recording devices to assist in self-analysis of her teaching. Therefore, the supplementing of supervision with recording media may not in itself insure training improvement in practicum.

Some program directors are particularly interested in personality measures, e.g., change in self-concept, as the trainee gains skills and assurance in practicum (Ginn, 1969; Walberg et al., 1968). Borg et al. (1970) used videotape feedback and microteaching methods for predicting success in practicum. They found a positive correlation between high ratings received by a student teacher and her scores on the Tennessee Self-Concept Scale. Yee (1967) found personality correlates of practicum success, measured in terms of practicum grades, among student-teachers. About one-third of student-teachers who were "cognitively oriented" (i.e., who said they preferred suprevisory help in learning and working to be better teachers) received C and D grades. "Affectively-oriented" trainees (who preferred supervisory support, sympathy, and warmth) received almost exclusively A and B grades. Thus, evaluation of practicum can illuminate the mechanisms and course not only of trainee development but of supervisory behaviors and effectiveness. In the above example, assessment of the supervision process suggested that factors other than trainee competence were possibly influencing supervisory ratings. Perhaps supervisors should be as alert to their own personality needs as to those of a trainee! Assessment may be focused on the ultimate consumer—the child— in most teacher-training programs. Measures of children's competencies may be fairly considered to reflect in some ways the effectiveness of trainee behaviors with these children (Bussis & Chittenden, 1970). Connors and Eisenberg (1966) reported the results of a six-week summer Head Start program in Baltimore: teachers who were rated positively on warmth in their teaching manner and in fostering intellectual growth had children who showed the greatest gains in intelligence as measured on the Peabody Picture Vocabulary Test.

The results of ongoing assessments should be a critical dimension in making decisions to change program variables. Supervisory tactics may have to be revised. The degree or number of competencies required of a particular trainee during a given time span may need to be modified. Additional components, such as films, role-playing, or private counseling, may need to be added to the trainee's program to hasten progress in certain areas. Cooper, Thomson, and Baer (1970) reported that when teacher behavior during practicum in preschool classrooms was observed and reviewed, teachers became more attentive to appropriate child responses. This effect was highly desirable since teacher attention was being used, in accordance with reinforcement theory, to improve and increase the frequency of desirable child behaviors. Thus, determination of practicum effects can serve as feedback in the training cycle and produce the acceleration of trainee development in specific competencies.

FAILURE IN PRACTICUM?

"Failure to thrive" in practicum may be discovered by the assessment personnel of a project or acutely realized by the trainee herself. In infancy, the "failure to thrive" syndrome usually results in the marshaling of available community health resources to identify and correct the problem involved. In the training program similar concern should be aroused.

Formal course work competence and practicum performance may not be highly correlated for a given trainee. Cooper (1969) analyzed the skills required of the teacher trainee in terms of competencies in subject matter, presentation, and professional decision-making. Realizing the necesstiy for practice in facing situations requiring such decisions, Cooper identified activities which allow for this practice: classroom simulation experiences which require teachers to face, to study, and to solve problems similar to those they will have in the classroom; microteaching and observational experiences—both live and videotaped; small group work; and practicum. One possible solution to practicum failures, therefore, would be to try assorted combinations of the above-recommended activities.

One of the authors once supervised an advanced M.A. student in a practicum which consisted of individually tutoring disadvantaged preschoolers. The student, with supervisory assistance, was to prepare and then carry out lessons, uniquely tailored for each youngster, in sensori-motor tasks, concept learning, and language development. She began each lesson as planned, but would yield helplessly and instantly if a child began to disorganize with the materials or use them aimlessly or repetitively. The student, who was terrified of a possible negative confrontation with a young child, profited from the kinds of activities suggested by Cooper. When she observed effective models, she particularly seemed to gain confidence. She began to set limits to a young child's behavior after she watched live and filmed teacher models who used behavior control techniques promptly and effectively, and yet were able to sustain a child happily at challenging activities and tasks. Supervisory encouragement for these efforts was generous and given initially for small successes in maintaining control of the tutorial situation.

Repeating Practicum

Provision for recycling a trainee through practicum experience when this might be necessary should be built into a program. Analyzing skill deficiencies and applying corrective procedures before recycling will increase the chance for success.

Some of the reasons for failure of an initial practicum experience have been detailed by Kaltsounis and Nelson (1968): "Practically every aspect of the teacher education program has been criticized by various groups and attacked as a causal factor in poor teaching. But . . . no one has seriously questioned the effectiveness of student teaching" (p. 277). They criticized student teaching on the grounds that not enough teaching models may be tried out; since few students fail practicum, trainees therefore do not put forth the requisite efforts; the educational system produces conformity so that the teacher supervision staff are also docile.

The first objection—that not enough teaching models may have been tried out—can be overcome by programmatic provision for planned variation in role-modeling by trainees in practica. Simulation techniques and exposure to institutional settings where such role model variants are observable can serve to acquaint the trainee with a variety of role models.

The second objection may be met if practicum failure is made a real possibility in a program. Antidotes to such failure have been mentioned, including the option of practicum repetition—in the same or in an alternative setting. If a competency-based training model is followed, it should then be possible to "fail" practicum, with provision for additional experiences, review of the trainee's goals and decisions for modification of his program objectives, or exit from the program.

It is more difficult to counteract educational system "conformity." Of course, pressures for conformity do not always come exclusively from within an educational system. Some parent and community groups may also react negatively to creative innovations by educational personnel trainees. Those on the training program staff have an obligation to initiate and maintain contacts with practicum sites or localities such as to assure the receptivity of these settings to creative trainee work. If such an atmosphere cannot be established, other settings should be explored.

Post-practicum Failure

The serious problem remains, of course, that success in a nurturant, accepting setting may not predict success in a conformist, overregimented, or even racist educational setting in which the trainee may find employment. One program which trains student teachers uses an experimental public school for the practicum setting. This school prides itself on promoting the "discovery" method of learning among the children and on receptivity to creative teaching. The decision of an administrator to train educational personnel only in such a school may invite failure not in practicum, but afterward, in other schools. Provision for diversified practica has already been suggested as one answer to problems of potential post-practicum failure.

FOLLOW-UPS OF PRACTICUM

The relationship of practicum experience to subsequent opportunities for job placement should be assessed. Too little attention has been paid, for example, to the ethical problems involved in recruiting and training both paraprofessionals and professionals without sufficiently attending to actual job opportunities available locally or regionally.

Changes in employment opportunities should shift and broaden institutional concerns so that practica can be provided at every level of child development. Future career responsibilities and roles may not always correspond to present educational job profiles. With the recent upsurge of interest in and the creation of new day-care centers for infants, trainees whose practicum dealt only with older preschoolers or elementary-school-age youngsters, may feel ill-prepared to assume care-giving or supervisory roles in infant centers. Follow-up data can help a program director keep attuned to and cope with such discrepancies.

Annual follow-up inquiries of the job skills and roles required of subsequently employed trainees can pinpoint both the adequacies and flaws in the existing practicum experience and give intelligent direction to modifying it. For example, such information can be used to fill in the training methods continuum from foundational techniques (learning and theorizing about phenomena through indirect experience, such as course work) to instrumental techniques (learning through direct experience, as in practicum) (Schueler & Lesser, 1967).

Feedback from former trainees can also help program directors break down some of the barriers between practicum and other course work or training methods. Beggs (1969) urged that "through a careful blending of campus and field experiences, the line that divides theory from practicum should be erased as nearly as possible" (p. 108). As has been noted, follow-up information on trainees can give valuable aid to program efforts to increase the effectiveness of the practicum and to coordinate it more closely with other training methods.

SUMMARY

Supervised practical experiences, offered as an integral and important component in the training of educational personnel, were examined. A distinction was made between practicum and internship, with the former term reserved for a method used earlier in a training program to build trainee skills within a practical setting. Depending on the depth and length of the experience and on the prior competence demanded of a trainee, practice teaching could be located at various points along the practicum-internship continuum. The historical importance of practicum as a training tool and current practices in its use were surveyed.

Major elements were identified for consideration in making decisions relative to the planning, carrying out, and assessment of practicum. Emphasis was placed on the need to specify objectives at every stage of this decision-making process and to adopt a competency-based curricular model for practicum. Different kinds of practica and training conditions could then be offered on an individualized basis to trainees who differed in educational and skill levels and in role expectations.

The facilitative effect of planned variation in practicum settings provided for a trainee was recognized. Traines could in this manner become acquainted with and understand the living and learning styles and the needs of different ethnic and linguistic groups. This attitude toward providing varied practice was contrasted with another viewpoint which emphasized the positive social impact of long-term trainee involvement in a single practicum setting on trainee-community relationships and functioning.

The particular effectiveness of practicum in training paraprofessionals as classroom aides or infant teachers was discussed. Also raised was the ethical issue of training students, whether professional or paraprofesional, for whom no community jobs may exist.

Abundant, high-quality supervision was found to be critically important to the success of practicum. Analysis of the supervisory role indicated the following as components of good supervision, apart from technical know-how: the need to value highly a trainee's ability to arouse curiosity, her sensitivity to the contributions of children's ideas, and her recognition of individual differences among children; the need to be a good listener, observer, and facilitator; the ability to motivate and extend the trainee's performance, and lead her to self-evaluation; the necessity of possessing effective observation and conceptualization skills; and the need for flexibility, adaptability, and maturity.

The issue of practicum failure was raised. In case of failure, provision for the recycling of a trainee through practicum can be made in conjunction with other remedial efforts after a diagnosis of the deficit functioning has been made.

Important outcomes of a follow-up process were presented: program modifications to enhance the trainee's development at many levels; determination of the relationship of practicum experience to current job opportunities; intelligent program alterations for more effectiveness in preparing trainees for subsequent job responsibilities; and establishment of a closer and more coordinated relationship between practicum and other curricular methods.

NOTES

1. For a fuller discussion of the implications of theory for pedagogical practice, see chapter 2.

2. On the other hand, a program director may decide that poor performance in practicum indicates that it is placed too early in the training program. He may decide to defer practicum in the curriculum sequence until a more adequate informational base has been acquired through other curricular methods in order to insure greater probability of success in practicum.

3. A good example, one that has implications for practicum, is provided by Bushnell's (1970) summary of the characteristics of objectives for improving curriculum: Objectives should be stated in operational terms; describe what is to be done and how it is to be done and at what level of acceptable per-

formance; be internally consistent; be consistent with what is intended by objectives; be comprehensive; provide for individual differences; allow for the unexpected to occur; provide cognizance of constraints and resources; and be obtainable by the ambitious in order to be challenging.

REFERENCES

Alex, R. H. How to prevent the student teaching blues. *Journal of Health, Education, and Recreation,* 1970, *41,* 93-95.

Anderson, R. M., & Little, H. A. A practicum oriented teacher education program. *Education and the Training of the Mentally Retarded,* 1968, *3*(2), 75-79.

Beggs, W. K. *The education of teachers.* New York: The Center for Applied Research in Education, 1969.

Borg, W. R., Kallenbach, W., Morris, G., & Friebel, A. Videotape feedback and microteaching methods for predicting success in practicum. *Journal of Teacher Education,* 1970, *21*(3), 357-361.

Bowman, G. W., & Klopf, G. J. *New careers and roles in the American school.* New York: Bank Street College of Education, 1968.

Burden, J. L., & Lanzillotti, K. (Eds.). *A reader's guide to the comprehensive models for preparing elementary teachers.* Washington, D.C.: Eric Clearinghouse on Teacher Education and American Association of Colleges for Teacher Education, 1969.

Bushnell, D. S. A suggested guide for developing a systems approach to curriculum improvement. *Education,* 1970, *90,* 351-362.

Bussis, A. M., & Chittenden, E. A. Analysis of an approach to open education. Interim Report PR-70-13. Princeton, N.J.: Educational Testing Service, 1970.

Butler, A. L. *Current research in early childhood education: A compilation and analysis for program planners.* Washington, D.C.: National Education Association Center, 1970.

Combs, A. W., & Snygg, D. *Individual behavior: A perceptual approach to behavior.* New York: Harper & Row, 1959.

Conant, J. B. *The education of American teachers.* New York: McGraw-Hill, 1963.

Conners, K., & Eisenberg, L. The effect of teacher behavior on intelligence in Operation Head Start children. Baltimore, Md.: Johns Hopkins School of Medicine, 1966.

Cooper, J. M. A guide to a model elementary teacher program. In S. L. Burdin & K. Lanzillotti (Eds.), *A reader's guide to the comprehensive models for preparing elementary teachers.* Washington, D.C.: Eric Clearinghouse on Teacher Education and American Association of Colleges for Teacher Education, 1969.

Cooper, M. L., Thomson, C. L., & Baer, D. M. The experimental modification of teacher-attending behavior. *Journal of Applied Behavior Analysis,* 1970, *3*(2), 153-157.

Corman, B. R., & Olmsted, A. G. *The internship in the preparation of elementary school teachers: A description and analysis of a program.* College of Education, Michigan State University, 1964.

Cross, J. S., & Nagle, J. M. Supervisory strategy for helping teachers improve students' thinking skills. *Peabody Journal,* 1970, *47,* 208-215.

Delp, H. A. An internship method for training special class teachers. *Exceptional Children,* 1968, *35*(2), 161-162.

Edmund, N. R., & Hemink, L. Ways in which supervisors help student teachers. *Educational Research Bulletin,* 1958, *37*(3), 57-60.

Fouracre, M. H. Student teaching in the professional preparation of the teacher of the mentally retarded. *Education and the Training of the Mentally Retarded,* 1966, *1*(3), 145-149.

Gardner, H., & Henry, M. A. Designing effective internships in teacher education. *Journal of Teacher Education,* 1968, *19,* 177-186.

Ginn, R. J. A Q sort study of the effect of a counseling practicum on the self-concept of a selected group of counselors in preparation at the University of Houston. *Dissertation Abstracts International,* 1969, *30,* 582-583.

Henry, M. Experimental program in summer student teaching. *Contemporary Education,* 1970, *42,* 28-30.

Honig, A. S., & Lally, J. R. *Infant caregiving: A design for training,* New York, Media Projects, Inc., 1972.

Johnson, J. A. *A brief history of student teaching.* De Kalb, Ill.: Creative Educational Materials, 1968a.

————. *Innovations in student teaching.* Multi-State Teacher Education Project Monograph IV, Washington, D.C.: Office of Education, U.S. Dept. of Health, Education, and Welfare, 1968b.

————. *A national survey of student teaching programs.* Multi-State Teacher Education Project, Monograph II, Washington, D.C.: Office of Education, U.S. Dept. of Health, Education, and Welfare, 1968c.

Johnson, W. D., & Knaupp, J. E. Trainee role expectations of the microteaching supervisor. *Journal of Teacher Education,* 1970, *21,* 396-401.

Joyce, B. R. A guide to the teacher-innovator: A program to prepare teachers. In S. L. Burdin & K. Lanzillotti (Eds.), *A reader's guide to the comprehensive models for preparing elementary teachers.* Washington, D.C.: Eric Clearinghouse on Teacher Education and American Association of Colleges for Teacher Education, 1969.

Kaltsounis, T., & Nelson, J. L. The mythology of student teaching. *Journal of Teacher Education,* 1968, *19,* 277-281.

Katz, L. G. Teaching in preschools: Roles and goals. *Children,* 1970, *17*(2), 42-48.

Katz, L. G., & Weir, M. K. Help for teachers in preschools: A proposal. Urbana, Ill.: Eric Clearinghouse on Early Childhood Education, University of Illinois, 1969.

Lally, J. R., Honig, A. S., & Caldwell, B. M. Training paraprofessionals for work with infants and toddlers. *Young Children,* 1973, *28*(3), 173-182.

Lazar, I., & Brown, S. To work with infants: A manual for trainers. Unpublished manuscript prepared for R. K. Parker, Director of Child Development, Day Care Resources Project, New York, N.Y., 1971.

Mayer, M. *The Schools.* New York: Harper Brothers, 1961.

Mitchell, M. M. A graduate level practicum: A practical model. *Education and the Training of the Mentally Retarded,* 1969, *4*(1), 17-19.

Readling, J. J., & Bloom, M. S. Team supervision: A humanistic approach to accountability. *Journal of Teacher Education,* 1970, *21,* 366-371.

Sarason, S. B., Davidson, K. S., & Blatt, B. *The preparation of teachers. An unstudied problem in education.* New York: John Wiley, 1962.

Schooler, V. E. A survey of the organization and administration of student teaching in selected teacher education institutions. *Bulletin of the School of Education.* Indiana University, 1965, *41*(6).

Schorling, R. *Student teaching: An experience program.* New York: McGraw-Hill, 1940.

Schueler, H., & Lesser, G. S. *Teacher education and the new media.* Washington, D.C.: American Association of Colleges for Teacher Education, 1967.

Shane, H. A curriculum continuum: Possible trends in the 70's. *Phi Delta Kappan,* 1970, *51,* 389-392.

Shaplin, J. T., & Powell, A. G. A comparison of internship programs. *The Journal of Teacher Education,* 1964, *15,* 175-183.

Smokoski, F. J. Teacher education: A change in emphasis. *Education and the Training of the Mentally Retarded,* 1969, *4*(2), 89-92.

Spodek, B. Constructing a model for a teacher education program in early childhood education. *Contemporary Education,* 1969, *40,* 145-149.

Stiles, L. J., Barr, A. S., Douglass, H. R., & Mills, H. H. *Teacher education in the United States.* New York: Ronald Press, 1960.

Tintera, J. B. Student teaching: Analysis of methods in which application of new communications media may improve teacher preparation in language, science, and mathematics. Research report, Wayne State University, Title VII Project Number 008-E, U.S. Department of Health, Education, and Welfare, 1961.

Troyer, M. E. *Evaluation in student teaching.* Syracuse, N.Y.: Syracuse University Press, 1947.

Walberg, H. J., Metzner, S., Todd, R., & Henry, P. M. Effects of tutoring and practice teaching on self-concept and attitudes in education students. *Journal of Teacher Education,* 1968, *19,* 283-291.

Whitelaw, J. B. The potentialities of the paid teaching internship. Report of six regional seminars, 1965, Washington, D.C., U.S. Department of Health, Education, and Welfare, Office of Education, Government Printing Office.

Wilhelms, F. T. Eleventh Charles W. Hunt Lecture: Realignments for teacher education. In E. D. Hemsing (Ed.), *Realignments for teacher education. Yearbook 1970.* Washington, D.C.: American Association of Colleges for Teacher Education, 1970.

Woellner, E. H., & Wood, M. A. *Requirements for certification* (36th ed.) Chicago: University of Chicago Press, 1971.

Yee, A. H. The student teaching triad: The relationship of attitudes among student teachers, college supervisors, and cooperating teachers. Research Report, 1967, University of Texas, Contract OE-6-10-309, U.S. Dept. of Health, Education, and Welfare, Office of Education.

PART III

EVALUATION, MEASUREMENT, AND DISSEMINATION

The four presentations which follow represent complementary views of a subject that has assumed an ever more prominent place in educational programs. They might be read as one views light through a prism. Inherent in each is the idea that the quality of any program may be and should be observed and measured quantitatively in order to test its efficiency and judge it fully. Each author deals with different facets of this common belief.

Goodwin presents the case for systematic evaluation as against the uninformed, undisciplined variety that furnishes data for judgments without clear evidence. He outlines several frameworks in which evaluation can take place.

Jones proposes a particular methodology through which educational concepts and goals can be made operational—an especially necessary but difficult process—and thereby more amenable to evaluation.

Evans outlines current measurement practices in early childhood education and offers a wealth of techniques and practices from which to choose, suggesting criteria to allow discriminating choices.

Peters, while pointing out the need to disseminate valuable program information, urges educators to be objective and responsible in publicizing their findings so as to insure that the resulting theories and policies will serve rather than hurt the interests of society.

More often than not, our society tends to judge the quality of life in terms of products, and to measure them in quantitative terms.

In the case of young children, the quality of a smile is difficult to measure even though we sense that it has great meaning. The motor skill of running is easier to record. Because we still lack adequate technology to assess the smile, should we limit ourselves to measuring the ability to run, and then claim for ourselves the ability to judge one educational program more effective than another?

One major purpose of evaluative systems and procedures is to assist a program toward perfection. Ideally, such evaluation is initiated and carried out by program personnel with professional guidance as needed. Another purpose is to make difficult decisions about the allocation of resources; hopefully, this can be implemented in a fair and responsible way.

Given our desire to test our programs through measuring everything undertaken, we must search for ways to represent the smile along with the running feet, and offer imaginative evaluative designs to help staff improve their guidance of the young child.

Chapter 8

Evaluation in
Early Childhood Education

WILLIAM L. GOODWIN

Several aspects of evaluation of programs in early childhood education considered in this chapter [1] are applicable both to programs for children and to programs preparing personnel to work with children. This is accomplished by presenting three major components: extended discussion of the pros and cons of evaluation; consideration of the distinctions between formative and summative evaluation with examples; and a unit containing brief sketches of evaluation models currently available for educational programs. Examples used throughout the chapter tend to be from preschool or early childhood settings.

THE CASE FOR EVALUATING:
OBJECTIONS OVERRULED

What is meant by evaluation? Evaluation is a systematic process by which judgments are made about the relative desirability, adequacy, effectiveness, or worth of something, often according to a definite criterion or standard, for specified purposes. Since evaluation is a process, it applies, in theory, equally well to any activity, program, or product, or to whatever is to be described and judged. Hopefully, judgments will be data-based, for the most part. The providing of a descriptive data base often, but not always, brings measurement into the evaluative process as a functional subcomponent. Measuring techniques, instruments, and procedures are given extensive coverage in a following chapter. The focus here is on the evaluation of early childhood programs—instructional programs for children as well as training programs for adults. Because of the extensiveness of the evaluation area, only selected topics are covered here. The interested reader is directed to the April 1970 issue of the *Review of*

Educational Research and to Worthen and Sanders (1973) for a more comprehensive review of the field.

This chapter begins by considering the case for not evaluating, in the form of commonly raised objections to evaluation. The assumption is that many of our readers belong, spiritually at least, to the club titled ONOE (pronounced "Oh, no!" and meaning the Organization for No Organized Evaluation). Why these readers belong is easy to understand, for most of us find ourselves members on one occasion or the other—e.g., when our employer's evaluation of us does not coincide with our own conceptions of self-worth or when students in our classes anonymously evaluate the dynamics of the college course we have instructed. (Curiously, students as a group seem to be very perceptive in their analyses of our colleagues, but are woefully off-target when they evaluate our own pedagogical efforts.)

Is evaluation a four-letter word? One might think so in reflecting upon the skeptical or even negative reception that evaluation reports often receive, or upon the lack of adherence to systematic evaluation plans in most areas of human activity. The role played by evaluation on projects or programs seems, in a sense, analogous to the treatment of mathematics in some elementary school classrooms: some teachers readily agree that mathematics is important, but schedule it as the last event of the day, as if hoping that circumstances will prevent its occurrence on many occasions. Likewise, evaluation is often endorsed enthusiastically throughout the life of many programs, but serious planning for evaluation is always second in priority or just over the horizon. In some cases, attention given to evaluation never exceeds the momentary frenzy in which the evaluation section of the initial proposal seeking funds was written.

The perceptive reader, noting that this chapter is entitled "Evaluation in Early Childhood Education" rather than "The Folly of Evaluation in Early Childhood," has undoubtedly already discerned how the plot will unfold. The author believes strongly in the sense (and cents) of evaluating, and hopes that you will increasingly believe likewise. At the same time, cognizance is given to the numerous, and to some extent persuasive, arguments against evaluation. We shall begin by giving them a hearing. Below are listed a series of objections that serve as explanations for this stubborn attitude toward evaluation; these are followed by pertinent counterpositions. Some objections listed might not be stated explicitly by opponents of evaluation as their personal reasons for not evaluating; they are nevertheless considered here because implicit objections for not evaluating might be as important as those explicitly stated.

Objection 1: Evaluation is too costly, in terms of both resources and time.

This objection to the worth of evaluation goes something like this: "We don't have enough money or time to run our program now the way we'd like. Yet you suggest that we take portions of these two extremely limited resources and place them into some complex evaluation that will probably only tell us what we already know. We're too busy to evaluate now; we'll evaluate when the program is over or at least when it's further along. And even if we could get our hands on more money, we wouldn't sink it into a complicated evaluation but would put it toward our program in ways that it would be immediately useful."

In essence, then, this first objection to evaluation is that the project can afford neither the funds nor the personnel to evaluate; it further implies that the typical evaluation is not worthwhile enough to justify its cost in time and money. The gist of the argument against this position is the premise that any project or organization hoping for some moderate degree of longevity can ill afford not to evaluate. In addition, it should be noted that immense variability is possible in the cost and complexity of evaluative activities.

Evaluation need not be costly in terms of either money or time. Costs will probably be markedly less than the savings effected (usually in terms of program efficiency) as a result of the evaluation. This is particularly true when the evaluation is planned *before* the program commences and focuses on the appraisal of program objectives. This before-the-fact cost reduction—or efficiency improvement, if you prefer—is well exemplified in an evaluation strategy preferred by a well-known evaluator.[2] Titled "cheapy competitor," this strategy involves the evaluator's playing the "devil's advocate" against his employing client by thinking up a program or product which *a priori* appears to have as high a probability of achieving the same objectives as the client's program or product and at less than half the cost. The classic example of a "cheapy competitor" occurred when a consumer research organization found that a solution of Tide was more effective for cleaning rugs than any of the foam-type rug cleaners being tested, and the Tide solution cost only one-tenth as much.

The considerable frequency with which evaluators can come up with feasible cheapy competitors, judged by experts to have good success probabilities, suggests that the strategy be used more often. (However, it could be noted in passing that the evaluator who uses only such a strategy might eventually reduce program costs to the point where the project was too small, financially, to hire an evaluator.) Generally, evaluation can result in substantial resource savings; the interested reader will want to pursue further the accountability references in the last section of this chapter.

Evaluation need not be complex. Some evaluations are, true enough, very complex. The Head Start and Follow Through evaluations (described in the next section) being conducted by Stanford Research Institute (SRI) are quite complex (and costly too, for that matter). The evaluations of Sesame Street and the Head Start Longitudinal Study conducted by Educational Testing Service (ETS) (also described later) are complex. Yet complexity is not a requirement; it is probable that the majority of evaluations are not complex.

As an example of a very simple evaluation, consider one conducted to determine the effectiveness with which students learned from hearing audiotapes played while they were aboard a school bus (Goodwin & Sanders, 1971). Via an innovative program in a rural mountainous district, five cartridge tape recorders and individual audio headsets were installed on a school bus. This system made it possible for each pupil to select any one of the five programs he considered appropriate in light of his needs and interests. During the development of the system, several questions were raised and answered via evaluative techniques. The question that was particularly germane to this evaluative study was whether listening to tapes aboard a bus would result in more or less learning by elementary school pupils than hearing the same tapes in the classroom.

Accordingly, a formative evaluation (see definition below) was designed and subsequently conducted in a single morning. Third- and fourth-grade pupils (N = 114) in one school, stratified on the basis of ability (I.Q.), grade, and sex, were randomly assigned to three groups. All three groups underwent their prescribed treatments simultaneously. Students in Group 1 were placed in the school bus and "taken for a ride," so to speak. A 20-minute taped presentation about Arizona was played during the trip. Students then returned to their regular classrooms. Students in Group 2 were placed in a classroom where they heard a copy of the same tape played to the Group 1 students. At the end of the 20-minute presentation, they returned to their regular classrooms. Group 3 students heard no taped materials and merely remained in their classrooms, working on materials which their teachers had scheduled for that day, or took their usual recess period. After all the students had returned to their regular classrooms, a 20-item factual knowledge test was given to pupils in all three groups at both grade levels. Tests were administered by the classroom teachers, but were scored by the experimenters.

Analysis of the data gathered in this evaluation indicated that the two groups hearing the tapes significantly outperformed the controls (p < .01), but did not perform significantly differently from each other. This example illustrates how quickly evaluation activities can be conducted, and that elements of the evaluation design need not be complex. This short experiment did not represent the entire evaluation design, but it did provide the information necessary to judge rationally certain aspects of the audio-bus program. Further studies of a similar nature were conducted to provide replications and to control for novelty.

Objection 2: Evaluation is unfair and stifling to the fledgling program just beginning.

This reason for not evaluating is often forthcoming when evaluation is suggested as important for a new program that has just been initiated. Program staff who resist evaluation at this point normally cite one or both of two bases for their feelings. First, they may indicate that it is unfair to expect a new program (as it disrupts the status quo and has growing pains) to compare favorably to other programs of long standing, particularly if only output or program outcomes are evaluated. Second, they may note that early evaluation could straitjacket a program. It could tunnel staff interest inordinately toward "good" performance on certain outcome measures, and dull staff to opportunities for intentional and serendipitous redirection of the program into more creative channels. The latter area of concern—that evaluation would suppress program creativeness and stifle creative redirection of the program—was of particular concern to directors of Title III, Elementary and Secondary Education Act (ESEA), innovative programs in the mid- and late 1960s (Miller, 1967, pp. 38-44).

This second objection to evaluation is genuine and often sincerely held; but it, too, is subject to much qualification and to counterarguments. First, it is debatable whether it is fair to compare a new program with an established one, a question possibly, but not certainly, answered by examination of the context of a particular proposed evaluation. For just as the program of longer standing has established procedures and tradition working in its favor, the new program typically has the novelty effect facilitating its efforts. The novelty effect in a given situation might be greater than or less than, or even counterbalanced with, the disruption effect brought about by the new program procedures (Bracht & Glass, 1968). Thus, it is an oversimplification to suggest that a new program not be evaluated because it is not yet on its feet or reaching its full potential.

It should be noted in passing that there is understandable concern that evaluations be so structured as to reduce the probability of unfair comparisons and undue influence of early returns upon program procedures. The potential influence of early returns has been documented in laboratory studies by Rosenthal (1966). Early returns in those investigations refer to the performance of, and outcomes from, the initial group of subjects who went through the experimental tasks. Experimenters may be unduly influenced by these early returns, even to the point that the new expectations thus formed have a definite influence upon subsequent results. It is likely that early evaluation returns in nonlaboratory studies also have effects. One noteworthy example of concern over this issue arose when national election results on the East Coast of the United States were announced over network media before the polls were closed in the West. A more recent example involved the early release of the Westinghouse Learning Corporation-Ohio University National Evaluation of the Head Start report, auspiciously, because of political pressure. The release occurred before the scientific community had ample opportunity to examine the methodology used and to suggest alternative explanations of the data (Smith & Bissell, 1970; White, 1969). Partly because of these reasons, certain current nationwide evaluations of a summative nature (see the section "Formative and Summative Evaluation" below for a definition of summative evaluations) are under a moratorium that prevents the release of results, and evaluation staffs have been quite careful about the release of data thus far collected.

In a general sense, the influence of early returns might cause Program B to make extensive changes in order to improve its outcomes relative to Program A. The possibility exists that an unaltered Program B might have been more effective in the long run. Once large alterations are made in B, massive confusion and disruption could result, as there seldom is time for training sessions or other preparatory activities; this disruption could further damage B's position on outcome measures. On the other hand, the alterations might permit Program B to become more effective than A. In any event, a summative evaluation should not change the programs it evaluates through and during the very process of evaluating them. One approach is to use designs that have established sheltered implementation or warm-up periods before a program is evaluated.

Another counterargument to the second objection to evaluation involves the realization that evaluation serves more roles than merely determining the overall worth or making fund/no fund decisions. The evaluation plan may be process-oriented rather than outcome-oriented, and therefore be entirely appropriate for the new programs. In the audio-bus evaluation described above, for example, emphasis was clearly on internal program improvement, sometimes referred to as formative evaluation. The roles of evaluation can be conceived as much broader than fund/no fund or go/no go decisions, or comparisons trying to determine which of several programs is most effective. This general topic is discussed more fully in a later section of this chapter.

Related to this counterargument is the clear implication that evaluation designs can be flexible and innovative themselves. Eisner (1967, p. 272) pointed out the need for innovative evaluation strategies. This point is only mentioned here and is developed more fully in response to several of the other objections to evaluation. Note, too, that evaluation studies can be designed to avoid any direct intervention in program activities (e.g., by evaluating objectives or by using only subtle measures for data collection).

Objection 3: Evaluation is inappropriate because it involves testing young children.

Objections 3, 4, and 5 center on the inappropriateness of evaluation because of presumed weaknesses in evaluation methodology. Concern over testing of preschoolers and children in the early grades reflects an implicit assumption that the experience is to some extent deleterious to the child. While this assumption has not been verified, neither has the counter-assumption that testing is not harmful. It is normally stipulated that many existing measuring instruments do not function ideally when used repeatedly with the same children over brief time periods. Likewise, relatively low reliability when testing young children can occur, particularly if careful attention is not paid to motivation, pacing, alertness, etc.

To counter the argument that young children should not be tested is not really the task of evaluation proponents. Young children can be tested, and are tested, and results therefrom serve as data and observations upon which evaluative judgments can be made. In the absence of evidence that testing is potentially harmful or traumatic, the evaluator seems under no special obligation to establish that it is harmless. It is appropriate, however, to note the widespread concern over how test results are used, rather than concern over the testing itself. If test data serve the purpose of creating low teacher expectations for some pupils, or if the data are misunderstood or misapplied, this is indeed unfortunate. Evaluators, and all others collecting test data, do have obligations to indicate precisely how the data will be used and to take all necessary precautions to prevent misuse or misinterpretation that would be detrimental to children.

Additionally, it should be noted that evaluation need not imply testing. Evaluation designs can be so structured that no testing is involved or extensive use is made of subtle, nonreactive measures. Another procedure is to limit the testing required of any one child to a moderate amount at most. The National Assessment of Educational Progress, for example, uses procedures that limit the number of items to which each student responds (Tyler, 1966); emphasis is on evaluating the national educational posture rather than on measuring children. This is accomplished by, first, sampling a considerable number of students to take part and, second, giving each student only a sample of the items designed for his age level in only one subject-matter area. Four age levels and 10 subject matter areas are involved in all. Thus, flexible approaches to evaluation should be able to counter, or at least balance, the concern about testing young children. This concern is elaborated in the measurement chapter.

Objection 4: Evaluation is inappropriate because it involves measuring instruments that are inappropriate.

Concern over the appropriateness of available measuring instruments is often mentioned as a methodological objection to evaluating. Instruments are challenged for being low-level, superficial, or limited in validity. An extensive case can be built against certain instruments (such as intelligence tests) because they are apparently biased against certain cultures and minority groups. Some attention is given to this issue in the measurement chapter; readers are also directed to a pertinent discussion in Cronbach (1970, chap. 9). Although it is easy to recognize the cultural-bias problem with measurement instruments, the question of how to alleviate or solve the problem is far from resolved. Not to test at all, the "solution" advocated by some, is an extreme position which cripples the beneficial outcomes that careful evaluation can provide.

Agreement exists, for the most part, that measures in the cognitive domain are best developed and less open to misinterpretation, and those in the affective domain least well developed. Further, some programs have charted as their major objectives pupil behaviors in both the cognitive and affective domains that are measured neither well nor easily. A brief digression to describe more fully one such program, nurtured by the Educational Development Center (EDC), seems in order at this juncture.

The basic elements of the Open Education Follow Through Project sponsored by EDC are difficult to describe in the present language of evaluation and measurement. The observations below are based on a report completed by staff from Educational Testing Service (ETS) (Bussis & Chittenden, 1970), and on a personal interview with the present director of EDC and two of his staff.[3] The program operates in kindergarten through grade three. For those readers familiar with several early education models, it can be noted that the EDC paradigm lies somewhere in the vicinity of the British Infant School and the Bank Street model (particularly the former), yet certainly it is not identical to either of them. EDC does not claim to have a model as such, but emphasizes a "plan for continuing growth" in both students and teachers. ETS coined the phrase "nonmodel" to describe EDC's efforts.

The nonmodel approach goes far beyond semantic puzzles. EDC does not publish specific guidelines for initiating its program at a Follow Through site. It does not judge or rank its sites on how well each is doing; rather, the effort is to nurture each site so that it can become as open as local personnel can support. The training of teachers or paraprofessionals for EDC classrooms is an open and unspecified process, and therefore hard to generalize to other potential trainers, for fixed teacher behaviors are considered of less importance than adults developing their own potential within a supportive classroom environment. EDC does not list prescriptions for learning deficits or recipes for learning; nor does it endorse lists of behavioral or performance objectives. Its approach seems to be more consonant with expressive objectives as defined by Eisner (1969), i.e., objectives that describe educational encounters or situations or tasks in which children are to engage, but do not specify what is to be learned from the encounters. Thus, emphasis seems to be placed more on transactions and experiences than on outcomes. (The importance of measuring and evaluating processes/transactions is well stated by Rosenshine, 1970; Sjogren, 1970; Stake, 1967.)

Another key element in understanding the EDC position is that the classrooms they hope to foster must manifest a climate which supports the development of the child and is conducive to the child's assuming initiative. The climate should also be supportive of teacher development and conducive to teacher initiative. Figure 8.1, adapted from Bussis and Chittenden (1970), displays this characteristic succinctly.

Teacher's Contributions

		LOW	HIGH
	HIGH	laissez-faire	open education
Child's Contributions	LOW	by-the-book: programmed instruction	traditional British

FIGURE 8.1

Teacher's and child's contributions to decisions regarding content and processes of learning.

The open education classroom desired by EDC is one which is both child- and teacher-centered; a classroom oriented toward open education is seen more as a process than as a goal. All EDC Follow Through classrooms do not fall in the upper right-hand quadrant, but movement by programs at EDC sites toward that quadrant would be considered desirable.

The brief presentation above of EDC's nonmodel is hardly comprehensive, and the interested reader is directed to the complete ETS report. Nevertheless, it has been presented in enough detail to suggest that unusual problems in evaluation and measurement are encountered. To the extent that the national evaluation of Follow Through conducted by Stanford Research Institute (described more fully below) focuses on outcome measures only (as it now predominantly does), EDC considers it inappropriate. The observational techniques used by SRI are fairly complex and are costly in terms of training and employing competent observers; less costly observational methods could be used, but reliability might be reduced. Even here, however, although the observational schedule focuses on process and transactions, EDC feels that the instrument is too teacher-behavior-oriented and not enough child-behavior-oriented. Interactions between the staffs of EDC and SRI have resulted in the addition of some categories to the observation schedule that are more consonant with the EDC viewpoint.

What behaviors of children do EDC staff believe to be important? They would include such things as initiative and self-direction (e.g., assuming responsibility for proper classroom behavior even when the teacher is out of the room); resourcefulness (e.g., solving problems that come up in the "real" world of the classroom rather than contrived problems in test situations, or having positive affect toward the solubility of problems); growth of problem-solving and problem-finding abilities; social development (e.g., teaching of one child by another, taking interest in other children's work, and empathy); improvement of self-image (e.g., willingness to take risks and undertaking to effect change in the classroom); positive task-oriented behaviors and attitudes (e.g., curiosity, perseverance, reflectiveness, and flexibility); language functioning (e.g., having a "real" conversation with visiting adults, using sentence structures that are diverse and complex, or utilizing information gained by asking questions); creativity and expressiveness (e.g., through spoken and written language, music, art, and dramatics); etc. For the most part, developers of measurement and evaluation techniques have not concentrated upon most of these dimensions.

The staff of EDC would like to see appropriate measures developed in the above areas. They feel that currently available standardized instruments are measuring behaviors that are often of minimal importance. They prefer measures that would concentrate on aspects of a child's growth which, from their point of view, are directed toward long-range outcomes of schooling—almost life measures, in a sense. (The general problem of an inappropriate match between program objectives and evaluation instruments is discussed by Kamii & Elliott, 1971; Minuchin, Biber, Shapiro & Zimiles, 1969; and Stephens, 1967.)

The best counterargument to the EDC position of lamenting the inappropriateness of current measuring instruments would seem to be agreeing with them—that is to say, *for their purposes,* the measures are not appropriate. In a sense, however, it is not necessary to construe the EDC position as antimeasurement and certainly not as anti-evaluation. EDC has never interfered with any of SRI's testing of children in Follow Through; rather, EDC has functioned to raise several important questions pertinent to SRI's evaluation. In general, their position is a protest against the particular types of measuring instruments currently being used to evaluate their program. These instruments do not tap the critical behaviors that

EDC staff hope will develop in children over time if the latter are given the appropriate experiences and encounters in school. Further, it is felt that many measuring instruments used in the current Follow Through evaluation are used because of their availability more than for any other reason. In other words, EDC staff do not seem to be against evaluation per se, but are against evaluation in terms of A, B, and C when it appears that A, B, and C were selected because they are the most easily measured behaviors. There can be real dangers of the measurement flea irritating the evaluation tail, and of the evaluation tail, in turn, wagging the program dog.

Nevertheless, the spirit and importance of evaluation are little diminished in all the foregoing; rather, the importance of developing numerous measuring instruments valid for specific purposes is highlighted.

In spite of measurement problems and unique programs, society at large cannot exempt programs from the responsibility of evaluating their effectiveness on reaching outcomes valued by the society. Any program in early childhood that accepts funding from federal or other sources can assuredly expect tests on outcome variables that are important to the financial supporters of the program (e.g., language development, knowledge of the alphabet, arithmetic skills, etc.). The position that instruments need to be developed to assess subtle program outcomes is certainly legitimate. Further, an excellent case can be made for evaluating agencies to be sensitive to local concerns and to community or local input when designing evaluations. In a word, evaluation at times should be "responsive" to the personnel and program being evaluated.

Objection 5: Evaluation is inappropriate when it involves the denial of services to control students.

Further elaboration of the inappropriateness of evaluation centers on the assumed impropriety of using control students in evaluation designs. Control students do not receive the special program, but are measured to determine program effects. The apparent assumption here is that the treatment or program being evaluated is good; therefore, children not involved in the program are being denied something from which they would benefit. Since the mid-1960s, local agencies have been required to evaluate annually their Head Start and Title I, ESEA, programs for the "disadvantaged." Only rarely have control groups been used in any of these evaluations, evidently because program directors feel compelled to involve all eligible children in the program. Note the reasoning implied in the following statements: (a) a definitive evaluation requires the use of control students who are in all ways similar to the program students; (b) since all eligible students are involved in the program, there are none available as appropriate controls; (c) the unavailability of controls makes definitive evaluation impossible; and (d) it is therefore impossible to evaluate. If one subscribes to this reasoning, then the case for not evaluating rests on limitations or constraints of evaluation within a given context. This does not, however, constitute a valid denial of the need for evaluation.

There seems to be little disagreement that the "true experimental design," in the Campbell-Stanley sense (1963), yields the most defensible cause and effect claims see (also Taba, 1966). Evaluators should be continuously striving to achieve design control through the use of control students whenever feasible and possible. This is not to suggest, however, that failure to achieve such control abrogates the need for evaluation; program evaluation should be conducted as rigorously as possible.

Several related points need to be made. First, the assumption that a treatment or program is "good" or "effective" (at least relatively more effective than no program at all, or more effective than the traditionally maligned "traditional program") is just that: an assumption. The ethics of introducing innovative educational programs into the schools require expectations that such programs will be effective. Nevertheless, the program introduced will likely have both unintended and unpredicted effects, and some of these effects may be deleterious. Still, there usually appears to be little glory in being in the control group, seemingly doomed to less learning or more cavities. The point is worth noting, though, that the context within which experimental groups find themselves in an evaluation must be examined. For example, as Walter Reed initiated his yellow fever studies, he undoubtedly was eminently more successful at locating control subjects; very few persons would have been itching to become experimental subjects.

A second related point, in part a counterargument to the contention that use of controls is undesirable, is that it is often possible to design a comparative evaluation in which all students are involved in one of several new programs, each believed to be beneficial. This design frequently may involve the random assignment of students to the various programs to achieve initial equivalency of groups (for a discussion of the merits of random assignment, see Campbell & Stanley, 1963). Then the different programs are compared on the same outcome measures. When an innovative program is instituted, often it is because new objectives have been established or because of dissatisfaction with the existing program. To continue some students in the traditional program, that is, to use it as one of the programs compared, may make little sense. In such a situation, two or more new programs might be instituted and evaluated, using a comparative design. Note also that the comparative experiment would permit the inclusion in the same study of a new "favorite," innovative program and a "cheapy competitor" that appears to have merit. This competition of the favorite with an inexpensive alternative often adds perspective to the actual merit of the favorite and increases the meaningfulness of the comparison.

When the traditional program is not included in the comparative experiment, all students are involved in some "new" program, circumventing what can be a sticky procedural problem for evaluators and administrators. Still, the traditional program often is one of the programs compared. This has the benefit of providing a known entity (i.e., the old program) for increasing the meaning of the comparison and of the generalizations made. In the comparative evaluation design, whether or not the traditional program is included, causal statements frequently can be made with greater assurance when one random group is included as a control receiving no program.

Although comparative evaluations have predominantly resulted in findings of no significant differences between programs on outcome measures, Scriven (1967) astutely points out that "no differences" should not imply "no knowledge." After all, knowledge has been gained that the programs are not differentially effective on selected outcome measures.

A third counterargument to this fifth objection to evaluation involves economic reality: new programs often lack sufficient resources to include all eligible participants. In such a case, it becomes appropriate for the program managers to follow a "deferred-treatment" policy (a term which has been used for some time in psychotherapy outcome studies instead of using "control group"). The deferred-treatment group does not receive the treatment, but is measured and used as a comparison group. As more resources become available, or as a second wave of program participants is initiated at some future time, the implication is that it will then be possible for many of those initially in the deferred-treatment group to receive the treatment and become active program participants.

A deferred treatment evaluation design recently was proposed by the author for use in the evaluation of an experimental preschool program in New Mexico. Except for several preschool programs for minority and disadvantaged children, New Mexico has until now had no statewide system of perschool education. In 1971 the state legislature provided funds to initiate 28 preschools on an experimental basis. Table 8.1 was suggested as an implementation design for certain of the 28 sites.

In this design, Groups 3, 4, and 5 are deferred-treatment groups. Group 1 receives a full year of preschool; Group 2 receives first semester only; Group 3 receives second semester only; and Group 4 receives only the summer preschool. Only Group 5 is a control group in the traditional sense—that is, it receives no time in preschool. If this was not feasible in New Mexico, the design would still be appropriate after excluding Group 5 and initially randomly assigning all available children to Groups 1 through 4.

A great number of meaningful comparisons are available. For example, the impact of one semester of preschool experience on relatively young children can be determined by comparing O_2 for Groups 1 and 2 with O_2 for Groups 3, 4, and 5. For relatively old children, the effect of a semes-

TABLE 8.1

New Mexico Preschool Implementation Design

	Sept. 1971	First Semester 1971	Jan. 1972	Second Semester 1972	May 1972	Summer 1972	Aug. 1972
Group 1:	R O_1	X_1	O_2	X_2	O_3	X_3	O_4
Group 2:	R O_1	X_1	O_2		O_3		O_4
Group 3:	R O_1		O_2	X_2	O_3		O_4
Group 4:	R O_1		O_2		O_3	X_3	O_4
Group 5:	R O_1		O_2		O_3		O_4

Where R = Random assignment to each of the five groups.
O = Observations or measurements.
X = Preschool experience.

ter of preschool experience results from a comparison of O_3 for Group 3 with O_3 for Groups 4 and 5. Twelve months' experience in preschool can be compared with a summer's preschool experience (O_4 for Group 1 and O_4 for Group 4) or with no preschool exposure at all (O_4 for Group 1 with O_4 for Group 5). The effects of early versus late preschool experience can be deduced by comparing the performance of Groups 2 and 3 at O_3 or of Groups 2, 3, and 4 at O_4. Many other comparisons are possible.

Comparisons of the above type can be made more meaningful if student aptitude level has been built into the design. By having students who are representatives of high, medium, and low intelligence in each of the five main groups, it is possible to determine whether any of the treatments is differentially effective for the three ability groups. For example, it might be that Treatment X_1 is more effective for low-ability students than Treatment X_3, while high-ability students respond better to X_3 than X_1. This design would allow examination of interactions between treatments and intellectual aptitude levels.

If the program directors or evaluators become concerned over the apparent excessive testing of youngsters, alternative procedures are apparent. The initial pretest, O_1, might be omitted, if random assignment was made and if it was expected that most children would perform at about the same level on the pretest. Another alternative would be to test a random portion of each group at each of the observation points rather than testing all children at all points.

Generally, then, in countering objection 5 (and to some extent also objections 2, 3, and 4), the flexibility of evaluation is emphasized. This flexibility applies to the time devoted to evaluation and to the instruments and designs used. Referring to the need for flexibility in the length of time that an evaluation takes, Stake [4] has suggested that evaluation results must be available much sooner than is currently the case. He feels that no evaluation of a social program should run more than a year before its major findings are in. Stake cites the tendency for evaluations typically to take too long, whether the evaluation runs for four years or is a crash two-week effort. He suggests that there is a Parkinson's law for evaluators: "No matter how short the evaluation period, the critical decisions will be made before the evaluation results are available." Thus, flexible time limits for evaluations, as well as timely reporting of results, are needed. Time problems often are caused by inefficient coding and processing of data once they are collected; advance attention given this potential bottleneck can speed the determination of results.

Flexibility in the instruments used has been alluded to in the discussion related to EDC's attitude toward the current Follow Through evaluation. The need for flexibility here is greater than the degree of flexibility possible, given our present arsenal of measurement instruments and techniques. Chapter 10 provides the reader with a good representation of the variety of instruments currently available. Much time-consuming instrument development remains to be done, particularly in affective areas.

Another promising approach is searching for and utilizing unobtrusive measures (Webb, Campbell, Schwartz & Sechrest, 1966). Unobtrusive measures are those that do not intrude upon or alter the event or person being measured. They are nonreactive measures; the person is not aware that his behavior is being observed. Examples would include examining archives data; measuring fear during a ghost story session by recording the shrinking diameter of a circle of seated children; discerning interest in Christmas by distortions in the size of children's drawing of Santa Claus; and determining preference for male offspring by ascertaining the male-female ratio of the last child born in families estimated to be complete.

Flexibility in the actual design of the evaluation also serves to attenuate several objections to evaluation. The use of control groups and deferred treatment groups has been suggested. Comparative evaluations offer another feasible approach, certainly more feasible at the present time (in the author's opinion) than is inferred by Kamii and Elliott (1971). Evaluation is a process and a very flexible one; waiting to evaluate in early childhood until all the subcomponents in the evaluation process are well developed would be foolish. Much usable and important data can be generated utilizing less-than-perfect measurement techniques and less-than-optimal statements of program objectives.

Not treated exhaustively here is the role that descriptive studies might play in the evaluation process. Description would seem to be most important in documenting the transactions that actually do take place. Accurate recording of what transpires (whether the observational scheme involves video recorders, tape recorders, human recorders, daily logs filled out by teachers, or other methods) constitutes critical data when attempting to relate outcomes to transactions that occurred.

In addition to controlled evaluation studies, comparative evaluations, and descriptive evaluations, flexibility in evaluation is possible through a number of innovative or adaptive approaches to evaluation design. Several sources are available for the interested reader (Campbell, 1969; Light & Smith, 1970; Stake & Denny, 1969). The effectiveness of using randomized experiments in actual evaluations related to important societal issues has been well documented (Reicken, Boruch, Campbell, Caplan, Glennan, Rees & Williams, 1974).

Objection 6: Evaluation is unnecessary because it is possible to "sense" when a program is effective.

This objection to evaluation suggests confidence in intuition about program success or failure. In contemporary slang, it's the "gut-level" feeling, the undivided certainty as to program effectiveness.

Curiously, this confidence and certainty in one's perceptual skills and one's emotional anatomy are often unshakable. Recently the author was serving as an outside independent evaluator of performance contracts between a commercial organization and several school districts. The contractor was guaranteeing reading gains of one year or more (on standardized reading comprehension tests) in junior high school pupils. For those students not experiencing a gain of one year or more, no payment would be made by the school districts. The design favored by the outside evaluator involved the use of deferred-treatment groups and extensive identification procedures to identify all eligible students and test them prior to assignment to program conditions. These events clearly were going to take considerable time and would delay the start of the program by 10 days. The spokesman for one school district insisted that the program commence immediately; he was certain that his past experiences would enable him to determine at the end of the year precisely how effective the program had been. He saw no need for deferred-treatment students, no need to control for possible sources of invalidity such as history, maturation, or the effect of repeated testing. His faith in his own gut-level evaluative system was virtually complete. The design preferred by the outside evaluator was implemented, but with considerable misgivings on the part of the official described (and of others, too, for that matter). It was as if the official went through the motions of evaluation when forced to, but he still placed more trust in his gut-level feelings.

Challenging this reason for not evaluating is probably easier than challenging any of the five objections discussed above. There is very little evidence for any consistent accuracy resulting from gut-level evaluation. Even predictive statements suggesting probable program outcomes are often notoriously unreliable if the program is subjected to a systematic, thorough evaluation. This is not to deny the existence of gut-level feelings about the worth of a program. Rather, it is suggested that evaluation involves both complete observation and thorough judgment. When exposed to solid, impartially gathered data, gut-level feelings can at times gain specificity and assist in unraveling the likely causes of program effects.

Objection 7: Evaluation is unnecessary because all evaluations are whitewashes.

This objection to evaluation is currently popular. Evaluation is viewed as a certain whitewash, always causing the program in question to appear in a positive light. Thus, the process becomes little more than frosting on the program cake, window-dressing for the program that has everything. Campbell (1969) sarcastically provides excellent advice for trapped administrators who must conduct an evaluation but cannot allow a program to appear as a failure. For example, he cites grateful testimonials from those who have been in the program as one of the most dependable ways of assuring a favorable evaluation. Also, he indicates that a positive outcome normally will result if the administrator confounds selection and treatment by insuring that the subjects chosen for the experimental group are more able and more likely to profit from the program.

A rebuttal is easily stated. Persons believing that evaluation inevitably results in program exoneration or praise are either naive or unaware of the facts. Not all evaluations are whitewashes; significant numbers have been unfavorable and some have been conflicting.

Evaluations can turn out to be whitewashes, but evaluation as a process should not be condemned because of this possibility. That there are political and ethical problems unavoidably intertwined with many evaluations is conceded, but many procedures are available to solve these technical problems. Some safeguard techniques that increase "honesty" of data collection and reporting and reduce the likelihood of biases contaminating evaluation are the use of more than one independent evaluator, implementing single-blind testing conditions, etc. Under single-blind testing conditions, the person doing the observing or testing does not know whether the subject has been in the experimental or control groups. Refusing to believe in evaluation because the outcome is always a whitewash is a position that is not easily defended.

Objection 8: Evaluation is inappropriate because it is inappropriate to compare programs having different goals.

This is a standard objection to evaluation. Program A has different goals from Program B. The argument is made that it does not make sense to compare their outcomes. After all, since the programs have different goals, how is it possible to evaluate them on a single set of criteria?

The answer to this objection is that it is legitimate to compare programs that do not have identical goals, and these comparisons are meaningful. In fact, such programs should be compared in three areas: on those goals specific to Program A; on those goals specific to Program B; and on those goals common to both A and B. For example, Program A's goals may be to improve math performance in systems of numeration, identities, long division, and set theory. Goals for Program B may be to improve math performance in the Venn diagrams, correspondences, long division, and set theory. Programs A and B can be compared, using measures in the areas of systems of numeration, identities, Venn diagrams, correspondences, long division, and set theory. One would expect Program A students to perform better on numeration and identities, and Program B students to do better on Venn diagrams and correspondences; these assumptions need to be verified. Achievement on A's and B's common goals, long divisions and set theory, can also be compared.

The programs can legitimately be compared, also, on goals desired by other potential consumers; program personnel may not even be aware of these goals. For example, a program may have the expressed goal of improving children's language functioning, while another agency might consider adoption because it believes that the program will increase children's achievement motivation. Further, it can also be noted that it is appropriate to evaluate directly the goals of Programs A and B (Scriven, 1967; Stake, 1970; Worthen & Sanders, 1973).

Objection 9: Evaluation is inappropriate because it does not explain why a program is effective.

This objection questions the depth of evaluation. An evaluation typically might conclude that Program A is moderately effective. In a comparative evaluation, the result might be that Program B is more effective than Program C. In neither case is it explained why A is moderately effective, or why Program B showed up better on outcome measures than Program C. The argument often continues that it is not possible to improve programs generally when reasons for more effective performance are not known.

A counterposition is not completely appropriate in this case, for it is true that evaluations normally do not answer the "why" question. Evaluations do not provide explanations, in most cases. The purpose of an evaluation is not to explain; its purpose is to determine worth. Via evaluation, information necessary to make rational judgments is collected. It is not likely that an evaluation will pick up explanations, for it is not directed toward producing explanations. Procedures other than evaluation must be initiated to determine why a program may be meritorious in a particular respect, or why certain outcomes were not achieved. Nevertheless, evaluation itself is a significant undertaking.

Objection 10: Evaluation is unnecessary because it makes little difference; little is changed by it.

This objection to evaluation quite possibly is more difficult to respond to than any of the preceding. The problem of providing prompt evaluation results has been discussed; often results do not become available until after critical decisions have already been faced and made. Additionally it is apparent that, at times, evaluation results are used selectively, responding to data that support one position and ignoring, defying, or repressing other data. Further, it would be hard to discern programs employing full-time evaluators as significantly more effective because of that fact than programs that are not evaluating to any marked extent. The same is true of school districts; those few which have established evaluation sections do not appear to have distinguished themselves, as a group, from districts without evaluation sections.

Possible immediate responses to this charge tend to seem somewhat trivial. Obviously, one should make sure that evaluation results are available on a timely basis. Refusal to use sound and complete evaluative data reflects a lack of good sense rather than a lack in the worth of evaluation. It is equally true that school districts employing many counselors do not distinguish themselves as a group from those employing a few counselors, and that programs having curriculum planning and developing staff sections do not leap to a salient position better than programs without planning and developing staff sections. But these points seem somewhat defensive and apologetic in nature.

A more solid rationale for evaluation might be forthcoming if we questioned whether or not evaluation has been systematically applied. Has evaluation been given a chance? Have resources budgeted for evaluation been 10 to 15 percent of program costs, particularly when programs are being initiated? Research and development costs in education have been a pittance compared to those costs in the automotive and drug industries. Have personnel with assigned evaluation responsibilities been competent evaluators? If not, were extensive provisions made for such training in evaluation? Have administrative personnel high in the organizational structure supported a systematic evaluation of organizational procedures and products (or, conversely, have they strongly suggested to internal evaluators the essential nature of the "results" that will be reached by the elevators)? It would seem that, in many cases, evaluation has not had a fair chance to influence anything or to demonstrate the benefits that can accrue from systematic evaluative efforts. It seems that educators have not looked to evaluation to provide the information necessary for rational decisions at the many choice points in personnel training programs and early childhood classrooms.

Apart from the above 10 objections, another reason, normally implicit, probably plays a role in programs that fail to evaluate and may underlie many of the explicit reasons stated. Essentially, there seems to be considerable anxiety over being evaluated, or having one's program evaluated. Evaluation may be experienced as a threat which triggers anxiety and avoidance symptoms (Phi Delta Kappa Commission on Evaluation, 1970). Anxiety to some degree and in some form is likely to accompany most evaluative efforts of any worth.

The necessity to budget adequately for evaluation has been noted.

It is important, too, that a program director approach a personal level of evaluation sophistication that will preclude being "conned" in evaluation. Program directors should develop competencies in judging the expertise of consultants, assigning appropriate amounts for evaluative services and assessing the quality of reports received from evaluators. Reports should clearly reflect the audience for whom the evaluation is intended; formats of evaluation reports should vary widely, depending on the constituencies for whom the reports are intended (Patterson, 1971).

The author feels that the case for evaluating is very strong. The recent popularity of the term *accountability* (discussed briefly at the end of this chapter) suggests that, despite the inertia of the educational establishment, there will be more demands to demonstrate the worth and value of most educational programs. Clearly, evaluation will have a large role to play. Program directors may be called upon to identify indicators of program effectiveness, analogous to the school effectiveness indicators discussed by Dyer (1970). The author believes that the challenge to evaluation will be healthy and that effective evaluation will have to be flexible evaluation. The necessity of breadth and flexibility in evaluation is illustrated by the following discussion of the distinction between formative and summative evaluation.

FORMATIVE AND SUMMATIVE EVALUATION

Several conceptual schemes bear more or less directly on distinctions between evaluative and research activities in education. Two schemes particularly relevant to formative and summative evaluation are discussed briefly below: decision- and conclusion-oriented inquiry; and elucidatory and evaluative inquiry.

In 1969 the Committee on Educational Research of the National Academy of Education released a report in which decision-oriented and conclusion-oriented inquiry were distinguished (Cronbach & Suppes, 1969). This distinction removed emphasis from the motivations of the investigators and the topics studied, and placed it on the conditions under which a study took place. Thus, in a decision-oriented study, the investigator primarily seeks information desired by a decision-maker. Freedom for the investigator to wander from the task or to fail to make target deadline dates is very limited. A conclusion-oriented study, on the other hand, has as its purpose to conceptualize or understand a phenomenon of the investigator's choosing. In this situation, the investigator ordinarily has more freedom to reframe questions as he proceeds and to set his own deadline dates. Decision-oriented research is clearly "applied" in the traditional sense, while conclusion-oriented studies might be either "basic" or "applied" (in the customary usage of those terms). Both types of inquiry, ideally, are equally disciplined and equally rigorous.

More recently, Glass (1971) has proposed a distinction between elucidatory and evaluative inquiry. Elucidatory inquiry is characterized by undertaking to satisfy curiosity and reach conclusions; seeking subsurface explanations, principles, scientific truth, and whys; having autonomy during inquiry; and probably studying generalizable phenomena. Evaluative inquiry, in contrast, is characterized by undertaking to solve (or to help solve) a practical problem and to reach decisions; seeking procedural descriptions of operations and social utility; having little autonomy during inquiry; and studying specific phenomena. In some respects, then, elucidatory inquiry seems to constitute research, and evaluative inquiry seems to constitute evaluation. Glass notes that each type of inquiry uses similar, rigorous investigative techniques, and concludes with the opinion that evaluative inquiry and educational development seem to hold more potential for improving education in the 1970s than does elucidatory inquiry.

Somewhat earlier than the schemes described above, the terms *formative* and *summative evaluation* were suggested by Scriven (1967) as having important implications for education. Although this initial exposure to the field was quite limited, the popularity and use of the terms have expanded markedly over the past few years. Cronbach and Suppes's decision-oriented inquiry and Glass's evaluative inquiry relate directly to, and in a sense include, both formative and summative evaluation. While summative evaluation (relative to formative evaluation) could be assumed to be closer to both conclusion-oriented and elucidatory inquiry, it approximates neither of them.

The clue to Scriven's use of these terms lies in the meaning of the terms themselves. Formative evaluation is directed toward ongoing activities or products currently being made, evaluating their merit, and feeding data back into the cycle to reform the activities or product. In effect, judgments are repeatedly being made about a product or activity as it is being formed or developed.

Summative evaluation relates more to a judgment of the overall worth of an activity or product, normally at an end or critical decision point. Obviously, it often takes the form of a comparative evaluation. Recalling the previously cited, audio-bus study, it is clearly an example of a comparative evaluation used in the formative sense. However, comparative evaluations seems less often used in formative evaluation activities. (In the opinion of the author, this situation is unfortunate.) These and other distinctions between formative and summative evaluation are highlighted in Table 8.2.

Some oversimplifications are presented in the table. For example, it is normally thought that summative evaluation will be performed by someone external to the program being evaluated. It is typically felt that

TABLE 8.2

Characteristics of Formative and Summative Evaluation

Characteristic	Formative Evaluation	Summative Evaluation
Primary purpose	Developmental improvement of activity or product	Determination of overall worth of activity or product
When used	Continually; provides feedback into developmental cycle	Normally at end of activity or in relation to finished product; or at go/no go, fund/no fund decision point
Investigative style	Rigorous, systematic, diagnostic	Rigorous, systematic, comparative
Personnel normally used	Internal staff or internal program evaluators	External personnel used as evaluators
Users of information collected	Program staff, developers, insiders	Market consumers, funding agencies, outsiders

pressures would be considerable on a person from the project who is placed in a summative evaluative role. If a summative evaluation is conducted by a person participating in the program, risks would always be present of either being biased in favor of the product or program, or overcompensating for such biases and underestimating the product or program. Nonetheless, instances do occur when internal summative evaluators are commissioned to conduct an evaluation. They are subject to cruel and unusual pressures—from employers, colleagues, and other program staff—and are liable to be known by such terms of endearment as "hatchet men," "turncoats," "double agents," and "executive officers."

Also, while the table implies that the formative evaluator is a person indigenous to the project, he could on occasion come from outside the parent organization or program. This is particularly likely to occur (a) when internal procedures for producing corrective evaluative feedback apparently break down and the decision is made to bring in a trouble-shooter; (b) when an organization or program initiates activities along a new line of endeavor quite unfamiliar to them; or (c) when the program staff is too small to have an evaluator. The more common practice, however, remains that of having the formative evaluator on staff, on payroll, and responsible for providing timely data to answer questions of immediate concern and to steer activities or product development in promising directions.

Use of Formative Evaluation by Program Director/Manager

Formative evaluation holds great potential payoff for the program itself, and this seems its primary justification for being. This is particularly true if directors approach evaluation as a flexible process and if they increasingly recognize comparative evaluation designs as having a legitimate role to play in formative evaluation. Without in any sense trying to be definitive, the listing in Table 8.3 suggests a few ideas in the formative paradigm. They should be of interest to directors of training programs for early childhood education personnel and of early childhood educational programs. The table is suggestive; individual directors/evaluators will want to add additional formative evaluation activities that fit their local concerns and program.

Again it should be emphasized that the table is neither prescriptive nor exhaustive; the context of each program will determine the characteristics of the specific formative evaluation techniques employed. The techniques used should be selected because they offer the greatest potential for answering questions that bear on decisions chosen by the director as matters of highest priority. The setting of objectives and priorities for areas to be examined via formative evaluation is of great importance, for there are always more questions than can be answered (Stake, 1970). Note also that formative evaluation techniques need not address the question of external validity or generalizability; of primary concern is answering a local question or providing information bearing on a local decision. Applying formative evaluation results to other settings or programs is normally of minimal concern and a risky process.

TABLE 8.3

Suggested Formative Evaluation Procedures

Area of formative evaluation concern	Suggestions for formative evaluation of programs training personnel to work in early childhood settings	Suggestions for formative evaluation of early childhood education programs
Goals/ objectives of program	1. Use of outside expert to review (with the program director) the program goals, objectives, and intended outcomes	1. Use of outside expert to evaluate formatively the early childhood education program by reviewing the value of program goals and objectives with program personnel and examining program content and procedures to determine degree of relationship to objectives and intended outcomes
	2. Determine whether objectives are stated so that progress toward them can be measured; ascertain appropriateness of instruments (both obtrusive and unobtrusive) for measuring progress toward objectives	2. Determine whether objectives are stated so that progress toward them can be measured; ascertain appropriateness of instruments (both obtrusive and unobtrusive) for measuring progress toward objectives
Client recruitment for program; program publicity assessment	1. Use debriefing techniques with all potential trainees to determine how they learned of the program (i.e., to learn which advertisement of the program was most effective); later, break down trainees into selected and unselected categories	1. Use debriefing techniques or questionnaire with parents of children enrolling to determine how they learned of the program (e.g., advertisements, personal testimony of former clients, etc.) and why they selected it over available alternative programs
	2. Vary recruitment techniques systematically in randomly selected subsections of the total area served; use newspaper ads in one locality, radio spot announcements in another, posters in community centers and grocery stores in another, mailed bro-	2. Vary recruitment techniques systematically in randomly selected subsections of the total area served; record numbers of children responding from each subsection in terms of number, quality, and eventual degree of success in the program

Area of formative evaluation concern	Suggestions for formative evaluation of programs training personnel to work in early childhood settings	Suggestions for formative evaluation of early childhood education programs
	chures in another and use all techniques in one locality; record response from each subsection in terms of number, quality, and eventual degree of success in the training program	
Instructional content/instructional methods of program	1. Initiate "follow-in" activities by which trainees categorized by source of recruitment, age, sex, mental ability, personality characteristics, etc., are compared as groups in terms of degree of success in the training program	1. Initiate "follow-in" activities by which children, categorized by source of recruitment, age, sex, mental ability, developmental level, ethnic group, personality characteristics, etc., are compared as groups in terms of success in the educational program
	2. Based in part on findings in 1, vary instructional methods systematically with different trainees and different categories of trainees to determine effectiveness of each method	2. Based in part on findings in 1, vary instructional methods systematically with different children and different categories of children to determine effectiveness of each method
	3. If training is established as a part-time activity or one involving the possibility of extensive reading/preparation at home, randomly assign trainees to receive maximum homework between sessions, moderate homework, or no homework at all; determine effect on performance in class and on criterion tests or performance criteria; in like manner, determine what type of homework assignments (e.g., material to read, written exercises, special TV shows,	3. Systematically observe children's preferences for materials of different types; determine relationships between these preferences and (a) children's preferred reinforcers, and (b) outcome measure performance by children

Table 8.3—Continued

Area of formative evaluation concern	Suggestions for formative evaluation of programs training personnel to work in early childhood settings	Suggestions for formative evaluation of early childhood education programs
Instructional content/instructional methods of program —Continued	etc.) are most effective in terms of subsequent trainee performance in class or on other criteria	
	4. Compare relative effects (on trainee performance) and efficiency of site visits (to early childhood center, daycare site, etc.) with having personnel from site come to the central training facility to work with trainees (this is done by randomly assigning some trainees to site visit while other trainees hear about the site without visiting)	4. Observe proportions of class time that are characterized by teacher-talk and teacher-initiation as distinguished from child-talk and child-initiation
	5. Determine trainee level of awareness of program objectives; possibly indoctrinate one random group of trainees with a saturation effort on the objectives and purposes of the program; determine effect on trainee class performance, test performance, etc.	5. Vary characteristics of the materials (e.g., number of prompts) and observe groups using the materials; note and record differences in completion time, compare performance of groups on outcome measures, etc.
	6. Establish an in-house group of trainees, elected/ selected by the trainees themselves, that serves as a collector of trainee complaints and bouquets about the merit of specific program content and training techniques; encourage group to meet monthly to provide (anonymous) feedback on training to director and instructional staff; reply to all trainees,	6. Record unobtrusively span of attention of children during different activities and different instructional techniques; analyze to suggest which techniques and activities have greater amounts of "holding power"; match more difficult content with activities and techniques having more holding power

Area of formative evaluation concern	Suggestions for formative evaluation of programs training personnel to work in early childhood settings	Suggestions for formative evaluation of early childhood education programs
	through the medium of this group, on matters of principal concern (this might be called the *omsbudsgroup*)	
	7. Set performance (behavioral) objectives for trainees; periodically observe, measure, or record (via video- or audiotape, or written means) and discuss with trainee degree of progress toward objectives	7. Vary systematically types and amounts of reinforcement used with different categories of children; record and analyze results to determine most effective procedures
	8. Provide periodic opportunities for trainees to evaluate anonymously quality of instruction they are receiving, as well as an opportunity to evaluate all other features of the instructional program	8. Set performance (behavioral) objectives for children; periodically observe, measure, or record (via video- or audiotape, or written means) to determine progress toward objectives, appropriateness of revising and reformulating objectives, etc. (these behavioral objectives obviously can focus on a wide range of behaviors, such as adequate performance on content measure, self-reliance, proclivity to initiate, relations with others, and language production and use)
Program staff involvement	1. Determine individual staff member's personal goals and reasons for working in the training program; periodically discuss with individual staff member his progress toward personal goals; record progress in some fashion	1. Determine individual staff member's or teacher's personal goals and reasons for working in the early childhood education program; periodically discuss progress toward these goals with the staff member; record progress in some fashion.
	2. Require staff to keep a running account or log of daily activities; monitor and	2. Require staff to keep a log of critical incidents occurring in the classroom; monitor

227

TABLE 8.3—Continued

Area of formative evaluation concern	Suggestions for formative evaluation of programs training personnel to work in early childhood settings	Suggestions for formative evaluation of early childhood education programs
Program staff involvement —Continued	discuss content of log periodically with the staff member	and discuss content of log periodically with the staff member
	3. Provide settings in which the staff can candidly react to proposed policies, give input on training methods used, discuss alternative procedures for evaluating staff, communicate with one another	3. Provide settings in which the staff can react candidly to proposed policies, give input on classroom activities and methods used, discuss alternative procedures for evaluating staff, communicate with one another, etc.
Institutional impact of program	1. Sample the opinions of personnel (in the parent institution in which the training program is housed) in regard to knowledge of program, attitude toward program, perceived effect of program on the institution	1. Sample the opinions of personnel in the parent institution (in which the program is housed) in regard to knowledge of program, attitude toward program, pereceived effect of program on the institution
	2. Determine the institutional level of commitment to the program in regard to in-kind cost sharing, financial outlays (current and future, after outside funding terminates), academic rank and other benefits for program staff, etc.	2. Determine the institutional level of commitment to the program in regard to financial outlays (current and future, after outside funding terminates), benefits for program staff, etc.
	3. Compare program objectives to institutional objectives (and to elementary education objectives in university settings); discuss with institutional officials areas where objectives are compatible and negotiate in those where possible conflict exists	3. Compare program objectives to institutional objectives; discuss with institutional officials areas where objectives are compatible and negotiate in those where possible conflict exists
Community rapport with program	1. Vary systematically procedures for informing randomly selected subsections of	1. Vary systematically procedures for informing randomly selected groups of

Area of formative evaluation concern	Suggestions for formative evaluation of programs training personnel to work in early childhood settings	Suggestions for formative evaluation of early childhood education programs
	the community about the training program (e.g., by using different combinations of television announcements, newspaper articles, trainees as speakers, staff as speakers); determine apparent effectiveness of each procedure for making decision on future use	parents about their children's school progress (e.g., by using parent conferences, newsletters sent home, open classroom for visitations, report forms); determine apparent effectiveness of each procedure for making decisions on future use
	2. Utilize a community advisory committee; solicit from it concerns about and suggestions for training; analyze this input, determine appropriate action (if any), and report back to advisory committee	2. Utilize a parental advisory committee; solicit from it concerns about and suggestions for the children's program; analyze this input, determine appropriate action (if any), and report back to advisory committee
	3. Select qualifying paraprofessionals (from randomly selected subsections of the community) to use as instructors or instructional assistants in the training program, observe and/or measure apparent effect on subsections of community (and on cost-effectiveness of the training)	3. Select qualifying paraprofessionals (from randomly selected subsections of the community) to use in classrooms, observe and/or measure apparent effect on subsections of the community (and on cost-effectiveness of the instructional program provided)
	4. Randomly select certain subsections of the community in which saturation public relations campaign will be launched; determine program rapport and knowledge of program in these subsections compared to subsections receiving no special attention	4. Randomly select parents (of children in the program) with whom extensive liaison will be effected concerning appropriate home activities for children; determine program rapport and knowledge of program by these parents compared to parents receiving no special attention (and also examine differential pupil progress for the children of the two groups of parents treated)

TABLE 8.3—Continued

Area of formative evaluation concern	Suggestions for formative evaluation of programs training personnel to work in early childhood settings	Suggestions for formative evaluation of early childhood education programs
Transfer effectiveness of program	1. Stratify graduates on basis of success in training program and randomly select groups of each to follow up and determine place of employment, salary level, job satisfaction, perceived strengths of training received, perceived weaknesses of training received, and job security	1. Stratify children completing the program on the basis of success in the program and randomly select groups of each to follow up and determine success in later educational pursuits, performance on standardized instruments, rate of development, apparent happiness, etc. (often, later teachers of the children are unaware of what specific programs children attended at an earlier age, and become good sources of information on the effectiveness of a given program, particularly if they rate all children in their class, remaining ignorant of knowledge about which children attended which programs)
	2. Stratify graduates on basis of success in training program and randomly select groups of each; send questionnaires to the employers of those selected to determine satisfaction of employer (e.g., comparison of employee to employees trained elsewhere, or entering the occupation via other avenues of entry, perceived strengths of the employee, perceived weaknesses of the employee)	2. Randomly select parents of former pupils and ask them to respond to questionnaire items and checklists that indicate pupil rate of progress after completing the program

Examples of Formative and Summative Evaluation

Some examples of formative and summative evaluation techniques in current early childhood education programs may be useful in clarifying the preceding discussion. All examples pertain to programs for children. No examples of evaluations of training programs for personnel preparing to work in early childhood education are given, primarily because the number of such evaluations that are well publicized is small and written documentation has been scant. Other examples of formative and summative evaluation, though not all from early childhood education, can be found in Bloom, Hastings, and Madaus (1971).

The first examples considered involve *Sesame Street,* which provides clear illustrations of both formative and summative evaluation activities as integral parts of that program. A second set of examples involves Follow Through; selected activities of two Follow Through models are cited as examples of formative evaluation, while Stanford Research Institute's program for summative evaluation of the entire Follow Through effort is also described. Finally, a longitudinal study of Head Start being conducted by Educational Testing Service is described. This one study embodies both summative and formative evaluation elements. The reader should not get the impression, based on the selection of these particular examples (primarily large-budget evaluations by teams of specialists), that evaluation can only be conducted on a grandiose scale. The examples were selected primarily because most readers will have some familiarity with the programs being evaluated, and secondarily because published material exists on the programs.

Before Children's Television Workshop (CTW) began the regular showing of *Sesame Street* on educational television networks in the fall of 1969, substantial in-house evaluation of program elements was conducted. An internal research/evaluation team headed by a full-time psychologist has had formative evaluation responsibilities from the beginning of the program. The primary charge for the team was to provide critical information needed by the production staff of the show (such as which segments of the show seem best to hold children's attention; which delivery style seems most effective in facilitating children's learning; what degree of redundancy of concept segments best facilitates children's learning; what interests, abilities, and other characteristics the target population had). Clearly the emphasis was formative, i.e., on improving a product by means of evaluating frequently, if not continuously, as an in-house activity and of feeding back the data thus generated into the production cycle.

To this end, the research-evaluation team undertook many activities (Palmer, 1969). One major activity involved three experimental studies conducted in the summer of 1969 in Philadelphia (one study with disadvantaged children and one with middle-class children) and in New York (with groups of students in a day-care center). The studies were to determine the instructional effectiveness of five *Sesame Street* test shows and to provide information on some tests that had been developed.

A second major activity in the formative evaluation motif involved a distracter study. The purpose was to determine the holding power of various *Sesame Street* segments when challenged by a series of varied slides simultaneously being shown. Experimental subjects individually viewed test shows Nos. 1 and 4 while, at a 45-degree angle from the child's line of vision to the television, 35 mm slides were being shown on a rear-projection screen the same size and height as the television screen. Slides were changed every 7.5 seconds. The dependent variable was the time spent looking at the *Sesame Street* show. By means of two recording observers flanking the child and by cumulative graphs continuously plotted over time, it was possible to link the viewing or nonviewing to specific segments of the test shows, for each segment previously had been timed exactly.

Had the purpose of the study been to generalize widely on the phenomenon of attention span, it would have been easy to criticize the study (for the potential threatening effect the two adult observers had on the four-year-old subjects, because the attractiveness of the slides per se had not been predetermined, because the slides were presented relatively slowly and the same slide recycled every 10 minutes while the test show did not recycle, because slides were used rather than sound or silent movie film, etc.). However, the purpose was to determine the holding power of various show segments compared with the given distracter stimulus, and this information was provided by the formative evaluation study. Incidentally, in this study, students watched show No. 1 90 percent of the potential viewing time and show No. 4 at an 88 percent attention level.

In addition to the formative evaluation activities of the internal research/evaluation team, summative evaluation of *Sesame Street* has been undertaken by Educational Testing Service (ETS). Under contract, ETS had responsibility for assessing and evaluating the impact of the show on children three through five years of age (Ball & Bogatz, 1970). Planning for the summative evaluation began in the summer of 1968, over a year before actual broadcasting began. The intervening year was thus available for measurement instrument development, and a wide variety of instruments was developed. Variety was necessary because of concerns which went beyond the primary question of whether viewers learned more than nonviewers. Questions almost as important included determining which groups of children benefited most from the show, what were their characteristics, how children reacted to techniques used on the show and whether these reactions were related to their learning, and the like.

The summative evaluation design involved one main effect (what was the overall impact of *Sesame Street?*) and questions about interactions between extent of viewing the program and several other variables. These variables were age, sex, former achievement, socioeconomic status, viewing in homes, viewing in preschools, Spanish-speaking or not, and home background conditions.

In the process of answering these questions, groups of children in five different locales in the United States (Boston, Massachusetts; Durham, North Carolina; suburban Philadelphia; Phoenix, Arizona; and northeastern California) were selected. Sampling and testing in these areas were conducted by local people after they had been trained by ETS staff. Tests used were specially developed for the most part and were designed to minimize the need for verbalization by the child. The pretest battery also included the Peabody Picture Vocabulary Test (in order to compare the *Sesame Street* sample with other groups of children). Posttests were similar to pretests (allowing for some revision based on pretest analysis) and also included a test of the child's familiarity with *Sesame Street,* which became part of a viewing index assessing the degree that children had watched the show.

Complete pretest and posttest data were available for slightly less than 1,000 students. Via a large number of different analyses, it was concluded that the over-all impact of *Sesame Street* during its first year was statistically and educationally significant in most goal areas. The complete report (Ball & Bogatz, 1970) contains more comprehensive results for all variables (e.g., high viewers at home far outgained low viewers at home, children watching *Sesame Street* in preschools benefited, etc.), and the reader is directed there for an elaborate, systmatic presentation of the results. The second-year summative evaluation conducted was also generally favorable (Bogatz & Ball, 1971).

In this case, the summative evaluations were highly complimentary to *Sesame Street.* Interestingly, the summative evaluation process itself has likewise been under evaluation on occasion by the ETS research advisory group. When the *Sesame Street* evaluation was presented to it, the advisory group functioned primarily as a "devil's advocate" society, suggesting possible alternate explanations of the data generated. For the most part, the major findings of the evaluative studies have weathered the storm of additional analyses performed to check out the suggested rival hypotheses.[5]

Turning attention now to the Follow Through program, consider a few selected examples of formative evaluation on some of the models. Follow Through was initiated in an attempt to make more permanent those gains experienced in preschool programs, particularly gains by disadvantaged children in Head Start and other special programs. In studies of graduates from special preschools it was noted that they gradually slipped to levels comparable to those of control students after a few years in public elementary schools (Biehler, 1971). Follow Through was to provide additional special programs for children during their first three years in public schools.

Community representative groups shopped—almost cafeteria-style—among 20 models, for one that each felt would be appropriate in its own community. Inadequate evaluation information on many of the models made the choice difficult. Sponsors were then to service and stimulate each of the sites, selecting their particular model. Sponsors of the various models and approaches—e.g., (Bereiter) Englemann-Becker; Primary Education Project/Individually Prescribed Instruction, Resnick; Behavioral Analysis, Bushell; Bank Street; Education Development Center; Responsive Environment, Nimnicht; Cognitively Oriented Curriculum, Weikart; Cultural Linguistic; Tucson Early Education; etc.—were thus, in a sense, immediately in competition with one another. Some model sponsors seemed to be relatively disinterested by the very thought of this competition; other sponsors seemed to thrive in anticipation of the competition (particularly since certain summative evaluations, such as the one described below by Stanford Research Institute, SRI, were planned).

Each of the Follow Through model sponsors make use of formative evaluation techniques. Some sponsors are much more explicit about this than others. The two specific instances below are cited because of their uniqueness and contrast; if all Follow Through models were examined, examples of formative evaluation in each could be cited.

One formative evaluation feature of the Systematic Use of Behavioral Principles Program (Engelmann and Becker, University of Oregon) involves the procedures established for rapid handling and analysis of progress data on each child. At each of the nearly 20 sites using the model, a uniform system of data collecting and reporting has been instituted (Mahan, 1971). The CARDS system (collect, analyze, retrieve, disseminate, and store) has been designed primarily to facilitate the evaluation of each student's learning progress. In clearly a formative-evaluative mode, CARDS permits ongoing evaluation and allows data-based intervention in the program at any point. Consider this example. Every two weeks a child is tested in reading, arithmetic, or language; thus, he takes a test in each area once every six weeks. Based on these test results and a monitoring of pupil progress through the materials, immediate action at the site can be taken, prescribing appropriate next steps for the learner or remedial work for a child weak in an area. Test data are also sent to the central Oregon office on port-a-punch cards, there to be analyzed by project managers and consultants. This serves as a check on action taken at the site. Test data are stored on magnetic tape, available either for quick determination of possible inadequate teaching approaches and weaknesses in materials or tests, or for more extensive evaluation analyses. This systematic approach to data handling permits rapid, data-based formative evaluation to take place. It stands as an interesting contrast to the long delays often experienced in the processing of data for evaluation purposes. The second example of a unique formative evaluation technique stands in marked contrast to the specificity of the Engelmann-Becker CARDS system. The Educational Development Center Follow Through Model makes only minimal provisions for the systematic collection of written data on children; after all, the instruments currently used often seem inappropriate to them. The EDC emphasis on process and development affects their notably informal style of formative evaluation. Advisors have organized themselves into three teams of five to six people, each team responsible for three to four communities. A team of advisors, or elements of a team, visits each EDC Follow Through site assigned. Two primary reasons for utilizing multiple advisors at a single site are: they provide independent checks on the observational data and impressions gained at the site, and they allow immediate interaction between advisors on their diagnosis of what might be done during the same visit to facilitate the process of the classroom moving more toward the "open education quadrant" (described earlier in this chapter). As they return from community visits, advisor teams undergo a self-evaluation debriefing. Via a reflective process, goals, procedures, and plans are considered and evaluated by the team with assistance from central EDC staff who play the role of friendly critics. Thus, the formative evaluation technique developed by EDC seems markedly in keeping with their over-all philosophy. Its use and apparent effects can be analyzed over time particularly if advisor teams have systematically recorded the rationale used in making redirective suggestions to their on-site Follow Through colleagues.

In contrast to formative evaluation internal to Follow Through programs, consider the summative evaluation design of Follow Through implemented by the Stanford Research Institute.[6] Under contract with the U.S. Office of Education, SRI is conducting an overall evaluation of the effects of the planned variation inherent in the Follow Through models. There are over 170 Follow Through sites in the United States. SRI has never included the full set in all its data collection activities; the number included has varied with the purpose and the instrumentation. For example, the spring 1972 sample includes 139 sites.

The basic design utilized has been quasi-experimental in a natural setting. For each of the Follow Through sites, SRI has sought a local comparison site that is not using a Follow Through model; there remain some locations for which no acceptable comparison site has been obtained. The logistic and administrative problems of pretesting and posttesting in so many sites over several years are easily imagined. However, the public relations and persuasive skills required to operate effectively with such diverse sponsors and to maintain contented control sites must be imagined at a level that boggles one's mind. Field data collection is conducted by SRI by training and employing 20 test supervisors around the country.

The basic strategy now being followed by SRI is fall and spring testing in the child's entering year (kindergarten or first grade) and spring testing each year thereafter through grade three.

To meet instrument needs, published tests have been used for the most part. Noting the extensive time and resources requirements necessary for adequate test development, SRI staff adapted (rather than developed) the remainder of the tests used. During the selection and adaptation of instruments, efforts were made to accommodate suggestions from various program sponsors. Measures used change somewhat from year to year, but are of two basic types: batteries of achievement tests, including verbal and linguistic skills, qualitative and computational skills, and perceptual and motor skills; and instruments of noncognitive growth (illustrative measures would include ethnic identity, school fearfulness, locus of control, intrinsic and extrinsic sources of motivation, and generalized school attitudes).

For certain sites, results from these measures are buttressed and complemented by results from an elaborate, SRI-devised observational system. It consists of three documents entitled *Classroom Observation Instrument, Classroom Observation Procedure,* and *Training Manual for Classroom Observation* (SRI, 1970). The training of personnel to use the observational model now requires five days.

Data were first collected during the 1969-70 school year, and collection will continue for several years, possibly until 1975-76; the exact time period will be determined by subsequent funding. As mentioned above, a moratorium on releasing results, broken down for each specific model sponsor, has been set. This practice allows a "sheltered" period for model sponsors to work out procedures and to develop programs more fully before public comparisons are made. Results for the first year are reported for five general categories of models; even though this is the case, manuals of results are not available for general distribution.

When results are finally released, it is hoped by SRI staff that a reporting model similar to a consumer's guide will be used. Intended are extensive descriptions of the antecedents or contextual givens (i.e., the nature of the community, children's characteristics, etc.), of the transactions (the Follow Through model used), and of the outcomes. It will then be up to the prospective consumers, presumably school districts or communities, to select the model they feel is appropriate for their local situation.

SRI has also been conducting a summative evaluation of the national Head Start program. The Head Start evaluation likewise entails planned variation, eight program models being involved. Chronologically, SRI's involvement in Head Start came after Follow Through, if one can imagine that. Their similarities are more striking than their differences; the Head Start evaluation likewise utilizes a quasi-experimental paradigm with local comparison sites. The measures used in each lack clear articulation, in part due to the different age levels of children involved, and the different sponsors at the U. S. Office of Education. Efforts are under way to increase measure similarity across the two evaluations if possible. As of June 1971, the Huron Institute of Cambridge has had responsibility for much of the data analyses, while SRI has retained data collection and some processing responsibilities.

Educational Testing Service's Head Start Longitudinal Study (Educational Testing Service, 1968; Shipman, 1970)[7] is not an evaluative study in the usual sense of the term. By means of it, though, a substantial pool of data is being generated that could have extensive applications to both formative and summative evaluation efforts. One notable feature of the study is the comprehensive and unusual battery of measuring instruments being used. The interested reader is directed to the two references previously cited for elaborate descriptions.

More germane to this presentation, and highly unique, is the design of the study. Each of the two SRI evaluations described above involves planned variations; in contrast, the ETS study involves naturalistic (i.e., nonmanipulated) variations. The basic strategy was to go into four communities (Lee County, Alabama; Portland, Oregon; St. Louis, Missouri; and Trenton, New Jersey), identify all children eligible for first grade in two years, assess these children on various measures *prior to any educational intervention,* and closely monitor their experiences and assess changes in test performance over a five-year period. Thus, a comprehensive study was launched in 1968 (initially with Office of Economic Opportunity funding, and now with funding from the Office of Child Development). It is designed to study and record the cognitive, personal, and social development of disadvantaged children during the crucial age period from four to nine years. It involves no random assignment of children to different groups; it involves no search for comparable control groups. Rather, it was assumed that natural events would result in certain of the children in the sample entering Head Start programs, others entering private preschools, others having no preschool experience, etc. This is a bold design, entailing extensive expenditures of resources, both monetary and time. It contains risks. One risk is that the relatively elaborate and extensive measuring process might disturb the very naturalness that the design is attempting to preserve. Another risk is that attrition rates due to unexpected movement patterns out of the sample area might reduce numbers in some samples to unacceptable levels before the longitudinal study has been completed. In fact, attrition problems have been severe in one of the four communities. Nevertheless, the design stands as a promising one, particularly if resources are provided in sufficient amounts.

Again, it is important to note that the large scale of most of these evaluation examples in no way obviates against the use of the same basic principles and procedures in evaluating programs of a much smaller scale. The program director need only be alert to those priority decisions that must be made, and then arrange for appropriate data collection and analysis. Formative evaluation techniques, successfully executed, provide a sound base for making decisions.

The focus of this chapter now shifts attention to several conceptual frameworks for educational evaluation. Frameworks are briefly outlined and referenced. In effect, emphasis is directed away from specific examples of evaluations and toward general topics that should be considered when designing, or contracting for, an evaluation of a program in early childhood education.

CONCEPTIONAL FRAMEWORKS IN EDUCATIONAL EVALUATION

This closing section contains brief descriptions of a number of conceptual frameworks available for evaluation in education.[8] The purpose of presenting them here is not to allow their immediate use. Rather, the intent is to give the reader enough information to allow him to make initial decisions about the potential fit between each framework and the evaluation he feels should be conducted for his project. It is then suggested that, for those frameworks with which the match appears particularly good, the reader consult the references cited and consider the more elaborate and complete presentation.

The reader should be alerted that use of the conceptual frameworks is most advantageous to evaluation during planning phases of the program, before a project or training program has begun, or at least early in the operational phase. Seldom is a framework adopted without modification. Further, it is a common pattern for an evaluator to borrow ideas from several conceptual frameworks.

The NLP fellows visited over 50 early childhood education programs and examined evaluation plans for them. Only a few of the programs had used any conceptual framework, and even in most of these cases, frameworks were not systematically applied during all program phases. Although it is rare for personnel to use a developed framework religiously throughout the life of a program, careful thinking about many elements in the conceptual frameworks can result in the identification of many areas for evaluation concern.

Accountability Framework [9]

Purpose: To establish a relationship wherein producers or sellers are accountable to their clientele.

Definition: Disclosing the nature of the service or product being offered, testing the service and product to determine performance characteristics, and providing redress when either disclosure has been misleading or performance has been inadequate.

Key Emphasis: Open specification of product or service characteristics to enable the consumer to hold the producer accountable.

Role of Evaluator: Specialist who conducts the performance testing and compares results to the disclosed promised performance or claims.

Relationship to Objectives: Objectives, in a sense, are implied in the disclosure statement. Evaluation by accountability determines the extent of congruency between disclosed claims and measured performance.

Relationship to Decision-Making: Evaluation provides decision-maker with data to substantiate or refute claims and to secure redress if warranted.

Types of Evaluation:
1. Educational audit to provide full disclosure.
2. Performance testing to determine claim accuracy.

Constructs Proposed:
1. Disclosure of performance specifications.
2. Performance testing.
3. Redress.

Criteria for Judging Evaluation:
1. Must insure that performance testing accurately reflects disclosed claims.
2. Must provide for performance testing to be conducted under rigorous conditions (e.g., blind testing, evaluation of alternative products or interventions, random assignment, etc.).

Implications for Design:
1. Will involve precise specification of service or product performance characteristics.
2. Will provide performance testing under controlled conditions.

Contributions:
1. Provides specific description of service or product claims.
2. Provides for rigorous performance testing.
3. Provides necessity for clear relationship between disclosed claims and performance testing.
4. Provides for positive action when discrepancies are found in claims or performance.

Limitations:
1. Avoids value concerns.
2. May be costly if performance testing is elaborate.
3. May be difficult to establish effective redress procedures in education.
4. Contains possible threat to personnel in producer role.

References:
1. Center for Instructional Research and Curriculum Evaluation (1971).
2. Phi Delta Kappan (1970).

Accreditation Framework

Purpose: To identify deficiencies in the education of teachers and students relevant to content and process.

Definition: Focusing attention on processes of education, using professional judgment. Development of standards of excellence for continued improvement of educational programs.

Key Emphasis: Personal judgment used in evaluating processes of education.

Role of Evaluator: Professional colleague who recommends or withholds program certification—a professional judge.

Relationship to Objectives: Self-study judgments are based on sets of predetermined standards published and available in advance.

Relationship to Decision-Making: When deficiencies are found, program certification is withheld, thus creating pressure to correct substandard conditions.

Type of Evaluation:
1. Self-study.
2. Visitation.
3. Annual reports.
4. Seven-year cycle reevaluations.

Construct Proposed: Standard evaluative criteria.

Criteria for Judging Evaluation:
1. Must reflect interests of school administrators.
2. Must follow evaluative criteria.

Implications for Design:
1. Will use standards (valued goals).
2. Will involve entire school and professional colleagues.

Contributions:
1. Is easy to implement; team can observe and make judgment.
2. Has little lag time between observations made, data collected, and feedback.
3. Breadth of variables noted is large.
4. Leads to self-study routine and self-improvement.

Limitations:
1. Objectivity and empirical basis are questionable.

2. Attention to process of education not balanced by attention to outcomes.

3. Replicability is questionable.

Reference: National Study of Secondary School Education (1960).

Hammond Framework

Purpose: To find out whether an innovation is effective in achieving expressed objectives.

Definition: Assessing effectiveness of current and innovative programs at the local level by comparing behavioral data with objectives.

Key Emphasis: Local program development. Evaluation functions as feedback to inform decision-maker on program development and revision.

Role of Evaluator: Consultant/researcher who should provide expertise in data collection and decision-making in local setting.

Relationship to Objectives: Evaluation centers on the definition and measurement of behavioral objectives.

Relationship to Decision-Making: Evaluation is source on which to base decisions about instructional, institutional, and behavioral dimensions.

Types of Evaluations:
1. Instructional.
2. Institutional.
3. Behavioral.
(Evaluation should take into account interaction of instructional, institutional, and behavioral dimensions.)

Constructs Proposed:
1. The application of evaluation design to existing programs.
2. Decisions about adequacy of current program in relationship to the objectives.
3. Feedback from (2) leads to innovation.
4. Application of evaluation to innovation itself.
5. Notion that feedback loops could continue if feasible.

Criteria for Judging Evaluation:
1. Must be related to behavioral objectives.
2. Must be an ongoing process.
3. Must provide feedback on goal achievement for program modification.
4. Must use local personnel and be part of the local education program.

Implications for Design:
1. Will generate empirical research.
2. Will require inclusion of local personnel.

Contributions:
1. Makes use of local personnel who can carry on evaluation process, once initiated.
2. Considers interaction of several dimensions and variables.
3. Provides feedback on program development and revision; stresses self-evaluation.
4. Requires specification of behavioral objectives.

Limitations:
1. Difficulty of quantifying data involving several dimensions and variables.
2. May be complex and time-consuming to set up.
3. Possible fixation of evaluation on the "cube."
4. Neglects judgmental dimension.
5. Motivation problem in local personnel.

Reference: Hammond (undated).

Metfessel-Michael Framework

Purpose: To formulate recommendations that furnish a basis for further implementation for modifications, and for revisions in broad goals and specific objectives.

Definition: Comparing measured performance with behavioral standards.

Key Emphasis: Specifying objectives and using multiple-criterion measures to assess outcomes; involving many different audiences.

Role of Evaluator: Measurement specialist who involves lay individuals, school personnel, and students in developing a set of recommendations.

Relationship to Objectives: Evaluation entails measurement of congruency of outcome behaviors with objectives.

Relationship to Decision-Making: Suggestions are made concerning revisions in objectives on program strategies. Feedback is given to all individuals involved in the school program.

Types of Evaluation: Eight-stage evaluation process using students, lay individuals, and professionals.

Construct Proposed: Multiple-criterion measurement.

Criteria for Judging Evaluation:
1. Must involve diverse audiences.

2. Must use specified objectives.
3. Must use valid, reliable, and objective measures.
4. Must use multiple-criterion measures.

Implications for Design:
1. Will involve eight-stage evaluation process.
2. Will involve various audiences; make recommendations to various audiences.
3. Will specify objectives.
4. Will make periodic observations, using multiple-criterion measures.

Contributions:
1. Involves various audiences, including reporting to them.
2. Forces specification of objectives.
3. Provides appendix.
4. Provides periodic observations and continuous feedback.
5. Applies easily.
6. Derives from measurement technology.

Limitations:
1. Primary focus on available instrumentation.
2. Focus only on outcome behaviors (little antecedent or process concern).
3. Lack of methodology for establishing standards or evaluating objectives.
Reference: Metfessel and Michael (1967).

Provus Discrepancy Framework

Purpose: To determine whether to improve, maintain, or terminate a program.

Definition: Comparing performance against standards.

Key Emphasis: Locating discrepancies, using team approach.

Role of Evaluator: A team member who aids program improvement and counsels administration in accordance with own rules and independently of program unit.

Relationship to Objectives: Agreement of evaluation team and program staff on standards. Comparison of performance against standards to see whether a discrepancy exists.

Relationship to Decision-Making: Evaluation staff collects information essential to program improvement and notes discrepancies between performance and standards. Every question involves a criterion, new information, and a decision; evaluation provides the new information.

Types of Evaluation:
1. Design: inputs, processes, outputs.

2. Installation: observation.
3. Process: cause and effect.
4. Cost: cost-benefit analysis and product discrepancy information.

Constructs Proposed:
1. Discrepancy concept.
2. Feedback and revision.

Criteria for Judging Evaluation:
1. Must provide for team involvement.
2. Must assume one-to-one correspondence between design and solution.
3. Must compare performance against standards as a tool for improvement and assessment.
4. Must provide periodic feedback.

Implications for Design:
1. Will provide continuous evaluation (feedback loops).
2. Will provide relevant and timely information for making decisions.
3. Will provide cost-benefit analysis.
4. Will involve evaluation in program development.

Contributions:
1. Provides continuous communication between program and evaluation staff through feedback loops.
2. Allows for program improvement as well as assessment either at early stages or at end.
3. Acknowledges alternative procedures in adjusting objectives and in changing treatments.
4. Forces explicit statement of standards.

Limitations:
1. Demands a lengthy time commitment; may be expensive to carry through.
2. Is inadequate methodology for establishing standards.
3. Requires large, expert, well-articulated staff.
4. Is designed for complete evaluation; partial evaluation not considered.

Reference: Provus (1969).

Scriven Framework

Purpose: To establish and justify merit or worth of certain entities for the consumer and producer; evaluation plays many roles.

Definition: Gathering and combining performance data with a weighted set of goal scales.

Key Emphasis: Justification of data-gathering instruments, weightings, and selection of goals. Heart of evaluation model: combining data on different performance scales into a single rating.

Role of Evaluator: Responsible for judging the merit of an educational practice for producers (formative) and consumers (summative).

Relationship to Objective: Moral obligation to look at goals and judge their worth; also to determine if they are being met.

Relationship to Decision-Making: Evaluation reports (with judgments, explicitly stated) for producers and/or consumers.

Types of Evaluation:
1. Formative-summative.
2. Comparative-noncomparative.
3. Intrinsic-payoff.
4. Mediated.

Constructs Proposed:
1. Distinction between goals (claims) and roles (functions).
2. Types of evaluation.

Criteria for Judging Evaluation:
1. Must be predicated on goals.
2. Must indicate worth.
3. Must have construct validity.
4. Must provide holistic program evaluation.

Implications for Design:
1. Will account for more factors; most complex and comprehensive.
2. Will be involved in value judgments.
3. Will require more conformance with scientific investigations.
4. Will evaluate from within (formative) and from without (summative).

Contributions:
1. Discriminates between formative (ongoing) and summative (end) evaluation.
2. Focuses on direct assessment of worth; focuses on value.
3. Is applicable in diverse contexts.
4. Provides analyses of instruments.
5. Delineates types of evaluation.

Limitations:
1. Equates performance on differing criteria and assigns relative weights to criteria thus creating methodological problems.
2. Has no methodology for assessing validity of judgments.
3. Contains several ambiguous, overlapping concepts.

Reference: Scriven (1967).

Stake Countenance Framework

Purpose: To describe and judge educational programs based on a formal inquiry process.

Definition: Describing educational program and judging strengths and weaknesses in order to recommend usability and function.

Key Emphasis: Collection of descriptive and judgmental data from various audiences; keep audience in mind for the final report.

Role of Evaluator: Specialist concerned with collection, processing, and interpreting descriptive and judgmental data.

Relationship to Objectives: Examination of goal specifications, priorities, progress reports. Identification of areas of failures and successes. Evaluator must assist in writing behavioral objectives.

Relationship to Decision-Making: Descriptive and judgmental data result in reports to various audiences and may result in recommendations. Judgments may be based on either absolute or relative standards.

Types of Evaluation:
1. Descriptive (intents and observations).
2. Judgmental (standards and judgments) of antecedents, transactions, and outcomes.

Constructs Proposed:
1. Data matrices: description (intents and observations) and judgment (standards and judgment).
2. Processing descriptive data: contingency among antecedents, transactions, and outcomes, and congruence between intents and observations.
3. Basis of forming judgment: absolute and relative.

Criteria for Judging Evaluation:
1. Must be panoramic, not microscopic.
2. Must include descriptive and judgmental data.
3. Must provide immediate relative answers for decision-making.
4. Must be formal (e.g., objective, scientific, reliable).

Implications for Design:
1. Will require general structure.
2. Will include matrices in design.

Contributions:
1. Provides a systematic method for arranging descriptive and judgmental data, thus emphasizing inter- and intrarelations between them.
2. Considers both absolute and relative judgments.
3. Requires explicit standard, thus minimizing power of any one person and allowing alternatives to be considered.
4. Provides a generalizable model.

Limitations:

1. Is inadequate methodology for obtaining information on key constructs.

2. Has cells of design matrix that overlap; distinctions not clear; constructs overlap.

3. Has possibility of leading to internal strife within program; value conflicts possible.

Reference: Stake (1967).

Stufflebeam CIPP Framework

Purpose: To provide relevant information to decision-maker.

Definition: Defining, obtaining, and using information for decision-making.

Key Emphasis: Decision-making.

Role of Evaluator: Specialist who provides evaluation information to decision-maker.

Relationship to Objectives: Terminal stage in context evaluation is setting objectives; input evaluation produces ways to reach objectives; product evaluation determines whether objectives are reached.

Relationship to Decision-Making: Provides information for use in decision-making; identifies alternatives and studies implications of each.

Types of Evaluation:
1. Context.
2. Input.
3. Process.
4. Product.

Constructs Proposed:
1. Context: planning decisions.
2. Input: programming decisions.
3. Process: implementing decisions.
4. Product: recycling decisions.

Criteria for Judging Evaluation:
1. Must have validity, internal and external.
2. Must have reliability.
3. Must have timeliness, relevance.
4. Must have pervasiveness, importance.
5. Must have credibility.
6. Must have objectivity.
7. Must have scope.
8. Must be efficient.

Implications for Design:
1. Will consider experimental design not applicable.
2. Will use systems approach for evaluation studies.
3. Will be directed by administrator.

Contributions:
1. Provides a service function by supplying data to administrators and decision-makers charged with conduct of the program.
2. Is sensitive to feedback.
3. Allows for evaluation to take place at any stage of the program.
4. Is holistic.

Limitations:
1. Avoids value concerns; tendency to overvalue efficiency.
2. Has decision-making process that is unclear; methodology undefined.
3. May be costly and complex if used entirely.
4. Contains some activities that are not clearly evaluative.

Reference: Stufflebeam (1969).

Tyler Framework

Purpose: To determine the extent to which purposes of learning activity are actually being realized; to measure student progress toward objectives.

Definition: Comparing student performance with behavioral goals.

Key Emphasis: Specification of objectives and measuring pupil competencies.

Role of Evaluator: Curriculum specialist.

Relationship to Objectives: Evaluation implies attainment of behavioral objectives stated at the beginning of the course.

Relationship to Decision-Making: Actual pupil performance data will provide information on strengths and weaknesses for the decision-maker to use.

Type of Evaluation: Pre- and post-measurement of performance.

Constructs Proposed:
1. Statements of objectives must be in behavioral terms.
2. Teaching objectives must be pupil-oriented.
3. Objectives must consider pupil's entry behavior; analysis of our culture; learning theories; school philosophy; new developments in teaching; etc.

Criteria for Judging Evaluation:
1. Must have clear, specific, and understandable behavioral objectives.

2. Must have objectives that contain references not only to course content but also to mental processes to be applied.

Implications for Design:
1. Will need to interpret and use results of assessment, especially in the affective domain.
2. Will develop designs to assess student progress.

Contributions:
1. Is easy to assess whether behavioral objectives are being attained.
2. Is easy for practitioners to design evaluative studies.
3. Has high degree of congruency between performance and objectives; forces clear definition of objectives.

Limitations:
1. Tends to oversimplify program and focus on terminal performance rather than on transactions and pre-program information.
2. Tends to focus directly and narrowly on objectives, with little attention to the worth of objectives.
3. Lacks concern for establishing causal claims.

Reference: Tyler (1958).

NOTES

1. Appreciation is expressed to Dr. Gene V Glass, Laboratory of Educational Research, University of Colorado, for his helpful comments on an earlier draft of this chapter.

2. Personal communication from Dr. Gene V Glass, Laboratory of Educational Research, University of Colorado, about one of his colleagues.

3. Appreciation is expressed to Dr. George Hein, Director of the Open Education Follow Through Project of the Educational Development Center, and to Margaret de Rivera and Claryce Lee Evans for their valuable suggestions.

4. Dr. Robert E. Stake, in an informal talk to colleagues and graduate students at the Laboratory of Educational Research, University of Colorado, summer 1970.

5. Personal communication from Dr. Gene V Glass, Laboratory of Educational Research, University of Colorado, one of the leading "devil's advocates."

6. Appreciation is extended to Dr. Phil Sorensen, Director of the Follow Through Evaluation, Dr. Daryl Dell . . . , Dr. Tor Meeland, and Dr. Jane Stallings, all of the Stanford Research Institute, for their valuable assistance.

7. Appreciation is extended to Dr. Virginia C. Shipman, the Project Director, and to Mrs. Anne M. Bussis, both of Educational Testing Service, for their valuable assistance.

8. Appreciation is expressed to Dr. James R. Sanders and Dr. Blaine R. Worthen for developing the basic material upon which most of this section is based. For elaborations, see Sanders (1971) and Worthen and Sanders (1974).

9. Appreciation is expressed to Dr. Gene V Glass for his insightful perspectives on accountability.

REFERENCES

Ball, S., & Bogatz, G. A. *The first year of Sesame Street: An evaluation,* PR
    70-15. Princeton, N.J.: Educational Testing Service, 1970.
Biehler, R. F. *Psychology applied to teaching.* Boston: Houghton-Mifflin, 1971.
Bloom, B. S., Hastings, T., & Madaus, G. *Formative and summative evaluation
    of student learning.* New York: McGraw-Hill, 1971.
Bogatz, G. A., & Ball, S. *The second year of Sesame Street: A continuing evalua-
    tion,* Vol. I. PR-71-21. Princeton, N.J.: Educational Testing Service, 1971.
Bracht, G. H., & Glass, G. V. The external validity of experiments. *American
    Educational Research Journal,* 1968, *5,* 437-474.
Bussis, A. M., & Chittenden, E. A. *Analysis of an approach to open education,*
    PR-70-13. Princeton, N.J.: Educational Testing Service, 1970.
Campbell, D. T. Reforms as experiments. *American Psychologist,* 1969, *24,*
    409-429.
Campbell, D. T., & Stanley, J. S. *Experimental and quasi-experimental designs
    for research.* Chicago: Rand McNally, 1963.
Center for Instructional Research and Curriculum Evaluation. *Accountability
    Notebook.* Urbana, Ill.: University of Illinois, 1971.
Cronbach, L. J. *Essentials of psychological testing.* (Third edition.) New York:
    Harper & Row, 1970.
Cronbach, L. J., & Suppes, P. (Eds.). *Researh for tomorrow's schools: Disci-
    plined inquiry for education.* Toronto, Ont.: Collier-MacMillan Canada
    Ltd., 1969.
Dyer, H. S. Toward objective criteria of professional accountability in the
    schools of New York City. *Phi Delta Kappan,* 1970, *52,* 206-211.
Educational Testing Service. *Theoretical considerations and measurement
    strategies,* PR 68-4. Princeton, N.J.: Educational Testing Service, 1968.
Eisner, E. W. The arts and cultural enrichment. In R. I. Miller (Ed.), *Notes
    and working papers concerning the administration of programs authorized
    under Title III, ESEA.* Washington, D.C.: U.S. Government Printing
    Office, 1967.
————. Instructional and expressive educational objectives: Their formulation
    and use in curriculum. In *AERA monograph series on curriculum evalua-
    tion: Instructional objectives,* Vol. 3. Chicago: Rand McNally, 1969.
Glass, G. V. The wisdom of scientific inquiry on education. Paper presented
    at meeting of National Association for Research on Science Teaching,
    Silver Springs, March 1971.
Goodwin, W. L., & Sanders, J. R. The effects on pupil performance of presen-
    tations made on an audio-bus. Paper presented at meeting of National
    Council on Measurement in Education, New York, February 1971.
Hammond, R. L. Evaluation at the local level. Tucson, Ariz.: EPIC Evaluation
    Center, undated.

Kamii, C., & Elliott, D. L. Evaluation of evaluation. *Educational Leadership,* 1971, *28,* 827-831.

Light, R. J., & Smith, P. V. Choosing a future: Strategies for designing and evaluating new programs. *Harvard Educational Review,* 1970, *40,* 1-28.

Mahan, J. M. Description of the CARDS data systems for the Engelmann-Becker Follow Through Project. Research Memorandum No. 14. Eugene, Ore.: Engelmann-Becker Follow Through Project, University of Oregon, 1971.

Metfessel, N. S., & Michael, W. S. A paradigm involving multiple-criterion measures for the evaluation of the effectiveness of school programs. *Educational and Psychological Measurement,* 1967, *27,* 931-943.

Miller, R. I. (Ed.). *Notes and working papers concerning the administration of programs authorized under Title III, ESEA.* Washington D.C.: U.S. Government Printing Office, 1967.

Minuchin, P., Biber, B., Shapiro, E., & Zimiles, H. *The psychological impact of school experience.* New York: Basic Books, 1969.

National Study of Secondary School Evaluation. *Evaluative criteria, 1960 edition.* Washington, D.C.: National Study of Secondary School Evaluation, 1960.

Palmer, E. L., Can television really teach? *American Education,* August-September 1969.

Patterson, J. M. Analyzing early childhood education programs: Evaluation. *Educational Leadership,* 1971, *28,* 809-811.

Phi Delta Kappa Commisison on Evaluation. *Educational evaluation and decision-making.* Bloomington, Ind.: Phi Delta Kappa International, 1970.

Phi Delta Kappan (Accountability Issue), *52*(4), 1970.

Provus, M. Evaluation of ongoing programs in the public school systems. In R. W. Tyler (Ed.), *Educational evaluation: New roles, new means.* Sixty-eighth Yearbook of National Society for the Study of Education, Part II. Chicago: University of Chicago Press, 1969.

Riecken, H. W., Boruch, R. F., Campbell, D. T., Caplan, N., Glennan, T. K., Pratt, J., Rees, A., & Williams W. *Social experiments for planning and evaluation.* New Work: Social Science Research Council 1974.

Rosenshine, B. Evaluation of classroom instruction. *Review of Educational Research,* 1970, *40,* 279-300.

Rosenthal, R. *Experimenter effects in behavioral research.* New York: Appleton-Century-Crofts, 1966.

Sanders, J. R. A descriptive summary of frameworks for planning evaluation studies. Research Paper No. 1, June 1971. Bloomington, Ind.: University of Indiana, Educational Research and Evaluation Laboratory.

Scriven, M. The methodology of evaluation. In *AERA monograph series on curriculum evaluation: Perspectives on curriculum evaluation.* Vol. 1. Chicago: Rand McNally, 1967.

Shipman, V. C. *Disadvantaged children and their first school experiences: Preliminary description of the initial sample prior to school enrollment,* Vol. I, PR 70-20. Princeton, N.J.: Educational Testing Service, 1970.

Sjogren, D. D. Measurement techniques in evaluation. *Review of Educational Research,* 1970, *40,* 301-320.

Smith, M. S., & Bissell, J. S. Report analysis: The impact of Head Start. *Harvard Educational Review*, 1970, *40*, 51-104.

Stake, R. E. The countenance of educational evaluation. *Teachers College Record*, 1967, *68*, 523-540.

——. Objectives, priorities, and other judgment data. *Review of Educational Research*, 1970, *40*, 181-212.

Stake, R. E., & Denny, T. Needed concepts and techniques for utilizing more fully the potential of evaluation. In R. W. Tyler (Ed.), *Educational evaluation: New roles, new means*. Sixty-eighth Yearbook of National Society for the Study of Education. Part II. Chicago: University of Chicago Press, 1969.

Stanford Research Institute. *Training manual for classroom observation; classroom observation procedure; and classroom observation instrument*. Menlo Park, California: Stanford Research Institute, 1970.

Stephens, J. M. *The process of schooling: A psychological examination*. New York: Holt, Rinehart and Winston, 1967.

Stufflebeam, D. L. Evaluation as enlightenment for decision-making. In W. H. Beatty (Ed.), *Improving educational assessment and an inventory of measures of affective behavior*. Washington, D.C.: Association for Supervision and Curriculum Development, NEA, 1969.

Taba, H. *Teaching strategies and cognitive functioning in elementary school children*. Cooperative Research Project No. 2404. San Francisco: San Francisco State College, 1966.

Tyler, R. W. The evaluation of teaching. In R. M. Cooper (Ed.), *The two ends of the leg*. Minneapolis: University of Minnesota Press, 1958.

——. The objectives and plans for a National Assessment of Educational Progress. *Journal of Educational Measurement*, 1966, *3*, 1-4.

Webb, E. J., Campbell, D. T., Schwartz, R. D., & Sechrest, L. *Unobtrusive measures: Nonreactive research in the social sciences*. Chicago: Rand McNally, 1966.

White, S. H. The national impact of Head Start. Unpublished manuscript, Harvard University, 1969.

Worthen, B. R., & Sanders, J. R. *Educational evaluation: Theory and practice*. Columbus, Ohio: Charles A. Jones, 1973.

Chapter 9

A Methodological Approach
to Evaluation

LEON JONES

In this chapter the rationale for a methodological approach to evaluation is presented. Further, the methodology is developed using a particular aspect of methodology: the operationalization of fuzzy concepts. Since the overall purpose of this book is to improve early childhood programs, the relevance of this methodological approach for that field is included.

EVALUATION METHODOLOGY—WHY?

The involvement of evaluation in education has recently expanded, and there is a critical need for the application of new and revised evaluation concepts. Evaluation methodology must encompass bold new horizons, clearly broader than those for measurement. Specialists in the field have before them challenging and uncharted territory.

In evaluation, a special demand is placed on methodology, that is, on the method of inquiry. For example, consider time as a variable. The researcher has available the luxury of being able to recreate a problem situation and repeat a study, if he desires. For the evaluator, however, time constraints are imposed from without, and events to be evaluated are not repeatable. Problems of ongoing programs are immediate, and evaluation activities must address them directly and without delay. Further contrasts between research and evaluation are presented in Table 9.1. It is noteworthy that research is conducted to determine the relationship between variables, whereas evaluation is undertaken to ascertain the value or worth of variables or programs and to mark the current status of programs relative to the attainment of some criteria or objectives.

Conceptually, evaluation is a process by which programs, institutions, processes, and individuals are examined to determine operational efficiency,

253

TABLE 9.1

Contrast between Research and Evaluation

Research	Evaluation
The purpose of research is to generate activity aimed at increasing the power to understand, predict, and control events of a given kind. All three of these features involve relationships between events or variables. The researcher:	The purpose of evaluation is to collect and analyze data to produce pertinent information on the worth or value of a program or the like. This information is used to facilitate decision-making by decision-makers. The evaluator process includes:
(a) understands an event by relating it logically to others;	(a) a commitment by the decision-makers to work closely with the evaluator;
(b) predicts an event by relating it empirically to antecedents in time;	(b) a commitment by the evaluator to preserve the decision-makers' goal intent;
(c) controls an event by manipulating the independent variables to which it is functionally related.	(c) a mutual commitment to maintain a distinction between the role of the evaluator and the decision-maker;
	(d) a commitment by the decision-makers to modify the enterprise during the evaluative process to become consistent with goal intentions.
Research requires:	Evaluation requires:
(a) preliminary conceptualization;	(a) planning conference;
(b) statement of the problem;	(b) statement of goals;
(c) definition of the problem in operational statements;	(c) operationalization of goals;
(d) design and procedures;	(d) design and procedures;
(e) instrumentation and assessment techniques;	(e) instrumentation and assessment techniques;
(f) data collection;	(f) data collection;
(g) data analysis;	(g) data analysis;
(h) report.	(h) report.

goal attainment effectiveness, and input-output relationships. This concept of evaluation and similar ones explicate a definite need for a methodology that will provide objective data about an enterprise in terms of its parts. The components of an enterprise may be people, processes, and products.

In this chapter, evaluation is defined as a procedure for collecting and analyzing data to produce pertinent information that can be used to facilitate decision-making by decision-makers (as noted in Table 9.1). The position of this author is that the role of the decision-maker should be delineated so that it can be meaningful in practice and, at the same time, apply to a variety of enterprises. A methodology is needed that will specify the roles of both the evaluator and the decision-maker throughout the evaluation period. A clear understanding of both roles would facilitate good evaluation practice. The methodology would require the evaluator to familiarize the decision-maker with the evaluative process.

HISTORICAL PERSPECTIVE

In the past, evaluation in education usually connoted curriculum or instructional evaluation (Tyler, 1950; Pace, 1968). Another historical trend involved the evolution of evaluation, as a discipline in its own right, out of the context of measurement. Some evaluators, such as Pace (1968) and Hutchinson (1970), feel that evaluation includes more than measurement (there is conceptual support for their position) and actually seeks to extend it, even to the point of highlighting current measurement inadequacies. Thus, evaluation includes and welcomes the use of psychometric techniques and instruments such as observations, interviews, checklists, questionnaires, testimonials, minutes of meetings, time logs, and many other relevant means of assembling information; yet evaluation still holds that psychometric theory is irrelevant in many undertakings. In like manner, evaluation has freed itself from many of the restrictions of the experimentalist's preoccupation with research design and hypothesis testing. There are many programs whose evaluation activities cannot be fitted into the experimentalist's paradigm.

Despite these awarenesses, ambiguities about the role and meaning of evaluation in education remain evident. New technologies and new social problems give rise to new evaluation problems, and some ambiguities exist because the concept of evaluation has changed to meet the increasing demands on it. Pace (1968) attributed much of the ambiguity to the ease with which the evaluation label is applied to a large assortment of quite diverse activities. His essential point is that the way we think about evaluation, and how we go about evaluating, are necessarily related to what, and why, we are evaluating.

Since the use of educational evaluation is widespread and rapidly increasing, the resources devoted to it may soon exceed those available for basic research. The current renaissance of educational evaluation occurred during the last half of the past decade. Historically, the milestones of evaluation can be categorized as follows:

1930s: Tests and measurements, emergence of evaluation as a broader concept.

1940s: Evaluation related to instruction, group processes, and improvement.

1950s: Self-study, new goals, emergence of new technologies.

1960s: Reemergence of evaluation—in relation to educational technologies—with respect to the consequences of large social programs.

With this brief consideration of the historical background of educational evaluation, attention is shifted to more recent trends in the field.

CURRENT PERSPECTIVE

In the 1970s, concepts such as educational auditing and accountability have become increasingly familiar. This concern with auditing and accountability is probably due to the vastly increased interest in educational evaluation. The substantial expansion in federal funding of educational programs, particularly under the Elementary and Secondary Education Act of 1965 and through the Office of Economic Opportunity (Head Start, Follow Through, etc.), brought with it evaluation demands. To a large extent, these demands caused the reemergence of evaluation in the late 1960s. Gage (1968) was inspired by Lortie's paper to take the position that whatever the future direction of American education, evaluation will be of major importance.

Several significant components reflecting the current status of evaluation in education are: (a) an appeal for a scientific approach to evaluation; (b) an appeal for a viable role for decision-makers; (c) consideration for both specific behavioral objectives and expressive objectives; (d) an explication of unresolved problems and new issues; and (e) the problems and difficulties that plague evaluation as a discipline. Stake (1968), Hutchinson (1970), and Stufflebeam et al. (1971) have dealt with the status of evaluation in education.

NEED FOR METHODOLOGY

A major reason for desiring a methodology is that it provides a frame of reference for ascertaining the value of the operations of an enterprise. If decision-makers are to act on the basis of judiciously sound information, evaluators must provide such information. This realization necessitates the call for a viable methodology. The ultimate criterion as to whether a methodology is viable depends on (a) the decision-maker using the data; and (b) the existence of other data that the decision-maker might want to use.

Increasingly, educational evaluators (Scriven, 1967; Provus, 1969; Stufflebeam et al., 1971) are concerned about the level of evaluation methodology presently in use. In searching for existing evaluation methodologies or procedures, Singh (1970) noted that there were at least six major designs or paradigms along which evaluation may proceed.

> First, the evaluation can be made in terms of the efficacy of a particular program. This phase of the evaluation is based upon empirical evidence gained from individuals actually participating in the program. Second, comparisons can be made with other similar programs; third, comparisons can be made with the results produced in control situations where no programs have been used; fourth, evaluation can be made in terms of the rationale upon which a particular program is based; fifth, an evaluation procedure can include an assessment of motivational and attitudinal variables relevant to the program; and sixth, an evaluation procedure can include an anecdotal description of the problems actually encountered in the "front lines" by the individuals implementing the program.

A review of these six paradigms makes apparent that there is no single mode of evaluation that encompasses all data and information. Further, existing methodology is inadequate, for education evaluation involves more than assessing programs and student performance. Stake (1969) felt that it included the task of gathering information about the nature and worth of educational programs in order to improve program management decisions.

Efforts to develop an adequate evaluation methodology have been plagued with problems. Two major difficulties have been the level of evaluator training and the credibility gap. Few schools of education provide relevant course work on evaluation. Up to the present time, according to Hutchinson (1970), practitioners in evaluation have received only piecemeal training in evaluation techniques: some was received in tests and measurement courses; some was acquired in educational statistics and psychology courses; and the rest was tacked on to methods courses. The status of evaluation in education is inadequate in part because of this lack of synthesis between these fragments of functional skill training.

A second problem blocking effective methodology development is the credibility gap. Evaluation requires sufficient methodology so that evaluators appear to be (and are) credible and can obtain ready acceptance and support from decision-makers. A current charge is that if present evaluation efforts are anything, they are noncredible. To some extent this noncreditability of evaluation causes symptoms in decision-makers of avoidance, anxiety, immobilization, and skepticism.

If evaluators would produce data that decision-makers respect, the latter would use the data and, in effect, bridge the credibility gap now evident. Stufflebeam and his colleagues (1971) took the position that evaluation is noncredible to both the decision-maker within the organization and to various audiences outside the organization. Their thesis was that evaluation should be an integral part of the process, not external to it, and that it should assist in shaping the enterprise, not merely in judging it. If such a situation materialized, they claimed, the decision-maker almost automatically perceived the evaluation as credible.

It is not enough merely to have the decision-maker party to the evaluative process. The way in which he is involved is critical. One main function of the decision-maker should be to assist in making his goals influence the evaluative process and, at the same time, preserving their original intent. It should be a responsibility of the decision-maker to translate his goal statements into explicit variables, and a responsibility of the evaluator to provide the methodology for decision-makers to facilitate that translation.

The methodology to be presented here concentrates on giving the decision-maker a lively role in the evaluation process. Further, it focuses on transforming goal statements into explicit variables. Let us consider the "Operationalization of Fuzzy Concepts" in some detail.

THE METHODOLOGICAL APPROACH

The methodology developed in this chapter is known as the "Operationalization of Fuzzy Concepts." It was developed several years before being put into practical use. The author, Hutchinson, formulated the methodology as a means of enhancing the human "thinking" process. Included in his work at the University of Massachusetts was the task of evaluating its new School of Education after its first year of operation. Among the problems facing him was that the School of Education had been operating in the absence of any formally expressed goals. During the process of obtaining the pertinent set of goals of the School of Education, he initiated the systematic use of the operationalization of fuzzy concepts.

The operationalization of fuzzy concepts is integral to the idea of a larger evaluation methodology. A methodology for evaluation should be generalizable to all educational enterprises. A consideration of decision-maker goals provides a convenient point of origin and a common starting point for all enterprises. It would then follow that each enterprise should operationalize its set of goals to the point at which a clear and unambiguous interpretation of each goal statement exists.

The definition of evaluation cited earlier—a procedure for collecting and analyzing data to produce pertinent information that can be used to facilitate decision-making by decision-makers—will undergird the methodological approach to be developed.

Rationale

The operationalization of fuzzy concepts purports to make available to evaluators a vehicle by means of which a goal (often stated in vague terms) can be delineated into explicit variables. At the same time, the process should preserve the real intent of the originator of the goal. In other words, application of the operationalization of fuzzy concepts of a goal yields a list of behaviorally stated variables that represents the decision-maker's real intent of the goal under consideration. The list makes up the set of variables that dictate the evaluation activity. A variable that implies behavior that is neither directly observable nor in measurable form is referred to as a fuzzy concept.

For purposes of this methodology, a variable is defined as the smallest element of a goal intent. Often the work of evaluators is facilitated by using explicit variables. An explicit variable is an unambiguously stated manifestation of a goal intent that can be observed directly. Usually explicit variables can be stated in the form of a simple sentence; the predicate of the sentence dictates the evaluation activity.

The concept of operationalization can be defined as a process that involves systematically thinking through several steps. It tries to provide the means whereby one can envision the ultimate characteristics of an intended outcome in vivid detail prior to actual manifestation of that outcome. It can also be noted that the operationalization of fuzzy concepts is cyclical in nature. Utilization of the methodology on particularly vague goal statements might require recycling the fuzzy portions of the goal repeatedly through the methodology until the real goal intent can be expressly stated via a set of explicit variables.

Procedure

The operationalization of fuzzy concepts as a methodology essentially consists of five phases. The phases, in their normal order of occurrence, are: (a) the procurement of goals; (b) the operationalization of goals; (c) the development of assessment techniques; (d) the implementation of assessment techniques; and (e) the summarization of the evaluation endeavor—the report. Each of these phases is now considered in some detail.

The Procurement of Goals. Procuring the goals of an enterprise is the evaluator's responsibility. The most direct, and often the simplest, way to get the goals is to ask the decision-maker for his goals. It is incumbent upon the decision-maker to articulate his goals to the evaluator. In turn, it is incumbent upon the evaluator to assist the decision-maker to transform his goals into meaningful behavioral statements. ("Goals" may be called different things by different people. Variously they may be referred to as objectives, aims, or desired program outcomes. In this discussion, the word *goals* is utilized.)

Every enterprise contains a set of goals. These goals may be written out in the form of a paragraph, phrases, or a series of sentences; they may manifest themselves through conversation with the decision-maker; or they may appear sporadically throughout pertinent documents in an unsystematic manner. Written phrases, sentences, and paragraphs can be translated into meaningful behavioral statements via the operationalization of fuzzy concepts with relatively little difficulty. An inherent disadvantage of verbally communicated goals is that they are often stated inferentially, awkwardly, and indirectly.

During the procurement of an enterprise's goals, a distinction between the roles of the evaluator and the decision-maker must be maintained at all times. It is important that the evaluator consult with the decision-maker about the priority of the goals. The decision-maker should rank-order the goals of the enterprise in terms of their importance.

The outcome of this combined effort of the decision-maker and the evaluator is a written statement of the set of goals ordered by importance. Given this rank-ordered list of goals, the evaluator considers them singly in terms of their operational implications. He then reports to the decision-maker, including in his report the following:

1. A preliminary operational procedure.
2. A feasibility speculation.
   a. A statement as to whether the decision-maker's ordering of goals is practical in terms of
      (1) contractual time;
      (2) material and equipment (facilities and space);
      (3) personnel;
      (4) implementation.
   b. A suggested reordering of goals based on their interrelatedness with respect to implementation.

The decision-maker considers the evaluator's report and ultimately decides on the final ordering of the goals.

The Operationalization of Goals. This phase of the methodology calls for considerable dialogue between evaluator and decision-maker. This dialogue results from sequentially carrying out the following steps:

1. Create a hypothetical situation where the fuzzy concept applies.

2. Analyze that hypothetical situation in terms of the observable and measurable events which take place (and which can be interpreted to mean that the fuzzy concept is present).

3. Create a hypothetical situation where the fuzzy concept is specifically absent and repeat Step 2, analyzing in terms of events that can be interpreted to mean that the concept is absent.

4. Generate alternative dimensions which can challenge the "list" of components arrived at in steps 1-3 in terms of completeness. (Note: The need here is for a complete list of all those elements which in the aggregate comprise the fuzzy concept [Hutchinson, 1970].)

The fourth step is sometimes called the "test of completeness." Essentially it is a technique requiring the decision-maker to repeatedly generate and reexamine all possible dimensions of the concept. The purpose of this test is to compel the decision-maker to explore a variety of alternative dimensions so that all aspects of his goal intent will be exhausted. Another reason for the decision-maker to delineate his goal intent via such an iterative process is to guarantee the preservation of the real meaning of his goal throughout the entire evaluative process. After all, if evaluation is to produce useful data for decision-making, the decision-maker must respect the data produced.

For clarification, an example using the preceding four steps will be presented. The fuzzy concept under consideration is: "Increase the range of knowledge and skills within regular subjects and be able to apply basic principles." The contextual setting for this fuzzy concept was a special section of the first grade class in a New England public school. The phrase "regular subjects" means reading, writing, arithmetic, social studies, and science.

To operationalize this fuzzy concept, it was first rewritten as three separate components.

1. Increase the range of knowledge within regular subjects.

2. Increase the range of skills within regular subjects.

3. Apply basic principles.

The rewriting or restating of goals, originally expressed as vague concepts, as simple sentences is fundamental to applying the operationalization of fuzzy concepts methodology. In the following extended dialogue, this process can be seen at work as the evaluator sequentially takes the decision-maker through several steps and levels using the methodology. Note also the great care that the evaluator takes to preserve the original intent of the decision-maker throughout while deriving essential variables from the goals. To conserve space, the evaluator's statements will be preceded simply by E, while those of the decision-maker will be marked D; quotation marks will not be used.

E: First, create in your mind a hypothetical construct where the fuzzy concept applies.

D: I don't understand what you mean.

E: Create mentally a situation with a group of people in it, a complete environment, buildings, furniture, and the like.

D: A whole city?

E: Yes, a whole city. Now consider a neighborhood having an elementary school in it.

D: Okay, I have that.

E: Imagine that the situation is conducive for your fuzzy concept to manifest itself.

D: You mean my objective, to increase the range of knowledge?

E: Yes. It is conducive and highly facilitative; that is, the range of knowledge within regular subjects does, in fact, increase.

D: Okay, I think I have that picture.

E: Now, look at that situation closely, observing everything in it, particularly the behavior patterns.

D: All right.

E: Now, write a list of the things the bear directly on your concept.

D: You mean increase the range of knowledge?

E: Yes. List the things that are happening in line with what you set out to do.

D: I see students demonstrating more knowledge about regular subjects than previously.

E: Is that all you see?

D: Yes. That's all that I see that relates to my objective.

This completes the initial dialogue concerning steps 1 and 2 of the methodology with respect to the objective, "Increase the range of knowledge within regular subjects." The record will show that only one variable was delineated. At this point, the evaluator and decision-maker continue to operationalize the objective:

E: Now, create a hypothetical situation where your concept is specifically absent. Try not to use merely opposite forms of variables that evolved out of the previous hypothetical situations.

D: Do you mean the concept, increase the range of knowledge?

E: Yes.

D: What do you want me to do with it?

E: Imagine that the range of knowledge does not increase.

D: I thought you wanted me to imagine that it increased.

E: This time I want you to imagine a situation where no range of knowledge incerases.

D: Okay, I see.

E: Imagine that there is a situation in which the range of knowledge does not increase.

D: What are you talking about? I got a group of kids who are at school.

E: I know. The purpose of this step is to get you to envision what the situation would be like if the concept was absent. The variables you identify will then be used only to the extent that they help you to delineate additional positive variables.

D: Okay, I think I have the picture.

E: Now, look at that situation closely, observing everything you see in it and, particularly, the behavior having nothing to do with your concept.

D: All right.

E: Write a list of the things that bear directly on, or reflect, the absence of your concept.

D: All right, I've listed these things. I see students going to sleep in class, throwing spit balls, and ignoring the teacher completely.

E: Now, examine each of these variables critically to see if you can think of variables that reflect what you mean by your concept.

D: But these variables have no direct bearing on my objective.

E: I know. The idea is that they may make you think of some variables that reflect what you do mean by your concept.

D: I see, but I am afraid that that is not the case.

E: All right. Next, we must generate a set of alternative variables that challenges the list of variables delineated. This process is known as the "test of completeness." The idea is to get someone else—preferably several people—to go through the same steps. So let me, as evaluator, put your fuzzy concept through the steps of his methodology as if the concept were mine.

First, I have visualized a hypothetical situation in which the fuzzy concept, "Increase the range of knowledge within regular subjects," applies. I've written down that I see students demonstrat-more legible writing skills, doing better on their tests, reading better and faster, reading books of increasing difficulty, choosing books of increasing difficulty on their own, working arithmetic problems on their own.

Second, I have envisioned a hypothetical situation in which your fuzzy concept is absent. Here I've written that I see students failing to do their school work at home, "goofing off" and not studying at school, and acting as though their range of knowledge of regular subjects has decreased.

The decision-maker looks at the two lists generated by the evaluator. He considers each variable and if it is a variable that he thinks he should have, he writes it on his list; if it is a variable that he does not like, he rejects, it; if the set of variables generated by the evaluator makes the decision-maker think of pertinent variables, he adds them to his list.

In the process of examining the variables delineated by the evaluator, the decision-maker chose as important variables: demonstrate improvement in reading comprehension; demonstrate increased reading rate; demonstrate improvement in composition writing skills.

This ends the first test of completeness.

There are essentially three tests of completeness. At the juncture, the evaluator and the decision-maker are beginning the second test of completeness.

E: Go back and look at the hypothetical situation. . . .

D: What! Again?

E: This time, I want you to look for something different in the hypothetical situation.

D: Oh! Well, all right. What am I to look for this time?

E: In that initial hypothetical situation that was conducive for the range of knowledge to increase, presumably there were things that you saw but did not write on your list because you felt they probably were not meaningful.

D: Oh!

E: Maybe this was the case. Think back and consider the things you saw but did not list.

D: All right, but I'm not sure I understand what you want.

E: Seriously consider the implications of the things you could have listed but felt were not meaningful variables.

D: Okay.

E: After reconsidering the variables that might possibly be meaningful, do you now see things which you should add to your list?

D: Well, let's see. I see students demonstrating more knowledge by the way they talk to their teacher and the other students.

E: Is that all you see?

D: I think so.

This ends the second test of completeness. The evaluator moves to begin the last test of completeness.

E: This time I want you to create a hypothetical. . . .

D: What? Again?

E: This hypothetical situation should have nothing to do with your fuzzy concept.

D: You mean my objective.

E: Yes, your objective: increase the range of knowledge within regular subjects.

D: Now, what am I supposed to do?

E: Create a hypothetical situation that is unrelated to your concept.

D: Any unrelated hypothetical situation?

E: Yes.

D: Okay: I think I have one.

E: Does this have any implications for your fuzzy concept?

D: I don't know. I was thinking of several first graders deciding whether they would rather play hop-scotch or jump rope. Do you see any implications?

E. Well, your fuzzy concept is "increase the range of knowledge within regular subjects."

E: Are there implications with respect to the fuzzy concept?

D: I don't see any.

This completes the first cycle of the methodology with respect to the objective: increase the range of knowledge within regular subjects. At this point the complete list that characterizes what the decision-maker means by his objective contains the following variables:

1. Demonstrate more knowledge about regular subjects than previously.

2. Demonstrate improvement in reading comprehension.

3. Demonstrate increased reading rate.

4. Demonstrate improvement in composition writing skills.

5. Demonstrate more knowledge in talking to teacher and other students.

For each of the variables on the list the decision-maker is asked to consider the question, "Can I observe that behavior directly?" The evaluator also considers this question with respect to each variable. Those variables implying behavior that can be observed directly are nonfuzzy concepts. They are recorded and filed to become a part of the final list for assessment and implementation. Variables implying behavior that cannot be observed directly continue to be fuzzy concepts.

At a glance, it can be determined that some of the variables delineated from the objective—increase the range of knowledge within regular subjects—still fit the fuzzy concept criterion. Note that each variable delineated from a goal via the methodology that continues to fit the fuzzy concept definition must undergo the methodological cycle again in the same manner. The variable—demonstrate more knowledge about regular subjects than previously—is the topic of the following dialogue:

E: Create in your mind a hypothetical situation where the fuzzy concept applies.

D: Do you mean a hypothetical situation where students are demonstrating more knowledge about regular subjects than previously?

E: Yes. Create a situation with a group of people in it, a complete environment, buildings, furniture, etc.

D: I got the picture, I think.

E: Now imagine that the situation is conducive for your fuzzy concept to manifest itself.

D: You mean my objective—demonstrate more knowledge than previously.

E: Yes, imagine that a high degree of excellence prevails and that the students are really demonstrating knowledge the way in which you expect them.

D: All right.

E: Now, write a list of the things that bear directly on your fuzzy concept.

D: I see students indicating a higher level of knowledge via objective measure, and indicating a higher level of knowledge via subjective measure.

E: Is this your complete list?

D: Yes, I think so.

E: Okay. Now create in your mind a hypothetical situation in which your concept is specifically absent. In this situation more knowledge about regular subjects is *not* being demonstrated.

D: What are you talking about?

E: Conceivably, we know what a situation is like when more knowledge is being demonstrated. Right?

D: Yes, I just listed two variables.

E: Now try to imagine what it is like when more knowledge is not evident.

D: Okay. I think I get the picture.

E: Analyze the hypothetical situation visually in terms of the observable and measurable events which take place in that situation that can be interpreted to mean that the concept is specifically absent.

D: How am I going to analyze my objective if it is absent?

E: What I want you to do is to examine the situation to see what behaviors exist that suggest that your concept is, indeed, absent.

D: I think I understand.

E: Okay, write a list of those things that you observe in this situation.

D: I see students judging their own level of knowledge. Also, I see students judging one another's level of knowledge.

E: Is this all you see in that situation?

D: Yes, I think that's it.

E: All right. We are now ready for the first test of completeness. This means that I must put the fuzzy concept through the same steps that you did. So by creating a hypothetical situation in which more knowledge is demonstrated than previously and analyzing the situation, I see students developing a high quality of achievement and a motivation for learning.

As I analyze the situation where the fuzzy concept is conspicuously absent, I see students singing a rhythmic song and building bridges with blocks. Consider the variables that I listed. Is there one that adds meaning to your fuzzy concept? If so, add it to your list. If not, reject it. If a variable makes you think of other pertinent variables, add them to your list.

D: As I look at your list, I don't see anything that I want to add to my list, and nothing reminds me of other pertinent variables.

E: All right. This ends the first test of completeness. Now go through the next level test of completeness.

D: Okay.

E: You understand that you will have to create your original hypothetical situation again.

D: Yes, I know.

E: I mean the one where you imagined that there was a high degree of excellence and that students were really demonstrating more knowledge than previously.

D: Yes, I got that.

E: Now, perhaps there were other things in that situation that you saw, but did not write on your list because you felt they probably were not important.

D: Oh! I don't think so.

E: Well, maybe. So think back and consider the things that you saw, but did not write on your list.

D: Okay.

E: Are there implications from the things you are now considering that might be important?

D: I don't think so.

E: Okay. Then this ends our second test of completeness. In order to do our last test of completeness, you must again create a hypothetical situation that is unrelated to your fuzzy concept.

D: That's right. This time I want a situation that has nothing to do with demonstrating knowledge. Right?

E: Yes, that is correct. Construct some variables that have nothing to do with demonstrating knowledge.

D: Like sitting quietly in the classroom.

E: Perhaps.

D: Like carrying out a daily schedule.

E: Doesn't that include demonstrating some knowledge?

D: Okay, but how about studying during study hall periods?

E: That could involve demonstrating knowledge too, I think.

D: All right, then. What about paying attention in class?

E: Let's think about the implications of this. Do these implications suggest any variables that you might want to add to your list?

D: Well, there could be. How about developing good study habits . . . and developing listening skills?

E: Good. Any more?

D: That's all can think of.

E: Well, this completes the cycle—the first-level cycle—with respect to the concept.

At this level some of the variables delineated meet the nonfuzzy criterion. These are recorded and filed to make up part of the master list for development of assessment techniques. Those variables which are still

classified as fuzzy concepts must be further operationalized. This is done
by repeating the methodological cycle.

Recall that this entire process was initiated by rewriting the decision-
maker's original goal intent into three subcomponents:

1. Increase the range of knowledge within regular subjects.
2. Increase the range of skills within regular subjects.
3. Apply basic principles.

The extended dialogue above represents just a portion of the effort
that was required to translate the decision-maker's vague goal into meaningful behavioral statements. Space limitations preclude going through the
entire dialogue that was exchanged in the actual situation before completing the methodological steps. It can be noted, though, that upon opera-
tionalizing subcomponents 1 and 2 (above), the decision-maker discovered
that he had also exhausted his goal intent concerning subcomponent 3.

Although it would be laborious to go through the actual dialogue of
the complete operationalization process, it is possible to present a summary list of all the explicit variables that ultimately were derived in this
actual situation. That summary list of all the operationalized variables of
the goal, "Increase the range of knowledge and skills within regular subjects and be able to apply basic principles," is presented below:

1. Score well on standardized tests.
2. Score well on teacher-made objective tests.
3. Score well on teacher-made subjective tests.
4. Rank well on regular subjects (via teacher opinion).
5. Talk about subject matter fluently with teacher.
6. Talk about subject matter fluently with peers (classmates).
7. Use improved study habits.
8. Use improved English in conversation.
9. Engage in conversation about regular subject matter and discuss
issues well enough to be understood by the listener.
10. Demonstrate an increased vocabulary.
11. Demonstrate improvement in reading comprehension.
12. Demonstrate increased reading rate.
13. Demonstrate improvement in verbal communication.
14. Demonstrate skill in listening attentively.
15. Demonstrate improvement in composition writing skills.
16. Demonstrate improvement in the skill to explain what one hears
in his own words.
17. Demonstrate improvement in the skill to act on what one hears.

This list does not meet completely the "nonfuzzy concept" criterion
because words like "well," "fluently," "improvement," and "increased"
need further operationalization. After consultation between the decision-

maker and the evaluator, the decision-maker defined these terms as follows:

"well"—at least the 85th percentile or a score of 85;
"fluently"—to be determined by teacher judgment;
"improvement"—better than the previous record;
"increased"—better than the previous record.

The Development of Assessment Techniques. An outcome of the sequential methodology used above to operationalize objectives is the establishment of a framework that is indicative of the variables to be assessed. The methodology used translates variables from vague statements into statements that are characterized by a particular behavior. How a particular behavior can be represented quantitatively is of paramount importance. It is so important that, for each variable, the behavior in question should influence the development of the assessment technique.

The rationale underlying the development of assessment techniques evolves as an integral part of the evaluative process. Once a goal has been operationalized so that its real intent is characterized by a set of either observable or measurable variables, it is then proper to make assessment. The logical step after quantifying those variables amenable to quantification is to develop assessment techniques for the required behavior. In this chapter, the term *assessment technique* is used to refer to those procedures that characterize a systematic way of measuring behaviors to obtain reliable and valid assesments of variables. Such behaviors are dictated by the explicit variables generated via the operationalization of fuzzy concepts methodology.

Thus, the development of assessment instruments and techniques involves two distinct steps: (1) variables behaviorally expressed must be quantified; (2) suitable assessment instruments must either be selected or developed. Considered first is the quantification of variables. Thorndike's statement, "Whatever exists at all exists in some amount," serves as the basis for quantifying variables. Since variables exist, they must exist in some amount, and hence can be quantified and measured. Pertinent here is explication of the standard way in which variables are classified as either nominal, ordinal, interval, or ratio (Stevens, 1951). An interesting discussion on classifying variables can be found in Torgerson (1958); yet Ferguson's treatment of the four categories (1966) is presented here because it appears to have high utility for the evaluator. Ferguson defined the classes as follows:

1. A nominal variable is a property of the members of a group defined by an operation which permits the making of statements only of equality or difference. A nominal variable may be viewed as a primitive type of variable. Color is a nominal variable.

2. An ordinal variable is a property defined by an operation which permits the rank ordering of the members of a group; that is, not only are statements of equality and difference possible, but also statements of the kind, greater than or less than. For instance, if a judge is required to order a group of individuals according to aggressiveness, or cooperativeness, or some other quality, the resulting variable is ordinal in type.

3. An interval variable is a property defined by an operation which permits the making of statements of sameness or difference or greater than or less than. An interval variable does not have a "true" zero point, although a zero point may for convenience be arbitrarily defined. Fahrenheit and centigrade temperature measurements constitute interval variables. Calendar time is also an interval variable with an arbitrarily defined zero.

4. A ratio variable is a property defined by an operation which permits the making of statements of equality of ratios in addition to all other kinds of statements discussed above. This means that the value of one variable may be spoken of as double or triple another, and so on. An absolute zero is always implied. (pp. 12-14)

The essential difference between an interval and a ratio variable is that for the latter the measurements are made from a true zero point, whereas for the former the measurements are made from an arbitrarily defined zero point or origin.

A variety of refinements and elaborations can be made on the distinctions between nominal, ordinal, interval, and ratio variables. Some writers distinguish between quantitative and qualitative variables without being explicit about the nature of this distinction.

Let us now consider the actual process of selecting or developing assessment instruments and techniques. Clearly the chief criterion operating is that the instrument or technique selected must be a valid measure of the behavior of interest and, secondarily, a reliable measure. Other frequently relevant questions are: Should it be a direct measure or unobtrusive? Should it involve test performance or an observational procedure? These questions must be considered and answered by the evaluator.

Another common dilemma concerns whether to use existing measures, whether to modify them, or whether to construct a new instrument or technique. The selection of already available instruments and assessment techniques obviously expedites the implementation phase. Thus, if valid and reliable measures of the required behaviors are available, they obviously should be used. Such instruments have a further advantage over a new instrument: they have established norms and an available history of pertinent and critical reviews. Still, there are potential dangers inherent in using ready-made instruments. A major danger is the fact that reliability and validity can be affected by transfer. That is, once an instrument has been tested out, using selected norms, standards, and sample populations, the validity and reliability indicators established may not be valid if the instrument is applied in an environment foreign to the criteria used to derive such indicators. Therefore, in addition to the responsibility of securing assessment instruments and techniques, the evaluator must examine them prior to endorsing their use. He must approve, disapprove, or modify them for use.

The alternative is developing the assessment technique or instrument. This is a time-consuming process, and further such development should include field tryout and modification before use in the actual evaluation. Clearly there are several ways in which one can arrive at assessment techniques. Assessment strategies will vary from assessor to assessor, however. It could be argued that assessment techniques should not be designed uniformly. The position of this author is that the development of assessment techniques should clearly reflect the behavior being measured. The following step-wise method is recommended:

1. Answer the question, "What is the behavior that is to be assessed?"
2. Answer the question, "What is the best practical technique that most accurately measures the behavior to be assessed?"
3. Describe the best practical measure.

This approach provides a procedure for evaluators to use in their efforts to produce a pertinent set of assessment techniques. Answers to these questions will set in motion the process of developing (or selecting) the required set of assessment techniques. The philosophy underlying the questions is consistent with the notion that evaluation as a process should be scientific. It incorporates the idea that one should be able to take a step-wise approach to evaluation and proceed in a sequential fashion throughout the entire evaluative process.

Note that during this phase of the evaluative process, the decision-maker's role differs markedly from his previous role. In the early phases of the evaluation of an enterprise, the decision-maker plays a dominant role. He identifies his goals and plays an active part in their operationalization. However, it is the responsibility of the evaluator to develop assessment techniques. During this phase, the decision-maker's role shifts and he becomes less active. He can be thought of as a consultant to the evaluator on matters regarding the feasibility of carrying out the assessment techniques for a given set of variables. It is not uncommon for decision-makers to offer critical advice on the set of assessment techniques, but their role is primarily to ascertain whether the assessment techniques are practical and permissible with regard to local policy, equipment resources, and other pertinent constraints. Feasibility considerations may require the revision of the assessment procedures developed.

An exemplary set of assessment techniques is shown in Table 9.2. Continuing the previous example, the techniques correspond to the variables generated by applying the operationalization procedures to the objective: "Increase the range of knowledge and skills within regular

TABLE 9.2

Assessment Techniques

Variable	Assessment Technique
1. Score well on standardized test.	1. Check test results.
2. Score well on teacher-made objective test.	2. Check teacher's record book.
3. Score well on teacher-made subjective test.	3. Check teacher's record book.
4. Rank well on regular subjects (via teacher opinion).	4. Ask teacher.
5. Talk fluently about subject matter with teacher.	5. Ask teacher.
6. Talk fluently about subject matter with peers (classmates).	6. Have teacher plan a lesson that calls for active group participation. Use tape recorder to tape students talking to peers. Analyze the tape.
7. Use improved study habits.	7. Discuss desired behavior with teacher. Consult with teacher about study habit criteria as it applies to study situation. Delineate the criterion and make the required observation.
8. Use improved English in conversation.	8. Have teacher engage students in informal conversations. Use tape recorder to record conversation. Do the same thing with control group. Make comparison.
9. Engage in conversation about regular subject matter.	9. Have students tell the people with whom they have talked about regular subject matter.
9a. Discuss issues well enough to be understood by the listener.	9a. Have students describe either the subject or principal focus of their most interesting conversation about regular subject matter. Have an observer rate it in terms of comprehensibility.
10. Demonstrate an increased vocabulary.	10. Check student record and ask teacher.

Variable	Assessment Technique
11. Demonstrate improvement in reading comprehension.	11. Check student record and ask teacher.
12. Demonstrate increased reading rate.	12. Check student record and ask teacher.
13. Demonstrate improvement in verbal communication.	13. Ask teacher.
14. Demonstrate skill in listening attentively.	14. Ask teacher.
15. Demonstrate improvement in composition writing skills.	15. Have outside judges read and grade pre- and post- compositions of students (unmarked as to whether pre- or post-).
16. Demonstrate improvement in the skill to explain what one hears in his own words.	16. Have teacher divide students into small groups of at least two students each. Have students engage in dialogue within groups. Have one student in each group make statements and the other member(s) of the group respond. Have each student record what he says during the conversation. Do the same thing with the control group. Make comparison.
17. Demonstrate improvement in the skill to act on what one hears.	17. Have teacher give the students three different instructive statements that they should be able to understand and carry out. Check the students' actions later. Compare what they did with what they were supposed to do.

subjects and be able to apply basic principles." The table is self-explanatory.

Implementation of Assessment Techniques. The concept of implementation of assessment techniques includes the following notions: collecting data or carrying out assessment techniques; and analyzing data.

Data collection consists of implementing the assessment techniques once developed or acquired. In practice, this task is usually delegated to members of the evaluative staff. The evaluator himself must be available to implement assessment techniques, depending on the kind of data to be collected.

Data collection techniques must take into account any need for special instructions relative to administering the instruments developed unless the evaluator himself is to administer the instrument. If an instrument likely to be unfamiliar to some participants is being used, care must be exercised to insure that participants understand the types of question and exactly how responses are to be made. If some participants fail to understand the types of questions used, a large portion of the variability in scores on the instrument may be attributable to differences in participants' perception of the instructions.

It can be noted that the evaluator is responsible for implementation of the assessment techniques. The role of the decision-maker, as in the selection/development phase, is that of consultant. The evaluator periodically informs the decision-maker of implementation progress.

To maximize the efficiency by which assessments can be made, required assessements are grouped and regrouped until the entire set is subdivided into categories amenable to similar implementation techniques. After having classified the entire set of assessment techniques into similar categories, the implementation procedure takes the following form:

1. The evaluator reconsiders the set of assessment techniques with regard to the newly formed groups and makes appropriate modifications.

2. He negotiates a calendar of activities with the specific aim of making the required assessments.

3. He consults the decision-maker, and they set up the schedule for carrying out the assessment techniques.

4. The assessment techniques are carried out in accordance with the schedule.

TABLE 9.3

Assessment Check List

Fill out a separate sheet for each student in the 6H program. Place a check mark (√) in the box that you feel to be most nearly correct. The response will be interpreted as follows:

"Rarely" implies 0% to 15% of the time.
"Sometimes" implies 16% to 35% of the time.
"Frequently" implies 36% to 65% of the time.
"Generally" implies 66% to 85% of the time.
"Almost always" implies 86% to 100% of the time.

Student _____

Date _____

	Rarely	Sometimes	Frequently	Generally	Almost always
1. Scores well on standardized test.					
2. Scores well on teacher-made objective test.					
3. Scores well on teacher-made subjective test.					
4. Ranks well on regular subjects (via teacher opinion).					
5. Talks fluently about subject matter with teacher.					
10. Demonstrates increased vocabulary.					
11. Demonstrates improvement in reading comprehension.					
12. Demonstrates increased reading rate.					
13. Demonstrates improvement in verbal communication.					
14. Demonstrates skill in listening attentively.					

Once data have been collected, the analysis commences. Careful preplanning as to the form of the data to be generated will reduce analysis time substantially. The extensive analysis procedures available are beyond the scope of this chapter, but are readily available in several excellent texts currently available. It should be kept in mind that the analysis should render the data into a form that has utility for the decision-maker.

Summarization of the Evaluation Endeavor—The Report. The evaluation report, much like a research report, usually includes sections on an applied methodology, data collection, results and interpretation, and conclusions.

The section on methodology describes the evaluative procedures and the instrumentation (how and why instruments were selected or developed).

The data collection section contains the raw data collected via the assessment techniques. Attention is given to problems encountered, constraints faced, and modifications made. If portions of the evaluation are purportedly either generalizable or replicable, this section must include sufficient detail to make apparent the generalizable or replicable features.

The results and their interpretation are usually contained in a single section. The data are analyzed, interpreted, and presented in a highly readable form, reflecting the common methods of analysis in common language. Whenever practical, results of the analysis of data are condensed in the form of tables or are graphically presented.

The conclusions are based on the results. They reflect the overall judgment about the data analyzed. Evaluative data should be used to influence systematic change while the operations of an enterprise are in progress. Therefore, comments that will improve the chances of accomplishing the goals under consideration often should be made prior to the actual drafting of the report and conclusions.

The principal user of the evaluation report is the decision-maker. However, the receiving audience of the report is usually much larger than the decision-maker. Therefore, in addition to the content described in the preceding paragraphs and specification of the intended audience, the report includes goals under consideration; operationalized variables (from the goals); problem areas; and evaluative suggestions.

The report should not contain judgmental statements of a managerial nature. It is the role of the evaluator to produce useful data for decision-making. It is the role of the decision-maker to use evaluative data for decision-making. Stufflebeam and his colleagues (1971) included judging—the act of choosing among several decision alternatives—as the central term in their definition of evaluation. Their position was that while the term *judging* is central to the definition of evaluation, the act of judging is *not* central to the evaluator's role. Stake (1967), however, argued that the evaluator who does participate in decision-making destroys his own objectivity, and, hence, his utility. Not all evaluators agree with this position. Scriven (1967), for example, regarded the evaluator who refuses to engage in decision-making as having abrogated his role.

EVALUATION AND EARLY CHILDHOOD PROGRAMS

Even a cursory view of federally funded programs throughout the country would reveal that seldom do program managers know enough about the purpose or the real intent of their goals to administer their programs efficiently. Rather, with a few notable exceptions, most programs are operated in a traditional manner, with little thought given to aims and objectives. Unfortunately, this condition is evident in many early childhood programs. Most early childhood programs do not have clearly defined objectives, although in that field, too, there is a trend toward fully identifiable objectives stated in behavioral terms.

These undesirable conditions support the present thrust to provide evaluation training and new concepts for program managers. One author (Rickover, 1960) suggested that most program managers operated in a similar manner, regardless of the nature or purpose of their programs. The operationalization of fuzzy concepts as a methodology purports to remedy some of these problems.

Evaluative Concerns

What can evaluation methodology do for program managers? One vital function is to produce useful data to influence decision-making. If evaluation is to be relevant for early childhood programs, some pertinent thoughts about a set of genuine concerns need to be verbalized. Among the thoughts are the following:

1. Identifying the decision-maker's goals.
2. Securing decision-maker participation and cooperation.
3. Coping with the decision-maker's perceived notion as to how to evaluate.
4. Reconciling evaluation issues; e.g., consequences of evaluation or multiaudience aspects.
5. Reconciling goal intention (in the case of more than one decision-maker).
6. Maintaining accesssibility of the decision-maker to the evaluator.
7. Establishing a set of variables that characterize goal intents.
8. Assessing resources.
9. Assuring the timeliness of the evaluation with respect to the age of the program—evaluation should be included in initial program planning.
10. Assessing time and other resources required to evaluate a goal completely.
11. Changing goal intents during the in-progress stage of the evaluation.
12. Modifying goal intents so that they are consistent with programmatic operations.

13. Modifying the program to become consistent with goal intentions.

The evaluator of any enterprise often faces problems such as these:

1. The timeliness of the evaluation report; i.e., the date that the evaluation is due often follows the time when decisions were made that should have been influenced by evaluation data.
2. The results of the evaluation are sometimes incongruent with the audience's expectation (see 4 above).
3. The methodology may challenge the decision-maker's ability to express the real intent of his goals in behavioral statements.
4. The duration of the evaluator/decision-maker dialogue may sometimes place the evaluator in the role of an imposer. Also, the nature of the dialogue may be somewhat threatening because the onus with respect to articulating the goal intent is placed clearly upon the decision-maker.

Summary

The state of the art of evaluation with respect to its impact on programs suggests that the evaluator of early childhood (EC) programs should examine the following questions:

1. Who wants the EC program evaluated?
2. How can the EC program be evaluated?
3. When is the EC program to be evaluated?
4. Why should the EC program be evaluated?

In answering the first question, the matters of identifying the decision-maker's goal, securing the decision-maker's cooperation and willing participation, and making resources available to the evaluator (including the dceision-maker's time) should be considered. In fact, some satisfactory resolution of these problem areas should be reached during the planning conference in the process of negotiating the evaluation arrangements.

In answering the question of how the EC program can be evaluated, the decision-maker's perceived notion of how to evaluate should be discussed and a rationale presented for not using his approach, if necessary. The accessibility of the decision-maker to the evaluator is essential in resolving this question. If more than one decision-maker exists, the likelihood of disagreement with respect to goal intents becomes more probable. This problem warrants careful consideration as one examines this second question.

The question of when the EC program is to be evaluated invites another question: "Evaluation for what purpose?" Included in the criteria necessary to answer the latter question is the position of Pace (1968), mentioned earlier: "The way in which we think about evaluation, and how we go about making evaluations, are necessarily related to what we are evaluating and why we are doing it." The answer to the third question, at least in part, depends on the evaluator's interest in data concerning persons, processes, and outcomes of the program.

A logical question from program managers is when to apply the evaluative technique. The position of this author is that formal or summative evaluation should be undertaken both during and at the end of early childhood programs. Formal evaluation activities should be oriented to the decision-maker's needs, and these needs should be articulated by program managers. Some salient features of formal evaluation include its multiaudience aspect and its varying appropriateness with respect to the age of the particular early childhood program. The formative or informal evaluation process should be continuous; that is, it should go on during the entire program operation. By means of the informal evaluation, program managers should have ready access to feedback.

In answer to the question of why the EC program should be evaluated, the consequence of conducting or not conducting an evaluation should be explored (see "The Case for Not Evaluating" in chapter 8. Also worthy of exploration is the matter of the decision-maker either changing his goal intents during the in-progress stage of the evaluation (because of beedback data or so that they are consistent with programmatic operations). In such an event, the goals governing the evaluation may no longer be consonant with the changes or modifications that have taken place and, hence, the evaluation data generated may not be valid.

In closing, it should be noted that early childhood programs should be evaluated because program managers need to be concerned with the extent to which goals of the program are being reached. By employing an evaluative methodology that provides useful results, it is reasonable to hope to find ways of eliminating existing deficiencies that may become evident. Evaluation should not be viewed as an extra chore imposed upon decision-makers or a distasteful task to be completed as quickly as possible. Rather, it should be viewed as an integral part of a good program manager's procedure in effectively conducting his program.

REFERENCES

Dyer, H. S. The role of evaluation in curriculum innovation. *Proceedings of the Assosciation for Supervision and Curriculum Development Pre-Conference Seminar,* Princeton, N.J.: Educational Testing Service, 1968.

Eisner, E. W. Instructional and expressive educational objectives: Their formulation and use in curriculum. Unpublished paper, Stanford University, Palo Alto, 1968.

Ferguson, G. A. *Statistical analysis in psychology and education.* (2nd edition.) New York: McGraw-Hill, 1966.

Fortune, J. C., & Hutchinson, T. E. Project upgrade: Evaluation design. Unpublished paper, University of Massachusetts, 1970.

Gage, N. L. Comments on Professor Lortie's paper entitled: The cracked cake of educational custom and emerging issues in evaluation. Report No. 21. Los Angeles: Center for the Study of Evaluation of Instructional Programs, University of California at Los Angeles Press, 1968.

Hammond, R. Context evaluation of instruction in local school districts. Educational Technology, 1969, 9(3), 11-38.

Hutchinson, T. E. Operationalization of fuzzy concepts: A methodology. Unpublished paper, University of Massachusetts, 1970.

Jones, L. The operationalization of educational objectives for the evaluation of an ongoing program. Unpublished doctoral dissertation, University of Massachusetts, 1971.

Mager, R. F. *Preparing instructional objectives.* Palo Alto: Fearon Publishers, 1962.

Pace, C. R. Evaluation perspectives. Paper presented at meeting of American Educational Research Association Presession, Chicago, 1968.

Popham, J. W. Objectives and instruction. *AERA Monograph Series on Curriculum Evaluation,* 1967, No. 3.

Provus, M. Evaluation of ongoing programs in the public school system. *Yearbook of the National Society for the Study of Education.* Part II. Chicago: University of Chicago Press, 1969.

Remmers, H. H., Gage, N. L., & Rummel, J. F. *A practical introduction to measurement and evaluation.* (2nd edition.) New York: Harper & Row, 1965.

Rickover, H. G. *Education and freedom.* New York: Dutton, 1960.

Sadker, D. Objectives in perspective. Unpublished manuscript, University of Massachusetts, 1969.

Scriven, M. The methodology of evaluation. *AERA Mimeograph Series on Curriculum Evaluation,* 1967, *1,* 39-81.

Singh, S. P. A strategy to evaluate a teacher-training program. *Educational Technology,* 1970, *10*(3), 13-18.

————, & Barnard, J. Evaluation of instructional materials: An approach. Southeastern Materials Center, University of South Florida Press, 1969.

Sjogren, D. D. Measurement techniques in evaluation. *Review of Educational Research,* 1969, *40*(2), 301.

Stake, R. E. The countenance of educational evaluation. *Teachers College Record,* 1967, *68,* 523-40.

————. Testing in the evaluation of curriculum development. *Review of Educational Research,* 1968, *38*(1). (a)

————. Two approaches to evaluating instructional materials. Paper presented at the meeting of the American Psychological Association, San Francisco, 1968b.

Stake, R. E., & Denny, T. Needed concepts and techniques for utilizing more fully the potential of evaluation. *Yearbook of the National Society for the Study of Education,* Part III. Chicago: University of Chicago Press, 1969.

Stevens, S. S. (Ed.). *Handbook of experimental psychology.* New York: John Wiley, 1951.

Stufflebeam, D. I., Foley, W. J., Gephart, W. J., Guba, E. G., Hammond, R. L., Merriman, H. O., & Provus, M. M. *Educational evaluation and decision making.* Itasca, Ill.: Peacock Publishers, 1971.

Thorndike, E. L. The nature, purposes, and general methods of measurements of educational products. *Yearbook of the National Society for the Study of Education.* Part II. Bloomington, Ill.: Public School Publishing Company, 1918.

Tiedeman, D. V., & Tatsuoka, M. M. Statistics and an aspect of scientific method in research on teaching. In N. L. Gage (Ed.), *Handbook on teaching.* Chicago: Rand McNally, 1967.

Torgerson, W. S. *Theory and methods of scaling.* New York: John Wiley, 1958.

Tyler, R. W. *Basic principles of curriculum and instruction: Syllabus for education 360.* Chicago: University of Chicago Press, 1950.

———. Changing concepts of educational evaluation. *AERA Monograph Series on Curriculum Evaluation,* 1967.

Wood, D. A. *Test construction.* Columbus, O.: Merrill Books, 1961.

Chapter 10

Measurement Practices in Early Childhood Education

ELLIS D. EVANS

Generalizations about child development and behavior, teacher effectiveness, and the worth of educational programs are no better than the data from which they come. Such data are in turn a function of the strategies and techniques used to measure behavior. In this chapter, current measurement strategies and techniques applicable to early childhood education are selectively examined; this will include a look at the basic measurement problems faced by both teacher educators and teachers of young children. Special emphasis is placed on how to measure behavior.

The task of writing this chapter was approached with all the verve of a Coronado searching for the Seven Cities of Gold. It was hoped that the spadework for this task would somehow uncover a wealth of sophisticated, precise measurement techniques, reflecting advances over the shopworn procedures that have so long dominated educational practice. While many variations on the traditional themes of testing and observation have emerged, along with a staggering proliferation of new, albeit conventional, measuring instruments, there have been few measurement techniques that are both valid and practical for widespread use in the field that could be termed innovative.

This view is shared by others who have recently dealt with the role of measurement in the evaluation of early childhood programs. For example, Kamii and Elliott (1971) have called for the development of measurement techniques which will more effectively match the program objectives of new curricula for young children. These authorities are especially critical of the use of conventional, standardized tests of intelligence, visual perception, vocabulary, and psycholinguistic abilities for the summative evaluation of early childhood programs. Such instruments simply are not designed for this purpose; they are usually constructed to classify children, diagnose possible learning disorders, or predict subsequent school achievement.

This problem applies also to procedures for comparing various instructional programs for young children. For example, during a review of research about early intervention programs, Butler (1970) remarked: "Instrumentation is a particular problem. What kind of instrumentation is valid if one wishes to compare the outcomes of a cognitive, direct-instruction program with a much more broadly based, informally organized program? What can changes in I.Q. indicate about the outcomes of these programs when other aspects are not measured?" (p. 18).

Since some readers will quarrel with the pessimistic tone of these conclusions, possible exceptions to the general situation should be noted. For example, considerable advances in the technique of computer-assisted branched testing have been made (Holtzman, 1971). However, the application of this technique depends upon an elaborate and expensive set of hardware and technical know-how seldom found in school settings. Perhaps even more exciting is the potential for unobtrusive or inconspicuous measures in various early childhood education endeavors (Webb, Campbell, Schwartz & Sechrest, 1966). To date, however, this potential has not been fully explored.

MEASUREMENT OF YOUNG
CHILDREN'S BEHAVIOR

Lest this perception of the measurement field be taken as too dismal, several encouraging trends in measurement practice can be noted.[1] In the main, they involve developments in the measurement of children's behavior, although a few incorporate more directly certain other variables such as curriculum components and institutional change. Consider first those trends specific to the measurement of young children's behavior.

At least seven trends can be identified here. First, the range of measures available for use with young children has increased rapidly in the past few years. For example, no longer is a practitioner concerned with preschoolers limited to the use of intelligence scales, developmental "schedules," and highly experimental measures of learning ability. (See the Appendix for a listing of recently published tests and scales designed for use with infants, preschoolers, and early school-age children.) Especially notable is the move toward comprehensive assessment of children's language development, until recently (except for vocabulary development) an area sadly neglected in many early childhood education programs. See Cazden (1971) for an overview of procedures for measuring young children's language development.

A second trend, related to the first, is a growing concern for the measurement of children's affect, including motives, attitudes, and values.

Reflecting the widespread belief among many early childhood educators that cultivation of a child's affective life is as important as cultivation of his intellect, an increasing number of early education programs include explicit goals for affective development. The work of Coopersmith (1967) on *self-esteem* exemplifies the dynamic interaction of affective and cognitive developmental factors in children, as does the research about such constructs as *intellectual achievement responsibility* (Crandall, Katkovsky & Crandall, 1965) and *achievement motivation* (Heckhausen, 1967).

Measurement specialists and educators are increasingly aware of the need to assess individual differences along cultural-linguistic lines. This third trend, described elsewhere as a decrease in the ethnocentrism of psychological assessment (Holtzman, 1971), is perhaps most apparent in the measurement of scholastic aptitude and language competence. For example, some authorities (e.g., Baratz, 1969) are pressing strongly for the construction and administration of tests in the dialect or native language of minority group children. Frequently, such authorities also recommend that test content be altered to reflect more accurately the cultural background of minorities. The educational advantages of such a move have yet to be fully explicated on empirical grounds. However, this approach stands in marked contrast to the practice of using, in the case of all ethnic minority children, measures of language and academic skills valued by white, middle-class adults (including psychologists). The general issue of cultural bias in testing will be more fully considered later in this chapter.

Fourth, there currently appears to be less emphasis on using formal tests alone for measuring the behavior of children (and teachers), and a greater emphasis on other techniques, including systematic observation (McReynolds, 1968). This is clearly reflected in the growing popularity of process observation procedures, such as interaction analysis and micro-teaching. It is also indicated by the focus on children's products (e.g., stories, scientific experiments, art work, and other creative outputs) by advocates of "open education." These notions are considered in more detail in the section of this chapter concerned with teacher-made tests.

A fifth trend concerns the development of systematic procedures for studying the school entry behavior of young children so that their pre-academic and early academic experiences can be tailored more specifically to their needs. These procedures, typically developed at the local school district level for specific programs, contrast with the traditional, global "readiness" test approach or with informal teacher ratings of developmental status. In addition to the general benefit of better educational planning for school beginners, screening measurements often provide data for the early detection of learning and behavior disorders. Examples of screening practices based upon the formal application of tests and scales include Ahr (1967), Conrad and Tobiessen (1967), and Rea and Rays

(1970). Rogolsky (1969) has provided a brief review of developments in this area. The value of early screening is also reflected in the creation of new tests of children's competence with concepts deemed basic to early school success (e.g., Boehm, 1969; Moss, 1970).

Sixth, there has been a marked increase in infant assessment in the past decade, especially in relation to infant stimulation studies (e.g., Painter, 1968; White, 1971). This interest indicates both a renewed concern for the diagnosis of early developmental status and a bias in developmental theory regarding the importance of early experiences for overall development (Stedman, 1966). Instruments for infant assessment are reviewed by Thomas (1970), and are largely concerned with early cognitive and sensorimotor behaviors. Practically no useful measures of early affective development (birth to age three) are reported in the recent literature about infancy.

Finally, a growing number of resource books and services relevant to measurement in early childhood education are appearing. Hopefully, this means that educators are becoming more aware of the need for and the value of judicious measurement practices in their work with young children. Examples include Beatty (1969); Bloom, Hastings, and Madaus (1971); Goolsby and Darby (1969); Hess, Kramer, Slaughter, Torney, Berry, and Hull (1967); Jenkins, Zeigfinger, Frengel, Birnbach, and Gold (1966); Johnson and Bommarito (1971); McReynolds (1968); Palmer (1970); and Savage (1968). To these resources can be added such information services as the *Test Collection Bulletin* published regularly by Educational Testing Service, Princeton, New Jersey. Finally, a publication devoted to the description and evaluation of tests keyed to the objectives of elementary school education (grades 1-6) is currently available (Center for the Study of Evaluation, 1970).

OTHER DEVELOPMENTS IN
CURRENT MEASUREMENT PRACTICE

At least two other developments in current early education measurement practice can be cited. The first involves the search for measurements of program variables other than those expressed solely in terms of pupil or teacher behavior. Three examples can serve to illustrate this trend.

A technique has been developed for assessing the organization of physical space within which early education occurs (Kritchevsky & Prescott, 1969). This seems particularly useful in view of the apparently significant, but often overlooked, relationship between spatial organization and the classroom-playground behavior of children and their teachers

(Prescott & Jones, 1967). Related to this technique are still more comprehensive attempts to measure educational environments, some of which can be adapted to the concerns of teacher educators (e.g., Astin & Holland, 1961; Creager & Astin, 1968), and measurement guidelines for the evaluation of a total school system (MGS, 1964).

A second example is the conceptualization of measurement criteria for purposes of evaluating instructional materials and equipment. Notable among specific developments along this avenue of measurement are procedures designed to measure the reading difficulty or "readability" of written materials (Bormuth, 1968; Klare, 1963). Other more preliminary efforts in this direction appear promising (Dick, 1968; Eash, 1969), although they have not yet been widely applied in the specific context of early childhood education.

A final example involves the analysis of measurable curriculum dimensions (e.g., pacing, variety, sequencing, and scope) on the basis of which early childhood education programs can be compared (Lay & Dopyera, 1971). Application of this measurement concept to early education research is in the embryonic stage; however, it does seem especially suitable for objectified assessments of diverse instructional programs.

A second broad development in the measurement of variables other than classroom behavior is represented by attempts to measure institutional change. This is notably the case within communities served by programs such as Project Head Start (Kirschner Associates, 1970). Quantitative institutional variables amenable to measurement include involvement of the poor in community decision-making activities, employment of local residents in paraprofessional occupations, and allocation of resources to the educational and health needs of poverty and minority groups. This approach to the measurement of change is significant, if for no other reason, because it encourages one to assess changes that extend beyond immediate pupil outcomes to possible broad-scale social benefits of early education programs. Pertinent sources of information about the use of social indicators of change include Bauer (1966) and Sheldon and Moore (1968).

FUNCTIONS OF MEASUREMENT IN
EARLY CHILDHOOD EDUCATION

As indicated in chapter 8, a need for evaluation pervades virtually every aspect of early childhood education, including the preparation of teacher personnel. If evaluation is to be based on empirical data, measurements are critical at various points in any program, whether the focus be personnel training or children and their parents. For example, important measurement functions at the preservice level of teacher education often include selection of trainees, diagnosis of trainee needs, measuring trainee progress and training outcomes, and predicting in-service teaching success. At the highest level of training, measurement again becomes focal in matters of selecting personnel and determining teacher effectiveness.

For children involved in early education programs, measurement is equally important. If the readiness principle is to be anything but a sterile cliché, children's entering behavior must be assessed along multiple dimensions and the data then used to facilitate individualized instruction where necessary. Many educators are interested in charting the developmental progress of children apart from specific curricular experiences; and, of course, the degree of children's progress in relation to explicit curriculum objectives must be measured in some way.

Measurement is also crucial in relation to parents variously involved in early education programs. Increased concern is being shown for measuring the quality and extent of parental involvement in early education, the outcomes of attempts to provide education for parents in matters of child development and family relations, and parental satisfaction with their children's participation and progress in certain early education programs.

BASIC PROBLEMS IN MEASUREMENT

Measurement is the description of data in terms of numbers (Guilford, 1954). More specifically, measurement involves the assignment of numerals to objects or events, according to certain rules, in order to represent magnitude (Stevens, 1951). Occasionally, one is interested in measurement only to determine the presence or absence of some property, without further quantification in terms of "more" or "less" (English & English, 1958). In this chapter the complexities of rules for assigning numbers, scaling procedures, and the like are not considered. Interested readers may review such topics elsewhere (e.g., Stevens, 1951; Nunnally, 1961). It is important, however, to point out that any use of measurement in educational settings involves at least three assumptions: the behavior of children and teachers can be symbolized numerically; the numerical description of behavior can be analyzed according to certain mathematical principles; and the results of such analyses can serve as useful and valid indications of the behavior involved (DuBois & Mayo, 1970). Once these assumptions are accepted, measurement can proceed. But at least three basic problems must be solved by anyone concerned with measuring behavior in an educational program for children or teachers: what, how, and when to measure (Webb, 1970).

The What of Measurement

The effectiveness of behavioral measurement in training programs is contingent upon the precision with which training outcomes are specified. Until one decides exactly what it is that a child (or teacher) should be doing differently as a result of a training experience, it is unlikely that measurement will be useful for one's intended purposes. This is the problem of establishing objectives, as has been discussed in previous chapters.

As Webb (1970) observes, at least two weaknesses often characterize this level of the measurement problem in practice. First, objectives frequently border on the intangible, making difficult any consensus about what constitutes evidence of the desired behavior. Consider, for example, the ambiguities involved in such kindergarten objectives as "responsiveness to beauty in all forms" or "realization of individuality and creative propensities" (Headley, 1965). Second, there is frequently a tendency to determine what to measure on the basis of expediency or convenience. Instead of gearing one's measurement policy to relevant program objectives, one opts for measuring what can easily or readily be measured. In the extreme case, one may refrain from measuring at all on the grounds that suitable techniques are not available, or that the "really important goals" are long-term, and therefore measurement at this time is inappropriate.

A measurement policy designed exclusively around program objectives may, of course, be too delimiting. The broader guideline for determining what to measure concerns *any* information that is either necessary, or useful in making decisions about programs and their participants; reporting to outside agencies, parents, and fellow professionals; and charting developmental changes for record-keeping purposes (e.g., height and weight in young children). Hopefully, a measurement policy is never based solely on custom or simply because it is the "thing to do."

The How of Measurement

Once decisions about what to measure have been made, one is faced with the two-pronged measurement techniques problem: determining the units of measurement that are most pertinent to tasks for which an individual is being groomed; and selecting or developing a technique that will yield valid and reliable measurements (Webb, 1970). Commonly used measurement units range from speed, amount, frequency, and accuracy to variety, quality, persistence, and originality. For example, a prospective teacher being trained in the successful application of classroom management techniques may be required to demonstrate that she is capable of handling a child's aggression quickly (speed) in several different ways (variety) that are based upon valid management principles (accuracy). Similarly, in the case of a child's being schooled in the techniques of creative problem-solving techniques, both persistence and originality, among others, are relevant units of measurement. Measurement of the acquisition of factual knowledge, or of extent of comprehension of concepts and principles, obviously calls for attention to both accuracy and amount. The point is that the units to be used depend upon the components of behavior that are focused on in-training. Again, this requires a careful analysis of the behavioral components reflected in program objectives.

The second prong of the problem about how to measure concerns specifically the matter of measurement strategy and technique. Measurement strategy is the method for determining the referents against which an individual's behavior can be measured. Measurement technique refers to the particular procedure for describing the behavior, usually in quantitative terms.

Basic measurement strategies

Perhaps the most basic distinction in measurement strategy is that between *norm-referenced* and *criterion-referenced* measurement (Glaser, 1963; Popham & Husek, 1969). A norm-referenced measure is one in which the meaning of an individual's behavior is derived from its relation to the behavior of others on the same measure. A comparison of persons whose behavior is measured by the same device is usually necessary for an interpretation of the behavior. The widely used *Preschool Inventory* (Caldwell, 1967) is an example of this approach to measurement. It is based upon the assumption that individual differences in intellectual attainments exist among children aged 4½ to 6½. A child's performance on this test is interpreted by comparing him with other children of the same age and socioeconomic standing. Thus, a child's performance can be described as "average," "above average," or "below average" in relation to how the scores of his comparison group are distributed. The distribution of test scores or other quantitative data constitutes the basis for test norms; hence the term *norm-referenced measurement*. Most standardized measures of intelligence, academic achievement, and even personality are norm-referenced measures.

Criterion-referenced measurement involves the determination of an individual's status in relation ot some preselected or established standard of performance. This standard or criterion, not other individuals, becomes the item against which performance is measured and interpreted. Performance tests, such as those involved in obtaining a driver's license and demonstrating swimming proficiency, are examples. Minimal but absolute standards of competence must be demonstrated in order to "pass." As far as a given individual is concerned, the performance of others on the same measures is irrelevant.

In early childhood education circles, the *Basic Concept Inventory* (Englemann, 1967) is an example of a criterion-referenced measure. This measure is based on the assumption that certain basic conceptual skills are critical for successful early academic progress. It can therefore be used to measure the degree of mastery of these various skills so that remedial instruction can be programmed. It can also be used to measure the effectiveness of an instructional program designed to develop mastery of these skills among young children.

Among the most recent and comprehensive applications of criterion-referenced achievement measures is the *Individually Prescribed Instruction* (IPI) evaluation program (Lindvall & Cox, 1970). Developed at the University of Pittsburgh, the program includes four main components: tests for the initial placement of pupils in the instructional program; pretests in relation to specific curriculum unit objectives; curriculum-embedded tests to measure individual pupil progress; and curriculum unit posttests for summative evaluation. Additionally, nontest information, including data obtained during personalized pupil-teacher conferences, are used to facilitate the design of individualized instruction and its evaluation.

The relative merits or weaknesses of criterion- and norm-referenced measurement strategies are perhaps incidental to the basis or rationale for choosing one or the other for use in the practical setting.[2] In both cases, this choice of strategy is contingent upon the kinds of decisions one will make from the measures obtained (Garvin, 1970). Some educational decisions involve the selection of a "fixed quota" from either the high or low end of a distribution of scores. For example, teacher trainers may wish to admit only those candidates for training whose scores on measures of academic competence and attitude toward children fall in the upper quartile. One may have room for only a small number of children in a compensatory education program and select for the special treatment only those who score at some point "below average." In both examples, norm-referenced measures would be appropriate. Where information is sought about the capacity of a given instructional program to increase the range of individual differences, norm-referenced measurement is also appropriate.

If, on the other hand, decisions are primarily oriented toward certifying competence with respect to some a priori standard, then criterion-referenced measurement is clearly indicated. When training programs have behaviorally defined objectives, criterion-referenced measurement is natural. In such cases, one is usually concerned with whether (or what proportion of) students master a given objective, not how they compare to some norm group (Sjogren, 1970).

It should also be noted that norm-referenced measures are often used as if they were measures of the criterion-reference type. A case in point is the use of a conventional intelligence test to "evaluate" the effectiveness of an early intervention program after children have been taught the test items directly. Yet norm-referenced measures typically are designed to "spread out" individuals along some dimension of behavior, and they usually represent only very broad samples of such behavior at that. Rarely can one find a norm-referenced measure that reflects in specific ways the objectives of most training programs. This point will again be considered, but in a different light, later in the chapter.

Finally, and in relation especially to criterion-referenced testing, increased attention is now being given to the formulation of various rate measures of learning; that is, measurements based on time needed by learners to achieve specified goals (Carroll, 1970). A consideration of rate measures involves a number of interacting variables: motivation (perseverance) of the learner, opportunity to learn, quality of instruction, and learner ability to comprehend and profit from instruction. These variables pose substantial measurement problems in themselves, but essentially this approach concerns measuring learning rate in terms of a ratio between amount of knowledge or skill gained and a specified unit of time. Interested readers should consult Carroll (1970) for details.

Measurement techniques

Measurement techniques can be classified according to: (a) the content or area measured (e.g., intelligence, interest, motor skill); (b) the way in which a measure is administered (e.g., group versus individual); (c) response mode (e.g., paper and pencil, free versus controlled response, verbal versus nonverbal response); (d) scoring method (e.g., subjective and judgmental versus objective); (e) target population (e.g., infants, preschoolers, or teachers); and (f) format of the measure (e.g., rating scale, performance test, process observation). It is convenient, however, to conceptualize measurement techniques along a broad dimension that transcends the foregoing classification schemes, namely, obtrusive-unobtrusive measurements (Shalock, 1968). By definition, an obtrusive measure is one in which an examiner or observer is present on the scene and the examinee or observee is aware that his behavior is being scrutinized. In general, unobtrusive measures represent the other side of this coin: physical traces (erosion and accretion), running records, episodic and private records, and the like. To date these measures have been little used in education, although they are potentially valuable, especially in combination with appropriate obtrusive measures (see Webb et al., 1966).

The present discussion generally is limited to obtrusive measures.

It should be recognized, however, that many observational procedures (both simple and contrived) herein discussed are essentially unobtrusive. Moreover, it is even possible that tests, to the extent they become simply another part of classroom routine, may take on the characteristics of an unobtrusive measure.

Obtrusive measures can be grouped into at least five broad categories: interviews, systematic observation, standardized objective measures, standard projective measures, and teacher-made tests. Only very general comments concerning such classes of measures will be advanced. The thrust instead will be in the direction of highlighting those that are currently being profitably used in the field or that seem to hold more than average promise. This survey is not limited to measures of children's behavior; attention is also given to examples of measures of teacher and parent behavior.

Interviews. Very few reports involving the use of interview measurements with children in early childhood education programs exist in the current literature. The clearest exception to this is the liberal use of Piaget's *méthode clinique* in curricula based on cognitive developmental theory (Kamii, 1971; Lavatelli, 1970). Such exploratory interviews are semi-structured in that they are designed, within broad limits, to determine the child's understanding of observed phenomena related to logical classification, seriation, numerical construction, conservation, and spatial concepts. According to Kamii and Peper (1969), the *méthode clinique* differs from psychometric methods in this dimension:

> In the psychometric method, the examiner is required to follow a standard set of procedures specified in the manual, without any deviation. The wording of a question cannot be changed, and the number of times the instruction can be repeated is specified. In the "exploratory method," on the other hand, the examiner has an outline and a hypothesis in mind at all times, and he tests these hypotheses by following the child's train of thought in a natural, conversational way. The examiner uses his ingenuity to make himself understood by the child in any way possible. (p. 13)

For educators interested in the child's conceptualization of Piaget-based tasks, this technique has the potential of yielding information not accessible in any other way. This comment is based on the dual assumption that an examiner will execute the *méthode clinique* correctly and will not be deceived by the child's language or his own biases.

Aside from this application, only a scattering of reports of formal interview measurement is apparent in the literature. Perhaps the most novel of these reports concerns the development of a standardized telephone interview procedure for obtaining speech samples from young children. Especially promising results from the use of this technique with disadvantaged children have been reported (Institute of Developmental Studies, 1968).

Interview measurement can also be helpful in the study of teacher behavior. Currently, however, the interview is largely restricted to two program aspects: selection and program evaluation. The interview has long been a popular procedure for selecting candidates for teacher training and hiring teachers for existing school programs. There is, however, little evidence to indicate that interview data alone predict success in either venture, which is probably due to the lack of common dimensions in interview measurements and a teacher's classroom behavior. Periodic interviews with teachers-in-training can be useful as a feedback mechanism for assessing training program effectiveness, although surprisingly few examples of this can be found in the current teacher education literature.

Perhaps the most extensive use of interviewing has been in the study of parental child-rearing practices. This method has been used profitably in recent years to measure parents' beliefs and perceptions about themselves as parents, including such things as child-rearing philosophy and preferred disciplinary practices (Baumrind, 1968). Within the context of early education programs, elaborate and promising interview methods have also been included in broad-scale evaluations of Head Start and Project Follow Through, such as those executed by Stanford Research Institute and the Educational Testing Service.

Systematic Observation. Observational techniques need not always be obtrusive. Observation conducted through one-way mirrors or by way of videotape recording for later analysis is unlikely to distract or otherwise affect the behavior of children or teachers being observed. However, outside of the psychological laboratory or child-research nursery school, such devices are rarely available (or used). Observation more typically occurs in the presence of children and teachers. Even then, systematic, direct-observation methods are problematical, especially with respect to reliability and the control of situational variables. Nevertheless, it is this writer's opinion that some of the most promising recent advances in measurement technique have been made in the area of systematic observation. For example, techniques of observation from the study of operant conditioning offer a great deal to persons concerned with measuring the effects of cueing procedures and reinforcement contingencies on response rate or frequency (see Honig, 1966; Baer, Wolf & Risley, 1968; Weiss, 1968). A major work on observation couched in the science of ethology is also a must for students of observational technique (Hutt & Hutt, 1970).

Methods for recording data obtained through observation include diary records, checklists, rating scales, rate and frequency counts, and anecdotal records. Details of these methods are given in many sources (e.g., Adams, 1964; Furth, 1958; Payne, 1968; Stanley, 1964); these should be consulted by readers unfamiliar with such methods. Included here will be basic features of observational systems suitable for use in early childhood education.

Traditionally, systems for observing young children have been focused on the individual child, his social and problem-solving skills, play activities, and interactions with materials in the classroom (Simon & Boyer, 1970). An example of a recently developed system for individual child observation is the *Personal Record of School Experience* (PROSE) (Medley, 1969). This system involves no rating, but simply the objective recording of observable events as they occur. One child at a time is observed and all his activity is recorded by means of a manageable coding system based on 11 categories of behavior (e.g., level of attention, manifest affect, and physical activity). Static conditions such as class organization, subject matter, and instructional materials in use can also be recorded. Codified data may be computer-analyzed. The PROSE is based upon the principle of OsCAR, a widely known system for observing teacher-pupil interaction (Medley, 1963).

Other examples of new observational schemes include systems for assessing preschool classroom environments (Stern & Gordon, 1967), nine aspects of young children's classroom behavior (Katz, 1968), and social and information-processing behaviors in natural settings (Honig, Caldwell & Tannenbaum, 1970; Cunningham & Boger, 1971). The Stern and Gordon (1967) inventory of checklists and scales is notable for its comprehensiveness. Categories for measurement include physical environment, materials and equipment; program structure, balance, and organization; play activities; predominant teaching mode, role of the teacher regarding verbal and nonverbal communication; group control and management; teacher involvement in children's social relations; classroom atmosphere; teacher "style and tone"; and general aspects of the teacher's relationship with children.

Systems for observing the relative strengths and abilities of teachers continue to be developed. A good example is B. B. Brown's *Teacher Practices Observation Record* (1970), which is being used in several Project Follow Through settings as an aid in developing effective behavior in both teachers and teacher aides.

The most extensive developments in classroom observational technique are based on the concept of *interaction analysis*. Impetus for such developments has been largely provided by Flanders' *Interaction Analysis Technique* (Flanders, 1966). The technique requires that an observer keep a running record of teacher-pupil exchanges at three-second intervals. These exchanges can be tabulated according to categories of behavior ranging from direct (e.g., giving commands, lecturing, justifying authority) to indirect teacher influences (e.g., accepting pupils' ideas and feelings, praising). Provision for recording extent of pupil talk is also made. Resulting data can be used to analyze prevailing patterns of teacher-student interaction and the relationship of such patterns to pupil achievement and attitudes.

Much research based on the Flanders system has accumulated in the past decade. For recent reviews, see Nuthall (1970) and Garrard (1966). Thus, if nothing else, this approach has been of great heuristic value. However, the technique also has immense practical value for guiding teacher behavior. Mild criticism has been leveled at the Flanders system because of its exclusive focus on verbal classroom behavior (especially of the teacher) and its predominant concern with affective components of classroom behavior.

Several extensions of this technique have been made and merit consideration by those involved in measuring and evaluating teacher behavior. These include greater provision for cognitive factors (Amidon, 1966; Reynolds, Abraham & Nelson, 1971) and nonverbal classroom interaction (French & Galloway, 1968). Perhaps the single most important finding from interaction analysis research for early childhood educators is that student teachers who are taught interaction analysis are generally more indirect, supporting, and accepting of their pupils than student teachers unfamiliar with this approach (Amidon, 1967).

Space limitations do not permit an elaborate review of all exciting developments in the area of classroom observation. However, a few additional systems deserve brief mention. These include systems designed especially for assessing student teachers (Sharpe, 1969), teacher skill in classroom management (Soar, Ragosta & Soar, 1971), a process approach to teacher's question-asking behavior (Zimmerman & Bergan, 1968), and the *Behavioral Analysis Instrument for Teachers* (1969). The latter is particularly useful for describing teacher skill in pedagogical technique, curriculum planning, and pupil evaluation-diagnosis. Perhaps the most comprehensive of all the newer systems are the *Indicators of Quality* (Teachers College, 1968) and the *Classroom Observation Instrument* (Stanford Research Institute, 1970). The latter system was developed specifically for use in evaluating Head Start and Project Follow Through. Finally, interested readers are encouraged to examine carefully Simon & Boyer's anthology (1970) of 79 classroom observation systems, and two major publications about the role of systematic observation for assessing and improving classroom behavior: Brown (1969) and Gallagher, Nuthall & Rosenshine, (1970).

There has been no extensive use of systematic observation techniques for measuring parental behavior in connection with early childhood education. There are at least two reasons for this: only recently have educators become sensitive to the vital role of parents in the formal early education enterprise; and it is extremely difficult to arrange for such observation, either in homes or schools. It is therefore much more common for parental behavior to be measured by interviews, questionnaires, and checklists. However, the potential of observing parent-child interaction to measure such things as parental teaching styles, the quality of parent-child relationships, and home stimulation cannot be overlooked. The value of such an approach is well illustrated by the work of Hess and Shipman (1965), Bee, Van Egeren, Streissguth, Nyman, and Leckie (1969), Brophy (1970), Schmidt and Hore (1970), and Caldwell, Heider, and Kaplan (1966). Observational procedures have also been utilized in evaluating maternal inservice training associated with preschool intervention programs (Hamilton, 1971).

A word about rating scale methods for tabulating observational data is also in order. It is clear from the literature that ratings of teachers by supervisors and of children by teachers continue to be a popular and expedient means for measuring classroom behavior. A recent survey of 53 of the nation's 60 largest school districts revealed that 50 of these districts currently use some type of rating scale to measure teacher performance (Queer, 1969). Problems and procedures associated with these and other techniques for measuring faculty instructional effectiveness are discussed by Blair (1968) and Cohen and Brawer (1969). Concerning effectiveness among teacher educators, it is not surprising that primary factors in "good" instruction include coursework in which objectives are clearly defined; a classroom atmosphere conducive to student ease; and a tolerant, responsive instructor who demonstrates both competence and enthusiasm (Bannister, 1961). Such characteristics would seem also to apply to teachers of young children. Research continues to highlight the importance of such qualities as empathy, nurturance, and communication skill for early childhood educators. For cues concerning the measurement of such qualities, see Hogan (1969) and O'Leary and Becker (1969).

The problems of reliability and validity inherent in rating scale approaches to measurement are well known. But the use of well-designed scales for measuring children's behavior by experienced teachers is often beneficial. For example, a rating scale adapted from the face sheet of the Stanford-Binet Intelligence Test form has been reported as being extremely useful in measuring three important motivational characteristics of children: achievement motivation, confidence in ability, and activity level (Hess et al., 1966). Promising rating scale devices for predicting kindergarten and primary grade academic achievement, learning difficulties, and behavior problems have also been reported (Attwell, Orpet & Meyers, 1967; Conrad & Tobiessen, 1967; Gross, 1970).

Rating scale methods also figure heavily in efforts to measure "socialization" of bilingual and ethnic group children (Cervenka, 1968), teachers' estimates of social competency among preschool and elementary school children (Levine & Elzey, 1968; Seagoe, 1970), and infant development (Hoopes, 1967).

Standardized, Objective Measures. This class of measures includes instruments for measuring intelligence and aptitude, achievement, personality, attitude, and interest. Such measures commonly appear in the form of tests that are constructed, administered, and scored according to prescribed rules (F. G. Brown, 1970). These rules govern the selection of item content, instructions for giving and taking the test, and recording and evaluating test responses. Strictly speaking, such tests are limited to the measurement of behavior in the *specific test situation,* a situation that is usually contrived. Consequently, any statements or conclusions about the person being tested represent an inference from that situation to the general class of responses presumably sampled by the test. That is, by way of inference one generalizes from sample of test behavior to the broader characteristic(s) of the individual. This is particularly true of norm-referenced measures.

Finally, it should be noted that not all tests are limited to a paper-and-pencil format, nor do all tests require formal arrangements. In this sense, any measure of performance can be called a "test." However, this section of the chapter is concerned largely with formal, obtrusive tests administered either individually or in groups.

With respect to standardized, objective measures of children's behavior, only a few points are made here. The reader is referred to the Appendix for an annotated bibliography of commercially available tests and scales for use with children; also, a handbook of such measures *not* commercially available has been published elsewhere (Johnson & Bommarito, 1971). Conventional measures of mental ability continue to be used extensively for purposes of diagnosing developmental status, guidance, and measuring the effects of therapy (Stott & Ball, 1965). By far the most frequently used measure of young children's intelligence is the Stanford-Binet. Other widely used measures are Goodenough's Draw-a-Man, the Weschler Intelligence Scales for preprimary and school-age children, the Gesell Schedules, the Cattell Infant Scale, Ammons Picture-Vocabulary, and the Merrill-Palmer Scale. For complete reviews of these and other conventional scales, see Stott and Ball (1965).

Alternatives to conventional measures of intelligence are finding favor among many psychologists and educators (Achenbach, 1970). This is particularly true for those who have been attracted to Piaget's cognitive-developmental theory of mental development. Piaget-based scales for use as early as infancy have been developed (e.g., Uzgiris & Hunt, 1969; Honig & Lally, 1970). Other scales for the measurement of precausal thinking, object permanence, classificatory development, and conservation have been devised (Laurendeau & Pinard, 1962; Decarie, 1965; Kofsky, 1966; Goldschmid & Bentler, 1968). Sullivan (1967) has provided a critical examination of this developmental approach to the measurement of cognition and its implications for practitioners.

There has been a tremendous surge of interest in the measurement of children's language competence since the advent of federal compensatory education programs. Newly developed language measures are appearing regularly in the literature; many are used to measure the outcomes of language training programs for disadvantaged and minority group children (e.g., Bierly, 1971; Mehrabian, 1970; Stern & Gupta, 1970). Research workers are beginning to explore ways of altering standardized testing procedures so that the language skills of disadvantaged preschoolers may be better assessed. For example, a modified Peabody Picture Vocabulary Test (see Appendix) has been devised whereby three important variables (expectancy for success, reinforcement, and specificity of task instructions) are accounted for in the test administration (Ali & Costello, 1971). The net effect of this modification has been positive in terms of enhanced test scores for preschool children who otherwise might have responded less well under "conventionally standard" conditions.

The influence of humanistic psychologies is apparent in the now widespread concern for children's affective development among early childhood educators. Unfortunately, the validity and other technical features of most measures of children's affect are unimpressive, if not poor. According to Hoepfner (1970), few worthwhile measures of achievement motivation, interest, activity level, and self-esteem are available. These are among the phenomena about which some educators are most concerned. In this writer's opinion, however, genuine attempts to develop better measures in these areas are becoming both more frequent and fruitful (e.g., Adkins, 1968; Bolea, 1970; Soares & Soares, 1969).

Not surprisingly, a majority of these attempts have focused on self-concept measures. An annotated bibliography of currently available measures of this construct designed for use with young children can be obtained through the ERIC Clearinghouse on Early Childhood Education (Coller, 1970). Unfortunately, most of these measures are marked by serious limitations: they invite socially desirable responses, depend heavily on young children's verbal facility, and utilize terminology that is subject to wide differences in interpretation. In view of such limitations, some rerearch workers (e.g., Long & Henderson, 1970; Yeatts & Bentley, 1971) have experimented with a nonverbal approach to self-esteem with modestly encouraging results. Other pertinent resources relevant to measurement in the affective domain are Beatty (1969), Bloom et al. (1971, chap. 10), and Eiss and Harbeck (1969). The latter two sources in particular deal with the knotty problem of affective objectives.

Finally, it should be noted that, apart from experimental programs in early childhood education, systematic use of standardized, objective measures by nursery and kindergarten teachers is apparently not extensive. Goslin, Epstein, and Hallock (1965) report little use of tests beyond reading readiness and individual intelligence tests at the kindergarten level. Gross I.Q. data are of little use to teachers faced with the complexities of educational planning (Neisworth, 1969). Even the results of reading readiness tests, when obtained, are not often put to good use (Goslin, 1967). These practices are due to at least two reasons. One is the limited number of educationally useful tests available to teachers in the past. Fortunately, this state of affairs is rapidly changing. Another reason may be that teachers of young children simply are not trained to select, administer, and interpret such measures. In this writer's judgment, training along these lines is important at both the pre- and in-service teaching levels. Such training for both testing and systematic observation conceivably can promote greater teacher initiative, cooperation, and responsibility concerning classroom measurement practices. As teacher involvement increases, it seems more likely that classroom measurements will be put appropriately to use. Certainly educators should not allow tests to be administered and interpreted by untrained personnel.

While the need for teacher skill in test selection, administration, and interpretation is critical, a precautionary word is in order. As Carroll (1970) has observed, standardized tests can be overused and too much reliance placed on their results. In his opinion, the problem is twofold: a given standardized test may not be sufficiently appropriate to the particular learning tasks in a local curriculum; and the overall score or grade level index derived from standardized test performance may be inadequate for determining what specific skills have and have not been well acquired by a student. These limitations must be kept in mind by practitioners who elect to use standardized tests.

Consider next the use of standardized, objective measures of teacher behavior. Like interview measures, tests and scales for measuring teacher behavior are most frequently used to select and predict instructional effectiveness. Occasionally, they are used to assess the effects of teacher training. Regardless, their use is more extensive at the preservice rather than the in-service level. Published tests that have received more than occasional use include the Allport-Vernon Study of Values (Allport, Vernon, Lindzey, 1951), the California Psychological Inventory (Gough, 1968), Minnesota Test of Teacher Attitudes (Yee & Fruchter, 1971), the Teacher Preference Schedule (Stern & Masling, 1958), the Watson-Glaser Test of Critical Thinking (Watson & Glaser, 1952), and the Tennessee Self-Concept Scale (Fitts, 1965). A measure with more than average usefulness for prediction purposes is addressed to the teacher's beliefs about learning and teaching and to the effect of such beliefs on classroom atmosphere (Harvey, White, Prather, Alter & Hoffmeister, 1966). Measures of teacher knowledge and ability to apply principles of good teaching in simulated problem situations have been developed (Popham, 1965; Murray, 1969); and a method of assessing teacher attitudes toward children's behavior problems is available (Tolor, Scarpatti & Lane, 1967).

The value of measures such as these depends on the purpose for which they are being used. It appears that a systematic observational approach is generally preferable, especially if some indication of teaching effectiveness is sought. More frequently, a low and positive insignificant relationship is obtained between teacher performance on paper-and-pencil tests and his or her behavior as perceived by disinterested classroom observers. The issue here concerns the degree of correspondence between observed skill and verbalized beliefs, attitudes, and professed knowledge about teaching. Among the more promising steps in the direction of measuring degree of correspondence between teacher intentions and actual practices has been that taken by Steele (1969). The resultant technique appears useful in determining the extent to which an instructional treatment is stably executed.

The common validity problem of paper-and-pencil tests of teaching skill is partly responsible for the development of performance tests of teaching effectiveness. Microteaching is one example of a technique that can be used to obtain some measure of actual performance. Still other performance approaches to the measurement of teaching proficiency have been attempted (e.g., Popham, 1971; Moody & Bauswell, 1971). However, such approaches have usually failed to differentiate experienced, formally trained teachers from inexperienced nonteachers. Perhaps the performance tests are faulty; perhaps such results indicate the inadequate nature of many teacher education programs.

Finally, standardized, objective measures of student opinion, attitudes toward instruction, and achievement are being increasingly used as indications of teaching effectiveness. However, this occurs mainly at the college level where preservice teachers rate or otherwise evaluate their teaching faculty. As yet, little work has been done to develop measures of preschool or early school pupil reactions to teachers. A notable exception is a report by Strickland (1970) of explorations with a school attitude questionnaire for young children. No attempt will be made here to review the vast literature of student evaluation of teaching. Sources of information about measurement in this area include Davidoff (1970), Evans (1969), Hayes (1968), Hoyt (1969), Justiz (1969), Lewis (1966), McKeachie (1969), and Paraskevopoulas (1968).

Parents, understandably, are not often tested in connection with early childhood education programs. When they are, it is usually in the form of scales to measure attitudes toward child-rearing practices and education or perceptions of themselves and their children in relation to training objectives (Caldwell, Mozell & Honig, 1966). Measurement of parental attitudes has a long history and has involved the development of a variety of scales for research use, some of which conceivably could be put to good use by educators (Baumrind, 1967; Lorr & Jenkins, 1963; Schaefer & Bell, 1958). Yet most measures of this kind are beset with problems of both validity and reliability. Caution in their application is therefore warranted. Measurement procedures used in home teaching and parent involvement projects are discussed by Kemble (1969), Orhan and Radin (1969) and Weikart and Lambie (1968). Finally, a scale designed to assess parental attitude change in relation to community action programs has been devised by Hanson, Stern, and Kitana (1968). For a review of published instruments for use in family measurement, see Straus (1969).

Teacher-Made Tests. This category of measurements includes short-answer, objectively scored tests, essay and written documents, and many pupil products (e.g., art work, written materials, constructions, and various classroom projects). Their nature, construction, and use are described in any basic textbook about educational measurements, and are familiar to most readers. Comments about teacher-made tests are therefore limited here to three incidental points.

First, behavioral objectives in any program of instruction in effect can themselves become measurements of the criterion-referenced type. That is, if one describes (a) an individual's behavior that is to be performed together with (b) the context conditions of performance specifically enough so that the behavior can (c) be recognized when it occurs, then one's measurement task is straightforward: observe and record the behavior. However, it is usually necessary also to specify a desired minimal level of performance (Mager, 1962). Such a suggestion is especially appropriate for those teachers who design their instructional programs around a mastery concept of achievement (Block, 1971).

Second, the potential of pupil products for measuring developmental progress, including academics, is frequently underestimated. However, there is some indication that a pupil product orientation is preferred even to conventional testing by many educators, especially those who identify with "open education." [3] For example, such educators maintain that the "best measure of a child's work is his work" (Barth, 1969). Any meaningful application of this principle obviously requires that careful records of children's work be kept. An analysis of the cumulative change in children's work on a longitudinal basis is also necessary. Admittedly, relatively "informal" measurements are extremely limited for research purposes. But children's conceptual functioning, problem-solving skills, and esthetic expression can all be revealed in unique ways by activities that result in pupil products of various kinds.

Third, there is a great need for improvement in the test-making skills of teachers in early childhood education programs. Too often, teacher education programs require no course at all, or only a general course, about tests and measurements in which descriptive statistics and item writing are stressed. Since the principal focus of such courses usually is on tests that require literacy, prospective early childhood personnel often see them as irrelevant. In short, more attention is needed to the development of skills in constructing checklists, tests of sensory discrimination and vocabulary, procedures for evaluating pupil products, and possibly even interview measurements among prospective preprimary teachers. Combined lack of skill in measurement technique and lack of understanding of how measurements can be used to facilitate instruction may also explain why teachers of young children often fail to incorporate a measurement perspective into their educational programs.

Fortunately, useful resources specifically concerned with the construction of informal measurement procedures are beginning to appear. For example, assessment tools for teachers of preprimary children with various language and learning disorders are described by Bangs (1968), who also provides curriculum suggestions once assessments are made. Another resource devoted to informal educational measurement deals with the areas of perceptual-motor development, reading and arithmetic skills, handwriting and spelling, speech and language disorders, and personal-social behavior (Smith, 1969).

Other Measurement Techniques. Thus far nothing has been said about projective measures, the measurement of social relations (sociometry), creativity measurement, and the medical approach to behavior measurement, including biological structure and function.[4] In a pragmatic sense, there is good reason for these "oversights." Projective measures of personality, for example, are rarely used outside the clinical setting. Even many clinicians seemingly have become disenchanted with projective techniques because of their low validity. Moreover, most teachers are not trained to administer and interpret projective measures; nor, in this writer's estimation, should they be. Readers interested in the use of projective techniques with children are referred to Levine (1966) and Blum (1968).

Sociometry has made a unique contribution to our understanding of such social phenomena as popularity and friendship, peer acceptance and rejection, leadership and influence power, group roles, and the relationship of sociability to school achievement. Insights concerning these phenomena have come mainly from the study of children beyond the preprimary level. But the successful use of sociometrics with nursery and kindergarten children has been reported (e.g., Northway, 1969a, 1969b; Hartup, 1970). Even so, sociometrics seems to be utilized largely by child development research workers, not by teachers and psychological specialists in the public schools. There are a number of probable reasons for this. One is lack of knowledge about and skill in using sociometric devices on the part of teachers. Another is that early childhood programs, while ostensibly devoted to promoting children's social development, infrequently reflect specific goals that call for systematic measurement in this area. Still another is the occasional ethical objection raised in connection with sociometrics: a reluctance to "meddle" in children's social lives. The irony of this should be self-evident. Nevertheless, in the writer's estimation, the potential of sociometrics for gaining a better understanding of children's social perceptions, competence, and acceptance has not been much capitalized upon by educators. Again, interested readers are referred to other sources for a more comprehensive treatment of sociometric theory and technique (Gronlund, 1959; Northway & Weld, 1957).

Creativity is a much discussed but little understood characteristic of human behavior. Not surprisingly, most empirical approaches to the measurement of creativity lack both a consensus about the behavior being measured and technical refinement (Tryk, 1968). Despite the measurement controversy, one cannot help being impressed with the vast amount of creativity research that has accumulated in recent years.[5] Most such research has been with older children, youth, and adults, but considerable effort has recently been deployed to measure young children's creative potential under experimental conditions. For example, behavioral tasks deemed relevant to such potential have been devised by Starkweather (1966). The tasks are purported to measure psychological freedom, willingness to try difficult tasks, curiosity, and originality. Ideational fluency, rate, uniqueness, expressive freedom, productivity, and communicability are criteria variously stressed in still other recent attempts to measure creativity in early childhood (Ward, 1969a, 1969b; Gross & Marsh, 1970; Singer & Whiton, 1971). Finally, it is claimed·that certain portions of the *Torrance Tests of Creative Thinking* are appropriate for children as young as age four (Torrance, 1966). For an overview of problems involved in measuring young children's creativity, see Starkweather (1964).

Early childhood personnel concerned with the assessment of physical growth, physiological functioning, sensory awareness, and the like, should consult the following sources for pertinent surveys of measurement technique and research methodology: Eichorn (1970), Kaye (1970), Macy and Kelly (1960), Meredith (1960), Reisen (1960), and Tanner (1970). Diverse approaches to the measurement of temperament, persistence, curiosity, impulse control, and reflectivity also merit the attention of educators. Not only are these measurable characteristics related to young children's school achievement, but they possibly can aid as indicators of affective development (Banta, 1970; Kagan, 1965; Maccoby, Dowley, Hagen & Degerman, 1965; Maw & Maw, 1970; Thomas, Chess & Birch, 1971). Finally, the *Illinois Test of Psycholinguistic Abilities* (1970) should be noted for its use as a frame of reference in diagnostic-prescriptive teaching.

The When of Measurement

Thus far, the *what* and *how* of measurement have occupied most of our attention. Theoretically, the question of *when* to measure should be answered according to one's evaluation plan. In chapter 8, much was said about formative and summative evaluation, both of which obviously call for measurement of one sort or another. There is little reason to elaborate further on this matter except a reminder that, in educational practice, most analyses require that measurements be taken at two points in time at least. Too often, measurement occurs only in the context of summative evaluation with little attempt to assess entering or baseline behavior. *When* is imbedded in the nature of the program, the needs of the children it serves. The developmental progress of individual children and/or teachers should dictate the timing.

The issue of immediate and long-term measurement of behavior is also applicable to the *when* question. In most training programs, measurement is limited to immediate outcome: performance during and/or at the end of a particular program (Webb, 1970). This emphasis is usually accompanied by the tacit assumption that performance at such times is an appropriate, if not good, indicator of how well one will perform in the future. If the skills being learned during teacher-training, for example, are directly linked to eventual classroom teaching performance, then the asumption is valid. However, the measurement of performance during training may be only remotely related to measurement of on-the-job proficiency.

In the case of both teachers in training and children in early education programs, a basic question is whether short-term measurements involve anything more than behavior developed over the short-term period. Related to this are the problems of determining how soon one can expect program effects to be realized, and of determining with certainty the stability and durability of the behavior changes brought about by programs (Caro, 1971). The ideal procedure to follow would involve repeated, if not continuous, measurement of program "output variables" (Caro, 1971). Unfortunately, in actual practice, one-time measurement in connection with immediate-term summative evaluation is probably more the rule than the exception. However, systematic follow-up measurement is a sound and potentially enlightening policy for both teacher educators and teachers of young children.

SELECTING AND EVALUATING
MEASUREMENT TECHNIQUES

In the earlier discussion of criterion- and norm-referenced measurement, the point was made that decisions about measurement strategy should be based on what decisions will be made from the measurements obtained. This decision-making process will necessitate a careful consideration of program objectives. The role of objectives is also to be considered in the selection of measurement techniques. Broadly speaking, there are at least two ways in which this selection can be made. First, measurement techniques can be determined in advance directly from specific program objectives. If such objectives are unique, measurement techniques often must be designed locally. Existing tests, scales, or other techniques simply may not be valid or otherwise suitable for measurement in relation to one's instructional objectives.

Second, one can approach this selection problem only with broad program goals in mind, and then select from "off the shelf" some existing measurement technique(s) for one's purposes. If so, the measurements obtained become either ipso facto instructional objectives and/or a sample of behavior that may be spuriously related to the content and objectives of one's curriculum.

The first procedure is generally preferable to the second, simply because it demands clear, systematic thinking about the exact purposes of a given instructional program. However, as suggested earlier in the chapter, measurement need not be limited to a narrow set of instructional objectives. One is often interested in determining change or outcomes for which specific curriculum experiences were not arranged. A teacher might be specifically concerned with measuring pupil progress in language skill development brought about through pattern drill. But this same teacher may also wish to obtain a measure of the extent to which children become more or less anxious about school during language instruction, even though the curriculum per se has no formal provision for modifying anxiety level. In fact, this notion is reflected in the thinking of others (e.g., Caro, 1971) who recommend that any possible unintended program effects, including those that are undesirable, should be both anticipated and measured.

The issue of selecting measurement techniques in relation to program objectives is essentially a matter of validity: Will a particular technique measure what I want to measure? While validity is unquestionably the most critical aspect of any measurement endeavor, other qualities of measurement techniques are also important. Unless a specific technique can measure behavior reliably or consistently from one time to the next, the interpretation of behavior changes in relation to an instructional program is impossible.

Practicality is still another important consideration. Even the most valid, reliable measures may not be feasible for use in some programs due to complexities in administration, scoring, cost, or other factors. Finally, in the case of norm-referenced measurements, the quality of norming procedures clearly is crucial, especially when important decisions about individuals are to be made. In short, the criteria of validity, reliability, and practicality are basic to any process of selecting and evaluating measurement techniques. Readers who wish more information about these criteria and their application to technique selection and evaluation tasks are referred to F. G. Brown (1970), Cronbach (1970), and the American Psychological Association publication concerning test standards (1966).

SPECIAL CONSIDERATIONS IN MEASUREMENT

Despite obvious values, the process of measurement is marked by many problems and issues that demand the attention of educators. These problems and issues can be grouped into three related categories: the problem of academic or cultural bias; the general impact of testing on students; and how test results are used (Bloom, 1969; Goslin, 1968). In this section, these related groupings of problems and issues in measurement are examined in order to stress the necessity for an ethical approach to educational measurement.

Academic or Cultural Bias

Most tests used with children of late preschool age and beyond already contain "academic" components that require specific language, discrimination, and conceptual skills (space, number, time) for successful performance. These tests also frequently call for various amounts of scholastic information (Stephens & Evans, 1973). For purposes of assessing achievement status and predicting subsequent scholastic success, this academic orientation is suitable *if* two conditions can be met. First, a child must have encountered the *opportunity* to become familiar with the test-related content in a general way. Second, a child must have at least a minimal repertoire of test-taking skills. Since many young children obviously can meet neither condition, a test with a strong academic flavor may be a very poor sample of their past learning.

Admittedly, a tester can do little about a child's limited familiarity with culturally or academically based test content except, of course, temper his interpretation of a child's performance accordingly and avoid misusing the test results. Therefore, the problem is not so much a matter of tests per se; it is more a problem of the test-user.

The problem of test-taking skills, however, is a matter about which a tester can do something more concrete. Personnel involved in test administration should provide children with those experiences that simulate test conditions prior to the formal test itself. This includes provisions for practice in following directions, handling test materials, and the like. A warm-up period prior to testing is also advisable. An example of this policy in action can be cited. Oakland and Weilert (1971) implemented special activities for disadvantaged children to develop their familiarity with tests and skills necessary for test performance. These activities had an initially strong, positive effect on the standardized test performance of these children as compared to peers who received no special training.

The problem of academic or cultural bias is basically one of test validity. This problem of test validity often is most apparent when tests are given to make decisions about children whose performance may be affected negatively by such factors as low reading ability, low test-taking motivation, lack of familiarity with the language and conceptual style of a test, negative attitudes toward school personnel and academics, and poorly designed test formats or instructions (Freeburg, 1970). These factors frequently are noted when conventional tests are used with children from impoverished circumstances or certain ethnic and minority groups.

The argument that tests based on standard English discriminate negatively and unfairly against children whose native language or dialect differs from the standard form has recently gained much support. This argument underlies, in part, the development of experimental measures of language competence and translations of conventional tests (e.g., the Stanford Binet Intelligence Scale) into nonstandard English forms. As far as variant English dialects are concerned, the overall results of such efforts are mixed. Some authorities (e.g., Baratz, 1969) report salutary effects when tests are administered and scored in terms of the child's native dialect. This is notably true in the case of measuring native dialect proficiency. Similarly, others (e.g., Garvey & McFarlane, 1970) have traced variations in standard English proficiency among black children from lower socioeconomic homes to interference from their normal language pattern rather than to academic ability differences.

In contrast, still other authorities (e.g., Quay, 1971) report that intelligence test performance among black children is little affected by the language of test administration (i.e., whether the test is given in standard English or black dialect) and no reliable performance differential has been observed among black children to whom a test of echoic responding was administered in either standard English or black dialect (Stern & Gupta, 1970).

Of course, there are at least two basic problems inherent in studies designed to compare children's performance on different linguistic forms of the same test. One is that tests translated from standard English to a second language (e.g., Spanish or French) may lose some validity in the very process of translation—to say nothing of the questionable practice of using norms from the original version of the test in order to describe performance on the translated version. A second problem is that no *one* English dialect is likely to characterize all children from different ethnic or racial minorities. Thus, comparisons of standard English with black dialect, for example, may be gross and misleading.

Clearly, extensive research is needed to clarify the influence of dialect on test-taking behavior. But certainly tests based on standard English are unsuitable for use with any child who neither understands nor can speak the language of the test. A teacher must first insure that a child is sufficiently competent in standard English if such competence is necessary for a valid test performance. Otherwise, alternative methods of measurement must be sought in order to obtain any reasonably accurate portrait of a child's achievement status. In short, one cannot condone the practice of early classifying or otherwise evaluating, with standard English measures, the intellectual competence of children whose native language is different from English. For an example of early intervention research in which a bilingual approach to measurement is illustrated, see Nedler and Sebera (1971).

General Impact of Testing on Students

As noted earlier, a particular testing program may have as its purpose nothing more than obtaining useful information. However limited the intended purposes of a testing program, the effect of testing will doubtless extend beyond this point (Stephens & Evans, 1973). Simply taking a test, or expecting one for that matter, is bound to have various effects on most children (Goodwin, 1966). Unfortunately, controlled research in this area of psychology has been meagre, but reasoned speculation combined with what little research has been done in this area can lead to the identification of some definite possibilities. For example, testing effects may occur in advance of actual testing by influencing the type and degree of preparation in which students engage themselves. In some cases, teachers (and parents) may even coach their charges, both in the tactics of test-taking and in the content of anticipated test situations.

Effects may also be realized during a test itself. For example, testing can act as a form of teaching (Stephens & Evans, 1973). In taking a test early in an educational program, students may learn something about what they will be studying (or evaluated on later) and also become sensitized to the material that will be stressed. Students may thus be led to pay more attention to this material when it is encountered (Entwhistle, 1961).

While this may often be desirable from a teacher's point of view (particularly in the case of criterion-referenced measurement), disadvantages may develop. Some students, for example, in advancing an erroneous answer, may become committed to that answer and encounter subsequent difficulty in overcoming their misconception or inaccuracy

(Stephens & Evans, 1973). Also students may become convinced that test-taking and strong test performance are the most important goals of education.

As Bloom (1969) suggests, the psychological effects on students during an actual examination may be comparatively light, except for such possibilities as excessive anxiety or emotional stress, frustration, self-doubt, or a feeling of failure (or accomplishment!) that may be associated with a test situation. Further, while fatigue at the end of an extended examination may occur among some children, it is likely that this effect is usually mild and short-lived.

Perhaps the most potentially serious outcome in this regard can come from "overtesting" children in connection with early intervention programs. Some evaluators simply schedule too much formal testing during the course of an early education program. Conceivably, the net adverse effect of this problem could be at least threefold. First, children may come to view testing negatively because it can mean unwelcome intrusions and undue pressures for performance. Second, teacher resentment over interruptions of their instructional program can accumulate to the point where their cooperation with testers may suffer. Third, overtesting is subject to the law of diminishing returns; that is, the time and expense involved in extensive testing may not be worth the additional results obtained. It is also possible that too much data can serve to complicate, rather than facilitate, the interpretation of program outcomes. This concern over excessive testing was also discussed in chapter 8.

There is no universal rule for determining how many of what kind of tests one should utilize in an evaluation plan. Nevertheless, a judicious perspective on this issue is imperative.

It has been suggested that temporary fatigue and/or the inconvenience occasionally associated with testing are comparatively minor problems. However, prolonged anxiety that may be engendered by testing and evaluation procedures is not minor. Among other things, the literature concerned with test anxiety indicates that teachers (testers) should avoid adding emotionalism to testing procedures by dramatizing the hazards of doing poorly or the idea that a student's future is at stake in the testing situation. It is extremely important to acknowledge the potentially debilitating effects that intense emotion may have on an individual's test performance, particularly where complex intellectual tasks are involved. There is good evidence to indicate that individual differences in test anxiety are apparent among children as early as kindergarten entrance, and that subsequent changes in measured anxiety level are linked to patterns of change in achievement and intelligence test performance throughout the elementary school period. In general, it is the highly anxious child or youth who stands to suffer the most in this regard

(Sarason, Davidson, Lighthall, Waite & Ruebush, 1960; Sarason, Hill & Zimbardo, 1964).

Thus far, a few ideas concerning the impact of testing on students before and during examination periods have been presented. While these dimensions of the problem are important, postexamination effects possibly are the most profound, depending upon what uses are made of test results. As Bloom (1969) has observed, these effects may be minimal or maximal, positive or negative, but they can neither be completely controlled nor entirely neutralized.

Aftereffects of testing are in part a function of the type of test utilized and the way in which tests are utilized. For example, at least three categories of tests carry a high potential for lasting effects: tests designed to measure significant and relatively stable human qualities, such as tests of intelligence and aptitudes; tests used to facilitate major educational decisions (e.g., tests for admission to certain academic programs, or for certification of satisfactory completion of an educational program); and tests whose results become a permanent part of a student's record or are made public for one reason or another (Bloom, 1969). Extreme care must therefore be exercised regarding the selection, administration, and interpretation of tests used for such purposes. This leads to an explicit ethical consideration of the way in which test results may be used.

The Ethical Use of Test Results

Concern about the possible misuses of test results is represented by an extensive literature (Black, 1963; Dyer, 1961; Ebel, 1964; Hoffman, 1962; Mehrens & Lehmann, 1969). Among the more critical potential misuses of tests discussed in this literature are four summarized by Ebel (1964). These misuses can serve both to illustrate the current and widespread professional concern about tests and suggest to the reader some guidelines for his own policy formulation about tests.

First, it is conceivable that imprudent educational testing can indelibly mark a student's intellectual status as superior, average, or inferior. If so, his subsequent academic or social status could be more or less predetermined by way of expectancies that become established among those privy to test results and decisions about educational programming that come about through testing. This need not necessarily be destructive to the individual. But an individual who is assigned a label of "weak student" on the basis of an intelligence test score may be adversely affected both in self-esteem and motivation for future achievement.

Second, it is possible that certain testing practices can generate a restricted concept of human abilities, one based largely on degrees of success in intellectual achievement situations. Consequently, this sort of concept may lead to a focus upon the attainment of limited goals, often at the expense of educational practices that are designed to facilitate the development of diverse talent.

A third possible misuse of test results concerns the exercise, by those in charge of testing programs, of excessive and unwarranted control over the personal destinies of children.

Finally, poorly conceived testing practices may foster rigid, mechanistic, and depersonalized approaches to measurement and evaluation, approaches that, in effect, could limit basic human rights and impede positive human relations within the schools.

Such distasteful outcomes are not inevitable, but steps must be taken to guarantee that these outcomes do not materialize. Tests should be viewed as one of several means for increasing student achievement by way of motivating and directing the energies of both students and teachers. Furthermore, the use of tests to *impose* upon others certain decisions and courses of action should be deferred as much as possible to their use in providing data for choice in individual decision-making (Ebel, 1964). As previously indicated, the issue therefore concerns more the way tests are used than it does the nature of tests.

This writer has often been impressed by the negative emotionalism associated with tests and their use by many parents, college students, and teachers. Frequently this emotionalism leads to exaggerated claims about the inhumane or even subversive nature of testing, particularly intelligence and personality testing. Such emotionalism undoubtedly is kindled by inadequate understanding of tests and their uses. However, instances of unwise test use in the school can provide justification for much criticism. At the extreme, tests may be confiscated and burned by opponents of psychometrics (Nettles, 1959; Eron & Walden, 1961). Less extreme, but indicative of resistance, is the refusal by parents to submit their children to testing in the school setting. Still another area of conflict for educators is the matter of when, by what means, and how extensively parents should be informed about their children's test performances. As a matter of course, professionals who are responsible for specific programs of childhood education and research must develop a judicious policy in relation to these problems. At the very least, this policy should include advance parental permission for testing and an acceptable method for communicating the purposes and outcomes to concerned parents. This recommendation, of course, is based on the assumption that parents have the right of access to their children's school records.

Unfortunately, virtually no empirical data exist concerning the effects on parents of receiving information about their children's test performances (Kirkland, 1971). Research in this area is sorely needed in order to glean better clues for policy formulation about school testing practices.[6] It is also pertinent to consider the social consequences of abandoning tests. In a broad sense, the case for no testing is much the same as that advanced against evaluation in general (see chapter 8). Ebel (1964) summarizes well a reasoned position on this matter:

> If the educational tests were abandoned, the encouragement and reward of individual efforts would be made more difficult. Excellence in programs of education would become less tangible as a goal and less demonstrable as an attainment. Educational opportunities would be extended less on the basis of aptitude and merit and more on the basis of ancestry and influence; social class barriers would become less permeable. Decisions on important issues of curriculum and method would be made less on the basis of solid evidence and more on the basis of prejudice or caprice. These . . . are likely to be the more harmful consequences, by far. Let us not forego the wise use of tests. (p. 334)

Implicit in this passage is the notion that problems of interpreting and using test results may occur largely because of certain lacks—for example, lack of knowledge about the limitations of tests and the technical and theoretical aspects of testing. Yet, if test results are to be useful, they must be communicated to those directly responsible for students, singly or in groups (Levine, 1966). Again, the task here is one of establishing sound policy for communication, a policy that includes safeguards for student welfare.

This section of the chapter can be concluded with a reference to a fairly recent position statement on psychological assessment adopted by the American Psychological Association (1970). The statement in fact represents a policy for testing and the use of test results formulated in relation to the essential features of psychological assessment. As such, it is an extremely important policy for consideration by school personnel everywhere.

1. Guaranteed protection must be provided for every individual against unwarranted inferences by educational personnel ill-equipped with necessary background knowledge and skill in testing.

2. Obsolete information that might lead to unfavorable evaluation of an individual must be periodically culled from personal records in order to protect that individual.

3. Unnecessary intrusions into one's privacy must be avoided; irrelevant tests and questions have no place in a well-designed assessment program.

4. Given the above modes of protection, procedures should be established to facilitate continual investigation of new and improved techniques of assessment.

While these guidelines are pertinent to ability testing, they are perhaps even more applicable to personality assessment. In either case, the key concept again is *relevance*. Measurement procedures should have demonstrable relevance to the peculiar purposes of evaluation, whether one wishes to evaluate academic competence, instructional effectiveness, or personal-social development. However, one must simultaneously determine relevance in relation to an ethical framework and criteria of social acceptability.

SUMMARY AND CONCLUSIONS

This chapter represents a selective overview of contemporary measurement practices in early childhood education. Although techniques for the measurement of young children's behavior received primary attention, comment was extended to procedures for measuring the behavior of teachers and parents.

A number of emergent trends concerning current measurement practice were cited. Those with perhaps the deepest implications for early education reflect attempts to broaden the spectrum of measurement in several directions, including a greater sensitivity to cultural or ethnic interests and a stronger focus upon children's affective development. However, much technical work remains to be done before field application of measures relevant to these foci can confidently be made.

Measurement was considered along three basic lines of thought: what, how, and when. An answer to the question of what to measure requires a careful scrutiny of educational objectives. In turn, the specification of objectives is instrumental in determining an answer to the how of measurement. Achievement of a consistency among program objectives, instructional content, and measurement procedures is imperative for sound curriculum evaluation.

It is clear that interviews, systematic observational procedures, and tests (standardized and otherwise) continue to dominate educational practice, and that many useful variations of these techniques have recently appeared. Moreover, a rebirth of mastery approaches to learning is apparent from the widespread interest in criterion-referenced measurement. Measurement is also being applied increasingly to variables other than strict behavioral outcomes of educational programs. These variables include curriculum components, curriculum materials, teacher-child interaction, and the physical environment for education. Among other things, this means that comprehensive measurement will include the input and process phases of instruction, as well as the traditional output phase. A precise conceptualization of basic input, process, and output variables can also serve better to answer the question of when to measure.

Finally, the research literature reviewed herein suggested that direct behavioral measures are generally preferable to those that provide only data for inferences about hypothetical constructs, primarily for reasons of validity. Validity is also a central issue in the special problems involved when many conventional measures are used with individuals from varying cultural backgrounds. Cultural bias, along with the possible psychological effects of testing on children and the ethical use of test results, were identified as phenomena that warrant the attention of teachers and research workers.

NOTES

1. For an overview of general trends in educational and psychological testing, see *Review of Educational Research*, 1965, Vol. 35, No. 1, and Deal and Wood (1968).

2. For a discussion of the merits and limitations of criterion-referenced measurement, see Ebel (1970).

3. Ostensibly, the open education movement represents more a commitment to the *process* of learning, including the enhancement of cognitive processes. Ultimately, however, some evidence of process—as reflected in the child's behavior (a product of *some* kind)—is necessary for evidence of process.

4. Measurement considerations associated with still another concept, *cost-benefit analysis,* are not dealt with in this chapter. For an introduction to this approach, see Alkin (1970).

5. For a recent and comprehensive review of creativity research, see Wallach (1970).

6. Readers interested in a further study of testing policy are referred to the *American Psychologist* (1965), Vol. 20, No. 11. The entire issue is devoted to issues and ethics associated with testing and public policy.

REFERENCES

Achenbach, T. M. The children's associative responding test: A possible alternative to group IQ tests. *Journal of Educational Psychology,* 1970, *61*(5), 340-348.

Adams, G. S. *Measurement and evaluation in education, psychology, and guidance.* New York: Holt, Rinehart and Winston, 1964.

Adkins, D. *Measurement of motivation to achieve in preschool children.* ERIC: ED 021 617, 1968.

Ahr, A. E. The development of a group preschool screening test of early school entrance potentiality. *Psychology in the Schools,* 1967, *4,* 59-63.

Ali, F., & Costello, J. Modification of the Peabody Picture Vocabulary Test. *Developmental Psychology,* 1971, *5,* 86-91.

Alkin, M. C. Evaluating the cost-effectiveness of instructional programs. In M. C. Wittrock & D. E. Wiley (Eds.), *The evaluation of instruction: Issues and problems.* New York: Holt, Rinehart and Winston, 1970.

Allport, G. W., Vernon, P. E., & Lindzey, G. *A study of values.* Boston: Houghton, 1951.

American Psychological Association. *Standards for educational and psychological tests and manuals.* Washington, D.C.: American Psychological Association, 1966.

————. Psychological assessment and public policy. *American Psychologist,* 1970, *25,* 264-267.

Amidon, E. Interaction analysis: Recent developments. Paper presented at meeting of American Educational Research Association, Chicago, February 1966.

————. *The effect upon the behavior and attitudes of student teachers of training cooperating teachers and student teachers in the use of interaction analysis as a classroom observational technique.* ERIC: ED 021 777, 1967.

Astin, A. W., & Holland, J. L. The environmental assessment technique: A way to measure college environments. *Journal of Educational Psychology,* 1961, *52,* 308-316.

Attwell, A. A., Orpet, R. E., & Meyers, C. E. Kindergarten behavior ratings as a predictor of academic achievement. *Journal of School Psychology,* 1967, *6,* 43-46.

Baer, D., Wolf, M., & Risley, T. Some current dimensions of applied behavior analysis. *Journal of Applied Behavior Analysis,* 1968, *1,* 91-97.

Bangs, T. E. *Language and learning disorders of the pre-academic child.* New York: Appleton-Century-Crofts, 1968.

Bannister, J. *Evaluating college teaching.* ERIC: ED 022 450, 1961.

Banta, T. J. Tests for the evaluation of early childhood education: The Cincinnati autonomy test battery. In J. Hellmuth (Ed.), *Cognitive studies.* Vol. 1. New York: Brunner-Mazel, 1970.

Baratz, J. C. A bi-dialectical task for determining language proficiency in economically disadvantaged Negro children. *Child Development,* 1969, *40,* 889-901.

Barth, R. S. Open education. *Theory and Philosophy of Education.* Kensington, Australia, 1969.

Bauer, R. A. (Ed.). *Social indicators.* Cambridge, Mass.: M.I.T. Press, 1966.

Baumrind, D. *Parent attitude inquiry: Research edition III.* Berkeley, Calif.: Department of Psychology, University of California, 1967.

————. *Naturalistic observation in the study of parent-child interaction.* ERIC: ED 027 073, 1968.

Beatty, W. H. *Improving educational assessment and an inventory of measures of affective behavior.* Washington, D.C.: Association for Supervision and Curriculum Development, NEA, 1969.

Bee, H., Van Egeren, L. F., Streissguth, A. P., Nyman, B. A., & Leckie, M. S. Social class differences in maternal teaching strategies and speech patterns. *Developmental Psychology,* 1969, *1,* 726-734.

Behavioral analysis instrument for teachers. Syracuse, N. Y.: Educational and Cultural Center, 1969.

Bierly, M. M. A validation of a method of assessing young children's language competence. Paper presented at meeting of American Educational Research Association, New York, February 1971.

Black, H. *They shall not pass.* New York: Morrow, 1963.

Blair, B. *Evaluation of faculty instruction.* ERIC: ED 029 642, 1968.

Block, J. H. (Ed.). *Mastery learning.* New York: Holt, Rinehart and Winston, 1971.

Bloom, B. S. Some theoretical issues relating to educational evaluation. In R. W. Tyler (Ed.), *Educational evaluation: New roles, new means.* Chicago: University of Chicago Press, 1969.

Bloom, B. S., Hastings, J. T., & Madaus, G. F. *Handbook of formative and summative evaluation of student learning.* New York: McGraw-Hill, 1971.

Blum, G. S. Assessment of psychodynamic variables by the Black Pictures. In P. McReynolds (Ed)., *Advances in psychological assessment.* Vol. 1. Palo Alto, Calif.: Science and Behavior Books, 1968.

Boehm, A. *Test of basic concepts.* New York: Psychological Corporation, 1969.

Bolea, A. S. *The development and validation of a pictorial self-concept scale for children in K-4.* ERIC: ED 037 780, 1970.

Bormuth, J. R. (Ed.). *Readability in 1968.* Washington, D. C.: National Conference on Research in English, National Council of Teachers of English, 1968.

Brophy, J. E. Mothers as teachers of their own preschool children: The influence of socioeconomic status and task structure on teaching specificity. *Child Development,* 1970, *41,* 79-94.

Brown, B. B. (Ed.). *Systematic observation: Relating theory and practice in the classroom.* ERIC: ED 031 444, 1969.

―――. Systematic observation and analysis of teaching. In R. LaCoste (Ed.), *Focus on kindergarten, early childhood education series.* Olympia, Wash.: State Department of Public Instruction, 1970.

Brown, F. G. *Principles of educational and psychological testing.* Hindsdale, Ill.: Dryden Press, 1970.

Butler, A. L. *Current research in early childhood education.* Washington, D. C.: American Association of Elementary-Kindergarten-Nursery Educators, 1970.

Caldwell, B. M. *The preschool inventory.* Princeton, N.J.: Educational Testing Service, 1967.

Caldwell, B. M., Heider, J., & Kaplan, B. The inventory of home stimulation. Paper presented at meeting of American Psychological Association, New York, 1966.

Caldwell, B. M., Mozell, C., & Honig, A. S. The implicit parental learning theory. Paper presented at meeting of American Psychological Association, New York, 1966.

Caro, F. G. Issues in the evaluation of social programs. *Review of Educational Research,* 1971, *41,* 87-114.

Carroll, J. B. Problems of measurement related to the concept of learning for mastery. *Educational Horizons,* 1970, *43,* 71-80.

Cazden, C. B. Evaluation of learning in preschool education: Early language development. In B. Bloom, J. T. Hastings, & G. F. Madaus (Eds.), *Handbook on formative and summative evaluation of student learning.* New York: McGraw-Hill, 1971.

Center for the Study of Evaluation. *Elementary school test evaluations.* Los Angeles: CSE, UCLA, 1970.

Cervenka, E. J. *Administrative manual for the inventory of socialization of bilingual children ages three to ten.* ERIC: ED 027 062, 1968.

Cohen, A. M., & Brawer, F. B. *Measuring faculty performance.* Washington, D.C.: American Association of Junior Colleges, 1969.

Coller, A. R. *An annotated bibliography of self-concept measures for the early childhood years.* Urbana, Ill.: ERIC Clearinghouse on Early Childhood Education, 1970.

Conrad, W. G., & Tobiessen, J. The development of kindergarten behavior rating scales for the prediction of learning and behavior disorders. *Psychology in the Schools,* 1967, *4,* 359-363.

Coopersmith, S. *The antecedents of self esteem.* San Francisco: Freeman, 1967.

Crandall, V. C., Katkovsky, W., & Crandall, V. J. Children's beliefs in their own control of reinforcements in intellectual-achievement situations. *Child Development,* 1965, *36,* 91-109.

Creager, J. A., & Astin, A. W. Alternative methods of describing characteristics of colleges and universities. *Educational and Psychological Measurement,* 1968, *28,* 719-734.

Cronbach, L. J. *Essentials of psychological testing.* (3rd ed.) New York: Harper & Row, 1970.

Cunningham, J. L., & Boger, R. P. Development of an observational rating schedule for preschool children's peer group behavior. Paper presented at meeting of American Educational Research Association, New York, February, 1971.

Davidoff, S. H. *The development of an instrument designed to secure student assessment of teaching behaviors that correlate with objective measures of student achievement.* Philadelphia: Office of Research and Evaluation, Philadelphia Public Schools, 1970.

Deal, T., & Wood, P. Testing the early educational and psychological development of children. *Review of Educational Research,* 1968, *38,* 12-18.

Decarie, T. T. *Intelligence and affectivity in early childhood.* New York: International Universities Press, 1965.

Dick, W. A methodology for the formative evaluation of instructional materials. *Journal of Educational Measurement,* 1968, *5,* 99-102.

DuBois, P. H., & Mayo, C. D. (Eds.). *Research strategies for eavluating training.* AERA Monograph Series on Curriculum Evlauation. Chicago: Rand McNally, 1970.

Dyer, H. S. Is testing a menace to education? *New York State Education,* 1961, *49,* 16-19.

Eash, M. J. Assessing curriculum materials: A preliminary instrument. *Educational Product Report 2,* 1969, *5,* 18-24.

Ebel, R. L. The social consequences of educational testing. *School and Society,* Nov. 1964, 331-334.

————. *Some limitations of criterion-referenced measurement.* ERIC: ED 038 670, 1970.

Eichorn, D. Physiological development. In P. Mussen (Ed.), *Carmichael's manual of child psychology.* (3rd ed.) New York: Wiley, 1970.

Eiss, A. F., & Harbeck, M. B. *Behavioral objectives in the affective domain.* Washington, D. C.: National Science Supervisors Association, 1969.

Engelmann, S. *Basic concept inventory.* Chicago: Follett, 1967.

English, H. B., & English, A. C. *A comprehensive dictionary of psychological and psychoanalytic terms.* New York: David McKay, 1958.

Entwhistle, D. Attensity: Factors of specific set in school learning. *Harvard Educational Review,* 1961, *31,* 84-101.

Eron, L., & Walden, L. O. Test burning: II. *American Psychologist,* 1961, *16,* 237-244.

Evans, E. D. Student activism and teaching effectiveness: Survival of the fittest? *Journal of College Student Personnel,* 1969, *10,* 102-208.

Fitts, W. H. *Tennessee self-concept scale.* Nashville: Counselor Recordings and Tests, 1965.

Flanders, N. A. *Interaction analysis in the classroom.* (Rev. ed.) Ann Arbor, Mich.: School of Education, University of Michigan, 1966.

Freeburg, N. E. Assessment of disadvantaged adolescents: A different approach to research and evaluation measures. *Journal of Educational Psychology,* 1970, *61,* 229-240.

French, R. L., & Galloway, C. M. *A description of teacher behavior: Verbal and nonverbal.* ERIC: 028 134, 1968.

Furth, E. J. *Constructing evaluation instruments.* New York: Longmans, Green and Co., 1958.

Gallagher, J. J., Nuthall, G. A., & Rosenshine, B. *Classroom observation.* AERA Monograph Series on Curriculum Evaluation. Chicago: Rand McNally, 1970.

Garrard, J. *Classroom interaction: Review of the literature.* ERIC: ED 013 988, 1966.

Garvey, C., & McFarlane, P. A measure of standard English proficiency of inner-city children. *American Educational Research Journal,* 1970, *7,* 29-40.

Garvin, A. D. *The applicability of criterion-referenced measurement by content area and level.* ERIC: ED 041 038, 1970.

Glaser, R. Instructional technology and the measurement of learning outcomes: Some questions. *American Psychologist,* 1963, *18,* 519-521.

Goldschmid, M. L., & Bentler, P. M. The dimensions and measurement of conservation. *Child Development,* 1968, *39,* 787-082.

Goodwin, W. L. Effect of selected methodological conditions of dependent measures taken after classroom experimentations. *Journal of Educational Psychology,* 1966, *57,* 350-358.

Goolsby, T. M., & Darby, B. M. *A bibliography of instrumentation method-

ology and measurement in early childhood learning. Athens, Ga.: University of Georgia, Research and Development Center in Educational Stimulation, 1969.

Goslin, D. *Teachers and testing.* New York: Russell Sage, 1967.

———. Standardized ability tests and testing. *Science,* 1968, *159,* 851-855.

Goslin, D., Epstein, R., & Hallock, B. *The use of standardized tests in elementary schools.* Technical Report No. 2: The Social Consequences of Testing. New York: Russell Sage, 1965.

Gough, H. G. An interpreter's syllabus for the California Psychological Inventory. In P. McReynolds (Ed.), *Advances in psychological assessment.* Vol. 1. Palo Alto, Calif.: Science and Behavior Books, 1968.

Gronlund, N. E. *Sociometry in the classroom.* New York: Harper, 1959.

Gross, M. B. Preschool prediction of academic achievement. *Psychological Reports,* 1970, *26,* 278.

Gross, R. B., & Marsh, M. An instrument for measuring creativity in young children: The gross geometric forms. *Developmental Psychology,* 1970, *3,* 267.

Guilford, J. P. *Psychometric methods.* (2nd ed.) New York: McGraw-Hill, 1954.

Hamilton, M. I. *Evaluation of a parent and child center program.* ERIC: 045 189, 1971.

Hanson, S. A., Stern, C., & Kitana, H. L. *Attitude differences related to economic status.* Los Angeles: Early Childhood Research, 1968.

Hartup, W. W. Peer interaction and social organization. In P. Mussen (Ed.), *Carmichael's manual of child psychology.* Vol. 2. (3rd ed.) New York: Wiley, 1970.

Harvey, O. J., White, B. J., Prather, M. S., Alter, R. D., & Hoffmeister, J. K. Teachers' belief systems and preschool atmospheres. *Journal of Educational Psychology,* 1966, *57,* 373-381.

Hayes, R. B. *A way to evaluate and to improve classroom teaching effectiveness.* ERIC: ED 048 095, 1968.

Headley, N. *The kindergarten: Its place in the program of education.* New York: Center for Applied Research in Education, 1965.

Heckhausen, H. *The anatomy of achievement motivation.* New York: Academic Press, 1967.

Hess, R. D., Kramer, R., Slaughter, D., Torney, J., Berry, C., & Hull, E. *Techniques for assessing cognitive and social abilities of children and parents in Project Head Start.* ERIC: ED 015 772, 1966.

Hess, R. D., & Shipman, V. C. Early experience and the socialization of cognitive modes in children. *Child Development,* 1965, *36,* 869-886.

Hoepfner, R. *Measuring normal affective states in children.* Los Angeles: UCLA, Center for the Study of Evaluation, 1970.

Hoffman, B. *The tyranny of testing.* New York: Crowell, 1962.

Hogan, R. Development of an empathy scale. *Journal of Consulting and Clinical Psychology,* 1969, *33,* 307-316.

Holtzman, W. H. The changing world of mental measurement and its social significance. *American Psychologist,* 1971, *26,* 546-553.

Honig, A. S., Caldwell, B. M., & Tannenbaum, J. Patterns of information processing used by and with young children in a nursery school setting. *Child Development,* 1970, *41,* 1045-1065.

Honig, A. S., & Lally, J. R. *Piagetian infancy scales.* Syracuse, N.Y.: Syracuse University Children's Center, 1970.

Honig, W. K. *Operant behavior: Areas of research and application.* New York: Appleton-Century-Crofts, 1966.

Hoopes, J. L. *An infant rating scale: Its validation and usefulness.* New York: Child Welfare League of America, Inc., 1967.

Hoyt, D. P. *Identifying effective teaching behavior.* ERIC: ED 039 197, 1969.

Hutt, S. J., & Hutt, C. *Direct observation and measurement of behavior.* Springfield, Ill.: Charles C. Thomas, 1970.

Illinois Test of Psycholinguistic Abilities. (Rev. ed.) Urbana, Ill.: University of Illinois Press, 1970.

Institute of Developmental Studies. *Development of a standardized telephone interview for the measurement of language changes in young children.* ERIC: ED 022 758, 1968.

Jenkins, W. O., Zeigfinger, S., Frengel, B., Birnbach, L., & Gold, H. *The status of behavioral measurement and assessment in children.* ERIC: ED 018 252, 1966.

Johnson, O. G., & Bommarito, J. *Tests and measurements in child development: A handbook.* San Francisco: Jossey-Bass, 1971.

Justiz, T. B. A reliable measure of teacher effectiveness. *Educational Leadership,* 1969, *27,* 49-55.

Kagan, J. Reflection-impulsivity and reading ability in primary grade children. *Child Development,* 1965, *36,* 609-628.

Kamii, C. Evaluation of learning in preschool education: Socioemotional, perceptual-motor, cognitive development. In B. Bloom, J. T. Hastings, & G. F. Madaus (Eds.), *Handbook on formative and summative evaluation of student learning.* New York: McGraw-Hill, 1971.

Kamii, C., & Elliot, D. L. Evaluation of evaluations. *Educational Leadership,* 1971, *28,* 827-831.

Kamii, C., & Peper, R. *A Piagetian method of evaluating preschool children's development in classification.* ERIC: ED 039 013, 1969.

Katz, L. G. *Child behavior survey instrument: Manual of instruction and definition.* Stanford, Calif.: Stanford University Center for Research and Development in Teaching, 1968.

Kaye, H. Sensory processes. In H. W. Reese & L. P. Lipsitt (Eds.), *Experimental Child Psychology.* New York: Academic Press, 1970.

Kemble, V. *A feasibility study of parent awareness programs.* (Final report.) ERIC: ED 040 742, 1969.

Kim, Y., Anderson, H. E., Jr., & Bashaw, W. L. The simple structure of social maturity at the second grade level. *Educational and Psychological Measurement.* 1968, *28,* 145-153.

Kirkland, M. C. The effects of tests on students and schools. *Review of Educational Research,* 1971, *41,* 303-350.

Kirschner Associates, Inc. *A national survey of the impacts of Head Start centers on community institutions.* Washington, D.C.: Office of Child Development, U.S. Office of Health, Education and Welfare, 1970.

Klare, G. R. *The measurement of readability.* Ames, Iowa: Iowa State University Press, 1963.

Kofsky, E. A scalogram study of classificatory development. *Child Development,* 1966, *37,* 191-204.

Kritchevsky, S., & Prescott, E. *Planning environments for young children: Physical space.* Washington, D.C.: National Association for the Education of Young Children, 1969.

Laurendeau, M., & Pinard, A. *Causal thinking in the child.* New York: International Universities Press, 1962.

Lavatelli, C. S. *Piaget's theory applied to an early education curriculum.* Boston: American Science and Engineering, 1970.

Lay, M., & Dopyera, J. *Analysis of early childhood programs: A search for comparative dimensions.* Urbana, Ill.: ERIC Clearinghouse on Early Childhood Education, 1971.

Levine, M. Psychological testing of children. In M. L. Hoffman & L. W. Hoffman (Eds.), *Review of child development research.* Vol. 2. New York: Russell Sage, 1966.

Levine, S., & Elzey, F. F. *Development of a social competency scale for preschool children.* ERIC: ED 020 004, 1968.

Lewis, G. M. *The evaluation of teaching.* ERIC: ED 030 602, 1966.

Lindvall, C. M., & Cox, R. C. *The IPI evaluation program.* AERA Monograph Series on Curriculum Evaluation. Chicago: Rand McNally, 1970.

Long, B. H., & Henderson, E. H. Social schemata of school beginners: Some demographic correlates. *Merrill-Palmer Quarterly,* 1970, *16,* 305-324.

Lorr, M., & Jenkins, R. Three factors in parent behavior. *Journal of Consulting Psychology,* 1963, *17,* 306-308.

Maccoby, E. E., Dowley, E. M., Hagen, J. W., & Degerman, R. Activity level and intellectual functioning in normal preschool children. *Child Development,* 1965, *16,* 761-770.

Macy, I. G., & Kelly, H. J. Chemical and physiologic growth. In P. Mussen (Ed.), *Handbook of research methods in child development.* New York: Wiley, 1960.

Mager, R. F. *Preparing instructional objectives.* Palo Alto, Calif.: Fearon, 1962.

Maw, W. H., & Maw, E. W. Self-concepts of high- and low-curiosity boys. *Child Development,* 1970, *41,* 123-129.

McKeachie, W. J. Student ratings of faculty. *American Association of University Professors Bulletin,* 1969, *55,* 439-444.

McReynolds, P. An introduction to psychological assessment. In P. McReynolds (Ed.), *Advances in psychological assessment.* Vol. 1. Palo Alto, Calif. Science and Behavior Books, 1968.

Medley, D. M. Experiences with the OsCAR technique. *Journal of Teacher Education,* 1963, *14,* 267-273.

―――. *OsCAR goes to nursery school: A new technique for recording pupil behavior.* Princeton, N.J.: Educational Testing Service, 1969.

Mehrabian, A. Measures of vocabulary and grammatical skills for children up to age six. *Developmental Psychology,* 1970, *2,* 439-446.

Mehrens, W. A., & Lehmann, I. J. *Standardized tests in education.* New York: Holt, Rinehart and Winston, 1969.

Meredith, H. V. Methods of studying physical growth. In P. Mussen (Ed.), *Handbook of research methods in child development.* New York: Wiley, 1960.

MGS. *The measure of a good school: A guide to evaluation of school systems adapted particularly for use in Kentucky School districts.* ERIC: ED 037 920, 1964.

Moody, W. B., & Bauswell, R. B. The effect of teacher experience on student achievement, transfer, and retention. Paper presented at meeting of American Educational Research Association, New York, February 1971.

Moss, M. H. *Tests of basic experiences.* Monterey, Calif.: CTB/McGraw-Hill, 1970.

Murray, C. K. The construct validity of the Teaching Situation Reaction Test. *Journal of Educational Research,* 1969, *62,* 323-328.

Nedler, S., & Sebera, P. Intervention strategies for Spanish-speaking children. *Child Development,* 1971, *42,* 259-267.

Neisworth, J. T. The educational irrelevance of intelligence. In R. M. Smith (Ed.), *Teacher diagnosis of educational difficulties.* Columbus, Ohio: Charles Merrill, 1969.

Nettles, G. Test burning in Texas. *American Psychologist,* 1959, *14,* 682-683.

Northway, M. L. The stability of young children's social relations. *Educational Research,* 1969, *11,* 54-57 (a)

————. The changing pattern of young children's social relations. *Educational Research,* 1969, *11,* 212-214. (b)

Northway, M. L., & Weld, L. *Sociometric testing: A guide for teachers.* Toronto: University of Toronto Press, 1957.

Nunnally, J. C. *Educational measurement and evaluation.* New York: McGraw-Hill, 1964.

Nuthall, G. A. A review of some selected recent studies of classroom interaction and teaching behavior. In J. J. Gallagher, G. A. Nuthall & B. Rosenshine (Eds.), *Classroom observation.* AERA Monograph Series on Curriculum Evaluation. Chicago: Rand McNally, 1970.

Oakland, T., & Weilert, E. The effects of test-wiseness materials on standardized test performance of preschool disadvantaged children. Paper presented at meeting of American Educational Research Association, New York, February 1971.

O'Leary, K. D., & Becker, W. C. The effects of the intensity of a teacher's reprimands on children's behavior. *Journal of School Psychology,* 1969, *7,* 8-11.

Orhan, S., & Radin, N. Teaching mothers to teach: A home counseling program for low income parents. *The Family Coordinator,* 1969, *18,* 326-311.

Painter, G. *Infant education.* San Rafael, Calif.: Dimensions Publishing, 1968.

Palmer, J. O. *The psychological assessment of children.* New York: Wiley, 1970.

Paraskevopoulos, How students rate their teachers. *Journal of Educational Research,* 1968, *62,* 25-29.

Payne, D. A. *The specification and measurement of learning outcomes.* Waltham, Mass.: Blaisdell, 1968.

Popham, W. J. Predicting student teachers' instructional behavior from a structured and unstructured test of professional knowledge. *California Journal of Educational Research,* 1965, *16,* 7-13.

————. Performance tests of teaching proficiency: Rationale, development and validation. *American Educational Research Journal,* 1971, *8,* 105-117.

Popham, W. J., & Husek, T. R. Implications of criterion-referenced measurement. *Journal of Educational Measurement,* 1969, *6,* 1-9.

Prescott, E., & Jones, E. *Group day care as a childrearing environment: An observational study of day care programs.* Pasadena, Calif.: Pacific Oaks College, 1967.

Quay, L. C. Language dialect, reinforcement, and the intelligence test performance of Negro children. *Child Development,* 1971, *42,* 5-15.

Queer, G. *An analysis of teacher rating scales: A national survey.* ERIC: ED 030 968, 1969.

Rea, R. E., & Rays, R. E. The comprehensive mathematics inventory: An experimental instrument for assessing youngsters entering school. *Journal of Educational Measurement,* 1970, *7,* 45-47.

Reisen, A. H. Receptor functions. In P. Mussen (Ed.), *Handbook of research methods in child development.* New York: Wiley, 1960.

Reynolds, W. R., Abraham, E. C., & Nelson, M. A. The classroom observational record. Paper presented at meeting of American Educational Research Association, New York, February 1971.

Rogolsky, M. M. Screening kindergarten children: A review and recommendations. *Journal of School Psychology,* 1969, *7,* 18-27.

Sapir, S. G., & Wilson, B. A developmental scale to assist in the prevention of learning disability. *Educational and Psychological Measurement,* 1967, *27,* 1061-1068.

Sarason, S. B., Davidson, K. S., Lighthall, F. F., Waite, R. R., & Ruebush, B. K. *Anxiety in elementary children.* New York: Wiley, 1960.

Sarason, S. B., Hill, K. T., & Zimbardo, P. G. A longitudinal study of the relation of test anxiety to performance on intelligence and achievement tests. *Monographs of the Society for Research in Child Development,* 1964, *29,* Ser. No. 98.

Savage, R. D. *Psychological assessment of the individual child.* Baltimore: Penguin Books, 1968.

Schaefer, E. S., & Bell, R. Q. Development of a parental attitude research instrument. *Child Development,* 1958, *29,* 336-361.

Schmidt, W. H. O., & Hore, T. Some nonverbal aspects of communication between mother and preschool child. *Child Development,* 1970, *41,* 889-896.

Seagoe, M. V. An instrument for the analysis of children's play as an index of degree of socialization. *Journal of School Psychology,* 1970, *8,* 139-145.

Shalock, H. D. *Appendix Z: Classes of measures used in the behavioral sciences, the nature of the data that derive from them, and some comments as to the advantages and disadvantages of each.* ERIC: ED 026 331, 1968.

Sharpe, D. M. *Isolating relevant variables in student teaching assessment.* ERIC: 028 999, 1969.

Sheldon, E., & Moore, W. *Indicators of social change.* New York: Russell Sage, 1968.

Simon, A., & Boyer, E. G. (Eds.). *Mirrors for behavior II.* Vols. A & B: *An anthology of observation instruments.* Philadelphia: Research for Better Schools, Inc., 1970.

Singer, D. L., & Whiton, M. B. Ideational creativity and expressive aspects of human figure drawing in kindergarten age children. *Developmental Psychology,* 1971, *4,* 366-369.

Sjogren, D. D. Measurement techniques in evaluation. *Review of Educational Research,* 1970, *40,* 301-320.

Smith, R. M. (Ed.). *Teacher diagnosis of educational difficulties.* Columbus, Ohio: Charles Merrill, 1969.

Soar, R. S., Ragosta, M., & Soar, R. M. The validation of an observation system for classroom management. Paper presented at meeting of American Educational Research Association, New York, February 1971.

Soares, A. T., & Soares, L. M. Self-perceptions of culturally disadvantaged children. *American Educational Research Journal,* 1969, *6,* 31-45.

Stanford Research Institute. *Classroom observation instrument.* Palo Alto, Calif.: SRI, 1970.

Stanley, J. C. *Measurement in today's schools.* (4th ed.) Englewood Cliffs, N.J.: Prentice-Hall, 1964.

Starkweather, E. K. Problems in the measurement of creativity in preschool children. *Journal of Educational Measurement,* 1964, *1,* 109-113.

————. *Potential creative ability and the preschool child.* ERIC: ED 018 900, 1966.

Stedman, D. J. *An approach to the study of infant behavior.* ERIC: ED 039 031, 1966.

Steele, J. M. *Things as they are: An evaluation procedure to assess intent and practice in instruction.* Unpublished dissertation, University of Illinois, 1969.

Stephens, J. M., & Evans, E. D. *The psychology of classroom learning.* (2nd ed.) New York: Holt, Rinehart & Winston, 1973.

Stern, C., & Gupta, W. Echoic responding of disadvantaged preschool children as a function of type of speech modeled. *Journal of School Psychology,* 1970, *8,* 24-27.

Stern, G. G., & Masling, J. M. *Unconscious factors in career motivation for teaching.* Washington, D.C.: U.S. Department of Health, Education, and Welfare, Office of Education, Contract No. SAE 6459, 1958.

Stern, V., & Gordon, A. *Head Start evaluation and research center, progress report, document 4: Development of observation procedures for assessing preschool classroom environment.* ERIC: ED 021 026, 1967.

Stevens, S. S. Mathematics, measurement, and psychophysics. In S. S. Stevens (Ed.), *Handbook of experimental psychology.* New York: Wiley, 1951.

Stott, L. H., & Ball, R. S. Infant and preschool mental tests: Review and evaluation. *Monographs of the Society for Research in Child Development,* 1965, *30,* Ser. No. 101.

Straus, M. A. *Family measurement techniques.* Minneapolis: University of Minnesota Press, 1969.

Strickland, G. *Development of a school attitude questionnaire for young children.* Los Angeles: UCLA, Center for the Study of Evaluation, 1970.

Sullivan, E. V. *Piaget and the school curriculum: A critical appraisal.* Toronto: Ontario Institute for Studies in Education, University of Ontario, Bulletin No. 2, 1967.

Tanner, J. M. Physical growth. In P. Mussen (Ed.), *Carmichael's manual of child psychology* (3rd ed.) New York: Wiley, 1970.

Teachers College. *Indicators of quality: A brochure.* New York: Institute of Administrative Research, Teachers College, Columbia University, 1968.

Thomas, A., Chess, S., & Birch, H. G. *Behavioral individuality in early childhood.* New York: New York University Press, 1971.

Thomas, H. Psychological assessment instruments for use with human infants. *Merrill-Palmer Quarterly,* 1970, *16,* 179-223.

Tolor, A., Scarpetti, W. L., & Lane, P. A. Teacher's attitudes toward children's behavior revisited. *Journal of Educational Psychology,* 1967, *58,* 175-180.

Torrance, E. P. *Torrance Tests of Creative Thinking.* Princeton: N.J.: Personnel Press, 1966.

Tryk, H. E. Assessment in the study of creativity. In P. McReynolds (Ed.), *Advances in psychological assessment.* Vol. 1. Palo Alto, Calif.: Science and Behavior Books, 1968.

Uzgiris, I. C., & Hunt, J. McV. *Toward ordinal scales of psychological development in infancy.* In preparation, 1969.

Wallach, M. A. Creativity. In P. Mussen (Ed.), *Carmichael's manual of child psychology.* Vol. 1 (3rd ed.) New York: Wiley, 1970.

Ward, W. C. Creativity and environmental cues in nursery school children. *Developmental Psychology,* 1969, *1,* 543-547 (a)

————. Rate and uniqueness in children's creative responding. *Child Development,* 1969, *40,* 869-878 (b).

Watson, G., & Glaser, E. M. *Manual, Watson-Glaser critical thinking appraisal.* Yonkers-on-Hudson, N.Y.: World Book, 1952.

Webb, E. J., Campbell, D. T., Schwartz, R. D., & Sechrest, L. *Unobtrusive measures: Nonreactive research in the social sciences.* Chicago: Rand McNally, 1966.

Webb, W. B. Measurement of learning in extensive training programs. In P. H. DuBois & C. D. Mayo (Eds.), *Research strategies for evaluating training.* Chicago: Rand McNally, 1970.

Weikart, D. P., & Lambie, D. Z. Preschool intervention through a home teaching program. In J. Hellmuth (Ed.), *Disadvantaged child.* Vol. 2. Seattle: Special Child Publications, 1968.

Weiss, R. L. Operant conditioning techniques in psychological assessment. In P. McReynolds (Ed.), *Advances in psychological assessment.* Vol. 1. Palo Alto, Calif.: Science and Behavior Books, 1968.

White, B. W. *Human infants.* New York: Prentice-Hall, 1971.

Williams, J., & Fox, A. M. Prediction of performance in student teaching. *Educational and Psychological Measurement,* 1967, *27,* 1169-1170.

Yeatts, P. P., & Bentley, E. L. The development of a non-verbal measure to assess the self-concept of young and low verbal children. Paper presented at meeting of American Educational Research Association, New York, February 1971.

Yee, A. H., & Fruchter, B. Factor content of the Minnesota Teacher Attitude Inventory. *American Educational Research Journal*, 1971, *8*, 119-133.

Zimmerman, B. J., & Bergan, J. R. *Intellectual operations in teacher-child interaction*. ERIC: ED 039 011, 1968.

APPENDIX

ANNOTATED BIBLIOGRAPHY OF PUBLISHED TESTS AND SCALES FOR EARLY CHILDHOOD DEVELOPMENT AND EDUCATION

Following is an annotated bibliography of recently published assessment devices for use with preschool and primary grade children. This bibliography is limited, with very few exceptions, to measures that are available through commercial outlets. Tests of reading achievement and intelligence scales of long-standing use by child development specialists are not included. Farr and Summers (1968) can be consulted for information about published reading tests; and Stott and Ball (1965) for a description of infant and preschool scales published prior to 1965. A handbook of preschool and kindergarten test evaluations has been published by the UCLA Graduate School of Education, Los Angeles, California (Hoefner, Stern, & Nunmedal, 1971). Measures of child development and behavior *not* published commercially are described by Johnson and Bommarito (1971). Finally, the Educational Resources Information Center (ERIC) reference system is an extremely useful source of data concerning behavioral measurement (see references at the end of this bibliography for examples).

The published measures herein described have been arranged into six major categories: developmental surveys, achievement and intelligence, language and audition, visual-motor behavior, socioemotional behavior, and "miscellaneous" measures. This was done with a full awareness that other possible classification schemes exist. In general, annotations do not include information about such factors as validity, reliability, cost, and time involved in administration. Readers are therefore cautioned to consider these factors carefully if any measures listed herein are selected for use with children.

Developmental Surveys

Ahr's Individual Development Survey (K–1). Skokie, Ill.: Priority Innovations, 1970. A three-part form (Family, Child, and School) designed for use by parents at the time they register their children for school. Developmental, behavioral, and medical data are sought. The usefulness of this procedure is thought to rest primarily in the collection of basic information about the child at initial school entry and as a possible aid to screening for suspected developmental difficulties.

Cassel Developmental Record (birth through adulthood). Jacksonville, Ill.: Psychologists and Educators Press. A form for deriving a developmental profile of six aspects of behavior: intellectual, social, psychosexual, emotional, educational, and physiological.

Developmental Examination (ages 5–10). Ilg, Frances & Ames, Louise. *School Readiness.* New York: Harper and Row, 1964. A general school readiness battery consisting of a structured interview, form copying, tests of directionality and sensorimotor coordination, from matching, memory for forms, naming, and the like. This battery requires roughly 30 minutes for administration to individual children.

Multidimensional Maturity Scale (K–12). Skokie, Illinois: Priority Innovations Inc., 1968. A device constructed to yield a profile of "maturational status" concerning physiological, emotional, psychosexual, mental, educational and social development.

Preprimary Profile (ages 4–5). Chicago: Science Research Associates, 1966. A rating scale for use by parents designed to provide information for teachers of beginning school children. The scale is organized into several areas that call for specific information about a child: self-sufficiency, social behavior, skill development and coordination, language and concept development, and environmental background and experience.

Preschool Attainment Record (ages 6 months–7 years). Circle Pines, Minnesota: American Guidance Service, 1966. A rating scale similar in format to the Vineland Social Maturity Scale. The PAR is designed to survey behavior in eight categories: ambulation, manipulation, rapport, communication, responsibility, general information, ideation, and creativity. Item placement has been determined by extrapolating age norms from other sources.

Riley Preschool Developmental Screening Inventory (preschool–Grade 1). Los Angeles: Western Psychological Services, 1969. Designed to indicate children's developmental age and self-concept.

Symptomatology and Identification of a Child with Learning Disabilities: Revised Edition (K–6). Skokie, Ill.: Priority Innovations, Inc., 1969. A checklist-type of instrument for use by education personnel to report any aspects of a child's behavior that may interfere with school progress. Among the facets of behavior checked are physical characteristics, specific learning problems, activity level, perceptual-motor functioning, coordination, speech and hearing impairments, visual functioning, aggressiveness, attention, impulsivity, sociability, and cognitive factors (memory, thinking).

Valett Developmental Survey of Basic Learning Ability (ages 5–12). Palo Alto, California: Fearon Publishers, 1968. An instrument developed to assist teachers and psychologists in the initial evaluation of elementary school children for whom learning disabilities are suspected. Its use extends to the formulation of specific educational therapy. Educational tasks in six primary areas of learning are sampled: sensorimotor integration, gross motor development, perceptual-motor skills, language development, conceptual skills, and social skills. This survey is not standardized. Rather, its appropriate use depends upon an examiner's subjective judgment and professional experience concerning diagnosis and remediation.

Measures of Achievement and Intelligence

Analysis of Learning Potential, Primary I and II (Grades 1 and 2–3). New York: Harcourt Brace Jovanovich, 1970. This two-part battery purports to be a measure of scholastic ability useful for predicting success in major areas of school learning. Both levels yield two scores: an Index of Learning Potential and a General Composite Standard Score. The administration of designated clusters of three or four subtests from the battery can also be used to obtain a Reading Prognosis and Mathematics Prognosis Score. Primary I subtests are: quantitative language, general information, word-picture association, listening comprehension, picture vocabulary, figure perception, and story sequence.

Primary II subtests include: word-picture association, figure series, number fluency, general information, number series, word meaning, and story sequence.

A Test of Understandings of Selected Properties of a Number System: Primary Form (grades 1–2). Bloomington, Indiana: Bureau of Educational Studies and Testing, School of Education, 1966. This test includes eight segments devoted to number system competence: one-to-one correspondence; cardinal number concepts; ordinal number concepts; recognition of numerals; place values (to hundreds); commutativity for addition; associativity for addition; and identity for addition.

Basic Concept Inventory (ages 3–9). Chicago: Follett Publishing Company, 1968. Most basically, the BCI is a criterion-referenced test for the Bereiter-Engelmann language program, although its use need not be limited to children who participate in this program. According to Engelmann, the Basic Concept Inventory measures five related classes of behavior. These include a child's ability to (a) follow basic instructions and understand key content words used in such instructions; (b) understand size, color, and relational concepts; (c) repeat statements and answer questions implied by them; (d) identify word-sound relationships and patterns; and (e) deal correctly with number statements. The BCI must be administered on a one-to-one basis. No statistical statements concerning validity or reliability are included in the test manual.

Bingham Button Test (ages 3–5). Lancaster, California: Antelope Valley College, 1967. This test purports to assess a child's mastery of concepts normally encountered during the primary grade period, including concepts of size, color, number, and relations between persons and objects and objects and objects. The test must be individually administered.

Boehm Test of Basic Concepts (ages 5–7). New York: The Psychological Corporation, 1969. A group test for the assessment of concept mastery crucial for initial school success. Its use leads to the identification of individual children who may need special attention due to low-level concept attainment, and specific concepts unfamiliar to large numbers of children of a given class. Pictorial items (50) are arranged in a hierarchy of increasing difficulty; administration is straightforward, simple, and ordinarily requires 30-40 minutes.

California Achievement Tests, 1970 edition: Levels 1 and 2 (grades 1.5–4). Monterey, California: CTB/McGraw-Hill, 1970. Both levels are concerned with assessing achievement in three areas: reading, mathematics, and language. These batteries are revisions of tests first published in 1957.

Cognitive Abilities Test (K–4). New York: Houghton-Mifflin, 1968. A group test comprising four short subtests—oral vocabulary, relational concepts, multimental ("one that doesn't belong"), and quantitative concepts—and designed to measure children's cognitive ability development during the early grades. Directions are given orally in conjunction with pictorial materials. A variety of norms is provided for this instrument, which is linked with the multilevel edition of the Lorge-Thorndike Intelligence Tests.

Concept Assessment Kit—Conservation (ages 4–7). San Diego: Educational and Industrial Testing Service, 1968. A Piaget-based measure of the conservation concept appropriate to the transition period from preoperational to concrete operational thought. Three scales, two of which are parallel forms, are included and measure conservation of two-dimensional space, number, substance, quantity, weight, discontinuous quantity, area, and length. The kit is also suitable for children as late as third or fourth grade. Norms are provided.

Contemporary School Readiness Test (K–1). Billings, Montana: Montana Reading Clinic Publications, 1970. An instrument designed to predict first grade success and for administration during the latter weeks of kindergarten or beginning weeks of first grade. A variety of subtests are involved: writing name; colors of the spectrum; science, health, and social studies; reading; handwriting readiness; numbers; visual and auditory discrimination; and listening comprehension.

Cooperative Preschool Inventory, revised edition (ages 3–6). Princeton, New Jersey: Educational Testing Service, 1970. The Preschool Inventory was originally designed in relation to Project Head Start. Its purpose is to assess achievement in areas regarded as necessary foundations for early school success. These areas have been labeled concept activation-sensory, concept activation-numerical, personal-social responsiveness, and associative vocabulary. The Preschool Inventory has been used as a rough diagnostic test, i.e., to identify selected "cultural handicaps" and as a gross measure of the impact of Head Start experience on children. Limited norms are provided (based on the performance of children from "lower-class" and "middle-class" backgrounds). Like so many preschool tests, this inventory must also be administered individually.

Cooperative Primary Tests (end of grade 1–grades 2 and 3). Princeton, New

Jersey: Educational Testing Service, 1967. A primary grade level instrument to measure "basic understandings of the verbal and quantitative world." The Primary Test Series includes six subsections: pilot test (orientation); listening; word analysis; mathematics; reading, and writing skills. The latter subtest involves grades 2 and 3 only. The battery clearly has a "basic skill" focus, is untimed, and can be administered in groups.

Cultural Fair Intelligence Test: Scale I (ages 4–8). Champaign, Illinois: Institute for Personality and Ability Testing (undated). A measure of general intelligence, relatively free of "cultural and educational influences," this scale contains eight subtests, four of which must be administered individually.

Delco Readiness Test (K–1). Media, Pennsylvania: Delco Readiness Test, 111 Linda Lane, 1970. Designed primarily as a reading readiness measure, this instrument provides a focus on visual discrimination and visual-motor skills. The manual lists behavior objectives in the area of "essential reading skills," along with suggested teaching activities for such objectives.

Fascinating Fives Learning Inventory (Kindergarten). Miami, Florida: Dade County Board of Public Instruction, 1969. A measure of achievement in traditional subject areas such as science, language arts, music, mathematics, social studies, art, and physical education. The test is designed for individual administration and requires the use of various props.

First Grade Screening Test (ages 5–6). Circle Pines, Minnesota: American Guidance Service, 1969. A group test for use in kindergarten and/or first grade. Its purpose is to screen beginning or potential first grade students so that those who will not make adequate progress without special assistance may be identified and helped.

Frengel-Jenkins Perceptual and Cognitive Battery (ages 4–5). Berger, Barbara. "A Longitudinal Investigation of Montessori and Traditional Pre-kindergarten Training with Inner City Children: A Comparative Assessment of Learning Outcomes." New York: Center for Urban Education, 105 Madison Ave., 1969. Seven subtests concerned with perceptual-cognitive skills in young children comprise this experimental battery. Included are tests of delayed memory, general information and comprehension, simple perceptual discrimination, relational concepts, immediate memory, discrimination learning, and problem-solving.

Gilliland Learning Potential Examination, 1970 revision (ages 6–15). Billings, Montana: Eastern Montana College, The Reading Clinic, 1970. A multipurpose test, unusual in that it is designed particularly for rural children and is accompanied by separate norms for American Indian children and youth who reside on reservations. The main focus of the test is scholastic aptitude: measures of visual memory, symbolic representation, relationships, listening comprehension, picture completion, and the like. However, portions of other segments—general information and interests—provide data concerning knowledge usually obtained through reading and the selection of reading materials for individual children.

Greater Cleveland Reading Test: First Level i.t.a. Reading Retention Test: Developmental Edition. Cleveland, Ohio: Educational Research Council of America, 1967. This instrument is designed to measure the reading responses of children who have experienced level one of the Greater Cleveland Reading Program, a program based on the initial teaching alphabet. Four subscores may be obtained: auditory-visual discrimination, phoneme-symbol identification, word recognition, and meaning (word and sentence).

Hammond-Skipper Pre-School Achievement Rating Scale (ages 3–5). Tallahassee, Florida: Florida State University, Department of Elementary Education, 1966. A teacher rating form for children's cognitive and social development intended to help in educational planning, guidance, and the assessment of individual progress.

Leicester Number Test (primary grades). London: University of London Press, 1970. This test is an outgrowth of curriculum experiences based on Piaget's theory about development of the number concept. Test components include the counting operation, conservation of number, seriation, grouping, number relativeness, proportion, and the four basic arithmetical operations.

Metropolitan Achievement Tests: Primary, Primary II, and Elementary, 1970 edition. New York: Harcourt Brace Jovanovich, 1970. Primary I (grades 1.5–2.4). Subtests include word knowledge, word analysis, reading stories, mathematics concepts, mathematics, computation. Primary II (grades 2.5–3.4). Same as I, with addition of spelling and mathematics problem-solving subtests. Elementary (grades 3.5–4.9). Subtests include word knowledge, reading, language, spelling, mathematics computation, mathematics concepts, and mathematics problem-solving.

Metropolitan Readiness Tests (ages 5–6). New York: Harcourt, Brace and World, 1965. Six subtests comprise the Metropolitan battery: word meaning, listening comprehension, perceptual recognition of similarities, recognition of lower-case alphabet letters, number knowledge, and perceptual-motor control (copying). In combination these tests are intended to provide an assessment of children's development in skills that contribute to "readiness for first grade instruction." The Metropolitan battery is ordinarily given at the end of kindergarten or beginning of first grade. Results may be used to classify pupils on a "readiness" continuum. Such a classification is presumed to be helpful for teachers who desire more efficient management of their instructional efforts. At least minimal skill in the use of writing instruments and paper is a prerequisite for children to whom the Metropolitan is administered. However, no special training is needed by teachers for the administration and scoring of these tests. Norms are based upon a nationwide sample of beginning first-graders. In general, the reliability of these tests is high and their prediction validity is encouraging. The Metropolitan is among the most popuplar of batteries currently used in public school kindergartens and primary grades.

New York City Project Materials (grade 1). Princeton, New Jersey: Educational Testing Service, 1965. A set of instructional and assessment materials, including written exercises for first-graders. These materials were designed especially to help teachers better understand, foster, and observe young children's intellectual development. Areas of emphasis include basic language skills, concepts of space and time, beginning logical concepts, beginning mathematical concepts, reasoning skills, and general development.

Parent Readiness Evaluation of Preschoolers (ages 4–6). Skokie, Illinois: Priority Innovations, Inc., 1968. An individual test for preschool and kindergarten children suitable for administration by parents. Domains sampled include general information, comprehension, opposites, verbal descriptions and associations, listening skills, motor coordination, auditory and visual memory, visual interpretation, and visual-motor association.

Peabody Individual Achievement Test (K–12). Los Angeles: Western Psychological Services, 1970. A survey measure of educational attainment in basic skills areas: mathematics, reading recognition, reading comprehension, spelling, and general information. Requires oral or pointing responses only. Purports to be useful with special populations, including disadvantaged, mentally handicapped, and children with learning disabilities. Developed for use in clinical settings for wide-range screening purposes.

Rhodes WISC Scatter Profile (ages 5–15). San Diego: Educational and Industrial Testing Service, 1969. A technique designed to facilitate the interpretation of level and pattern of performance on the Wechsler Intelligence Scale for Children.

Short Form Test of Academic Aptitude. Level I (grades 1.5–2); Level II (grades 3–4). Monterey, California: CTB/McGraw-Hill, 1970. Children's intellectual level and potential for rate of progress in school are the focus of this instrument. Level I requires no reading and consists of four main subtests: vocabulary, analogies, sequences, and memory. Items consist only of pictures, letters, numerals, or various designs. The parent test of this "short form" is the California Test for Mental Maturity. Level II consists of similar subtests.

Stanford Early School Achievement Test. Level I. New York: Harcourt, Brace and World, 1969. Formerly the Stanford Pre-primary Test, the focus of this new edition remains those learnings of children acquired prior to school entrance, Included are tests of the environment (social studies and sciences), mathematics, letters and sounds, and aural comprehension. A new primary grades version of the Stanford Achievement Test is also available.

Stanford Early School Achievement Test: Level II (K–1). New York: Harcourt Brace Jovanovich, 1970. A cognitive abilities measure suitable for use only with children who have experienced formal instruction. Six subscores can be derived from the SESAT Level II: letters and sounds, aural comprehension, word reading, sentence reading, mathematics, and the environment (science and social studies).

Sprigle School Readiness Screening Test (ages 4½–6). Herbert A. Sprigle (1936 San Marco Blvd., Jacksonville, Florida), 1965. This test is designed to measure the extent to which requisite school skills and abilities have been acquired. Nine subtests are involved in this individually administered measure: verbal comprehension, size relationships, visual discrimination, reasoning, number understanding, analogies, information, vocabulary, and spatial relations.

Tests of Basic Experiences: Level K, preliminary edition, (preschool-kindergarten). Level L (K–1). Monterey, California: CTB/McGraw-Hill, 1970. This battery is designed to measure the child's acquisition of knowledge and understandings believed essential for successful progress and participation in school. Subtests include language, science, social studies, mathematics, and general concepts. The composition of *Level L* is essentially the same as *Level K* except, of course, that more advanced concepts are included.

The ABC Inventory (ages 4–9 to 4–11). Muskegon, Michigan: Educational Studies and Development (1357 Forest Park Road), 1965. An orally administered school readiness screening instrument for individual preschoolers. Subtests include naming, common knowledge, elementary counting, and simple drawings.

The APELL Test (ages 4½–7). Orange, California: EDCODYNE (3724 West Chapin Avenue), 1969. APELL represents a system of instructional diagnosis and design for use by teachers to identify children's individual needs. The test can be used with children younger than 4½, although such use must be based on individual administration. Areas covered include visual discrimination, auditory association, letter names, discrimination of attributes, number concepts, number facts, nouns, pronouns, verbs, adjectives, plurals, and prepositions.

The Matrix Test (preschool–primary). New York: Research Division, Bank Street College of Education, 1967. This test is purported to measure young children's inferential thinking and classification skills. Piagetian theory provides the framework for item construction.

Word Recognition Test (Ages 4–8½). London: University of London Press, 1970. A test suitable for group administration and engineered to assess word recognition skills from initial letter knowledge through competences typically achieved by eight years of age. This instrument comprises four major aspects: comprehension of spoken language, ability to analyze sounds, ability to organize a series of visual symbols, and the interaction of aural and visual abilities.

Zip Test (ages 5–12). California State Department of Education: Bureau of Community Services and Migrant Education (undated). A brief measure of basic proficiencies for migrant or Spanish-speaking children, including readiness and skill in mathematics, conceptual ability in English, and reading comprehension in English. Test data are thought to be useful for assessing learning-level or grade-level placement and/or as clues for instructional planning.

Measures of Language and Audition

Arizona Articulation Proficiency Scale, revised edition (ages 3 and over). Los Angeles: Western Psychological Services, 1970. This measure is best described by its title.

Assessment of Children's Language Comprehension, Research Edition for Preschool Planning. Palo Alto, California: Consulting Psychologists Press, 1969. An experimental technique for the measurement of comprehension based on standard English.

Expressive Vocabulary Inventory for Children (preschool–kindergarten). Los

Angeles: Early Childhood Research Center, 1968. This inventory is suitable for use with children who must make verbal responses within a context of individual administration. Word content is a sample of the vocabulary that children are usually expected to have mastered at point of kindergarten entry.

Goldman-Fristse-Woodcock Test of Auditory Discrimination (ages 4 and over). Circle Pines, Minnesota: American Guidance Service, 1970. An individually administered test of children's ability to discriminate speech sounds under conditions of both quiet and distracting noise.

Illinois Test of Psycholinguistic Processes, revised edition (ages 2–10). Urbana, Illinois: University of Illinois Press, 1970. The ITPA purports to assess twelve aspects of psycholinguistic functioning ranging from auditory and visual reception to visual sequential memory and sound blending. These aspects have been conceptualized in terms of three dimensions. First, children's auditory-vocal and visual-motor behaviors constitute abilities labeled *channels of communication.* Receptive, organizing, and expressive processes are the second major dimension, the *psycholinguistic processes.* The third dimension consists of two *levels of organization,* the automatic and the representational. Assessment by way of the ITPA leads to the charting of individual profiles or to intra-individual differences in terms of the aforementioned dimensions. Emphasis has been placed upon the identification of major psycholinguistic deficits or disabilities which may require remediation. The ITPA is administered individually. Special training is required for use of the ITPA.

Laradon Articulation Scale (ages 1–8). Los Angeles: Western Psychological Services (12031 Wilshire Blvd), revised 1963. A measure of phonemic skill, individually administered, resulting in ranking of children according to pronunciation skill; the 10 percent who may require clinical speech therapy are identified.

Massad Mimicry Test II (ages 3½–9). Princeton, New Jersey: Educational Testing Service, 1969. An individual test of phoneme articulation, word articulation, and applied knowledge of sentence properties. A tape recorder is required for this individually administered test.

Oregon Language Profile (ages 3 months–8 years). Corvallis, Oregon: Continuing Education Publications, Oregon State University (undated). A rating scale approach for the evaluation of language skills during infancy and early childhood. Principal focuses include verbal comprehension, oral expression, intelligibility, phonology, and articulation.

Peabody Picture Vocabulary Test (preschool and beyond). Minneapolis: American Guidance Service, 1959. The PPVT is assumed to measure recognition (hearing) vocabulary by having a child identify correct pictorial representations (from among four alternatives) in a series as the examiner speaks a word corresponding to each picture. It was originally designed to predict school success, and results obtained from its use are often taken to estimate roughly a child's "verbal intelligence." Items are arranged from simple to complex. This test is suitable for use with children of preschool age and beyond, and is easily administered. Further, the PPVT requires little in the way of special training for scoring and interpretation. In general, the reliability of this test is satisfactory and scores derived from its use are correlated positively with a wide range of other measures of verbal behavior. Of studies performed to date, relevant to the validity of the PPVT for predicting school success, it appears to be more effective with children beyond age 7 than with those of nursery and kindergarten age. Extensive use has been made of the PPVT for the study of mentally retarded children.

Preschool Language Scale (preschool–primary grades). Columbus, Ohio: Charles E. Merrill, 1969. A scale designed to detect language strengths and deficiencies. Two distinct sections—auditory comprehension and verbal ability—provide the means to derive a language quotient for individual children.

The "Stycar" Hearing Tests, revised edition (ages 6 months–11 years). Great Britain: N.F.E.R. Publishing Co. Ltd., 1968. An instrument to measure children's capacity to hear with comprehension. Involved is a series of simple auditory screening tests which make use of words and objects commonly found in the child's environment.

Templin-Darley Tests of Articulation, 2nd edition (ages 3–8). University of Iowa: Bureau of Educational Research and Service, 1969. An instrument with ten subtests ranging from consonant singles (initial and final) to diphthongs and combinations, all of which are designed to assess articulation proficiency and identify possible articulation difficulty.

Verbal Language Development Scale (ages 1–15). Circle Pines, Minnesota: American Guidance Service, 1958. An extension of the communication portion of the Vineland Social Maturity Scale. As such, the informant-interview method of administration is utilized.

Measures of Visual-Motor Behavior

Dennis Visual Perception Scale (grades 1-6). Los Angeles: Western Psychological Services, 1969. A paper-and-pencil test for screening children for perceptual difficulties thought to affect learning adversely.

Kindergarten Test Chart (K-1). Woodside, New York: Graham-Field Surgical Co. (undated). A vision-screening device for children who cannot read or who have difficulties in reading. Pictures and symbols are substituted for letters.

Lincoln-Oseretsky Motor Development Scale (ages 6-14). Sloan, W. "Manual for the Lincoln-Oseretsky Motor Development Scale," *Genetic Psychology Monographs,* 1955, *51,* 185–252. A standardized scale for the assessment of general motor proficiency. Administration is complex and best executed by trained persons working with individual children in the clinical setting. Heavy emphasis is placed on hand and arm movements regarding speed, dexterity, coordination, and rhythm. Gross motor items involve balance and jumping. (See Savage, 1968, pp. 72-78, for description of more specific motor measures.)

Marianne Frostig Developmental Test of Visual Perception (preschool and beyond). Palo Alto, California: Consulting Psychologists Press, 1969. A diagnostic test of visual-perceptual "subfunctions" thought relevant to school performance, especially reading. Purportedly the test measures five relatively independent subfunctions: eye-hand coordination, figure-ground perception, form constancy, position in space, and spatial relationships. Recent factor analytic research indicates, however, that only one general perceptual factor may be involved. The test is designed for use in conjunction with a perceptual training program.

Primary Visual Motor Test (ages 4-8). New York: Grune and Stratton, 1970. Standardized on children from various socioeconomic backgrounds, this instrument is designed to measure the following dimensions: rotation or reversal, line configuration, linear, segmentation, fragmentation, closure, omission, addition, distortion, directionality, alignment, boundary, no resemblance, and gross signs.

Purdue Perceptual-Motor Survey (ages 5-10). Columbus, Ohio: Charles E. Merrill, 1966. A survey instrument developed to assess qualitatively the perceptual-motor abilities of children in the early school years (standardized in children from grades 1-4). This survey must be administered individually and requires training for proper use. Among the behavioral domains sampled are generalized movement, reflex activities, movement patterns, laterality, perceptual-motor match and directionality. The relationship of perceptual-motor development to general academic achievement is basic to the design of this survey.

Southern California Perceptual-Motor Tests (ages 4-8). Los Angeles: Western Psychological Services, 1968. This battery of tests is designed to measure imitation of postures, crossing midline of body, bilateral motor coordination, right-left discrimination, standing balance (eyes open) and standing balance (eyes closed).

U.C.L.A. Visual Discrimination Inventory (ages 3-6). Los Angeles: Early Childhood Research Center, 1968. Children are asked to point to a picture that is identical to a stimulus picture. Designed for individual administration.

Measures of Socioemotional Behavior

Classroom Behavior Inventory (K-3). New York: Westinghouse Learning Corporation, 1968. Ratings of children's behavior in the classroom and other observable characteristics are taken as an indication of achievement motivation.

Draw-A-Classroom Test (K-4). Toronto: Research Department, Toronto Board of Education, 1969. This is a tool for obtaining information about how children perceive and conceptualize the world by way of objects and people that are present in the classroom.

Bristol Social Adjustment Guides (ages 5 and above). San Diego: Educational and Industrial Testing Service, 1967. A rating scale for social adjustment involving two broad dimensions of child behavior: school (or residential care) and home (family).

California Preschool Social Competency Scale (ages 2½-5½). Palo Alto,

California: Consulting Psychologists Press, 1980. A teacher's rating scale devised for the diagnosis, placement, or measurement of young children's developmental progress.

Children's Attitudinal Range Indicator (K-3). New York: Westinghouse Learning Corporation, 1968. A measure of children's attitudes, both positive and negative, toward peers, home, school, and society. Based upon the projective technique.

Children's Personality Questionnaire (ages 8-12). San Diego: Educational and Industrial Testing Service, 1963. A general assessment of personality development that purports to measure fourteen traits ranging from reserved–outgoing and deliberate–excitable to obedient–assertive and relaxed–tense. Standardization procedures and statistical data are fully reported in the manual. The CPQ has been used with children as young as age 6.

Early School Personality Questionnaire (ages 6-8). Champaign, Illinois: Institute for Personality and Ability Testing (undated). An individually- or group-administered test of "personality." Thirteen "factors" are presumably measured, including such traits as reserved–outgoing, humble–assertive, vigorous–doubting, relaxed–tense, undisciplined self-conflict–controlled, expedient–conscientious, and forthright–shrewd.

Inferred Self Concept Judgment Scale (K-6). McDaniel, Elizabeth. Los Angeles: Institute of Aerospace Management, University of Southern California, 1969. Teacher perceptions of children's self-concepts as influenced by school experiences are recorded in an effort to describe self-esteem among students.

Junior Eysenck Personality Inventory (ages 7-16). San Diego: Educational and Industrial Testing Service, 1965. A downward extension of the Eysenck Personality Inventory designed to measure two personality dimensions: extraversion and neuroticism. A lie scale has also been incorporated. Reliability of the instrument increases with age; norms presented separately for each year group for both sexes. A Spanish-language edition (1970) of this inventory is also available, complete with norms for Mexican-American children.

Peabody Scale for Rating Emotional Behavior. Nashville, Tennessee: Child Study Center, George Peabody College for Teachers, 1967. A rating scale-type of measurement technique for use by parents in describing their children's behavior traits: gregarious–unsocial, bright–dull, emotionally stable–neurotic, dominant–submissive, cheerful–depressed, adventurous–timid, and socialized–unsocialized.

Politte Sentence Completion Test (grades 1-8). Jacksonville, Illinois: Psychologists and Educators Press, 1970. A quasi-projective test much of which concerns the child's situation in school. Either oral or written responses may be obtained according to the age of the child.

Primary Academic Sentiment Scale (preschool-grade 1). Skokie, Illinois: Priority Innovations, Inc., 1968. A group test for the purpose of assessing young children's motivation for learning, maturity, and independence from parents.

Sarason Scales for General and Test Anxiety (grades 1-6). Sarason, S. B. *Anxiety in Elementary School Children.* New York: Wiley, 1960. Self-report, paper-and-pencil measures of anxiety. These scales can be administered to younger children by reading the items; children may then respond verbally or by checkmark in terms of simple "yes–no." Individual or group administration procedures may be followed, depending on one's particular situation. Changes in anxiety as measured by these scales have been correlated with educational achievement, particularly reading progress throughout the elementary school period.

Self-Concept Adjective Checklist (K-8). Jacksonville, Ill.: Psychologists and Educators Press, 1971. A simply administered instrument to achieve insight into how children describe themselves.

Student Referral for Psychological Services (K-12). Los Angeles: Western Psychological Services, 1969. A form for obtaining various information concerning a child and his problems, to be completed by a person who refers the child for psychological services.

Student Evaluation Scale (K-12). Jacksonville, Illinois: Psychologists and Educators Press, 1970. A rating scale technique applied to student behavior by teachers. Ratings of educational response and social-emotional response are used to evaluate general student behavior and student approach to learning tasks.

Target Game (ages 3–5). Starkweather, Elizabeth K. Stillwater, Oklahoma; Oklahoma State University, 1967. A performance test, individually administered, that is designed to measure children's willingness to attempt difficult tasks independent of their ability to perform them.

The Birthday Test (preschool-grade 6). Northway, Mary L. Toronto, Canada: Institute of Child Study, University of Toronto, 1966. A measure of children's preferences for adults or peers based upon the sociometric approach. Test situation involves having the child pretend that he is planning a birthday party and must determine his guest list. Doll figures are used in administering this test.

The Children's Self-Concept Index (K-3). New York: Westinghouse Learning Corporation, 1968. A group-administered test that attempts to measure degree of positive self-concept. Children are required to make a first-choice response to items that have both a positive and negative alternative. Focal areas include peer relations and positive reinforcement at home and in school.

Thomas Self-Concept Values Test (ages 3-9). Grand Rapids, Michigan: Educational Service Company, 1967. A polaroid photograph of the child is used in this individual approach to value measurement. Factors examined include happiness, size, sociability, ability for sharing, male acceptance, fear of things, fear of people, strength, cleanliness, health, attractiveness, material independence. A total self-concept score is also yielded. Referents are the child's mother, peers, teacher, and the child himself.

Miscellaneous Measures

Cincinnati Autonomy Test Battery (preschool–primary grades). Banta, T. J. "Tests for the evaluation of early childhood education: The Cincinnati

Autonomy Test Battery." In Jerome Hellmuth (ed.). *Cognitive Studies,* Vol. I. New York: Brunner-Mazel, 1970, pp. 424-491. The CATB was designed to measure "self-directed behaviors that facilitate effective problem-solving among children." Several relatively distinct aspects of self-regulating behavior pertinent to the development of problem-solving skills are reportedly measured by the CATB. These aspects include curiosity, exploratory behavior, persistence, resistance to distraction, impulse control, reflectivity, analytic perceptual processes, innovative behavior, and social competence. From a theoretical standpoint, the CATB represents an "eclectic" approach to child development theory; it is further based upon a diverse package of current research interests in developmental psychology. Language responses required of children for performance throughout the CATB are not stringent. Neither are the instructions given to children excessively verbal.

Evanston Early Identification Scale: Field Research Edition (ages 5-6). Chicago: Follett Educational Corporation, 1967. A "draw-a-person" test that purports to identify children whose school progress is less than favorable. Administered individually or in groups.

Gross Geometric Forms (ages 4-6½). Cincinnati. University of Cincinnati (Ruth B. Gross, Asst. Professor), 1970. This test purports to measure three aspects of young children's creative potential: ideational productivity, ideational communicability, and "richness" in thinking. It must be administered individually.

Kindergarten Health Check for Parents. Los Angeles: Los Angeles City School Districts, 1968. A checklist covering such things as cleanliness, posture habits, dental health, eyes, ears, nose, rest and sleep habits, eating habits, prevention and control of disease, social health, growth and development, and community cleanliness and health.

Originality Test (ages 3½-6½). Starkweather, Elizabeth K. Stillwater, Oklahoma: Oklahoma State University, 1968. This test is described by its author as a measure of creative potential. It must be individually administered and involves the child in the identification of forty plastic pieces of varying shapes and colors.

Secondary Vigilance Test (ages 5-6). Albuquerque, New Mexico: Southwestern Cooperative Development Laboratory (undated). Ostensibly a method for the measurement and manipulation of children's attention in the classroom setting.

Torrance Tests of Creative Thinking (ages 5 and above). Princeton, New Jersey: Personnel Press, 1966. Two sections, verbal and figural tests, make up this experimental or research battery. The first section includes four measures of verbal behavior: flexibility, fluency, elaboration, and originality. The second section is based upon the same four criteria but requires instead responses that are essentially drawing or pictorial in nature. Conceptually, these tests are based upon Torrance's extensive research into the development of creativity (divergent production) among children, much of which is referenced throughout the literature. The verbal portion is best used with children beyond grade 3 because of the writing requirements involved. It can, however, be administered individually to children as young as age 5. The figural form of the test is suitable for kindergarten children and beyond. Persons interested in using this battery should familiarize themselves completely with Torrance's major works, including criteria for scoring children's test responses. Reliability and validity data for this battery seem adequate for research purposes.

APPENDIX REFERENCES

A readiness test for disadvantaged preschool children. ERIC: ED 037 253, 1970.

Farr, R., and Summers, E. G. *Guide to tests and measuring instruments for reading.* ERIC: ED 022 973, 1968.

Haspiel, G. S., and Siegenthaler, B. M. *Evaluation of two measures of speech hearing for hearing impaired children.* ERIC: ED 024 207, 1968.

Johnson, O. G. and Bommarito, J. W. *Tests and measurements in child development: A handbook.* San Francisco: Jossey-Bass, 1971.

Kresh, Esther, and Green, B. F., Jr. *Preschool academic skills test.* ERIC: ED 028 045, 1969.

Lampe, J. M. *An evaluative study of color-vision tests for kindergarten and first grade pupils.* ERIC: ED 028 816, 1968.

Morris, June E., and Nolan, C. Y. *Bibliography on tests and testing of the blind.* ERIC: ED 025 075, 1967.

Rosenberg, L. A. *The Johns Hopkins Perceptual Test: The development of a rapid intelligence test for the preschool child.* ERIC: ED 020 787, 1966.

Ross, A. O. *The development of a behavior checklist for boys.* ERIC: ED 023 468, 1965.

Ross, M., and Lerman, J. *A picture identification test for hearing impaired children.* ERIC: ED 023 248, 1968.

Stott, L., and Ball, Rachel. "Infant and preschool mental tests: Review and evaluation." *Monographs of the society for research in child development,* 1965, 30, Ser. No. 101.

Van Riper, C., and Erickson, R. *Cross validation of a predictive screening test for children with articulatory speech defects.* ERIC: ED 024, 200, 1968.

Chapter 11

Dissemination

DONALD L. PETERS

Since early childhood education is a rapidly growing field, the dissemination of information in all its aspects, including the training of personnel, is essential. Many professionals and agencies are engaged in similar programs and can certainly benefit from sharing ideas and knowledge gained. Mistakes can be avoided and new efforts can be built upon the honestly evaluated experience of others. Also, where new concepts and innovative procedures abound the general public must be kept abreast of change. Only an informed community can be expected to accept and support new programs.

MULTIMEDIA DISSEMINATION

Dissemination of program information can take different forms. The selection of a particular medium will depend upon the target audience and upon the purpose of dissemination. For example, the traditional mimeo report to a funding agency meets both agency and program needs for accountability. However, if the information is to be more widely shared the publication of journal articles or books is preferable.

If the purpose is general publicity, a newspaper release may serve. Where the desire is to share new teaching techniques some form of film (a 16mm motion picture or videotape) may be most appropriate. Here too, choices are involved.

The variety of media available is large and each has its own virtues and limitations. Most programs will want to engage in a variety of dissemination activities for each of several potential audiences.

ETHICAL CONCERNS IN EVALUATION
AND DISSEMINATION

Dissemination of program information and evaluative reports should be an integral part of all programs, but dissemination places additional respon-

343

sibilities on all program personnel. At each juncture, responsibilities should be assessed and alternatives weighed carefully. There are two main areas of concern: professional ethics and the credibility of evaluative research.

The Professional Ethic

We hear with increasing frequency that the ivory-tower scholar can no longer pursue his interest in social-scientific topics divorced from the implications of his findings for the world around him (Sugarman, 1970; Beals, 1970; Moynihan, 1970; Cohen, 1970). His work has become political ammunition in the battle for social change (Mitchell, 1970; Caldwell, 1970). He now finds his advice sought far beyond the academic community, frequently on topics beyond the realm of his expertise, by those less concerned with scientific rigor than with immediate practical solutions to pressing problems (Fraser, 1970). More importantly, what the researcher says often influences the fiscal life-and-death decisions for large-scale social and educational programs which affect the lives of great numbers of people.

When evaluations are used as arguments for public policymaking and for legislative decisions, the researcher is confronted with a dilemma (Cohen, 1970; Berlak, 1970). He finds himself torn between the pursuit and dissemination of scientific information and his concern for the welfare and best interests of his target population, urban poor children for example.

These two considerations have not always been incompatible. However, the potential for conflict between them is becoming increasingly clear. Several statements recently published in professional publications indicate the magnitude of the problem.

In an article entitled, "Who Shall Rule Research?" Ralph Beals comments:

> Another critical issue is the protection of the rights of groups and individuals. Virtually all social research involves some invasion of privacy and rests upon the consent of the subjects. Some social scientists still place their research above the welfare of their subjects. Yet as early as 1948 the American Anthropological Association officially stressed the necessity to protect the individuals, communities or groups. Given the lack of legal protection for confidentiality, *individual researchers should accept the suppression or even destruction of their data if there is a possibility of its misuse.* (Beals, 1970; emphasis added)

Earlier in the article Beals makes reference to the fact that governments (including our own) may misuse social science to implement and support policies which the researcher himself could not approve.

How then shall such decisions concerning the best interests of society be made? Jule Sugarman has recommended that the research community accept

> the view that researchers should delay public discussion of research findings which they believe require changes in public policy until the responsible agency and a [panel of eminent researchers] have had a reasonable time to review—but not in any way change—the findings. (Sugarman, 1970).

Such a recommendation sounds reasonable, but Caldwell (1970) indicates that, in relation to the Coleman report, the thirty-three page summary coming from the Office of Education was characterized by Daniel Moynihan as having "withheld from all but the *cognoscenti* any suggestion that major, and in effect, heretical findings had appeared" (Caldwell, 1970).

Representing a somewhat different point of view, James Mitchell, Associate Dean of the College of Education at the University of Rochester, has candidly written about the rejection of a paper evaluating an "intercultural enrichment" program integrating a suburban school with inner-city black children. One of the reasons for the rejection by the American Psychological Association program committee, and, according to Mitchell, the critical one, he quotes as being that "the results of your study might be subject to misinterpretation, *particularly in the press."*

Mitchell comments:

> It was apparently felt that the results and conclusions of the paper could serve as ammunition for opponents of integration. But the fact that the research findings can be put to undesirable as well as desirable uses, interpreted properly or improperly, should have no bearing on the researcher's freedom and right to communicate. A professional's right to communicate with other professionals was now being denied by a super-professional on quite pernicious grounds.
>
> There is an increasing tendency on the part of many people, including professionals, to be party to various forms of subtle suppression of information when it is not quite in accord with their purposes and beliefs. The social and political passions of the day have caused us to become politically shrewd about what should and should not be said, and some fundamental freedoms are lost sight of or treated lightly as we assess all utterances in the light of political expediency. It is an unfortunate and dangerous tendency, for by blinding us to certain problems that must be solved before we can achieve our goals, it can effectively prevent the attainment of those goals. It is ubiquitous in the relationship between the practitioner and the researcher. The researcher often recognizes quite early the subtle signs conveying the message that the project he is evaluating *must* be successful. (Mitchell, 1970)

This conflict between freedom of inquiry and considerations of the best interests of society has been intensified by the demand for rapid dissemination of research findings and their speedy translation into legislated programs. In the last five to seven years this has been extraordinarily true of research with "disadvantaged" children and early childhood education. In the latter area in particular, the demand for dissemination has outstripped the capacity of the normal public channels, which have the safety valve of the colleague-referee system, and has relied upon films, ditto, and the spoken word for the transmission of evaluational information. This has led to another major problem area.

The Credibility of Evaluative Research

The political and social climate of the last five years has made child-related research good news copy. Newspapers, magazines, and television have provided their audiences with glimpses of research evidence, which are often chosen from bias, misconstrued, blown out of proportion, overgeneralized, or used without the cautions and reservations the researcher himself would impose. (Sugarman, 1970). This occurs even when materials for dissemination are carefully prepared, refereed by competent colleagues, and published in such a way as to make them generally accessible. Under less controlled conditions the possibility of misuse and misunderstanding is even greater.

The growing skepticism about the power of the social sciences and the use of that power is reflected in such facetious statements as those of Moynihan (1970):

> I have been guilty of optimism about the use of knowledge gained through social science in the management of public affairs.

and

> In time it may turn out that the real disaster of the '60's was in the area of the social sciences, that is to say, in those studies that seek to enlighten and improve the public mind with respect to social phenomena such as race relations.

It is also evident in the warnings of Jules Sugarman:

> It is my judgment that the enthusiasm for using evaluation information and the confidence of many people in its validity has far outrun the state of the art.
> The real possibility is that the uses which are being made of research reports are generating a cynicism which may so undermine public and

political confidence that research and evaluation studies will not be used at all. (Sugarman, 1970)

There is already some evidence that federally funded ESEA Title III programs that have the largest budgets for evaluation and dissemination are the ones least likely to survive when federal funds are reduced (Hearn, 1970).

Given this situation, it is important that evaluators and administrators direct their attention toward those factors which bear directly on the validity, generalizability, and dissemination of their findings. Educational evaluation can ill afford the overzealous and extravagant claims, based on highly questionable data and methodology, that have so much public appeal. The much publicized book, *Pygmalion in the Classroom* (Rosenthal and Jacobson, 1968), is a glaring example of what should not be done. The reviews by Thorndyke (1968) and Snow (1969) leave little doubt concerning the untrustworthiness of this study. Snow comments on the greater dangers involved:

> *Pygmalion,* inadequately and prematurely reported in book and magazine form, has performed a disservice to teachers and schools, to users of mental tests, and perhaps worst of all, to parents and children whose newly gained expectations may not prove quite so self-fulfilling. (Snow, 1969)

Unfortunately these critiques rarely reach as wide an audience as does the original publication.

It is apparent that the evaluator and all program personnel have a responsibility to provide the best information possible for the resolution of society's problems and to provide direction for its growth.

It is necessary for the researcher to be cognizant of and explicit about his assumptions and his own value system. These bear directly upon the activities he engages in, the kinds of research and evaluation programs he devises, and ultimately upon his definition of what is the proper or improper use of his findings. In other roles (for example, reviewer or expert witness) his assumptions and values will determine the type of information he will accept or provide for others.

It is necessary for the evaluator to bring to bear the very best tools of his trade on each problem he studies. His research must be objective and soundly designed. It must be interpreted with due caution. To insure this the researcher should seek the critiques of colleagues before disseminating his fiindings widely.

The evaluator and the program administrator must bear the responsibility of doing all in their power to insure the careful dissemination of information and to prevent erroneous or extravagant publicity for ques-tionable findings.

REFERENCES

Beals, R. L. Who will rule research? *Psychology Today,* 1970, *4,* 44-47, 75.

Berlak, H. Values, goals, public policy and educational evaluation. *Review o, Educational Research,* 1970, *40,* 261-278.

Caldwell, C. Social science as ammunition. *Psychology Today,* 1970, *4,* 38-41 72.

Cohen, D. Politics and research: evaluation of social action programs in educa tion. *Review of Educational Research,* 1970, *40,* 213-238.

Fraser, D. Congress and the psychologist. *American Psychologist,* 1970, *25* 323-327.

Hearn, N. When sugar daddy's gone, does baby starve? (or) A study of the adoption rate of ESEA Title III innovations when federal funds are ter-minated. *Phi Delta Kappan,* September, 1970, 59-61.

Mitchell, J. On the perils of conducting socially significant research. *Phi Delta Kappan,* November, 1970, 182-184.

Moynihan, D. Eliteland. *Psychology Today,* 1970, *4,* 35-37, 66.

Rosenthal, R., and Jacobson, L. *Pygmalion in the Classroom.* New York: Holt Rinehart, Winston, 1968.

Snow, R. Review: *Pygmalion in the Classroom. Contemporary Psychology* 1969, *14* 197-199.

Sugarman, J. Research, Evaluation, and Public Policy. *Child Development* 1970, *41,* 263-266.

Thorndike, R. Review: *Pygmalion in the Classroom. American Educationa Research Journal,* 1968, *5,* 708-711.

Index

349